SOLAS

Consolidated Edition, 2004

Consolidated text of
the International Convention for
the Safety of Life at Sea, 1974,
and its Protocol of 1988:
articles, annexes and certificates

*Incorporating all amendments
in effect from 1 July 2004*

INTERNATIONAL
MARITIME
ORGANIZATION
London, 2004

Published by the
INTERNATIONAL MARITIME ORGANIZATION
4 Albert Embankment, London SE1 7SR

First edition, 1992
Second edition, 1997
Third edition, 2001
Fourth edition, 2004

Printed in the United Kingdom by The Bath Press, Bath

2   4   6   8   10   9   7   5   3   1

ISBN 92-801-4183-X

IMO PUBLICATION
Sales number: ID110E

Foreword

Introduction

1   The International Convention for the Safety of Life at Sea (SOLAS), 1974, currently in force, was adopted on 1 November 1974 by the International Conference on Safety of Life at Sea, which was convened by the International Maritime Organization (IMO), and entered into force on 25 May 1980. It has since been amended twice by means of protocols:

.1   by the Protocol adopted on 17 February 1978 by the International Conference on Tanker Safety and Pollution Prevention (1978 SOLAS Protocol), which entered into force on 1 May 1981; and

.2   by the Protocol adopted on 11 November 1988 by the International Conference on the Harmonized System of Survey and Certification (1988 SOLAS Protocol), which entered into force on 3 February 2000 and replaced and abrogated the 1978 Protocol, as between Parties to the 1988 Protocol.

2   In addition, the 1974 SOLAS Convention has been amended by means of resolutions adopted either by IMO's Maritime Safety Committee (MSC) in its expanded form specified in SOLAS article VIII or by Conferences of SOLAS Contracting Governments, also specified in article VIII, as follows:

.1   by the 1981 amendments, which were adopted by resolution MSC.1(XLV) and entered into force on 1 September 1984;

.2   by the 1983 amendments, which were adopted by resolution MSC.6(48) and entered into force on 1 July 1986;

.3   by the April 1988 amendments, which were adopted by resolution MSC.11(55) and entered into force on 22 October 1989;

.4   by the October 1988 amendments, which were adopted by resolution MSC.12(56) and entered into force on 29 April 1990;

.5   by the November 1988 amendments, which were adopted by resolution 1 of the Conference of Contracting Governments to SOLAS, 1974, on the Global Maritime Distress and Safety System and entered into force on 1 February 1992;

.6   by the 1989 amendments, which were adopted by resolution MSC.13(57) and entered into force on 1 February 1992;

.7   by the 1990 amendments, which were adopted by resolution MSC.19(58) and entered into force on 1 February 1992;

.8   by the 1991 amendments, which were adopted by resolution MSC.22(59) and entered into force on 1 January 1994;

.9   by the April 1992 amendments, which were adopted by resolutions MSC.24(60) and MSC.26(60) and entered into force on 1 October 1994;

.10   by the December 1992 amendments, which were adopted by resolution MSC.27(61) and entered into force on 1 October 1994;

.11   by the May 1994 amendments, which were adopted by resolution MSC.31(63) and entered into force on 1 January 1996 (annex 1) and on 1 July 1998 (annex 2);

.12   by the May 1994 amendments, which were adopted by resolution 1 of the Conference of Contracting Governments to SOLAS, 1974, which entered into force on 1 January 1996 (annex 1) and on 1 July 1998 (annex 2);

.13   by the December 1994 amendments, which were adopted by resolution MSC.42(64) and entered into force on 1 July 1996;

.14   by the May 1995 amendments, which were adopted by resolution MSC.46(65) and entered into force on 1 January 1997;

.15   by the November 1995 amendments, which were adopted by resolution 1 of the Conference of Contracting Governments to SOLAS, 1974, and entered into force on 1 July 1997;

.16   by the June 1996 amendments, which were adopted by resolution MSC.47(66) and entered into force on 1 July 1998;

.17   by the December 1996 amendments, which were adopted by resolution MSC.57(67) and entered into force on 1 July 1998;

.18   by the June 1997 amendments, which were adopted by resolution MSC.65(68) and entered into force on 1 July 1999;

.19   by the November 1997 amendments which were adopted by resolution 1 of the Conference of Contracting Governments to SOLAS 1974 and entered into force on 1 July 1999;

.20   by the May 1998 amendments, which were adopted by resolution MSC.69(69) and entered into force on 1 July 2002;

.21   by the May 1999 amendments, which were adopted by resolution MSC.87(71) and entered into force on 1 January 2001;

.22 by the May 2000 amendments, which were adopted by resolution MSC.91(72) and entered into force on 1 January 2002;

.23 by the November 2000 amendments, which were adopted by resolution MSC.99(73) and entered into force on 1 July 2002;

.24 by the June 2001 amendments, which were adopted by resolution MSC.117(74) and entered into force on 1 January 2003;

.25 by the May 2002 amendments, which were adopted by resolution MSC.123(75) and entered into force on 1 January 2004;

.26 by the December 2002 amendments, which were adopted by resolution MSC.134(76) and entered into force on 1 July 2004;

.27 by the December 2002 amendments, which were adopted by resolution 1 of the Conference of Contracting Governments to the International Convention for the Safety of Life at Sea, 1974 and entered into force on 1 July 2004. The entry into force of the new chapter XI (Special measures to enhance maritime security) will give effect to the International Code for the Security of Ships and of Port Facilities (ISPS Code); and

.28 by the June 2003 amendments, which were adopted by resolution MSC.142(77). At the time of their adoption, the Maritime Safety Committee determined that these amendments shall be deemed to have been accepted on 1 January 2006 and will enter into force on 1 July 2006, unless, prior to 1 January 2006, more than one third of the Contracting Governments to the SOLAS Convention, or Contracting Governments the combined merchant fleet of which constitute not less than 50% of the gross tonnage of the world's merchant fleet, have notified their objections to the amendments.

.29 by the May 2004 amendments, which were adopted by resolutions MSC.151(78) (regulation II-1/3-6), MSC.152(78) (chapters III and IV and the appendix to the annex) and MSC.153(78) (chapter V). At the time of their adoption, the Maritime Safety Committee determined that these amendments shall be deemed to have been accepted on 1 July 2005, 1 January 2006 and 1 January 2006 respectively, unless, prior to these dates, more than one third of the Contracting Governments to the Convention, or Contracting Governments the combined merchant fleets of which constitute not less than 50% of the gross tonnage of the world's merchant fleet, have notified their objections to the amendments. If these amendments are accepted, they will enter into force on 1 January 2006, 1 July 2006 and 1 July 2006 respectively.

3   The 1988 SOLAS Protocol has been amended by the May 2000 amendments, which were adopted by resolution MSC.92(72) and entered into force on 1 January 2002, and by the May 2002 amendments, which were adopted by resolution MSC.124(75). The conditions for their entry into force were met on 1 July 2003, and the amendments entered into force on 1 January 2004. The 1988 Protocol has also been amended by the May 2004 amendments, which were adopted by resolution MSC.154(78). At the time of their adoption, the Maritime Safety Committee determined that these amendments shall be deemed to have been accepted on 1 January 2006 unless, prior to that date, more than one third of the Parties to the 1988 SOLAS Protocol, or Parties the combined merchant fleets of which constitute not less than 50% of the gross tonnage of the world's merchant fleet, have notified their objections to the amendments. If they are accepted, the amendments will enter into force on 1 July 2006.

Content of the consolidated text

4   This publication contains a consolidated text of the 1974 SOLAS Convention, the 1988 SOLAS Protocol, and all subsequent amendments thereto up to and including the December 2002 amendments. The resulting text has been compiled by the IMO Secretariat and is intended to provide an easy reference to SOLAS requirements applicable as on 1 July 2004.

5   The publication has been arranged in two parts:

   .1   part 1, which contains the 1974 SOLAS Convention and 1988 SOLAS Protocol articles, requirements and certificates; and

   .2   part 2, which contains resolution A.883(21) on the Global and uniform implementation of the harmonized system of survey and certification (HSSC), a list of certificates and documents* to be carried on board ships, a list of resolutions adopted by the aforementioned SOLAS Conferences and the text of regulation 12-2 of chapter II-1 of SOLAS.

6   The operational requirements contained in this consolidated text are, in general, applicable to all ships, whilst the requirements for ship construction and equipment apply to ships constructed on or after the dates specified in the various regulations. To identify construction and equipment requirements applicable to ships constructed before 2001, previous texts of the 1974 SOLAS Convention, the 1988 SOLAS Protocol and the amendments to the Convention should be consulted. For instance, special requirements for existing passenger ships are contained only in part F

---

* The list of certificates includes brief descriptions of the purpose of all certificates and documents specified therein for the purpose of assisting shore staff, officials and shipmasters in evaluating the documents and certificates, which are necessary for port State control and for the smooth operation of ships in ports.

of chapter II-2 of the original 1974 SOLAS Convention but neither in chapter II-2 of the 1981 amendments nor in this consolidated text.

7   Those provisions of chapter I and of the appendix to the annex to the 1974 SOLAS Convention which have been modified by the 1988 SOLAS Protocol are indicated by the symbol P88 . No similar symbol is shown for provisions of the 1974 SOLAS Convention which were modified by the 1978 SOLAS Protocol because, whilst, in respect of chapter I of the Convention, the provisions thereof have been replaced and abrogated by the 1988 SOLAS Protocol, as between Parties to the Protocol, for provisions in other chapters of the Convention, they have been superseded by SOLAS amendments subsequently adopted.

8   In general, this publication reproduces the text of the 1974 SOLAS Convention and the 1988 SOLAS Protocol and includes the modifications and amendments thereto given in their authentic texts. In addition, it includes some minor editorial changes, which, while not altering the substance, aim at achieving a degree of consistency between the texts of the 1974 SOLAS Convention and the 1988 SOLAS Protocol and the various SOLAS amendments. In particular:

.1   while the decimal numbering system is used for paragraphs and subparagraphs of regulations in chapters II-1, II-2, III, IV, V, VI and VII, which were completely rewritten in the 1981, 1983, 1988, 1991 and 2000 amendments, the original numbering system is retained in chapters I and VIII;

.2   the references to regulations, paragraphs and chapters in the texts adopted in the 1981 and subsequent amendments use an abbreviated form (e.g. "regulation II-2/55.5"), whereas the original reference system is retained in unamended regulations (e.g. "regulation 5 of this chapter", "paragraph (a) of this regulation", etc.);

.3   the term *tons gross tonnage* has been replaced by the term *gross tonnage* in view of the Assembly's decision (resolution A.493(XII)) that the term *tons gross tonnage* used in IMO instruments should be considered as having the same meaning as *gross tonnage* as determined under the 1969 Tonnage Convention; and

.4   metric values of the SI system have been used in accordance with resolution A.351(IX).

Status of footnotes

9   The footnotes given in this consolidated text (which do not, as noted by the MSC, form part of the Convention but are inserted for ease of reference) refer to codes, guidelines and recommendations relating to a particular text and were updated by the Secretariat at the time of

publication. In addition, certain explanatory footnotes have been inserted based on relevant texts of codes, guidelines, recommendations and other decisions of the MSC. In all cases, the reader must make use of the latest versions of the referenced texts, bearing in mind that such texts may have been revised or superseded by updated material since publication of this consolidated edition of the 1974 SOLAS Convention, as amended.

Contents

Part 1

Part 2

Index   557

Part 1

Articles of the International Convention for the Safety of Life at Sea, 1974

THE CONTRACTING GOVERNMENTS

BEING DESIROUS of promoting safety of life at sea by establishing in a common agreement uniform principles and rules directed thereto,

CONSIDERING that this end may best be achieved by the conclusion of a Convention to replace the International Convention for the Safety of Life at Sea, 1960, taking account of developments since that Convention was concluded,

HAVE AGREED as follows:

Article I
General obligations under the Convention

(a) The Contracting Governments undertake to give effect to the provisions of the present Convention and the annex thereto, which shall constitute an integral part of the present Convention. Every reference to the present Convention constitutes at the same time a reference to the annex.

(b) The Contracting Governments undertake to promulgate all laws, decrees, orders and regulations and to take all other steps which may be necessary to give the present Convention full and complete effect, so as to ensure that, from the point of view of safety of life, a ship is fit for the service for which it is intended.

Article II
Application

The present Convention shall apply to ships entitled to fly the flag of States the Governments of which are Contracting Governments.

Article III
Laws, regulations

The Contracting Governments undertake to communicate to and deposit with the Secretary-General of the Inter-Governmental Maritime Consultative Organization* (hereinafter referred to as "the Organization"):

(a)   a list of non-governmental agencies which are authorized to act in their behalf in the administration of measures for safety of life at sea for circulation to the Contracting Governments for the information of their officers;

(b)   the text of laws, decrees, orders and regulations which shall have been promulgated on the various matters within the scope of the present Convention;

(c)   a sufficient number of specimens of their certificates issued under the provisions of the present Convention for circulation to the Contracting Governments for the information of their officers.

Article IV
Cases of force majeure

(a)   A ship, which is not subject to the provisions of the present Convention at the time of its departure on any voyage, shall not become subject to the provisions of the present Convention on account of any deviation from its intended voyage due to stress of weather or any other case of *force majeure*.

(b)   Persons who are on board a ship by reason of *force majeure* or in consequence of the obligation laid upon the master to carry shipwrecked or other persons shall not be taken into account for the purpose of ascertaining the application to a ship of any provisions of the present Convention.

Article V
Carriage of persons in emergencies

(a)   For the purpose of evacuating persons in order to avoid a threat to the security of their lives a Contracting Government may permit the carriage of a larger number of persons in its ships than is otherwise permissible under the present Convention.

---

* The name of the Organization was changed to "International Maritime Organization" (IMO) by virtue of amendments to the Organization's Convention which entered into force on 22 May 1982.

(b)   Such permission shall not deprive other Contracting Governments of any right of control under the present Convention over such ships which come within their ports.

(c)   Notice of any such permission, together with a statement of the circumstances, shall be sent to the Secretary-General of the Organization by the Contracting Government granting such permission.

Article VI
Prior treaties and conventions

(a)   As between the Contracting Governments, the present Convention replaces and abrogates the International Convention for the Safety of Life at Sea which was signed in London on 17 June 1960.

(b)   All other treaties, conventions and arrangements relating to safety of life at sea, or matters appertaining thereto, at present in force between Governments parties to the present Convention shall continue to have full and complete effect during the terms thereof as regards:

    (i)   ships to which the present Convention does not apply;

    (ii)   ships to which the present Convention applies, in respect of matters for which it has not expressly provided.

(c)   To the extent, however, that such treaties, conventions or arrangements conflict with the provisions of the present Convention, the provisions of the present Convention shall prevail.

(d)   All matters which are not expressly provided for in the present Convention remain subject to the legislation of the Contracting Governments.

Article VII
Special rules drawn up by agreement

When in accordance with the present Convention special rules are drawn up by agreement between all or some of the Contracting Governments, such rules shall be communicated to the Secretary-General of the Organization for circulation to all Contracting Governments.

Article VIII
Amendments

(a)   The present Convention may be amended by either of the procedures specified in the following paragraphs.

(b)   Amendments after consideration within the Organization:

    (i)   Any amendment proposed by a Contracting Government shall be submitted to the Secretary-General of the Organization, who shall then circulate it to all Members of the Organization and all Contracting Governments at least six months prior to its consideration.

    (ii)   Any amendment proposed and circulated as above shall be referred to the Maritime Safety Committee of the Organization for consideration.

    (iii)   Contracting Governments of States, whether or not Members of the Organization, shall be entitled to participate in the proceedings of the Maritime Safety Committee for the consideration and adoption of amendments.

    (iv)   Amendments shall be adopted by a two-thirds majority of the Contracting Governments present and voting in the Maritime Safety Committee expanded as provided for in subparagraph (iii) of this paragraph (hereinafter referred to as "the expanded Maritime Safety Committee") on condition that at least one third of the Contracting Governments shall be present at the time of voting.

    (v)   Amendments adopted in accordance with subparagraph (iv) of this paragraph shall be communicated by the Secretary-General of the Organization to all Contracting Governments for acceptance.

    (vi)   (1)   An amendment to an article of the Convention or to chapter I of the annex shall be deemed to have been accepted on the date on which it is accepted by two thirds of the Contracting Governments.

        (2)   An amendment to the annex other than chapter I shall be deemed to have been accepted

            (aa)   at the end of two years from the date on which it is communicated to Contracting Governments for acceptance; or

            (bb)   at the end of a different period, which shall not be less than one year, if so determined at the time of its adoption by a two-thirds majority of the Contracting Governments present and voting in the expanded Maritime Safety Committee.

        However, if within the specified period either more than one third of Contracting Governments, or Contracting Governments the combined merchant fleets of which constitute not less than fifty per cent of the gross tonnage of the world's merchant fleet, notify the Secretary-General of the Organization that they object to the amendment, it shall be deemed not to have been accepted.

(vii) (1) An amendment to an article of the Convention or to chapter I of the annex shall enter into force with respect to those Contracting Governments which have accepted it, six months after the date on which it is deemed to have been accepted, and with respect to each Contracting Government which accepts it after that date, six months after the date of that Contracting Government's acceptance.

(2) An amendment to the annex other than chapter I shall enter into force with respect to all Contracting Governments, except those which have objected to the amendment under subparagraph (vi)(2) of this paragraph and which have not withdrawn such objections, six months after the date on which it is deemed to have been accepted. However, before the date set for entry into force, any Contracting Government may give notice to the Secretary-General of the Organization that it exempts itself from giving effect to that amendment for a period not longer than one year from the date of its entry into force, or for such longer period as may be determined by a two-thirds majority of the Contracting Governments present and voting in the expanded Maritime Safety Committee at the time of the adoption of the amendment.

(c) Amendment by a Conference:

(i) Upon the request of a Contracting Government concurred in by at least one third of the Contracting Governments, the Organization shall convene a Conference of Contracting Governments to consider amendments to the present Convention.

(ii) Every amendment adopted by such a Conference by a two-thirds majority of the Contracting Governments present and voting shall be communicated by the Secretary-General of the Organization to all Contracting Governments for acceptance.

(iii) Unless the Conference decides otherwise, the amendment shall be deemed to have been accepted and shall enter into force in accordance with the procedures specified in subparagraphs (b)(vi) and (b)(vii) respectively of this article, provided that references in these paragraphs to the expanded Maritime Safety Committee shall be taken to mean references to the Conference.

(d)   (i)   A Contracting Government which has accepted an amendment to the annex which has entered into force shall not be obliged to extend the benefit of the present Convention in respect of the certificates issued to a ship entitled to fly the flag of a State the Government of which, pursuant to the provisions of subparagraph (b)(vi)(2) of this article, has objected to the amendment and has not withdrawn such an objection, but only to the extent that such certificates relate to matters covered by the amendment in question.

     (ii)   A Contracting Government which has accepted an amendment to the annex which has entered into force shall extend the benefit of the present Convention in respect of the certificates issued to a ship entitled to fly the flag of a State the Government of which, pursuant to the provisions of subparagraph (b)(vii)(2) of this article, has notified the Secretary-General of the Organization that it exempts itself from giving effect to the amendment.

(e)   Unless expressly provided otherwise, any amendment to the present Convention made under this article, which relates to the structure of a ship, shall apply only to ships the keels of which are laid or which are at a similar stage of construction, on or after the date on which the amendment enters into force.

(f)   Any declaration of acceptance of, or objection to, an amendment or any notice given under subparagraph (b)(vii)(2) of this article shall be submitted in writing to the Secretary-General of the Organization, who shall inform all Contracting Governments of any such submission and the date of its receipt.

(g)   The Secretary-General of the Organization shall inform all Contracting Governments of any amendments which enter into force under this article, together with the date on which each such amendment enters into force.

Article IX
Signature, ratification, acceptance, approval and accession

(a)   The present Convention shall remain open for signature at the Headquarters of the Organization from 1 November 1974 until 1 July 1975 and shall thereafter remain open for accession. States may become parties to the present Convention by:

     (i)   signature without reservation as to ratification, acceptance or approval; or

(ii) signature subject to ratification, acceptance or approval, followed by ratification, acceptance or approval; or

(iii) accession.

(b) Ratification, acceptance, approval or accession shall be effected by the deposit of an instrument to that effect with the Secretary-General of the Organization.

(c) The Secretary-General of the Organization shall inform the Governments of all States which have signed the present Convention or acceded to it of any signature or of the deposit of any instrument of ratification, acceptance, approval or accession and the date of its deposit.

Article X
Entry into force

(a) The present Convention shall enter into force twelve months after the date on which not less than twenty-five States, the combined merchant fleets of which constitute not less than fifty per cent of the gross tonnage of the world's merchant shipping, have become parties to it in accordance with article IX.

(b) Any instrument of ratification, acceptance, approval or accession deposited after the date on which the present Convention enters into force shall take effect three months after the date of deposit.

(c) After the date on which an amendment to the present Convention is deemed to have been accepted under article VIII, any instrument of ratification, acceptance, approval or accession deposited shall apply to the Convention as amended.

Article XI
Denunciation

(a) The present Convention may be denounced by any Contracting Government at any time after the expiry of five years from the date on which the Convention enters into force for that Government.

(b) Denunciation shall be effected by the deposit of an instrument of denunciation with the Secretary-General of the Organization who shall notify all the other Contracting Governments of any instrument of denunciation received and of the date of its receipt as well as the date on which such denunciation takes effect.

(c) A denunciation shall take effect one year, or such longer period as may be specified in the instrument of denunciation, after its receipt by the Secretary-General of the Organization.

Article XII
Deposit and registration

(a)   The present Convention shall be deposited with the Secretary-General of the Organization who shall transmit certified true copies thereof to the Governments of all States which have signed the present Convention or acceded to it.

(b)   As soon as the present Convention enters into force, the text shall be transmitted by the Secretary-General of the Organization to the Secretary-General of the United Nations for registration and publication, in accordance with Article 102 of the Charter of the United Nations.

Article XIII
Languages

The present Convention is established in a single copy in the Chinese, English, French, Russian and Spanish languages, each text being equally authentic. Official translations in the Arabic, German and Italian languages shall be prepared and deposited with the signed original.

IN WITNESS WHEREOF the undersigned,* being duly authorized by their respective Governments for that purpose, have signed the present Convention.

DONE AT LONDON this first day of November one thousand nine hundred and seventy-four.

---

* Signatures omitted.

Protocol of 1988 relating to the International Convention for the Safety of Life at Sea, 1974

THE PARTIES TO THE PRESENT PROTOCOL,

BEING PARTIES to the International Convention for the Safety of Life at Sea, done at London on 1 November 1974,

RECOGNIZING the need for the introduction into the above-mentioned Convention of provisions for survey and certification harmonized with corresponding provisions in other international instruments,

CONSIDERING that this need may best be met by the conclusion of a Protocol relating to the International Convention for the Safety of Life at Sea, 1974,

HAVE AGREED as follows:

Article I
General obligations

1   The Parties to the present Protocol undertake to give effect to the provisions of the present Protocol and the annex hereto, which shall constitute an integral part of the present Protocol. Every reference to the present Protocol constitutes at the same time a reference to the annex hereto.

2   As between the Parties to the present Protocol, the provisions of the International Convention for the Safety of Life at Sea, 1974, as amended, (hereinafter referred to as "the Convention") shall apply subject to the modifications and additions set out in the present Protocol.

3   With respect to ships entitled to fly the flag of a State which is not a Party to the Convention and the present Protocol, the Parties to the present Protocol shall apply the requirements of the Convention and the present Protocol as may be necessary to ensure that no more favourable treatment is given to such ships.

Article II
Prior treaties

1   As between the Parties to the present Protocol, the present Protocol replaces and abrogates the Protocol of 1978 relating to the Convention.

2   Notwithstanding any other provisions of the present Protocol, any certificate issued under, and in accordance with, the provisions of the Convention and any supplement to such certificate issued under, and in accordance with, the provisions of the Protocol of 1978 relating to the Convention which is current when the present Protocol enters into force in respect of the Party by which the certificate or supplement was issued, shall remain valid until it expires under the terms of the Convention or the Protocol of 1978 relating to the Convention, as the case may be.

3   A Party to the present Protocol shall not issue certificates under, and in accordance with, the provisions of the International Convention for the Safety of Life at Sea, 1974, as adopted on 1 November 1974.

Article III
Communication of information

The Parties to the present Protocol undertake to communicate to, and deposit with, the Secretary-General of the International Maritime Organization (hereinafter referred to as "the Organization"):

(a)   the text of laws, decrees, orders and regulations and other instruments which have been promulgated on the various matters within the scope of the present Protocol;

(b)   a list of nominated surveyors or recognized organizations which are authorized to act on their behalf in the administration of measures for safety of life at sea for circulation to the Parties for information of their officers, and a notification of the specific responsibilities and conditions of the authority delegated to those nominated surveyors or recognized organizations; and

(c)   a sufficient number of specimens of their certificates issued under the provision of the present Protocol.

Article IV
Signature, ratification, acceptance, approval and accession

1   The present Protocol shall be open for signature at the Headquarters of the Organization from 1 March 1989 to 28 February 1990 and shall thereafter remain open for accession. Subject to the provisions of paragraph 3, States may express their consent to be bound by the present Protocol by:

(a)   signature without reservation as to ratification, acceptance or approval; or

(b)   signature subject to ratification, acceptance or approval, followed by ratification, acceptance or approval; or

(c)   accession.

2   Ratification, acceptance, approval or accession shall be effected by the deposit of an instrument to that effect with the Secretary-General of the Organization.

3   The present Protocol may be signed without reservation, ratified, accepted, approved or acceded to only by States which have signed without reservation, ratified, accepted, approved or acceded to the Convention.

Article V
Entry into force

1   The present Protocol shall enter into force twelve months after the date on which both the following conditions have been met:

(a)   not less than fifteen States, the combined merchant fleets of which constitute not less than fifty per cent of the gross tonnage of the world's merchant shipping, have expressed their consent to be bound by it in accordance with article IV, and

(b)   the conditions for the entry into force of the Protocol of 1988 relating to the International Convention on Load Lines, 1966, have been met,

provided that the present Protocol shall not enter into force before 1 February 1992.

2   For States which have deposited an instrument of ratification, acceptance, approval or accession in respect of the present Protocol after the conditions for entry into force thereof have been met but prior to the date of entry into force, the ratification, acceptance, approval or accession shall take effect on the date of entry into force of the present Protocol or three months after the date of deposit of the instrument, whichever is the later date.

3   Any instrument of ratification, acceptance, approval or accession deposited after the date on which the present Protocol enters into force shall take effect three months after the date of deposit.

4   After the date on which an amendment to the present Protocol is deemed to have been accepted under article VI, any instrument of ratification, acceptance, approval or accession deposited shall apply to the present Protocol as amended.

Article VI
Amendments

The procedures set out in article VIII of the Convention shall apply to amendments to the present Protocol, provided that:

(a) references in that article to the Convention and to Contracting Governments shall be taken to mean references to the present Protocol and to the Parties to the present Protocol respectively;

(b) amendments to the articles of the present Protocol and to the Annex thereto shall be adopted and brought into force in accordance with the procedure applicable to amendments to the articles of the Convention or to chapter I of the annex thereto; and

(c) amendments to the appendix to the annex to the present Protocol may be adopted and brought into force in accordance with the procedure applicable to amendments to the annex to the Convention other than chapter I.

Article VII
Denunciation

1   The present Protocol may be denounced by any Party at any time after the expiry of five years from the date on which the present Protocol enters into force for that Party.

2   Denunciation shall be effected by the deposit of an instrument of denunciation with the Secretary-General of the Organization.

3   A denunciation shall take effect one year, or such longer period as may be specified in the instrument of denunciation, after its receipt by the Secretary-General of the Organization.

4   A denunciation of the Convention by a Party shall be deemed to be a denunciation of the present Protocol by that Party. Such denunciation shall take effect on the same date as denunciation of the Convention takes effect according to paragraph (c) of article XI of the Convention.

Article VIII
Depositary

1   The present Protocol shall be deposited with the Secretary-General of the Organization (hereinafter referred to as "the depositary").

2   The depositary shall:

(a) inform the Governments of all States which have signed the present Protocol or acceded thereto of:

   (i)   each new signature or deposit of an instrument of ratification, acceptance, approval or accession, together with the date thereof;

   (ii) the date of entry into force of the present Protocol;

(iii)   the deposit of any instrument of denunciation of the present Protocol together with the date on which it was received and the date on which the denunciation takes effect;

(b)   transmit certified true copies of the present Protocol to the Governments of all States which have signed the present Protocol or acceded thereto.

3   As soon as the present Protocol enters into force, a certified true copy thereof shall be transmitted by the depositary to the Secretariat of the United Nations for registration and publication in accordance with Article 102 of the Charter of the United Nations.

Article IX
Languages

The present Protocol is established in a single original in the Arabic, Chinese, English, French, Russian and Spanish languages, each text being equally authentic. An official translation into the Italian language shall be prepared and deposited with the signed original.

DONE AT LONDON this eleventh day of November one thousand nine hundred and eighty-eight.

IN WITNESS WHEREOF the undersigned*, being duly authorized by their respective Governments for that purpose, have signed the present Protocol.

---

* Signatures omitted.

Consolidated text of
the annex to the 1974 SOLAS Convention

CHAPTER I
General provisions

Chapter I: General provisions
Contents

Part C – *Casualties*

Part A
Application, definitions, etc.

Regulation 1
Application

(a)   Unless expressly provided otherwise, the present regulations apply only to ships engaged on international voyages.

(b)   The classes of ships to which each chapter applies are more precisely defined, and the extent of the application is shown, in each chapter.

Regulation 2
Definitions

For the purpose of the present regulations, unless expressly provided otherwise:

(a)   *Regulations* means the regulations contained in the annex to the present Convention.

(b)   *Administration* means the Government of the State whose flag the ship is entitled to fly.

(c)   *Approved* means approved by the Administration.

(d)   *International voyage* means a voyage from a country to which the present Convention applies to a port outside such country, or conversely.

(e)   A *passenger* is every person other than:

    (i)   the master and the members of the crew or other persons employed or engaged in any capacity on board a ship on the business of that ship; and

    (ii)   a child under one year of age.

(f)   A *passenger ship* is a ship which carries more than twelve passengers.

(g)   A *cargo ship* is any ship which is not a passenger ship.

19

(h) A *tanker* is a cargo ship constructed or adapted for the carriage in bulk of liquid cargoes of an inflammable* nature.

(i) A *fishing vessel* is a vessel used for catching fish, whales, seals, walrus or other living resources of the sea.

(j) A *nuclear ship* is a ship provided with a nuclear power plant.

P88 **(k)** *New ship* means a ship the keel of which is laid or which is at a similar stage of construction on or after 25 May 1980.

(l) *Existing ship* means a ship which is not a new ship.

(m) A *mile* is 1,852 m or 6,080 ft.

P88 **(n)** *Anniversary date* means the day and the month of each year which will correspond to the date of expiry of the relevant certificate.

Regulation 3
Exceptions

(a) The present regulations, unless expressly provided otherwise, do not apply to:

    (i) Ships of war and troopships.

    (ii) Cargo ships of less than 500 gross tonnage.

    (iii) Ships not propelled by mechanical means.

    (iv) Wooden ships of primitive build.

    (v) Pleasure yachts not engaged in trade.

    (vi) Fishing vessels.

(b) Except as expressly provided in chapter V, nothing herein shall apply to ships solely navigating the Great Lakes of North America and the River St Lawrence as far east as a straight line drawn from Cap des Rosiers to West Point, Anticosti Island and, on the north side of Anticosti Island, the 63rd meridian.

---

* "Inflammable" has the same meaning as "flammable".

Regulation 4
Exemptions*

(a)   A ship which is not normally engaged on international voyages but which, in exceptional circumstances, is required to undertake a single international voyage may be exempted by the Administration from any of the requirements of the present regulations provided that it complies with safety requirements which are adequate in the opinion of the Administration for the voyage which is to be undertaken by the ship.

(b)   The Administration may exempt any ship which embodies features of a novel kind from any of the provisions of chapters II-1, II-2, III and IV of these regulations the application of which might seriously impede research into the development of such features and their incorporation in ships engaged on international voyages. Any such ship shall, however, comply with safety requirements which, in the opinion of that Administration, are adequate for the service for which it is intended and are such as to ensure the overall safety of the ship and which are acceptable to the Governments of the States to be visited by the ship. The Administration which allows any such exemption shall communicate to the Organization particulars of same and the reasons therefor which the Organization shall circulate to the Contracting Governments for their information.

Regulation 5
Equivalents

(a)   Where the present regulations require that a particular fitting, material, appliance or apparatus, or type thereof, shall be fitted or carried in a ship, or that any particular provision shall be made, the Administration may allow any other fitting, material, appliance or apparatus, or type thereof, to be fitted or carried, or any other provision to be made in that ship, if it is satisfied by trial thereof or otherwise that such fitting, material, appliance or apparatus, or type thereof, or provision, is at least as effective as that required by the present regulations.

(b)   Any Administration which so allows, in substitution, a fitting, material, appliance or apparatus, or type thereof, or provision, shall communicate to the Organization particulars thereof together with a report on any trials made and the Organization shall circulate such particulars to other Contracting Governments for the information of their officers.

---

* Refer to SLS.14/Circ.115, as amended, on the issue of exemption certificates under the 1974 SOLAS Convention and amendments thereto.

Part B
*Surveys and certificates**

[P88] # Regulation 6
Inspection and survey

(a) The inspection and survey of ships, so far as regards the enforcement of the provisions of the present regulations and the granting of exemptions therefrom, shall be carried out by officers of the Administration. The Administration may, however, entrust the inspections and surveys either to surveyors nominated for the purpose or to organizations recognized by it.

(b) An Administration nominating surveyors or recognizing organizations to conduct inspections and surveys as set forth in paragraph (a) shall as a minimum empower any nominated surveyor or recognized organization to:

    (i) require repairs to a ship;

    (ii) carry out inspections and surveys if requested by the appropriate authorities of a port State.

The Administration shall notify the Organization of the specific responsibilities and conditions of the authority delegated to nominated surveyors or recognized organizations.

(c) When a nominated surveyor or recognized organization determines that the condition of the ship or its equipment does not correspond substantially with the particulars of the certificate or is such that the ship is not fit to proceed to sea without danger to the ship, or persons on board, such surveyor or organization shall immediately ensure that corrective action is taken and shall in due course notify the Administration. If such corrective action is not taken the relevant certificate should be withdrawn and the Administration shall be notified immediately; and, if the ship is in the port of another Party, the appropriate authorities of the port State shall also be notified immediately. When an officer of the Administration, a nominated surveyor or a recognized organization has notified the appropriate authorities of the port State, the Government of the port State concerned shall give such officer, surveyor or organization any necessary assistance to carry out their obligations under this regulation. When

---

* Refer to "Global and uniform implementation of the harmonized system of survey and certification (HSSC)" and to the "Revised survey guidelines under the harmonized system of survey and certification" adopted by the Organization by resolutions A.883(21) and A.948(23) respectively.

applicable, the Government of the port State concerned shall ensure that the ship shall not sail until it can proceed to sea, or leave port for the purpose of proceeding to the appropriate repair yard, without danger to the ship or persons on board.

(d) In every case, the Administration shall fully guarantee the completeness and efficiency of the inspection and survey, and shall undertake to ensure the necessary arrangements to satisfy this obligation.

[P88] Regulation 7
*Surveys of passenger ships**

(a) A passenger ship shall be subject to the surveys specified below:

(i) an initial survey before the ship is put in service;

(ii) a renewal survey once every 12 months, except where regulation 14(b), (e), (f) and (g) is applicable;

(iii) additional surveys, as occasion arises.

(b) The surveys referred to above shall be carried out as follows:

(i) the initial survey shall include a complete inspection of the ship's structure, machinery and equipment, including the outside of the ship's bottom and the inside and outside of the boilers. This survey shall be such as to ensure that the arrangements, materials and scantlings of the structure, boilers and other pressure vessels and their appurtenances, main and auxiliary machinery, electrical installation, radio installations including those used in life-saving appliances, fire protection, fire safety systems and appliances, life-saving appliances and arrangements, shipborne navigational equipment, nautical publications, means of embarkation for pilots and other equipment fully comply with the requirements of the present regulations, and of the laws, decrees, orders and regulations promulgated as a result thereof by the Administration for ships of the service for which it is intended. The survey shall also be such as to ensure that the workmanship of all parts of the ship and its equipment is in all respects satisfactory, and that the ship is provided with the lights, shapes, means of making sound signals and distress signals as required by the provisions of the present regulations and the International Regulations for Preventing Collisions at Sea in force;

(ii) the renewal survey shall include an inspection of the structure, boilers and other pressure vessels, machinery and equipment, including the outside of the ship's bottom. The survey shall be

---

* Refer to resolution A.794(19) on surveys and inspections of ro–ro passenger ships and MSC/Circ. 956, Guidelines for unscheduled inspections of ro–ro passenger ships by flag States.

such as to ensure that the ship, as regards the structure, boilers and other pressure vessels and their appurtenances, main and auxiliary machinery, electrical installation, radio installations including those used in life-saving appliances, fire protection, fire safety systems and appliances, life-saving appliances and arrangements, shipborne navigational equipment, nautical publications, means of embarkation for pilots and other equipment is in satisfactory condition and is fit for the service for which it is intended, and that it complies with the requirements of the present regulations and of the laws, decrees, orders and regulations promulgated as a result thereof by the Administration. The lights, shapes, means of making sound signals and distress signals carried by the ship shall also be subject to the above-mentioned survey for the purpose of ensuring that they comply with the requirements of the present regulations and of the International Regulations for Preventing Collisions at Sea in force;

(iii) an additional survey either general or partial, according to the circumstances, shall be made after a repair resulting from investigations prescribed in regulation 11, or whenever any important repairs or renewals are made. The survey shall be such as to ensure that the necessary repairs or renewals have been effectively made, that the material and workmanship of such repairs or renewals are in all respects satisfactory, and that the ship complies in all respects with the provisions of the present regulations and of the International Regulations for Preventing Collisions at Sea in force, and of the laws, decrees, orders and regulations promulgated as a result thereof by the Administration;

(c) (i) the laws, decrees, orders and regulations referred to in paragraph (b) of this regulation shall be in all respects such as to ensure that, from the point of view of safety of life, the ship is fit for the service for which it is intended;

(ii) they shall among other things prescribe the requirements to be observed as to the initial and subsequent hydraulic or other acceptable alternative tests to which the main and auxiliary boilers, connections, steam pipes, high pressure receivers and fuel tanks for internal combustion engines are to be submitted including the test procedures to be followed and the intervals between two consecutive tests.

[P88] Regulation 8
Surveys of life-saving appliances and other equipment of cargo ships

(a) The life-saving appliances and other equipment of cargo ships of 500 gross tonnage and upwards as referred to in paragraph (b)(i) shall be subject to the surveys specified below:

(i) an initial survey before the ship is put in service;

(ii) a renewal survey at intervals specified by the Administration but not exceeding 5 years, except where regulation 14(b), (e), (f) and (g) is applicable;

(iii) a periodical survey within three months before or after the second anniversary date or within three months before or after the third anniversary date of the Cargo Ship Safety Equipment Certificate which shall take the place of one of the annual surveys specified in paragraph (a)(iv);

(iv) an annual survey within 3 months before or after each anniversary date of the Cargo Ship Safety Equipment Certificate;

(v) an additional survey as prescribed for passenger ships in regulation 7(b)(iii).

(b) The surveys referred to in paragraph (a) shall be carried out as follows:

(i) the initial survey shall include a complete inspection of the fire safety systems and appliances, life-saving appliances and arrangements except radio installations, the shipborne navigational equipment, means of embarkation for pilots and other equipment to which chapters II-1, II-2, III and V apply to ensure that they comply with the requirements of the present regulations, are in satisfactory condition and are fit for the service for which the ship is intended. The fire control plans, nautical publications, lights, shapes, means of making sound signals and distress signals shall also be subject to the above-mentioned survey for the purpose of ensuring that they comply with the requirements of the present regulations and, where applicable, the International Regulations for Preventing Collisions at Sea in force;*

(ii) the renewal and periodical surveys shall include an inspection of the equipment referred to in paragraph (b)(i) to ensure that it complies with the relevant requirements of the present regulations and the International Regulations for Preventing Collisions at Sea in force, is in satisfactory condition and is fit for the service for which the ship is intended;

(iii) the annual survey shall include a general inspection of the equipment referred to in paragraph (b)(i) to ensure that it has been maintained in accordance with regulation 11(a) and that it remains satisfactory for the service for which the ship is intended.

---

* Refer to the Record of approved cargo ship safety equipment (SLS.14/Circ.1).

(c)   The periodical and annual surveys referred to in paragraphs (a)(iii) and (a)(iv) shall be endorsed on the Cargo Ship Safety Equipment Certificate.

[P88]Regulation 9
Surveys of radio installations of cargo ships

(a)   The radio installations, including those used in life-saving appliances, of cargo ships to which chapters III and IV apply shall be subject to the surveys specified below:

(i)   an initial survey before the ship is put in service;

(ii)   a renewal survey at intervals specified by the Administration but not exceeding five years, except where regulation 14(b), (e), (f) and (g) is applicable;

(iii)   a periodical survey within three months before or after each anniversary date of the Cargo Ship Safety Radio Certificate;

(iv)   an additional survey as prescribed for passenger ships in regulation 7(b)(iii).

(b)   The surveys referred to in paragraph (a) shall be carried out as follows:

(i)   the initial survey shall include a complete inspection of the radio installations of cargo ships, including those used in life-saving appliances, to ensure that they comply with the requirements of the present regulations;

(ii)   the renewal and periodical surveys shall include an inspection of the radio installations of cargo ships, including those used in life-saving appliances, to ensure that they comply with the requirements of the present regulations.

(c)   The periodical surveys referred to in paragraph (a)(iii) shall be endorsed on the Cargo Ship Safety Radio Certificate.

[P88]Regulation 10
Surveys of structure, machinery and equipment
of cargo ships

(a)   The structure, machinery and equipment (other than items in respect of which a Cargo Ship Safety Equipment Certificate and a Cargo Ship Safety Radio Certificate are issued) of a cargo ship as referred to in paragraph (b)(i) shall be subject to the surveys and inspections specified below:

(i)   an initial survey including an inspection of the outside of the ship's bottom before the ship is put in service;*

(ii) a renewal survey at intervals specified by the Administration but not exceeding 5 years, except where regulation 14(b), (e), (f) and (g) is applicable;

(iii) an intermediate survey within three months before or after the second anniversary date or within three months before or after the third anniversary date of the Cargo Ship Safety Construction Certificate, which shall take the place of one of the annual surveys specified in paragraph (a)(iv);

(iv) an annual survey within 3 months before or after each anniversary date of the Cargo Ship Safety Construction Certificate;

(v)   a minimum of two inspections of the outside of the ship's bottom during any five year period, except where regulation 14(e) or (f) is applicable. Where regulation 14(e) or (f) is applicable, this five year period may be extended to coincide with the extended period of validity of the certificate. In all cases the interval between any two such inspections shall not exceed 36 months;

(vi) an additional survey as prescribed for passenger ships in regulation 7(b)(iii).

(b)   The surveys and inspections referred to in paragraph (a) shall be carried out as follows:

(i)   the initial survey shall include a complete inspection of the structure, machinery and equipment. This survey shall be such as to ensure that the arrangements, materials, scantlings and workmanship of the structure, boilers and other pressure vessels, their appurtenances, main and auxiliary machinery including steering gear and associated control systems, electrical installation and other equipment comply with the requirements of the present regulations, are in satisfactory condition and are fit for the service for which the ship is intended and that the required stability information is provided. In the case of tankers such a survey shall also include an inspection of the pump-rooms, cargo, bunker and ventilation piping systems and associated safety devices;

(ii) the renewal survey shall include an inspection of the structure, machinery and equipment as referred to in paragraph (b)(i) to ensure that they comply with the requirements of the present

---

* Refer to the circular concerning inspection of the outside of the ship's bottom (PSLS.2/Circ.5).

regulations, are in satisfactory condition and are fit for the service for which the ship is intended;

(iii) the intermediate survey shall include an inspection of the structure, boilers and other pressure vessels, machinery and equipment, the steering gear and the associated control systems and electrical installations to ensure that they remain satisfactory for the service for which the ship is intended. In the case of tankers, the survey shall also include an inspection of the pump-rooms, cargo, bunker and ventilation piping systems and associated safety devices and the testing of insulation resistance of electrical installations in dangerous zones;

(iv) the annual survey shall include a general inspection of the structure, machinery and equipment referred to in paragraph (b)(i), to ensure that they have been maintained in accordance with regulation 11(a) and that they remain satisfactory for the service for which the ship is intended;

(v) the inspection of the outside of the ship's bottom and the survey of related items inspected at the same time shall be such as to ensure that they remain satisfactory for the service for which the ship is intended.

(c) The intermediate and annual surveys and the inspections of the outside of the ship's bottom referred to in paragraphs (a)(iii), (a)(iv) and (a)(v) shall be endorsed on the Cargo Ship Safety Construction Certificate.

P88 **Regulation 11**
Maintenance of conditions after survey

(a) The condition of the ship and its equipment shall be maintained to conform with the provisions of the present regulations to ensure that the ship in all respects will remain fit to proceed to sea without danger to the ship or persons on board.

(b) After any survey of the ship under regulations 7, 8, 9 or 10 has been completed, no change shall be made in the structural arrangements, machinery, equipment and other items covered by the survey, without the sanction of the Administration.

(c) Whenever an accident occurs to a ship or a defect is discovered, either of which affects the safety of the ship or the efficiency or completeness of its life-saving appliances or other equipment, the master or owner of the ship shall report at the earliest opportunity to the Administration, the nominated surveyor or recognized organization responsible for issuing the relevant certificate, who shall cause investigations to be initiated to determine whether a survey, as required by regulations 7, 8, 9 or 10, is necessary. If the ship is in a port of another Contracting Government, the master or owner shall also report immediately to the appropriate authorities of the port State and the nominated surveyor or recognized organization shall ascertain that such a report has been made.

[P88] Regulation 12
*Issue or endorsement of certificates**

(a) **(i)** a certificate called a Passenger Ship Safety Certificate shall be issued after an initial or renewal survey to a passenger ship which complies with the relevant requirements of chapters II-1, II-2, III, IV and V and any other relevant requirements of the present regulations;

(ii) a certificate called a Cargo Ship Safety Construction Certificate† shall be issued after an initial or renewal survey to a cargo ship which complies with the relevant requirements of chapters II-1 and II-2 (other than those relating to fire safety systems and appliances and fire control plans) and any other relevant requirements of the present regulations;

(iii) a certificate called a Cargo Ship Safety Equipment Certificate† shall be issued after an initial or renewal survey to a cargo ship which complies with the relevant requirements of chapters II-1, II-2, III and V and any other relevant requirements of the present regulations;

(iv) a certificate called a Cargo Ship Safety Radio Certificate shall be issued after an initial or renewal survey to a cargo ship which complies with the relevant requirements of chapter IV and any other relevant requirements of the present regulations;

(v) (1) a certificate called a Cargo Ship Safety Certificate may be issued after an initial or renewal survey to a cargo ship which complies with the relevant requirements of chapters II-1, II-2, III, IV and V and any other relevant requirements of the present regulations, as an alternative to the certificates referred to in paragraph (a)(ii), (a)(iii) and (a)(iv);

(2) whenever in this chapter reference is made to a Cargo Ship Safety Construction Certificate, Cargo Ship Safety Equipment Certificate or Cargo Ship Safety Radio Certificate, it shall apply to a Cargo Ship Safety Certificate, if it is used as an alternative to these certificates.

---

* Refer to resolution A.791(19) on application of the International Convention on Tonnage Measurement of Ships, 1969, to existing ships.
† Refer to the circular concerning issue of supplements and attachments (PSLS.2/Circ.1).

(vi) the Passenger Ship Safety Certificate, the Cargo Ship Safety Equipment Certificate, the Cargo Ship Safety Radio Certificate and the Cargo Ship Safety Certificate, referred to in subparagraphs (i), (iii), (iv) and (v), shall be supplemented by a Record of Equipment;

(vii) when an exemption is granted to a ship under and in accordance with the provisions of the present regulations, a certificate called an Exemption Certificate shall be issued in addition to the certificates prescribed in this paragraph;

(viii) the certificates referred to in this regulation shall be issued or endorsed either by the Administration or by any person or organization authorized by it. In every case, that Administration assumes full responsibility for the certificates.

(b) A Contracting Government shall not issue certificates under, and in accordance with, the provisions of the International Convention for the Safety of Life at Sea, 1960, 1948 or 1929, after the date on which acceptance of the present Convention by the Government takes effect.

[P88] Regulation 13
Issue or endorsement of certificates by another Government

A Contracting Government may, at the request of the Administration, cause a ship to be surveyed and, if satisfied that the requirements of the present regulations are complied with, shall issue or authorize the issue of certificates to the ship and, where appropriate, endorse or authorize the endorsement of certificates on the ship in accordance with the present regulations. Any certificate so issued shall contain a statement to the effect that it has been issued at the request of the Government of the State the flag of which the ship is entitled to fly, and it shall have the same force and receive the same recognition as a certificate issued under regulation 12.

[P88] Regulation 14
Duration and validity of certificates

(a) A Passenger Ship Safety Certificate shall be issued for a period not exceeding 12 months. A Cargo Ship Safety Construction Certificate, Cargo Ship Safety Equipment Certificate and Cargo Ship Safety Radio Certificate shall be issued for a period specified by the Administration which shall not exceed five years. An Exemption Certificate shall not be valid for longer than the period of the certificate to which it refers.

(b) **(i)** notwithstanding the requirements of paragraph (a), when the renewal survey is completed within three months before the expiry date of the existing certificate, the new certificate shall be valid from the date of completion of the renewal survey to:

(1)   for a passenger ship, a date not exceeding 12 months from the date of expiry of the existing certificate;

(2)   for a cargo ship, a date not exceeding five years from the date of expiry of the existing certificate;

(ii)   when the renewal survey is completed after the expiry date of the existing certificate, the new certificate shall be valid from the date of completion of the renewal survey to:

(1)   for a passenger ship, a date not exceeding 12 months from the date of expiry of the existing certificate;

(2)   for a cargo ship, a date not exceeding five years from the date of expiry of the existing certificate;

(iii)   when the renewal survey is completed more than three months before the expiry date of the existing certificate, the new certificate shall be valid from the date of completion of the renewal survey to:

(1)   for a passenger ship, a date not exceeding 12 months from the date of completion of the renewal survey;

(2)   for a cargo ship, a date not exceeding five years from the date of completion of the renewal survey.

(c)   If a certificate other than a Passenger Ship Safety Certificate is issued for a period of less than five years, the Administration may extend the validity of the certificate beyond the expiry date to the maximum period specified in paragraph (a), provided that the surveys referred to in regulations 8, 9 and 10 applicable when a certificate is issued for a period of 5 years are carried out as appropriate.

(d)   If a renewal survey has been completed and a new certificate cannot be issued or placed on board the ship before the expiry date of the existing certificate, the person or organization authorized by the Administration may endorse the existing certificate and such a certificate shall be accepted as valid for a further period which shall not exceed 5 months from the expiry date.

(e)   If a ship at the time when a certificate expires is not in a port in which it is to be surveyed, the Administration may extend the period of validity of the certificate but this extension shall be granted only for the purpose of allowing the ship to complete its voyage to the port in which it is to be surveyed, and then only in cases where it appears proper and reasonable to do so. No certificate shall be extended for a period longer than three months, and a ship to which an extension is granted shall not, on its arrival in the port in which it is to be surveyed, be entitled by virtue of such extension to leave that port without having a new certificate. When the renewal survey is completed, the new certificate shall be valid to:

(i)   for a passenger ship, a date not exceeding 12 months from the date of expiry of the existing certificate before the extension was granted;

(ii)   for a cargo ship, a date not exceeding 5 years from the date of expiry of the existing certificate before the extension was granted.

(f)   A certificate issued to a ship engaged on short voyages which has not been extended under the foregoing provisions of this regulation may be extended by the Administration for a period of grace of up to one month from the date of expiry stated on it. When the renewal survey is completed, the new certificate shall be valid to:

(i)   for a passenger ship, a date not exceeding 12 months from the date of expiry of the existing certificate before the extension was granted;

(ii)   for a cargo ship, a date not exceeding 5 years from the date of expiry of the existing certificate before the extension was granted.

(g)   In special circumstances, as determined by the Administration, a new certificate need not be dated from the date of expiry of the existing certificate as required by paragraphs (b)(ii), (e) or (f). In these special circumstances, the new certificate shall be valid to:

(i)   for a passenger ship, a date not exceeding 12 months from the date of completion of the renewal survey;

(ii)   for a cargo ship, a date not exceeding five years from the date of completion of the renewal survey.

(h)   If an annual, intermediate or periodical survey is completed before the period specified in the relevant regulations then:

(i)   the anniversary date shown on the relevant certificate shall be amended by endorsement to a date which shall not be more than three months later than the date on which the survey was completed;

(ii)   the subsequent annual, intermediate or periodical survey required by the relevant regulations shall be completed at the intervals prescribed by these regulations using the new anniversary date;

(iii)   the expiry date may remain unchanged provided one or more annual, intermediate or periodical surveys, as appropriate, are carried out so that the maximum intervals between the surveys prescribed by the relevant regulations are not exceeded.

(i)   A certificate issued under regulation 12 or 13 shall cease to be valid in any of the following cases:

    (i)   if the relevant surveys and inspections are not completed within the periods specified under regulations 7(a), 8(a), 9(a) and 10(a);

    (ii)   if the certificate is not endorsed in accordance with the present regulations;

    (iii)   upon transfer of the ship to the flag of another State. A new certificate shall only be issued when the Government issuing the new certificate is fully satisfied that the ship is in compliance with the requirements of regulation 11(a) and (b). In the case of a transfer between Contracting Governments, if requested within three months after the transfer has taken place, the Government of the State whose flag the ship was formerly entitled to fly shall, as soon as possible, transmit to the Administration copies of the certificates carried by the ship before a transfer and, if available, copies of the relevant survey reports.

P88 Regulation 15
Forms of certificates and records of equipment

The certificates and records of equipment shall be drawn up in the form corresponding to the models given in the appendix to the annex to the present Convention. If the language used is neither English nor French, the text shall include a translation into one of these languages.*

P88 Regulation 16
Availability of certificates

The certificates issued under regulations 12 and 13 shall be readily available on board for examination at all times.

Regulation 17
Acceptance of certificates

Certificates issued under the authority of a Contracting Government shall be accepted by the other Contracting Governments for all purposes covered by the present Convention. They shall be regarded by the other Contracting Governments as having the same force as certificates issued by them.

---

* Refer to resolution A.561(14) on translation of the text of certificates.

Regulation 18
Qualification of certificates

(a) If in the course of a particular voyage a ship has on board a number of persons less than the total number stated in the Passenger Ship Safety Certificate and is in consequence, in accordance with the provisions of the present regulations, free to carry a smaller number of lifeboats and other life-saving appliances than that stated in the certificate, an annex may be issued by the Government, person or organization referred to in regulation 12 or 13 of this chapter.

(b) This annex shall state that in the circumstances there is no infringement of the provisions of the present regulations. It shall be annexed to the certificate and shall be substituted for it in so far as the life-saving appliances are concerned. It shall be valid only for the particular voyage for which it is issued.

P88 Regulation 19
Control[*]

(a)
Every ship when in a port of another Contracting Government is subject to control by officers duly authorized by such Government in so far as this control is directed towards verifying that the certificates issued under regulation 12 or regulation 13 are valid.

(b) Such certificates, if valid, shall be accepted unless there are clear grounds for believing that the condition of the ship or of its equipment does not correspond substantially with the particulars of any of the certificates or that the ship and its equipment are not in compliance with the provisions of regulation 11(a) and (b).

(c) In the circumstances given in paragraph (b) or where a certificate has expired or ceased to be valid, the officer carrying out the control shall take steps to ensure that the ship shall not sail until it can proceed to sea or leave the port for the purpose of proceeding to the appropriate repair yard without danger to the ship or persons on board.

(d) In the event of this control giving rise to an intervention of any kind, the officer carrying out the control shall forthwith inform, in writing, the Consul or, in his absence, the nearest diplomatic representative of the State whose flag the ship is entitled to fly of all the circumstances in which intervention was deemed necessary. In addition, nominated surveyors or recognized organizations responsible for the issue of the certificates shall also

---

[*] Refer to the Procedures for port State control adopted by the Organization by resolution A.787(19), as amended by resolution A.882(21).

be notified. The facts concerning the intervention shall be reported to the Organization.

(e) The port State authority concerned shall notify all relevant information about the ship to the authorities of the next port of call, in addition to parties mentioned in paragraph (d), if it is unable to take action as specified in paragraphs (c) and (d) or if the ship has been allowed to proceed to the next port of call.

(f) When exercising control under this regulation all possible efforts shall be made to avoid a ship being unduly detained or delayed. If a ship is thereby unduly detained or delayed it shall be entitled to compensation for any loss or damage suffered.

Regulation 20
Privileges

The privileges of the present Convention may not be claimed in favour of any ship unless it holds appropriate valid certificates.

Part C
Casualties

Regulation 21
Casualties

(a)   Each Administration undertakes to conduct an investigation of any casualty occurring to any of its ships subject to the provisions of the present Convention when it judges that such an investigation may assist in determining what changes in the present regulations might be desirable.[*]

(b)   Each Contracting Government undertakes to supply the Organization with pertinent information concerning the findings of such investigations. No reports or recommendations of the Organization based upon such information shall disclose the identity or nationality of the ships concerned or in any manner fix or imply responsibility upon any ship or person.

---

[*] Refer to the following resolution adopted by the Organization:

   Resolution A.849(20): Code for the investigation of marine casualties and incidents, as amended by resolution A.884(21).

Refer also to:

   MSC/Circ.953 – MEPC/Circ.372: Reports on marine casualties and incidents. Revised harmonized reporting procedures – Reports required under SOLAS regulation I/21 and MARPOL 73/78 articles 8 and 12.

CHAPTER II-1
Construction – Structure, subdivision and stability, machinery and electrical installations

37

Chapter II-1: Construction – structure, stability, installations
Contents

Part B-1 – *Subdivision and damage stability of cargo ships*

Part C – *Machinery installations*

Chapter II-1: Construction – structure, stability, installations
Contents

Part D – *Electrical installations*

Part E – *Additional requirements for periodically unattended machinery spaces*

Part A
General

Regulation 1
Application

1.1   Unless expressly provided otherwise, this chapter shall apply to ships the keels of which are laid or which are at a similar stage of construction on or after 1 July 1986.

1.2   For the purpose of this chapter, the term *a similar stage of construction* means the stage at which:

> **.1**   construction identifiable with a specific ship begins; and

> **.2**   assembly of that ship has commenced comprising at least 50 tonnes or one per cent of the estimated mass of all structural material, whichever is less.

1.3   For the purpose of this chapter:

> **.1**   the expression *ships constructed* means ships the keels of which are laid or which are at a similar stage of construction;

> **.2**   the expression *all ships* means ships constructed before, on or after 1 July 1986;

> **.3**   a cargo ship, whenever built, which is converted to a passenger ship shall be treated as a passenger ship constructed on the date on which such a conversion commences.

2   Unless expressly provided otherwise, for ships constructed before 1 July 1986 the Administration shall ensure that the requirements which are applicable under chapter II-1 of the International Convention for the Safety of Life at Sea, 1974, as amended by resolution MSC.1(XLV), are complied with.

3.1   All ships which undergo repairs, alterations, modifications and outfitting related thereto shall continue to comply with at least the requirements previously applicable to these ships. Such ships if constructed before 1 July 1986 shall, as a rule, comply with the requirements for ships constructed on or after that date to at least the same extent as they did before undergoing such repairs, alterations, modifications or outfitting. Repairs, alterations and modifications of a major character* and outfitting related thereto shall meet the requirements for ships constructed on or after 1 July 1986 in so far as the Administration deems reasonable and practicable.†

3.2 Notwithstanding the provisions of paragraph 3.1, passenger ships which undergo repairs, alterations and modifications to meet the requirements of regulation 8-1 shall not be deemed to have undergone repairs, alterations and modifications of a major character.

4 The Administration of a State may, if it considers that the sheltered nature and conditions of the voyage are such as to render the application of any specific requirements of this chapter unreasonable or unnecessary, exempt from those requirements individual ships or classes of ships entitled to fly the flag of that State which, in the course of their voyage, do not proceed more than 20 miles from the nearest land.

5 In the case of passenger ships which are employed in special trades for the carriage of large numbers of special trade passengers, such as the pilgrim trade, the Administration of the State whose flag such ships are entitled to fly, if satisfied that it is impracticable to enforce compliance with the requirements of this chapter, may exempt such ships from those requirements, provided that they comply fully with the provisions of:

   .1   the rules annexed to the Special Trade Passenger Ships Agreement, 1971; and

   .2   the rules annexed to the Protocol on Space Requirements for Special Trade Passenger Ships, 1973.

Regulation 2
Definitions

For the purpose of this chapter, unless expressly provided otherwise:

1.1 *Subdivision load line* is a waterline used in determining the subdivision of the ship.

1.2 *Deepest subdivision load line* is the waterline which corresponds to the greatest draught permitted by the subdivision requirements which are applicable.

2 *Length of the ship* is the length measured between perpendiculars taken at the extremities of the deepest subdivision load line.

---

* Refer to MSC/Circ.650 on interpretation of alterations and modifications of a major character.
† Refer to MSC/Circ.609 on interpretation of regulation II-1/1.3 of the 1974 SOLAS Convention.

3   *Breadth of the ship* is the extreme width from outside of frame to outside of frame at or below the deepest subdivision load line.

4   *Draught* is the vertical distance from the moulded base line amidships to the subdivision load line in question.

5   *Bulkhead deck* is the uppermost deck up to which the transverse watertight bulkheads are carried.

6   *Margin line* is a line drawn at least 76 mm below the upper surface of the bulkhead deck at side.

7   *Permeability of a space* is the percentage of that space which can be occupied by water. The volume of a space which extends above the margin line shall be measured only to the height of that line.

8   *Machinery space* is to be taken as extending from the moulded base line to the margin line and between the extreme main transverse watertight bulkheads, bounding the spaces containing the main and auxiliary propulsion machinery, boilers serving the needs of propulsion, and all permanent coal bunkers. In the case of unusual arrangements, the Administration may define the limits of the machinery spaces.

9   *Passenger spaces* are those spaces which are provided for the accommodation and use of passengers, excluding baggage, store, provision and mail rooms. For the purposes of regulations 5 and 6, spaces provided below the margin line for the accommodation and use of the crew shall be regarded as passenger spaces.

10   In all cases volumes and areas shall be calculated to moulded lines.

11   *Weathertight* means that in any sea conditions water will not penetrate into the ship.

12   An *oil tanker* is the oil tanker defined in regulation 1 of Annex I of the Protocol of 1978 relating to the International Convention for the Prevention of Pollution from Ships, 1973.

13   *Ro–ro passenger ship* means a passenger ship with ro–ro cargo spaces[*] or special category spaces as defined in regulation II-2/3.

Regulation 3
Definitions relating to parts C, D and E

For the purpose of parts C, D and E, unless expressly provided otherwise:

1   *Steering gear control system* is the equipment by which orders are transmitted from the navigation bridge to the steering gear power units.

---

[*] This relates to the chapter II-2 in force before 1 July 2002. The equivalent term in the amended chapter II-2 is "ro–ro spaces".

Steering gear control systems comprise transmitters, receivers, hydraulic control pumps and their associated motors, motor controllers, piping and cables.

2 *Main steering gear* is the machinery, rudder actuators, steering gear power units, if any, and ancillary equipment and the means of applying torque to the rudder stock (e.g. tiller or quadrant) necessary for effecting movement of the rudder for the purpose of steering the ship under normal service conditions.

3 *Steering gear power unit* is:

.1 in the case of electric steering gear, an electric motor and its associated electrical equipment;

.2 in the case of electrohydraulic steering gear, an electric motor and its associated electrical equipment and connected pump;

.3 in the case of other hydraulic steering gear, a driving engine and connected pump.

4 *Auxiliary steering gear* is the equipment other than any part of the main steering gear necessary to steer the ship in the event of failure of the main steering gear but not including the tiller, quadrant or components serving the same purpose.

5 *Normal operational and habitable condition* is a condition under which the ship as a whole, the machinery, services, means and aids ensuring propulsion, ability to steer, safe navigation, fire and flooding safety, internal and external communications and signals, means of escape, and emergency boat winches, as well as the designed comfortable conditions of habitability are in working order and functioning normally.

6 *Emergency condition* is a condition under which any services needed for normal operational and habitable conditions are not in working order due to failure of the main source of electrical power.

7 *Main source of electrical power* is a source intended to supply electrical power to the main switchboard for distribution to all services necessary for maintaining the ship in normal operational and habitable condition.

8 *Dead ship condition* is the condition under which the main propulsion plant, boilers and auxiliaries are not in operation due to the absence of power.

9 *Main generating station* is the space in which the main source of electrical power is situated.

10 *Main switchboard* is a switchboard which is directly supplied by the main source of electrical power and is intended to distribute electrical energy to the ship's services.

11 *Emergency switchboard* is a switchboard which in the event of failure of the main electrical power supply system is directly supplied by the emergency source of electrical power or the transitional source of emergency power and is intended to distribute electrical energy to the emergency services.

12 *Emergency source of electrical power* is a source of electrical power, intended to supply the emergency switchboard in the event of failure of the supply from the main source of electrical power.

13 *Power actuating system* is the hydraulic equipment provided for supplying power to turn the rudder stock, comprising a steering gear power unit or units, together with the associated pipes and fittings, and a rudder actuator. The power actuating systems may share common mechanical components, i.e., tiller, quadrant and rudder stock, or components serving the same purpose.

14 *Maximum ahead service speed* is the greatest speed which the ship is designed to maintain in service at sea at the deepest seagoing draught.

15 *Maximum astern speed* is the speed which it is estimated the ship can attain at the designed maximum astern power at the deepest seagoing draught.

16 *Machinery spaces* are all machinery spaces of category A and all other spaces containing propelling machinery, boilers, oil fuel units, steam and internal combustion engines, generators and major electrical machinery, oil filling stations, refrigerating, stabilizing, ventilation and air conditioning machinery, and similar spaces, and trunks to such spaces.

17 *Machinery spaces of category A* are those spaces and trunks to such spaces which contain:

.1   internal combustion machinery used for main propulsion; or

.2   internal combustion machinery used for purposes other than main propulsion where such machinery has in the aggregate a total power output of not less than 375 kW; or

.3   any oil-fired boiler or oil fuel unit.

18 *Control stations* are those spaces in which the ship's radio or main navigating equipment or the emergency source of power is located or where the fire recording or fire control equipment is centralized.

19 *Chemical tanker* is a cargo ship constructed or adapted and used for the carriage in bulk of any liquid product listed in either:

.1   chapter 17 of the International Code for the Construction and Equipment of Ships Carrying Dangerous Chemicals in Bulk adopted by the Maritime Safety Committee by resolution MSC.4(48), hereinafter referred to as "the International Bulk Chemical Code", as may be amended by the Organization; or

.2   chapter VI of the Code for the Construction and Equipment of Ships Carrying Dangerous Chemicals in Bulk adopted by the Assembly of the Organization by resolution A.212(VII), hereinafter referred to as "the Bulk Chemical Code", as has been or may be amended by the Organization;

whichever is applicable.

20   *Gas carrier* is a cargo ship constructed or adapted and used for the carriage in bulk of any liquefied gas or other products listed in either:

.1   chapter 19 of the International Code for the Construction and Equipment of Ships Carrying Liquefied Gases in Bulk adopted by the Maritime Safety Committee by resolution MSC.5(48) hereinafter referred to as "the International Gas Carrier Code", as may be amended by the Organization; or

.2   chapter XIX of the Code for the Construction and Equipment of Ships Carrying Liquefied Gases in Bulk adopted by the Organization by resolution A.328(IX), hereinafter referred to as "the Gas Carrier Code", as has been or may be amended by the Organization;

whichever is applicable.

21   *Deadweight* is the difference in tonnes between the displacement of a ship in water of a specific gravity of 1.025 at the load waterline corresponding to the assigned summer freeboard and the lightweight of the ship.

22   *Lightweight* is the displacement of a ship in tonnes without cargo, fuel, lubricating oil, ballast water, fresh water and feedwater in tanks, consumable stores, and passengers and crew and their effects.

Part A-1
Structure of ships

Regulation 3-1
Structural, mechanical and electrical requirements for ships

In addition to the requirements contained elsewhere in the present regulations, ships shall be designed, constructed and maintained in compliance with the structural, mechanical and electrical requirements of a classification society which is recognized by the Administration in accordance with the provisions of regulation XI/1, or with applicable national standards of the Administration which provide an equivalent level of safety.

Regulation 3-2
Corrosion prevention of seawater ballast tanks

1   This regulation applies to oil tankers and bulk carriers constructed on or after 1 July 1998.

2   All dedicated seawater ballast tanks shall have an efficient corrosion prevention system, such as hard protective coatings or equivalent. The coatings should preferably be of a light colour. The scheme for the selection, application and maintenance of the system shall be approved by the Administration, based on the guidelines adopted by the Organization.* Where appropriate, sacrificial anodes shall also be used.

Regulation 3-3
Safe access to tanker bows

1   For the purpose of this regulation and regulation 3-4, tankers include oil tankers as defined in regulation 2.12, chemical tankers as defined in regulation VII/8.2 and gas carriers as defined in regulation VII/11.2.

---

* Refer to the Guidelines for the selection, application and maintenance of corrosion prevention systems of dedicated seawater ballast tanks adopted by the Organization by resolution A.798(19).

2 Every tanker constructed on or after 1 July 1998 shall be provided with the means to enable the crew to gain safe access to the bow even in severe weather conditions. For tankers constructed before 1 July 1998, such means of access shall be provided at the first scheduled dry-docking after 1 July 1998, but not later than 1 July 2001. Such means of access shall be approved by the Administration based on the guidelines developed by the Organization.[*]

Regulation 3-4
Emergency towing arrangements on tankers

1 Emergency towing arrangements shall be fitted at both ends on board every tanker of not less than 20,000 tonnes deadweight.

2 For tankers constructed on or after 1 July 2002:

  .1 the arrangements shall, at all times, be capable of rapid deployment in the absence of main power on the ship to be towed and easy connection to the towing ship. At least one of the emergency towing arrangements shall be pre-rigged ready for rapid deployment; and

  .2 emergency towing arrangements at both ends shall be of adequate strength taking into account the size and deadweight of the ship, and the expected forces during bad weather conditions. The design and construction and prototype testing of emergency towing arrangements shall be approved by the Administration, based on the Guidelines developed by the Organization.

3 For tankers constructed before 1 July 2002, the design and construction of emergency towing arrangements shall be approved by the Administration, based on the Guidelines developed by the Organization.[†]

Regulation 3-5
New installation of materials containing asbestos

1 This regulation shall apply to materials used for the structure, machinery, electrical installations and equipment covered by the present Convention.

---

[*] Refer to the Guidelines for safe access to tanker bows adopted by the Maritime Safety Committee by resolution MSC.62(67).

[†] Refer to the Guidelines on emergency towing arrangements for tankers adopted by the Maritime Safety Committee by resolution MSC.35(63), as may be amended.

2   For all ships, new installation of materials which contain asbestos shall be prohibited except for:

.1   vanes used in rotary vane compressors and rotary vane vacuum pumps;

.2   watertight joints and linings used for the circulation of fluids when, at high temperature (in excess of 350°C) or pressure (in excess of 7×10^6 Pa), there is a risk of fire, corrosion or toxicity; and

.3   supple and flexible thermal insulation assemblies used for temperatures above 1,000°C.

Regulation 3-6
Access to and within spaces in the cargo area
of oil tankers and bulk carriers

1   Application

1.1   Except as provided for in paragraph 1.2, this regulation applies to oil tankers of 500 gross tonnage and over and bulk carriers, as defined in regulation IX/1, of 20,000 gross tonnage and over, constructed on or after 1 January 2005.

1.2   Oil tankers of 500 gross tonnage and over constructed on or after 1 October 1994 but before 1 January 2005 shall comply with the provisions of regulation II-1/12-2 adopted by resolution MSC.27(61).[*]

2   Means of access to cargo and other spaces

2.1   Each space within the cargo area shall be provided with a permanent means of access to enable, throughout the life of a ship, overall and close-up inspections and thickness measurements of the ship's structures to be carried out by the Administration, the Company, as defined in regulation IX/1, and the ship's personnel and others as necessary. Such means of access shall comply with the requirements of paragraph 5 and with the Technical provisions for means of access for inspections, adopted by the Maritime Safety Committee by resolution MSC.133(76), as may be amended by the Organization, provided that such amendments are adopted, brought into force and take effect in accordance with the provisions of article VIII of the present Convention concerning the amendment procedures applicable to the annex other than chapter I.

2.2   Where a permanent means of access may be susceptible to damage during normal cargo loading and unloading operations or where it is

---

[*] Refer to annex 4.

impracticable to fit permanent means of access, the Administration may allow, in lieu thereof, the provision of movable or portable means of access, as specified in the Technical provisions, provided that the means of attaching, rigging, suspending or supporting the portable means of access forms a permanent part of the ship's structure. All portable equipment shall be capable of being readily erected or deployed by ship's personnel.

2.3 The construction and materials of all means of access and their attachment to the ship's structure shall be to the satisfaction of the Administration. The means of access shall be subject to survey prior to, or in conjunction with, its use in carrying out surveys in accordance with regulation I/10.

3   Safe access to cargo holds, cargo tanks, ballast tanks and other spaces

3.1 Safe access* to cargo holds, cofferdams, ballast tanks, cargo tanks and other spaces in the cargo area shall be direct from the open deck and such as to ensure their complete inspection. Safe access* to double bottom spaces may be from a pump-room, deep cofferdam, pipe tunnel, cargo hold, double hull space or similar compartment not intended for the carriage of oil or hazardous cargoes.

3.2 Tanks, and subdivisions of tanks, having a length of 35 m or more, shall be fitted with at least two access hatchways and ladders, as far apart as practicable. Tanks less than 35 m in length shall be served by at least one access hatchway and ladder. When a tank is subdivided by one or more swash bulkheads or similar obstructions which do not allow ready means of access to the other parts of the tank, at least two hatchways and ladders shall be fitted.

3.3 Each cargo hold shall be provided with at least two means of access as far apart as practicable. In general, these accesses should be arranged diagonally, for example one access near the forward bulkhead on the port side, the other one near the aft bulkhead on the starboard side.

4   Ship Structure Access Manual

4.1 A ship's means of access to carry out overall and close-up inspections and thickness measurements shall be described in a Ship Structure Access Manual approved by the Administration, an updated copy of which shall be kept on board. The Ship Structure Access Manual shall include the following for each space in the cargo area:

    .1   plans showing the means of access to the space, with appropriate technical specifications and dimensions;

---

* Refer to the Recommendations for entering enclosed spaces aboard ships, adopted by the Organization by resolution A.864(20).

.2 plans showing the means of access within each space to enable an overall inspection to be carried out, with appropriate technical specifications and dimensions. The plans shall indicate from where each area in the space can be inspected;

.3 plans showing the means of access within the space to enable close-up inspections to be carried out, with appropriate technical specifications and dimensions. The plans shall indicate the positions of critical structural areas, whether the means of access is permanent or portable and from where each area can be inspected;

.4 instructions for inspecting and maintaining the structural strength of all means of access and means of attachment, taking into account any corrosive atmosphere that may be within the space;

.5 instructions for safety guidance when rafting is used for close-up inspections and thickness measurements;

.6 instructions for the rigging and use of any portable means of access in a safe manner;

.7 an inventory of all portable means of access; and

.8 records of periodical inspections and maintenance of the ship's means of access.

4.2 For the purpose of this regulation "critical structural areas" are locations which have been identified from calculations to require monitoring or from the service history of similar or sister ships to be sensitive to cracking, buckling, deformation or corrosion which would impair the structural integrity of the ship.

5   General technical specifications

5.1 For access through horizontal openings, hatches or manholes, the dimensions shall be sufficient to allow a person wearing a self-contained air-breathing apparatus and protective equipment to ascend or descend any ladder without obstruction and also provide a clear opening to facilitate the hoisting of an injured person from the bottom of the space. The minimum clear opening shall not be less than 600 mm × 600 mm. When access to a cargo hold is arranged through the cargo hatch, the top of the ladder shall be placed as close as possible to the hatch coaming. Access hatch coamings having a height greater than 900 mm shall also have steps on the outside in conjunction with the ladder.

5.2 For access through vertical openings, or manholes, in swash bulkheads, floors, girders and web frames providing passage through the length and breadth of the space, the minimum opening shall be not less than

600 mm × 800 mm at a height of not more than 600 mm from the bottom shell plating unless gratings or other foot holds are provided.

5.3   For oil tankers of less than 5,000 tonnes deadweight, the Administration may approve, in special circumstances, smaller dimensions for the openings referred to in paragraphs 5.1 and 5.2, if the ability to traverse such openings or to remove an injured person can be proved to the satisfaction of the Administration.

Part B
*Subdivision and stability**

(Part B applies to passenger ships and to cargo
ships, as indicated in the regulations)

Regulation 4
Floodable length in passenger ships

1   The floodable length at any point of the length of a ship shall be
determined by a method of calculation which takes into consideration the
form, draught and other characteristics of the ship in question.

2   In a ship with a continuous bulkhead deck, the floodable length at a
given point is the maximum portion of the length of the ship, having its
centre at the point in question, which can be flooded under the definite
assumptions set forth in regulation 5 without the ship being submerged
beyond the margin line.

3.1   In the case of a ship not having a continuous bulkhead deck, the
floodable length at any point may be determined to an assumed continuous
margin line which at no point is less than 76 mm below the top of the deck
(at side) to which the bulkheads concerned and the shell are carried
watertight.

3.2   Where a portion of an assumed margin line is appreciably below the
deck to which bulkheads are carried, the Administration may permit a
limited relaxation in the watertightness of those portions of the bulkheads
which are above the margin line and immediately under the higher deck.

Regulation 5
Permeability in passenger ships

1.1   The definite assumptions referred to in regulation 4 relate to the
permeability of the spaces below the margin line.

1.2   In determining the floodable length, a uniform average permeability

---

* Instead of the requirements in this part, the Regulations on subdivision and stability of
passenger ships as an equivalent to part B of chapter II of the International Convention for the
Safety of Life at Sea, 1960, adopted by the Organization by resolution A.265(VIII), may be
used, if applied in their entirety.

shall be used throughout the whole length of each of the following portions of the ship below the margin line:

 .1 the machinery space as defined in regulation 2;

 .2 the portion forward of the machinery space; and

 .3 the portion abaft the machinery space.

2.1 The uniform average permeability throughout the machinery space shall be determined from the formula:

$$85 + 10\left(\frac{a-c}{v}\right)$$

where:

 a = the volume of the passenger spaces, as defined in regulation 2, which are situated below the margin line within the limits of the machinery space;

 c = the volume of between-deck spaces below the margin line within the limits of the machinery space which are appropriated to cargo, coal or stores;

 v = the whole volume of the machinery space below the margin line.

2.2 Where it is shown to the satisfaction of the Administration that the average permeability as determined by detailed calculation is less than that given by the formula, the detailed calculated value may be used. For the purpose of such calculation, the permeability of passenger spaces, as defined in regulation 2, shall be taken as 95, that of all cargo, coal and store spaces as 60, and that of double bottom, oil fuel and other tanks at such value as may be approved in each case.

3 Except as provided in paragraph 4, the uniform average permeability throughout the portion of the ship forward of or abaft the machinery space shall be determined from the formula:

$$63 + 35\frac{a}{v}$$

where:

 a = the volume of the passenger spaces, which are situated below the margin line, forward of or abaft the machinery space; and

 v = the whole volume of the portion of the ship below the margin line forward of or abaft the machinery space.

4.1 In the case of special subdivision required in regulation 6.5, the uniform average permeability throughout the portion of the ship forward of or abaft the machinery space shall be:

$$95 - 35\frac{b}{v}$$

where:

b = the volume of the spaces below the margin line and above the tops of floors, inner bottom, or peak tanks, as the case may be, which are appropriated to and used as cargo spaces, coal or oil fuel bunkers, store-rooms, baggage and mail rooms, chain lockers and fresh water tanks, forward of or abaft the machinery space; and

v = the whole volume of the portion of the ship below the margin line forward of or abaft the machinery space.

4.2   In the case of ships engaged on services where the cargo holds are not generally occupied by any substantial quantities of cargo, no part of the cargo spaces is to be included in calculating b.

5   In the case of unusual arrangements the Administration may allow, or require, a detailed calculation of average permeability for the portions forward of or abaft the machinery space. For the purpose of such calculation, the permeability of passenger spaces as defined in regulation 2 shall be taken as 95, that of spaces containing machinery as 85, that of all cargo, coal and store spaces as 60, and that of double bottom, oil fuel and other tanks at such value as may be approved in each case.

6   Where a between-deck compartment between two watertight transverse bulkheads contains any passenger or crew space, the whole of that compartment, less any space completely enclosed within permanent steel bulkheads and appropriated to other purposes, shall be regarded as passenger space. Where, however, the passenger or crew space in question is completely enclosed within permanent steel bulkheads, only the space so enclosed need be considered as passenger space.

Regulation 6
Permissible length of compartments
in passenger ships

1   Ships shall be as efficiently subdivided as is possible having regard to the nature of the service for which they are intended. The degree of subdivision shall vary with the length of the ship and with the service, in such manner that the highest degree of subdivision corresponds with the ships of greatest length, primarily engaged in the carriage of passengers.

2   Factor of subdivision

2.1   The maximum permissible length of a compartment having its centre at any point in the ship's length is obtained from the floodable length by multiplying the latter by an appropriate factor called the factor of subdivision.

2.2   The factor of subdivision shall depend on the length of the ship, and for a given length shall vary according to the nature of the service for which the ship is intended. It shall decrease in a regular and continuous manner,

.1   as the length of the ship increases, and

.2   from a factor A, applicable to ships primarily engaged in the carriage of cargo, to a factor B, applicable to ships primarily engaged in the carriage of passengers.

2.3   The variations of the factors A and B shall be expressed by the following formulae (1) and (2) where L is the length of the ship as defined in regulation 2:

$$A = \frac{58.2}{L - 60} + 0.18 \quad (L = 131 \text{ m and upwards}) \tag{1}$$

$$B = \frac{30.3}{L - 42} + 0.18 \quad (L = 79 \text{ m and upwards}) \tag{2}$$

3   Criterion of service

3.1   For a ship of given length the appropriate factor of subdivision shall be determined by the criterion of service numeral (hereinafter called the criterion numeral) as given by the following formulae (3) and (4) where:

C_s =   the criterion numeral;

L =   the length of the ship (metres), as defined in regulation 2;

M =   the volume of the machinery space (cubic metres), as defined in regulation 2; with the addition thereto of the volume of any permanent oil fuel bunkers which may be situated above the inner bottom and forward of or abaft the machinery space;

P =   the whole volume of the passenger spaces below the margin line (cubic metres), as defined in regulation 2;

V =   the whole volume of the ship below the margin line (cubic metres);

P_1 = KN

where:

N =   the number of passengers for which the ship is to be certified, and

K = $0.056L$

3.2   Where the value of KN is greater than the sum of P and the whole volume of the actual passenger spaces above the margin line, the figure to be taken as P_1 is that sum or two-thirds KN, whichever is the greater.

When P_1 is greater than P:

$$C_s = 72\,\frac{M + 2P_1}{V + P_1 - P} \tag{3}$$

and in other cases:

$$C_s = 72\,\frac{M + 2P}{V} \tag{4}$$

3.3 For ships not having a continuous bulkhead deck the volumes are to be taken up to the actual margin lines used in determining the floodable lengths.

4 Rules for subdivision of ships other than those covered by paragraph 5

4.1 The subdivision abaft the forepeak of ships of 131 m in length and upwards having a criterion numeral of 23 or less shall be governed by the factor A given by formula (1); of those having a criterion numeral of 123 or more by the factor B given by formula (2); and of those having a criterion numeral between 23 and 123 by the factor F obtained by linear interpolation between the factors A and B, using the formula:

$$F = A - \frac{(A - B)(C_s - 23)}{100} \tag{5}$$

Nevertheless, where the criterion numeral is equal to 45 or more and simultaneously the computed factor of subdivision as given by formula (5) is 0.65 or less, but more than 0.5, the subdivision abaft the forepeak shall be governed by the factor 0.5.

4.2 Where the factor F is less than 0.4 and it is shown to the satisfaction of the Administration to be impracticable to comply with the factor F in a machinery compartment of the ship, the subdivision of such compartment may be governed by an increased factor, which, however, shall not exceed 0.4.

4.3 The subdivision abaft the forepeak of ships of less than 131 m but not less than 79 m in length having a criterion numeral equal to S, where:

$$S = \frac{3,574 - 25L}{13}$$

shall be governed by the factor unity; of those having a criterion numeral of 123 or more by the factor B given by the formula (2); of those having a criterion numeral between S and 123 by the factor F obtained by linear interpolation between unity and the factor B using the formula:

$$F = 1 - \frac{(1 - B)(C_s - S)}{123 - S} \qquad (6)$$

4.4   The subdivision abaft the forepeak of ships of less than 131 m but not less than 79 m in length and having a criterion numeral less than S, and of ships of less than 79 m in length shall be governed by the factor unity, unless, in either case, it is shown to the satisfaction of the Administration to be impracticable to comply with this factor in any part of the ship, in which case the Administration may allow such relaxation as may appear to be justified, having regard to all the circumstances.

4.5   The provisions of paragraph 4.4 shall apply also to ships of whatever length, which are to be certified to carry a number of passengers exceeding 12 but not exceeding:

$\dfrac{L^2}{650}$, or 50, whichever is the less.

5   Special subdivision standards for ships complying with regulation III/21.1.2

5.1.1   In the case of ships primarily engaged in the carriage of passengers, the subdivision abaft the forepeak shall be governed by a factor of 0.5 or by the factor determined according to paragraphs 3 and 4, if less than 0.5.

5.1.2   In the case of such ships of less than 91.5 m in length, if the Administration is satisfied that compliance with such factor would be impracticable in a compartment, it may allow the length of that compartment to be governed by a higher factor provided the factor used is the lowest that is practicable and reasonable in the circumstances.

5.2   Where, in the case of any ship whether of less than 91.5 m or not, the necessity of carrying appreciable quantities of cargo makes it impracticable to require the subdivision abaft the forepeak to be governed by a factor not exceeding 0.5, the standard of subdivision to be applied shall be determined in accordance with the following subparagraphs .1 to .5, subject to the condition that where the Administration is satisfied that insistence on strict compliance in any respect would be unreasonable, it may allow such alternative arrangement of the watertight bulkheads as appears to be justified on merits and will not diminish the general effectiveness of the subdivision.

.1   The provisions of paragraph 3 relating to the criterion numeral shall apply with the exception that in calculating the value of P_1 for berthed passengers K is to have the value defined in paragraph 3, or 3.5 m^3, whichever is the greater, and for unberthed passengers K is to have the value 3.5 m^3.

.2   The factor B in paragraph 2 shall be replaced by the factor BB determined by the following formula:

$$BB = \frac{17.6}{L - 33} + 0.20 \qquad (L = 55 \text{ m and upwards})$$

.3   The subdivision abaft the forepeak of ships of 131 m in length and upwards having a criterion numeral of 23 or less shall be governed by the factor A given by formula (1) in paragraph 2.3; of those having a criterion numeral of 123 or more by the factor BB given by the formula in paragraph 5.2.2; and of those having a criterion numeral between 23 and 123 by the factor F obtained by linear interpolation between the factors A and BB, using the formula:

$$F = A - \frac{(A - BB)(C_s - 23)}{100}$$

except that if the factor F so obtained is less than 0.5 the factor to be used shall be either 0.5 or the factor calculated according to the provisions of paragraph 4.1, whichever is the smaller.

.4   The subdivision abaft the forepeak of ships of less than 131 m but not less than 55 m in length having a criterion numeral equal to S_1 where:

$$S_1 = \frac{3,712 - 25L}{19}$$

shall be governed by the factor unity; of those having a criterion numeral of 123 or more by the factor BB given by the formula in paragraph 5.2.2; of those having a criterion numeral between S_1 and 123 by the factor F obtained by linear interpolation between unity and the factor BB using the formula:

$$F = 1 - \frac{(1 - BB)(C_s - S_1)}{123 - S_1}$$

except that in either of the two latter cases if the factor so obtained is less than 0.5 the subdivision may be governed by a factor not exceeding 0.5.

.5   The subdivision abaft the forepeak of ships of less than 131 m but not less than 55 m in length and having a criterion numeral less than S_1 and of ships of less than 55 m in length shall be governed by the factor unity, unless it is shown to the satisfaction of the Administration to be impracticable to comply with this factor in particular compartments, in which event the Administration may allow such relaxations in respect of those compartments as appear to be justified, having regard to all the circumstances, provided that the aftermost compartment and as many as possible of the forward compartments (between the forepeak and the after end of the machinery space) shall be kept within the floodable length.

5.3 The special provisions regarding permeability given in regulation 5.4 shall be employed when calculating the floodable length curves.

5.4 Where the Administration is satisfied that, having regard to the nature and conditions of the intended voyages compliance with the other provisions of this chapter and of chapter II-2 is sufficient, the requirements of this paragraph need not be complied with.

Regulation 7
Special requirements concerning passenger ship subdivision

1 Where in a portion or portions of a ship the watertight bulkheads are carried to a higher deck than in the remainder of the ship and it is desired to take advantage of this higher extension of the bulkheads in calculating the floodable length, separate margin lines may be used for each such portion of the ship provided that:

.1 the sides of the ship are extended throughout the ship's length to the deck corresponding to the upper margin line and all openings in the shell plating below this deck throughout the length of the ship are treated as being below a margin line, for the purposes of regulation 17; and

.2 the two compartments adjacent to the "step" in the bulkhead deck are each within the permissible length corresponding to their respective margin lines, and, in addition, their combined length does not exceed twice the permissible length based on the lower margin line.

2.1 A compartment may exceed the permissible length determined by the rules of regulation 6 provided the combined length of each pair of adjacent compartments to which the compartment in question is common does not exceed either the floodable length or twice the permissible length, whichever is the less.

2.2 If one of the two adjacent compartments is situated inside the machinery space, and the second is situated outside the machinery space, and the average permeability of the portion of the ship in which the second is situated differs from that of the machinery space, the combined length of the two compartments shall be adjusted to the mean average permeability of the two portions of the ship in which the compartments are situated.

2.3 Where the two adjacent compartments have different factors of subdivision, the combined length of the two compartments shall be determined proportionately.

3   In ships of 100 m in length and upwards, one of the main transverse bulkheads abaft the forepeak shall be fitted at a distance from the forward perpendicular which is not greater than the permissible length.

4   A main transverse bulkhead may be recessed provided that all parts of the recess lie inboard of vertical surfaces on both sides of the ship, situated at a distance from the shell plating equal to one fifth the breadth of the ship, as defined in regulation 2, and measured at right angles to the centreline at the level of the deepest subdivision load line. Any part of a recess which lies outside these limits shall be dealt with as a step in accordance with paragraph 5.

5   A main transverse bulkhead may be stepped provided that it meets one of the following conditions:

   .1   the combined length of the two compartments, separated by the bulkhead in question, does not exceed either 90% of the floodable length or twice the permissible length, except that, in ships having a factor of subdivision greater than 0.9, the combined length of the two compartments in question shall not exceed the permissible length;

   .2   additional subdivision is provided in way of the step to maintain the same measure of safety as that secured by a plane bulkhead;

   .3   the compartment over which the step extends does not exceed the permissible length corresponding to a margin line taken 76 mm below the step.

6   Where a main transverse bulkhead is recessed or stepped, an equivalent plane bulkhead shall be used in determining the subdivision.

7   If the distance between two adjacent main transverse bulkheads, or their equivalent plane bulkheads, or the distance between the transverse planes passing through the nearest stepped portions of the bulkheads, is less than 3 m plus 3% of the length of the ship, or 11 m, whichever is the less, only one of these bulkheads shall be regarded as forming part of the subdivision of the ship in accordance with the provisions of regulation 6.

8   Where a main transverse watertight compartment contains local subdivision and it can be shown to the satisfaction of the Administration that, after any assumed side damage extending over a length of 3 m plus 3% of the length of the ship, or 11 m, whichever is the less, the whole volume of the main compartment will not be flooded, a proportionate allowance may be made in the permissible length otherwise required for such compartment. In such a case the volume of effective buoyancy assumed on the undamaged side shall not be greater than that assumed on the damaged side.

9   Where the required factor of subdivision is 0.5 or less, the combined length of any two adjacent compartments shall not exceed the floodable length.

Regulation 8
Stability of passenger ships in damaged condition[*]

(Subject to the provisions of regulation 8-1, paragraphs 2.3.1 to 2.3.4, 2.4, 5 and 6.2 apply to passenger ships constructed on or after 29 April 1990. Paragraphs 7.2, 7.3 and 7.4 apply to all passenger ships)

1.1   Sufficient intact stability shall be provided in all service conditions so as to enable the ship to withstand the final stage of flooding of any one main compartment which is required to be within the floodable length.

1.2   Where two adjacent main compartments are separated by a bulkhead which is stepped under the conditions of regulation 7.5.1 the intact stability shall be adequate to withstand the flooding of those two adjacent main compartments.

1.3   Where the required factor of subdivision is 0.5 or less but more than 0.33 intact stability shall be adequate to withstand the flooding of any two adjacent main compartments.

1.4   Where the required factor of subdivision is 0.33 or less the intact stability shall be adequate to withstand the flooding of any three adjacent main compartments.

2.1   The requirements of paragraph 1 shall be determined by calculations which are in accordance with paragraphs 3, 4 and 6 and which take into consideration the proportions and design characteristics of the ship and the arrangement and configuration of the damaged compartments. In making these calculations the ship is to be assumed in the worst anticipated service condition as regards stability.

2.2   Where it is proposed to fit decks, inner skins or longitudinal bulkheads of sufficient tightness to seriously restrict the flow of water, the Administration shall be satisfied that proper consideration is given to such restrictions in the calculations.

---

[*] Refer to MSC/Circ.541 (as may be revised): Guidance notes on the integrity of flooding boundaries above the bulkhead deck of passenger ships for proper application of regulations II-1/8 and 20, paragraph 1, of SOLAS 1974, as amended.

2.3 The stability required in the final condition after damage, and after equalization where provided, shall be determined as follows:

2.3.1 The positive residual righting lever curve shall have a minimum range of 15° beyond the angle of equilibrium. This range may be reduced to a minimum of 10°, in the case where the area under the righting lever curve is that specified in paragraph 2.3.2, increased by the ratio:

$$\frac{15}{\text{range}}$$

where the range is expressed in degrees.

2.3.2 The area under the righting lever curve shall be at least 0.015 metre-radians, measured from the angle of equilibrium to the lesser of:

   .1   the angle at which progressive flooding occurs;

   .2   22° (measured from the upright) in the case of one-compartment flooding, or 27° (measured from the upright) in the case of the simultaneous flooding of two or more adjacent compartments.

2.3.3 A residual righting lever is to be obtained within the range of positive stability, taking into account the greatest of the following heeling moments:

   .1   the crowding of all passengers towards one side;

   .2   the launching of all fully loaded davit-launched survival craft on one side;

   .3   due to wind pressure;

as calculated by the formula:

$$\text{GZ (in metres)} = \frac{\text{heeling moment}}{\text{displacement}} + 0.04$$

However, in no case is this righting lever to be less than 0.1 m.

2.3.4 For the purpose of calculating the heeling moments in paragraph 2.3.3, the following assumptions shall be made:

   .1   Moments due to crowding of passengers:

   .1.1   four persons per square metre;

   .1.2   a mass of 75 kg for each passenger;

   .1.3   passengers shall be distributed on available deck areas towards one side of the ship on the decks where muster stations are located and in such a way that they produce the most adverse heeling moment.

.2   Moments due to launching of all fully loaded davit-launched survival craft on one side:

.2.1   all lifeboats and rescue boats fitted on the side to which the ship has heeled after having sustained damage shall be assumed to be swung out fully loaded and ready for lowering;

.2.2   for lifeboats which are arranged to be launched fully loaded from the stowed position, the maximum heeling moment during launching shall be taken;

.2.3   a fully loaded davit-launched liferaft attached to each davit on the side to which the ship has heeled after having sustained damage shall be assumed to be swung out ready for lowering;

.2.4   persons not in the life-saving appliances which are swung out shall not provide either additional heeling or righting moment;

.2.5   life-saving appliances on the side of the ship opposite to the side to which the ship has heeled shall be assumed to be in a stowed position.

.3   Moments due to wind pressure:

.3.1   a wind pressure of 120 N/m^2 to be applied;

.3.2   the area applicable shall be the projected lateral area of the ship above the waterline corresponding to the intact condition;

.3.3   the moment arm shall be the vertical distance from a point at one half of the mean draught corresponding to the intact condition to the centre of gravity of the lateral area.

2.4   In intermediate stages of flooding, the maximum righting lever shall be at least 0.05 m and the range of positive righting levers shall be at least $7°$. In all cases, only one breach in the hull and only one free surface need be assumed.

3   For the purpose of making damage stability calculations the volume and surface permeabilities shall be in general as follows:

Spaces	Permeability
Appropriated to cargo, coal or stores	60
Occupied by accommodation	95
Occupied by machinery	85
Intended for liquids	0 or 95[*]

Higher surface permeabilities are to be assumed in respect of spaces which, in the vicinity of the damage waterplane, contain no substantial quantity of

---

[*] Whichever results in the more severe requirements.

accommodation or machinery and spaces which are not generally occupied by any substantial quantity of cargo or stores.

4   Assumed extent of damage shall be as follows:

    .1   longitudinal extent: 3 m plus 3% of the length of the ship, or 11 m, whichever is the less. Where the required factor of subdivision is 0.33 or less the assumed longitudinal extent of damage shall be increased as necessary so as to include any two consecutive main transverse watertight bulkheads;

    .2   transverse extent (measured inboard from the ship's side, at right angles to the centreline at the level of the deepest subdivision load line): a distance of one fifth of the breadth of the ship, as defined in regulation 2; and

    .3   vertical extent: from the base line upwards without limit;

    .4   if any damage of lesser extent than that indicated in paragraphs 4.1, 4.2 and 4.3 would result in a more severe condition regarding heel or loss of metacentric height, such damage shall be assumed in the calculations.

5   Unsymmetrical flooding is to be kept to a minimum consistent with efficient arrangements. Where it is necessary to correct large angles of heel, the means adopted shall, where practicable, be self-acting, but in any case where controls to cross-flooding fittings are provided they shall be operable from above the bulkhead deck. These fittings together with their controls shall be acceptable to the Administration. The maximum angle of heel after flooding but before equalization shall not exceed 15°. Where cross-flooding fittings are required the time for equalization shall not exceed 15 min. Suitable information concerning the use of cross-flooding fittings shall be supplied to the master of the ship.*

6   The final conditions of the ship after damage and, in the case of unsymmetrical flooding, after equalization measures have been taken shall be as follows:

    .1   in the case of symmetrical flooding there shall be a positive residual metacentric height of at least 50 mm as calculated by the constant displacement method;

    .2   in the case of unsymmetrical flooding, the angle of heel for one-compartment flooding shall not exceed 7°. For the simultaneous flooding of two or more adjacent compartments, a heel of 12° may be permitted by the Administration;

---

* Refer to the Recommendation on a standard method for establishing compliance with the requirements for cross-flooding arrangements in passenger ships adopted by the Organization by resolution A.266(VIII).

.3   in no case shall the margin line be submerged in the final stage of flooding. If it is considered that the margin line may become submerged during an intermediate stage of flooding, the Administration may require such investigations and arrangements as it considers necessary for the safety of the ship.

7.1   The master of the ship shall be supplied with the data necessary to maintain sufficient intact stability under service conditions to enable the ship to withstand the critical damage. In the case of ships requiring cross-flooding the master of the ship shall be informed of the conditions of stability on which the calculations of heel are based and be warned that excessive heeling might result should the ship sustain damage when in a less favourable condition.

7.2   The data referred to in paragraph 7.1 to enable the master to maintain sufficient intact stability shall include information which indicates the maximum permissible height of the ship's centre of gravity above keel (KG), or alternatively the minimum permissible metacentric height (GM), for a range of draughts or displacements sufficient to include all service conditions. The information shall show the influence of various trims taking into account the operational limits.

7.3   Each ship shall have scales of draughts marked clearly at the bow and stern. In the case where the draught marks are not located where they are easily readable, or operational constraints for a particular trade make it difficult to read the draught marks, then the ship shall also be fitted with a reliable draught indicating system by which the bow and stern draughts can be determined.

7.4   On completion of loading of the ship and prior to its departure, the master shall determine the ship's trim and stability and also ascertain and record that the ship is in compliance with stability criteria in the relevant regulations. The determination of the ship's stability shall always be made by calculation. The Administration may accept the use of an electronic loading and stability computer or equivalent means for this purpose.

8.1   No relaxation from the requirements for damage stability may be considered by the Administration unless it is shown that the intact metacentric height in any service condition necessary to meet these requirements is excessive for the service intended.

8.2   Relaxations from the requirements for damage stability shall be permitted only in exceptional cases and subject to the condition that the Administration is to be satisfied that the proportions, arrangements and other characteristics of the ship are the most favourable to stability after damage which can practically and reasonably be adopted in the particular circumstances.

Regulation 8-1
*Stability of ro–ro passenger ships in damaged condition**

Ro-ro passenger ships constructed before 1 July 1997 shall comply with regulation 8, as amended by resolution MSC.12(56), not later than the date of the first periodical survey after the date of compliance prescribed below, according to the value of A/A_{max} as defined in the annex of the Calculation Procedure to assess the survivability characteristics of existing ro–ro passenger ships when using a simplified method based upon resolution A.265(VIII), developed by the Maritime Safety Committee at its fifty-ninth session in June 1991 (MSC/Circ.574).[†]

Value of A/A_{max}	Date of compliance
less than 85%	1 October 1998
85% or more but less than 90%	1 October 2000
90% or more but less than 95%	1 October 2002
95% or more but less than 97.5%	1 October 2004
97.5% or more	1 October 2005

Regulation 8-2
Special requirements for ro–ro passenger ships carrying 400 persons or more

Notwithstanding the provisions of regulations 8 and 8-1:

.1 Ro–ro passenger ships certified to carry 400 persons or more constructed on or after 1 July 1997 shall comply with the provisions of paragraph 2.3 of regulation 8, assuming the damage applied anywhere within the ship's length L; and

.2 Ro–ro passenger ships certified to carry 400 persons or more constructed before 1 July 1997 shall comply with the requirements of subparagraph .1 not later than the date of the first periodical survey after the date of compliance prescribed in subparagraph .2.1, .2.2 or .2.3 which occurs the latest:

.2.1

Value of A/A_{max}	Date of compliance
less than 85%	1 October 1998
85% or more but less than 90%	1 October 2000
90% or more but less than 95%	1 October 2002
95% or more but less than 97.5%	1 October 2004
97.5% or more	1 October 2010

---

* For the application of specific stability requirements to ro–ro passenger ships, refer to resolution 14 of the 1995 SOLAS Conference and resolution MSC.141(76), Revised model test method under resolution 14 of the 1995 SOLAS Conference.

† Refer to MSC/Circ.649, Interpretations of provisions of resolution MSC.26(60) and MSC/Circ.574.

.2.2   Number of persons permitted to be carried

1,500 or more	1 October 2002
1,000 or more but less than 1,500	1 October 2006
600 or more but less than 1,000	1 October 2008
400 or more but less than 600	1 October 2010

.2.3   **Age of the ship equal to or greater than 20 years,**

where the age of the ship means the time counted from the date on which the keel was laid or the date on which it was at a similar stage of construction or from the date on which the ship was converted to a ro–ro passenger ship.

Regulation 8-3
Special requirements for passenger ships, other than ro–ro
passenger ships, carrying 400 persons or more

Notwithstanding the provisions of regulation 8, passenger ships, other than ro–ro passenger ships, certified to carry 400 persons or more constructed on or after 1 July 2002 shall comply with the provisions of paragraphs 2.3 and 2.4 of regulation 8, assuming the damage applied anywhere within the ship's length *L*.

Regulation 9
Ballasting of passenger ships

1   Water ballast should not in general be carried in tanks intended for oil fuel. In ships in which it is not practicable to avoid putting water in oil fuel tanks, oily-water separating equipment to the satisfaction of the Administration shall be fitted, or other alternative means, such as discharge to shore facilities, acceptable to the Administration shall be provided for disposing of the oily-water ballast.

2   The provisions of this regulation are without prejudice to the provisions of the International Convention for the Prevention of Pollution from Ships in force.

Regulation 10
Peak and machinery space bulkheads, shaft tunnels, etc.,
*in passenger ships**

1   A forepeak or collision bulkhead shall be fitted which shall be watertight up to the bulkhead deck. This bulkhead shall be located at a

---

* Refer to MSC/Circ.855, Interpretation of the position of the forward perpendicular for the purpose of SOLAS regulation II-1/10.

distance from the forward perpendicular of not less than 5% of the length of the ship and not more than 3 m plus 5% of the length of the ship.

2   Where any part of the ship below the waterline extends forward of the forward perpendicular, e.g. a bulbous bow, the distances stipulated in paragraph 1 shall be measured from a point either:

    .1   at the mid-length of such extension; or

    .2   at a distance 1.5% of the length of the ship forward of the forward perpendicular; or

    .3   at a distance 3 m forward of the forward perpendicular;

whichever gives the smallest measurement.

3   Where a long forward superstructure is fitted, the forepeak or collision bulkhead on all passenger ships shall be extended weathertight to the next full deck above the bulkhead deck. The extension shall be so arranged as to preclude the possibility of the bow door causing damage to it in the case of damage to, or detachment of, a bow door.

4   The extension required in paragraph 3 need not be fitted directly above the bulkhead below, provided that all parts of the extension are not located forward of the forward limit specified in paragraph 1 or paragraph 2. However, in ships constructed before 1 July 1997:

    .1   where a sloping ramp forms part of the extension, the part of the extension, which is more than 2.3 m above the bulkhead deck, may extend no more than 1 m forward of the forward limits specified in paragraph 1 or paragraph 2; and

    .2   where the existing ramp does not comply with the requirements for acceptance as an extension to the collision bulkhead and the position of the ramp prevents the siting of such extension within the limits specified in paragraph 1 or paragraph 2, the extension may be sited within a limited distance aft of the aft limit specified in paragraph 1 or paragraph 2. The limited distance aft should be no more than is necessary to ensure non-interference with the ramp. The extension to the collision bulkhead shall open forward and comply with the requirements of paragraph 3 and shall be so arranged as to preclude the possibility of the ramp causing damage to it in the case of damage to, or detachment of, the ramp.

5   Ramps not meeting the above requirements shall be disregarded as an extension of the collision bulkhead.

6   In ships constructed before 1 July 1997, the requirements of paragraphs 3 and 4 shall apply not later than the date of the first periodical survey after 1 July 1997.

7   An afterpeak bulkhead, and bulkheads dividing the machinery space, as defined in regulation 2, from the cargo and passenger spaces forward and aft, shall also be fitted and made watertight up to the bulkhead deck. The afterpeak bulkhead may, however, be stepped below the bulkhead deck, provided the degree of safety of the ship as regards subdivision is not thereby diminished.

8   In all cases stern tubes shall be enclosed in watertight spaces of moderate volume. The stern gland shall be situated in a watertight shaft tunnel or other watertight space separate from the stern tube compartment and of such volume that, if flooded by leakage through the stern gland, the margin line will not be submerged.

Regulation 11
*Peak and machinery space bulkheads and stern tubes
in cargo ships*

*(Paragraphs 8 and 9 of this regulation apply to ships
constructed on or after 1 February 1992)*

1   For the purpose of this regulation *freeboard deck, length of ship* and *forward perpendicular* have the meanings as defined in the International Convention on Load Lines in force.

2   A collision bulkhead shall be fitted which shall be watertight up to the freeboard deck. This bulkhead shall be located at a distance from the forward perpendicular of not less than 5% of the length of the ship or 10 m, whichever is the less, and, except as may be permitted by the Administration, not more than 8% of the length of the ship.

3   Where any part of the ship below the waterline extends forward of the forward perpendicular, e.g. a bulbous bow, the distances stipulated in paragraph 2 shall be measured from a point either:

   .1   at the mid-length of such extension; or

   .2   at a distance 1.5% of the length of the ship forward of the forward perpendicular; or

   .3   at a distance 3 m forward of the forward perpendicular;

whichever gives the smallest measurement.

4   The bulkhead may have steps or recesses provided they are within the limits prescribed in paragraph 2 or 3. Pipes piercing the collision bulkhead shall be fitted with suitable valves operable from above the freeboard deck and the valve chest shall be secured at the bulkhead inside the forepeak. The valves may be fitted on the after side of the collision bulkhead provided that the valves are readily accessible under all service conditions and the space in which they are located is not a cargo space. All valves shall be of steel, bronze or other approved ductile material. Valves of ordinary cast iron or similar material are not acceptable. No door, manhole, ventilation duct or any other opening shall be fitted in this bulkhead.

5   Where a long forward superstructure is fitted the collision bulkhead shall be extended weathertight to the deck next above the freeboard deck. The extension need not be fitted directly above the bulkhead below provided it is located within the limits prescribed in paragraph 2 or 3 with the exemption permitted by paragraph 6 and the part of the deck which forms the step is made effectively weathertight.

6   Where bow doors are fitted and a sloping loading ramp forms part of the extension of the collision bulkhead above the freeboard deck the part of the ramp which is more than 2.3 m above the freeboad deck may extend forward of the limit specified in paragraph 2 or 3. The ramp shall be weathertight over its complete length.

7   The number of openings in the extension of the collision bulkhead above the freeboard deck shall be restricted to the minimum compatible with the design and normal operation of the ship. All such openings shall be capable of being closed weathertight.

8   Bulkheads shall be fitted separating the machinery space from cargo and passenger spaces forward and aft and made watertight up to the freeboard deck.

9   Stern tubes shall be enclosed in a watertight space (or spaces) of moderate volume. Other measures to minimize the danger of water penetrating into the ship in case of damage to stern tube arrangements may be taken at the discretion of the Administration.

Regulation 12
Double bottoms in passenger ships

1   A double bottom shall be fitted extending from the forepeak bulkhead to the afterpeak bulkhead as far as this is practicable and compatible with the design and proper working of the ship.

    .1   In ships of 50 m and upwards but less than 61 m in length a double bottom shall be fitted at least from the machinery space to the forepeak bulkhead, or as near thereto as practicable.

    .2   In ships of 61 m and upwards but less than 76 m in length a double bottom shall be fitted at least outside the machinery space, and shall extend to the fore and after peak bulkheads, or as near thereto as practicable.

    .3   In ships of 76 m in length and upwards, a double bottom shall be fitted amidships, and shall extend to the fore and after peak bulkheads, or as near thereto as practicable.

2   Where a double bottom is required to be fitted its depth shall be to the satisfaction of the Administration and the inner bottom shall be continued out to the ship's sides in such a manner as to protect the bottom to the turn of the bilge. Such protection will be deemed satisfactory if the line of intersection of the outer edge of the margin plate with the bilge plating is not lower at any part than a horizontal plane passing through the point of intersection with the frame line amidships of a transverse diagonal line inclined at 25° to the base line and cutting it at a point one half the ship's moulded breadth from the middle line.

3   Small wells constructed in the double bottom in connection with drainage arrangements of holds, etc., shall not extend downwards more than necessary. The depth of the well shall in no case be more than the depth less 460 mm of the double bottom at the centreline, nor shall the well extend below the horizontal plane referred to in paragraph 2. A well extending to the outer bottom is, however, permitted at the after end of the shaft tunnel. Other wells (e.g. for lubricating oil under main engines) may be permitted by the Administration if satisfied that the arrangements give protection equivalent to that afforded by a double bottom complying with this regulation.

4   A double bottom need not be fitted in way of watertight compartments of moderate size used exclusively for the carriage of liquids, provided the safety of the ship, in the event of bottom or side damage, is not, in the opinion of the Administration, thereby impaired.

5   In the case of ships to which the provisions of regulation 1.5 apply and which are engaged on regular service within the limits of a short international voyage as defined in regulation III/3.22, the Administration may permit a double bottom to be dispensed with in any part of the ship which is subdivided by a factor not exceeding 0.50, if satisfied that the fitting of a double bottom in that part would not be compatible with the design and proper working of the ship.

Regulation 12-1
Double bottoms in cargo ships other than tankers

(This regulation applies to ships constructed on or after 1 February 1992)

1   A double bottom shall be fitted extending from the collision bulkhead to the afterpeak bulkhead, as far as this is practicable and compatible with the design and proper working of the ship.

2   Where a double bottom is required to be fitted, its depth shall be to the satisfaction of the Administration and the inner bottom shall be continued out to the ship's side in such a manner as to protect the bottom to the turn of the bilge.

72

3   Small wells constructed in the double bottom, in connection with the drainage arrangements of holds, shall not extend in depth more than necessary. A well extending to the outer bottom, may, however, be permitted at the after end of the shaft tunnel of the ship. Other wells may be permitted by the Administration if it is satisfied that the arrangements give protection equivalent to that afforded by a double bottom complying with this regulation.

4   A double bottom need not be fitted in way of watertight compartments used exclusively for the carriage of liquids, provided the safety of the ship in the event of bottom damage is not, in the opinion of the Administration, thereby impaired.

Regulation 13
Assigning, marking and recording of subdivision load lines for passenger ships

1   In order that the required degree of subdivision shall be maintained, a load line corresponding to the approved subdivision draught shall be assigned and marked on the ship's sides. A ship having spaces which are specially adapted for the accommodation of passengers and the carriage of cargo alternatively may, if the owners desire, have one or more additional load lines assigned and marked to correspond with the subdivision draughts which the Administration may approve for the alternative service conditions.

2   The subdivision load lines assigned and marked shall be recorded in the Passenger Ship Safety Certificate, and shall be distinguished by the notation C.1 for the principal passenger condition, and C.2, C.3, etc., for the alternative conditions.

3   The freeboard corresponding to each of these load lines shall be measured at the same position and from the same deck line as the freeboards determined in accordance with the International Convention on Load Lines in force.

4   The freeboard corresponding to each approved subdivision load line and the conditions of service for which it is approved, shall be clearly indicated on the Passenger Ship Safety Certificate.

5   In no case shall any subdivision load line mark be placed above the deepest load line in salt water as determined by the strength of the ship or the International Convention on Load Lines in force.

6   Whatever may be the position of the subdivision load line marks, a ship shall in no case be loaded so as to submerge the load line mark appropriate to the season and locality as determined in accordance with the International Convention on Load Lines in force.

7   A ship shall in no case be so loaded that when it is in salt water the subdivision load line mark appropriate to the particular voyage and condition of service is submerged.

Regulation 14
Construction and initial testing of watertight bulkheads, etc.,
in passenger ships and cargo ships

1   Each watertight subdivision bulkhead, whether transverse or longitudinal, shall be constructed in such a manner that it shall be capable of supporting, with a proper margin of resistance, the pressure due to the maximum head of water which it might have to sustain in the event of damage to the ship but at least the pressure due to a head of water up to the margin line. The construction of these bulkheads shall be to the satisfaction of the Administration.

2.1   Steps and recesses in bulkheads shall be watertight and as strong as the bulkhead at the place where each occurs.

2.2   Where frames or beams pass through a watertight deck or bulkhead, such deck or bulkhead shall be made structurally watertight without the use of wood or cement.

3   Testing main compartments by filling them with water is not compulsory. When testing by filling with water is not carried out, a hose test shall be carried out where practicable. This test shall be carried out in the most advanced stage of the fitting out of the ship. Where a hose test is not practicable because of possible damage to machinery, electrical equipment insulation or outfitting items, it may be replaced by a careful visual examination of welded connections, supported where deemed necessary by means such as a dye penetrant test or an ultrasonic leak test or an equivalent test. In any case a thorough inspection of the watertight bulkheads shall be carried out.

4   The forepeak, double bottoms (including duct keels) and inner skins shall be tested with water to a head corresponding to the requirements of paragraph 1.

5   Tanks which are intended to hold liquids, and which form part of the subdivision of the ship, shall be tested for tightness with water to a head up to the deepest subdivision load line or to a head corresponding to two thirds of the depth from the top of keel to the margin line in way of the tanks, whichever is the greater; provided that in no case shall the test head be less than 0.9 m above the top of the tank.

6   The tests referred to in paragraphs 4 and 5 are for the purpose of ensuring that the subdivision structural arrangements are watertight and are not to be regarded as a test of the fitness of any compartment for the storage of oil fuel or for other special purposes for which a test of a superior character may be required depending on the height to which the liquid has access in the tank or its connections.

Regulation 15
Openings in watertight bulkheads in passenger ships
(This regulation applies to ships constructed on or after 1 February 1992)

1   The number of openings in watertight bulkheads shall be reduced to the minimum compatible with the design and proper working of the ship; satisfactory means shall be provided for closing these openings.

2.1   Where pipes, scuppers, electric cables, etc., are carried through watertight subdivision bulkheads, arrangements shall be made to ensure the watertight integrity of the bulkheads.

2.2   Valves not forming part of a piping system shall not be permitted in watertight subdivision bulkheads.

2.3   Lead or other heat sensitive materials shall not be used in systems which penetrate watertight subdivision bulkheads, where deterioration of such systems in the event of fire would impair the watertight integrity of the bulkheads.

3.1   No doors, manholes, or access openings are permitted:

 .1 in the collision bulkhead below the margin line;

 .2 in watertight transverse bulkheads dividing a cargo space from an adjoining cargo space or from a permanent or reserve bunker, except as provided in paragraph 10.1 and in regulation 16.

3.2   Except as provided in paragraph 3.3, the collision bulkhead may be pierced below the margin line by not more than one pipe for dealing with fluid in the forepeak tank, provided that the pipe is fitted with a screwdown valve capable of being operated from above the bulkhead deck, the valve chest being secured inside the forepeak to the collision bulkhead. The Administration may, however, authorize the fitting of this valve on the after side of the collision bulkhead provided that the valve is readily accessible under all service conditions and the space in which it is located is not a cargo space.

3.3   If the forepeak is divided to hold two different kinds of liquids the Administration may allow the collision bulkhead to be pierced below the margin line by two pipes, each of which is fitted as required by paragraph 3.2, provided the Administration is satisfied that there is no practical alternative to the fitting of such a second pipe and that, having regard to the additional subdivision provided in the forepeak, the safety of the ship is maintained.

4.1 Watertight doors fitted in bulkheads between permanent and reserve bunkers shall always be accessible, except as provided in paragraph 9.4 for between-deck bunker doors.

4.2 Satisfactory arrangements shall be made by means of screens or otherwise to prevent the coal from interfering with the closing of watertight bunker doors.

5 Subject to paragraph 11, not more than one door, apart from the doors to bunkers and shaft tunnels, may be fitted in each main transverse bulkhead within spaces containing the main and auxiliary propulsion machinery including boilers serving the needs of propulsion and all permanent bunkers. Where two or more shafts are fitted, the tunnels shall be connected by an intercommunicating passage. There shall be only one door between the machinery space and the tunnel spaces where two shafts are fitted and only two doors where there are more than two shafts. All these doors shall be of the sliding type and shall be so located as to have their sills as high as practicable. The hand gear for operating these doors from above the bulkhead deck shall be situated outside the spaces containing the machinery.

6.1 Watertight doors, except as provided in paragraph 10.1 or regulation 16, shall be power-operated sliding doors complying with the requirements of paragraph 7 capable of being closed simultaneously from the central operating console at the navigation bridge in not more than 60 s with the ship in the upright position.

6.2 The means of operation whether by power or by hand of any power-operated sliding watertight door shall be capable of closing the door with the ship listed to 15° either way. Consideration shall also be given to the forces which may act on either side of the door as may be experienced when water is flowing through the opening applying a static head equivalent to a water height of at least 1 m above the sill on the centreline of the door.

6.3 Watertight door controls, including hydraulic piping and electric cables, shall be kept as close as practicable to the bulkhead in which the doors are fitted, in order to minimize the likelihood of them being involved in any damage which the ship may sustain. The positioning of watertight doors and their controls shall be such that if the ship sustains damage within one fifth of the breadth of the ship, as defined in regulation 2, such distance being measured at right angles to the centreline at the level of the deepest subdivision load line, the operation of the watertight doors clear of the damaged portion of the ship is not impaired.

6.4 All power-operated sliding watertight doors shall be provided with means of indication which will show at all remote operating positions whether the doors are open or closed. Remote operating positions shall only be at the navigation bridge as required by paragraph 7.1.5 and at the location where hand operation above the bulkhead deck is required by paragraph 7.1.4.

6.5   In ships constructed before 1 February 1992, doors which do not comply with paragraphs 6.1 to 6.4 shall be closed before the voyage commences, and shall be kept closed during navigation; the time of opening such doors in port and of closing them before the ship leaves port shall be entered into the log-book.

7.1   Each power-operated sliding watertight door:

.1   shall have a vertical or horizontal motion;

.2   shall, subject to paragraph 11, be normally limited to a maximum clear opening width of 1.2 m. The Administration may permit larger doors only to the extent considered necessary for the effective operation of the ship provided that other safety measures, including the following, are taken into consideration:

.2.1   special consideration shall be given to the strength of the door and its closing appliances in order to prevent leakages;

.2.2   the door shall be located outside the damage zone $\frac{B}{5}$;

.2.3   the door shall be kept closed when the ship is at sea, except for limited periods when absolutely necessary as determined by the Administration;

.3   shall be fitted with the necessary equipment to open and close the door using electric power, hydraulic power, or any other form of power that is acceptable to the Administration;

.4   shall be provided with an individual hand-operated mechanism. It shall be possible to open and close the door by hand at the door itself from either side, and in addition, close the door from an accessible position above the bulkhead deck with an all round crank motion or some other movement providing the same degree of safety acceptable to the Administration. Direction of rotation or other movement is to be clearly indicated at all operating positions. The time necessary for the complete closure of the door, when operating by hand gear, shall not exceed 90 s with the ship in the upright position;

.5   shall be provided with controls for opening and closing the door by power from both sides of the door and also for closing the door by power from the central operating console at the navigation bridge;

.6   shall be provided with an audible alarm, distinct from any other alarm in the area, which will sound whenever the door is closed remotely by power and which shall sound for at least 5 s but no more than 10 s before the door begins to move and shall continue sounding until the door is completely closed. In the case of remote hand operation it is sufficient for the audible alarm to sound only when the door is moving. Additionally, in passenger areas and areas of high ambient noise the Administration may require the audible alarm to be supplemented by an intermittent visual signal at the door; and

.7 shall have an approximately uniform rate of closure under power. The closure time, from the time the door begins to move to the time it reaches the completely closed position, shall in no case be less than 20 s or more than 40 s with the ship in the upright position.

7.2 The electrical power required for power-operated sliding watertight doors shall be supplied from the emergency switchboard either directly or by a dedicated distribution board situated above the bulkhead deck. The associated control, indication and alarm circuits shall be supplied from the emergency switchboard either directly or by a dedicated distribution board situated above the bulkhead deck and be capable of being automatically supplied by the transitional source of emergency electrical power required by regulation 42.3.1.3 in the event of failure of either the main or emergency source of electrical power.

7.3 Power-operated sliding watertight doors shall have either:

.1 a centralized hydraulic system with two independent power sources each consisting of a motor and pump capable of simultaneously closing all doors. In addition, there shall be for the whole installation hydraulic accumulators of sufficient capacity to operate all the doors at least three times, i.e. closed–open–closed, against an adverse list of 15°. This operating cycle shall be capable of being carried out when the accumulator is at the pump cut-in pressure. The fluid used shall be chosen considering the temperatures liable to be encountered by the installation during its service. The power operating system shall be designed to minimize the possibility of having a single failure in the hydraulic piping adversely affect the operation of more than one door. The hydraulic system shall be provided with a low-level alarm for hydraulic fluid reservoirs serving the power-operated system and a low gas pressure alarm or other effective means of monitoring loss of stored energy in hydraulic accumulators. These alarms are to be audible and visual and shall be situated on the central operating console at the navigation bridge; or

.2 an independent hydraulic system for each door with each power source consisting of a motor and pump capable of opening and closing the door. In addition, there shall be a hydraulic accumulator of sufficient capacity to operate the door at least three times, i.e. closed–open–closed, against an adverse list of 15°. This operating cycle shall be capable of being carried out when the accumulator is at the pump cut-in pressure. The fluid used shall be chosen considering the temperatures liable to be encountered by the installation during its service. A low gas pressure group alarm or other effective means of monitoring loss of stored energy in hydraulic accumulators shall be provided at the central operating console on the navigation bridge. Loss of stored energy indication at each local operating position shall also be provided; or

.3   an independent electrical system and motor for each door with each power source consisting of a motor capable of opening and closing the door. The power source shall be capable of being automatically supplied by the transitional source of emergency electrical power as required by regulation 42.4.2 – in the event of failure of either the main or emergency source of electrical power and with sufficient capacity to operate the door at least three times, i.e. closed–open–closed, against an adverse list of 15°.

For the systems specified in 7.3.1, 7.3.2 and 7.3.3, provision should be made as follows:

Power systems for power-operated watertight sliding doors shall be separate from any other power system. A single failure in the electric or hydraulic power-operated systems excluding the hydraulic actuator shall not prevent the hand operation of any door.

7.4   Control handles shall be provided at each side of the bulkhead at a minimum height of 1.6 m above the floor and shall be so arranged as to enable persons passing through the doorway to hold both handles in the open position without being able to set the power closing mechanism in operation accidentally. The direction of movement of the handles in opening and closing the door shall be in the direction of door movement and shall be clearly indicated.

7.5   As far as practicable, electrical equipment and components for watertight doors shall be situated above the bulkhead deck and outside hazardous areas and spaces.

7.6   The enclosures of electrical components necessarily situated below the bulkhead deck shall provide suitable protection against the ingress of water.*

7.7   Electric power, control, indication and alarm circuits shall be protected against fault in such a way that a failure in one door circuit will not cause a failure in any other door circuit. Short circuits or other faults in the alarm or

---

* Refer to the following IEC publication 60529 (1989), as amended by its amendment 1 (1999):
    .1   electrical motors, associated circuits and control components; protected to IPX7 standard;
    .2   door position indicators and associated circuit components; protected to IPX8 standard; and
    .3   door movement warning signals; protected to IPX6 standard.
Other arrangements for the enclosures of electrical components may be fitted provided the Administration is satisfied that an equivalent protection is achieved. The water pressure testing of the enclosures protected to IPX8 shall be based on the pressure that may occur at the location of the component during flooding for a period of 36 h.

indicator circuits of a door shall not result in a loss of power operation of that door. Arrangements shall be such that leakage of water into the electrical equipment located below the bulkhead deck will not cause the door to open.

7.8   A single electrical failure in the power operating or control system of a power-operated sliding watertight door shall not result in a closed door opening. Availability of the power supply should be continuously monitored at a point in the electrical circuit as near as practicable to each of the motors required by paragraph 7.3. Loss of any such power supply should activate an audible and visual alarm at the central operating console at the navigation bridge.

8.1   The central operating console at the navigation bridge shall have a "master mode" switch with two modes of control: a "local control" mode which shall allow any door to be locally opened and locally closed after use without automatic closure, and a "doors closed" mode which shall automatically close any door that is open. The "doors closed" mode shall permit doors to be opened locally and shall automatically reclose the doors upon release of the local control mechanism. The "master mode" switch shall normally be in the "local control" mode. The "doors closed" mode shall only be used in an emergency or for testing purposes. Special consideration shall be given to the reliability of the "master mode" switch.

8.2   The central operating console at the navigation bridge shall be provided with a diagram showing the location of each door, with visual indicators to show whether each door is open or closed. A red light shall indicate a door is fully open and a green light shall indicate a door is fully closed. When the door is closed remotely, the red light shall indicate the intermediate position by flashing. The indicating circuit shall be independent of the control circuit for each door.

8.3   It shall not be possible to remotely open any door from the central operating console.

9.1   All watertight doors shall be kept closed during navigation except that they may be opened during navigation as specified in paragraphs 9.2, 9.3 and 9.4. Watertight doors of width of more than 1.2 m permitted by paragraph 11 may only be opened in the circumstances detailed in that paragraph. Any door which is opened in accordance with this paragraph shall be ready to be immediately closed.

9.2   A watertight door may be opened during navigation to permit the passage of passengers or crew, or when work in the immediate vicinity of the door necessitates it being opened. The door must be immediately closed when transit through the door is complete or when the task which necessitated it being open is finished.

9.3   Certain watertight doors may be permitted to remain open during navigation only if considered absolutely necessary; that is, being open is determined essential to the safe and effective operation of the ship's machinery or to permit passengers normally unrestricted access throughout the passenger area. Such determination shall be made by the Administration only after careful consideration of the impact on ship operations and survivability. A watertight door permitted to remain thus open shall be clearly indicated in the ship's stability information and shall always be ready to be immediately closed.

9.4 Sliding watertight doors fitted between bunkers in the between-decks below the bulkhead deck may sometimes be open at sea for the purpose of trimming coal. The opening and closing of these doors shall be recorded in such log-book as may be prescribed by the Administration.

10.1 If the Administration is satisfied that such doors are essential, watertight doors of satisfactory construction may be fitted in watertight bulkheads dividing cargo between deck spaces. Such doors may be hinged, rolling or sliding doors but shall not be remotely controlled. They shall be fitted at the highest level and as far from the shell plating as practicable, but in no case shall the outboard vertical edges be situated at a distance from the shell plating which is less than one fifth of the breadth of the ship, as defined in regulation 2, such distance being measured at right angles to the centreline at the level of the deepest subdivision load line.

10.2 Such doors shall be closed before the voyage commences and shall be kept closed during navigation; the time of opening such doors in port and of closing them before the ship leaves port shall be entered in the log-book. Should any of the doors be accessible during the voyage, they shall be fitted with a device which prevents unauthorized opening. When it is proposed to fit such doors, the number and arrangements shall receive the special consideration of the Administration.

11 Portable plates on bulkheads shall not be permitted except in machinery spaces. Such plates shall always be in place before the ship leaves port, and shall not be removed during navigation except in case of urgent necessity at the discretion of the master. The times of removal and replacement of any such portable plates shall be recorded in the log-book, and the necessary precautions shall be taken in replacing them to ensure that the joints are watertight. The Administration may permit not more than one power-operated sliding watertight door in each main transverse bulkhead larger than those specified in paragraph 7.1.2 to be substituted for these portable plates, provided these doors are closed before the ship leaves port and remain closed during navigation except in case of urgent necessity at the discretion of the master. These doors need not meet the requirements of paragraph 7.1.4 regarding complete closure by hand-operated gear in 90 s. The time of opening and closing these doors, whether the ship is at sea or in port, shall be recorded in the log-book.

12.1 Where trunkways or tunnels for access from crew accommodation to the stokehold, for piping, or for any other purpose are carried through main transverse watertight bulkheads, they shall be watertight and in accordance with the requirements of regulation 19. The access to at least one end of each such tunnel or trunkway, if used as a passage at sea, shall be through a trunk extending watertight to a height sufficient to permit access above the margin line. The access to the other end of the trunkway or tunnel may be through a watertight door of the type required by its location in the ship. Such trunkways or tunnels shall not extend through the first subdivision bulkhead abaft the collision bulkhead.

12.2   Where it is proposed to fit tunnels piercing main transverse watertight bulkheads, these shall receive the special consideration of the Administration.

12.3   Where trunkways in connection with refrigerated cargo and ventilation or forced draught trunks are carried through more than one watertight bulkhead, the means of closure at such openings shall be operated by power and be capable of being closed from a central position situated above the bulkhead deck.

Regulation 16
Passenger ships carrying goods vehicles
and accompanying personnel

1   This regulation applies to passenger ships regardless of the date of construction designed or adapted for the carriage of goods vehicles and accompanying personnel where the total number of persons on board, other than those specified in regulation I/2(e)(i) and (ii), exceeds 12.

2   If in such a ship the total number of passengers which includes personnel accompanying vehicles does not exceed $N = 12 + A/25$, where A = total deck area (square metres) of spaces available for the stowage of goods vehicles and where the clear height at the stowage position and at the entrance to such spaces is not less than 4 m, the provisions of regulation 15.10 in respect of watertight doors apply except that the doors may be fitted at any level in watertight bulkheads dividing cargo spaces. Additionally, indicators are required on the navigation bridge to show automatically when each door is closed and all door fastenings are secured.

3   When applying the provisions of this chapter to such a ship, N shall be taken as the maximum number of passengers for which the ship may be certified in accordance with this regulation.

4   In applying regulation 8 for the worst operating conditions, the permeability for cargo spaces intended for the stowage of goods vehicles and containers shall be derived by calculation in which the goods vehicles and containers shall be assumed to be non-watertight and their permeability taken as 65. For ships engaged in dedicated services the actual value of permeability for goods vehicles or containers may be applied. In no case shall the permeability of the cargo spaces in which the goods vehicles and containers are carried be taken as less than 60.

Regulation 17
Openings in the shell plating of passenger ships below the margin line

1   The number of openings in the shell plating shall be reduced to the minimum compatible with the design and proper working of the ship.

2   The arrangement and efficiency of the means for closing any opening in the shell plating shall be consistent with its intended purpose and the position in which it is fitted and generally to the satisfaction of the Administration.

3.1   Subject to the requirements of the International Convention on Load Lines in force, no sidescuttle shall be fitted in such a position that its sill is below a line drawn parallel to the bulkhead deck at side and having its lowest point 2.5% of the breadth of the ship above the deepest subdivision load line, or 500 mm, whichever is the greater.

3.2   All sidescuttles the sills of which are below the margin line, as permitted by paragraph 3.1 shall be of such construction as will effectively prevent any person opening them without the consent of the master of the ship.

3.3.1   Where in a between-decks, the sills of any of the sidescuttles referred to in paragraph 3.2 are below a line drawn parallel to the bulkhead deck at side and having its lowest point 1.4 m plus 2.5% of the breadth of the ship above the water when the ship departs from any port, all the sidescuttles in that between-decks shall be closed watertight and locked before the ship leaves port, and they shall not be opened before the ship arrives at the next port. In the application of this paragraph the appropriate allowance for fresh water may be made when applicable.

3.3.2   The time of opening such sidescuttles in port and of closing and locking them before the ship leaves port shall be entered in such log-book as may be prescribed by the Administration.

3.3.3   For any ship that has one or more sidescuttles so placed that the requirements of paragraph 3.3.1 would apply when it was floating at its deepest subdivision load line, the Administration may indicate the limiting mean draught at which these sidescuttles will have their sills above the line drawn parallel to the bulkhead deck at side, and having its lowest point 1.4 m plus 2.5% of the breadth of the ship above the waterline corresponding to the limiting mean draught, and at which it will therefore be permissible to depart from port without previously closing and locking them and to open them at sea on the responsibility of the master during the voyage to the next port. In tropical zones as defined in the International Convention on Load Lines in force, this limiting draught may be increased by 0.3 m.

4   Efficient hinged inside deadlights so arranged that they can be easily and effectively closed and secured watertight, shall be fitted to all sidescuttles except that abaft one eighth of the ship's length from the forward perpendicular and above a line drawn parallel to the bulkhead deck at side and having its lowest point at a height of 3.7 m plus 2.5% of the breadth of the ship above the deepest subdivision load line, the deadlights may be portable in passenger accommodation other than that for steerage passengers, unless the deadlights are required by the International Convention on Load Lines in force to be permanently attached in their proper positions. Such portable deadlights shall be stowed adjacent to the sidescuttles they serve.

5   Sidescuttles and their deadlights which will not be accessible during navigation shall be closed and secured before the ship leaves port.

6.1   No sidescuttles shall be fitted in any spaces which are appropriated exclusively to the carriage of cargo or coal.

6.2   Sidescuttles may, however, be fitted in spaces appropriated alternatively to the carriage of cargo or passengers, but they shall be of such construction as will effectively prevent any person opening them or their deadlights without the consent of the master.

6.3   If cargo is carried in such spaces, the sidescuttles and their deadlights shall be closed watertight and locked before the cargo is shipped and such closing and locking shall be recorded in such log-book as may be prescribed by the Administration.

7   Automatic ventilating sidescuttles shall not be fitted in the shell plating below the margin line without the special sanction of the Administration.

8   The number of scuppers, sanitary discharges and other similar openings in the shell plating shall be reduced to the minimum either by making each discharge serve for as many as possible of the sanitary and other pipes, or in any other satisfactory manner.

9.1   All inlets and discharges in the shell plating shall be fitted with efficient and accessible arrangements for preventing the accidental admission of water into the ship.

9.2.1   Subject to the requirements of the International Convention on Load Lines in force, and except as provided in paragraph 9.3, each separate discharge led through the shell plating from spaces below the margin line shall be provided with either one automatic non-return valve fitted with a positive means of closing it from above the bulkhead deck or with two automatic non-return valves without positive means of closing, provided that the inboard valve is situated above the deepest subdivision load line and is always accessible for examination under service conditions. Where a valve with positive means of closing is fitted, the operating position above the bulkhead deck shall always be readily accessible and means shall be provided for indicating whether the valve is open or closed.

9.2.2 The requirements of the International Convention on Load Lines in force shall apply to discharges led through the shell plating from spaces above the margin line.

9.3 Machinery space main and auxiliary sea inlets and discharges in connection with the operation of machinery shall be fitted with readily accessible valves between the pipes and the shell plating or between the pipes and fabricated boxes attached to the shell plating. The valves may be controlled locally and shall be provided with indicators showing whether they are open or closed.

9.4 All shell fittings and valves required by this regulation shall be of steel, bronze or other approved ductile material. Valves of ordinary cast iron or similar material are not acceptable. All pipes to which this regulation refers shall be of steel or other equivalent material to the satisfaction of the Administration.

10.1 Gangway, cargo and coaling ports fitted below the margin line shall be of sufficient strength. They shall be effectively closed and secured watertight before the ship leaves port, and shall be kept closed during navigation.

10.2 Such ports shall in no case be so fitted as to have their lowest point below the deepest subdivision load line.

11.1 The inboard opening of each ash-chute, rubbish-chute, etc., shall be fitted with an efficient cover.

11.2 If the inboard opening is situated below the margin line, the cover shall be watertight, and in addition an automatic non-return valve shall be fitted in the chute in an easily accessible position above the deepest subdivision load line. When the chute is not in use both the cover and the valve shall be kept closed and secured.

Regulation 17-1
Openings in the shell plating below the bulkhead deck of passenger ships and the freeboard deck of cargo ships

Notwithstanding the requirements of regulation 17, ships constructed on or after 1 July 1998 shall comply with the requirements of regulation 17 where a reference to "margin line" shall be deemed to mean a reference to the bulkhead deck of passenger ships and the freeboard deck of cargo ships.

Regulation 18
Construction and initial tests of watertight doors,
sidescuttles, etc., in passenger ships and cargo ships

1   In passenger ships:

.1   the design, materials and construction of all watertight doors, sidescuttles, gangway, cargo and coaling ports, valves, pipes, ash-chutes and rubbish-chutes referred to in these regulations shall be to the satisfaction of the Administration;

.2   the frames of vertical watertight doors shall have no groove at the bottom in which dirt might lodge and prevent the door closing properly.

2   In passenger ships and cargo ships each watertight door shall be tested by water pressure to a head up to the bulkhead deck or freeboard deck respectively. The test shall be made before the ship is put into service, either before or after the door is fitted.

Regulation 19
Construction and initial tests of watertight decks,
trunks, etc., in passenger ships and cargo ships

1   Watertight decks, trunks, tunnels, duct keels and ventilators shall be of the same strength as watertight bulkheads at corresponding levels. The means used for making them watertight, and the arrangements adopted for closing openings in them, shall be to the satisfaction of the Administration. Watertight ventilators and trunks shall be carried at least up to the bulkhead deck in passenger ships and up to the freeboard deck in cargo ships.

2   In ro–ro passenger ships where a ventilation trunk passing through a structure penetrates the bulkhead deck, the trunk shall be capable of withstanding the water pressure that may be present within the trunk, after having taken into account the maximum heel angle allowable during intermediate stages of flooding, in accordance with regulation 8.5.*

3   In ro–ro passenger ships where all or part of the penetration of the bulkhead deck is on the main ro–ro deck, the trunk shall be capable of withstanding impact pressure due to internal water motions (sloshing) of water trapped on the ro–ro deck.*

---

* The Maritime Safety Committee, at its sixty-eighth session, agreed that paragraphs 2, 3 and 4 should commence with the words "In ro–ro passenger ships".

4   In ro–ro passenger ships constructed before 1 July 1997, the requirements of paragraphs 2 and 3 shall apply not later than the date of the first periodical survey after 1 July 1997.*†

5   After completion, a hose or flooding test shall be applied to watertight decks and a hose test to watertight trunks, tunnels and ventilators.

Regulation 20
Watertight integrity of passenger ships above the margin line

1   The Administration may require that all reasonable and practicable measures shall be taken to limit the entry and spread of water above the bulkhead deck. Such measures may include partial bulkheads or webs. When partial watertight bulkheads and webs are fitted on the bulkhead deck, above or in the immediate vicinity of main subdivision bulkheads, they shall have watertight shell and bulkhead deck connections so as to restrict the flow of water along the deck when the ship is in a heeled damaged condition. Where the partial watertight bulkhead does not line up with the bulkhead below, the bulkhead deck between shall be made effectively watertight.‡

2   The bulkhead deck or a deck above it shall be weathertight. All openings in the exposed weather deck shall have coamings of ample height and strength and shall be provided with efficient means for expeditiously closing them weathertight. Freeing ports, open rails and scuppers shall be fitted as necessary for rapidly clearing the weather deck of water under all weather conditions.

3   In passenger ships constructed on or after 1 July 1997, the open end of air pipes terminating within a superstructure shall be at least 1 m above the waterline when the ship heels to an angle of 15°, or the maximum angle of heel during intermediate stages of flooding, as determined by direct calculation, whichever is the greater. Alternatively, air pipes from tanks other than oil tanks may discharge through the side of the superstructure. The provisions of this paragraph are without prejudice to the provisions of the International Convention on Load Lines in force.

4   Sidescuttles, gangway, cargo and coaling ports and other means for closing openings in the shell plating above the margin line shall be of efficient design and construction and of sufficient strength having regard to

---

* The Maritime Safety Committee, at its sixty-eighth session, agreed that paragraphs 2, 3 and 4 should commence with the words "In ro–ro passenger ships".

† The Maritime Safety Committee, at its sixty-seventh session, agreed that the expression "paragraph 2" should be replaced by the expression "paragraphs 2 and 3".

‡ Refer to MSC/Circ.541 (as may be amended): Guidance notes on the integrity of flooding boundaries above the bulkhead deck of passenger ships for proper application of regulations II-1/8 and 20, paragraph 1, of SOLAS 1974, as amended.

the spaces in which they are fitted and their positions relative to the deepest subdivision load line.*

5   Efficient inside deadlights, so arranged that they can be easily and effectively closed and secured watertight, shall be provided for all sidescuttles to spaces below the first deck above the bulkhead deck.

Regulation 20-1
Closure of cargo loading doors

1   This regulation applies to all passenger ships.†

2   The following doors, located above the margin line, shall be closed and locked before the ship proceeds on any voyage and shall remain closed and locked until the ship is at its next berth:

> **.1**   cargo loading doors in the shell or the boundaries of enclosed superstructures;
>
> **.2**   bow visors fitted in positions, as indicated in paragraph 2.1;
>
> **.3**   cargo loading doors in the collision bulkhead;
>
> **.4**   weathertight ramps forming an alternative closure to those defined in paragraphs 2.1 to 2.3 inclusive.

Provided that where a door cannot be opened or closed while the ship is at the berth, such a door may be opened or left open while the ship approaches or draws away from the berth, but only so far as may be necessary to enable the door to be immediately operated. In any case, the inner bow door must be kept closed.

3   Notwithstanding the requirements of paragraph 2.1 and 2.4, the Administration may authorize that particular doors can be opened at the discretion of the master, if necessary for the operation of the ship or the embarking and disembarking of passengers, when the ship is at safe anchorage and provided that the safety of the ship is not impaired.

4   The master shall ensure that an effective system of supervision and reporting of the closing and opening of the doors referred to in paragraph 2 is implemented.

5   The master shall ensure, before the ship proceeds on any voyage, that an entry in the log-book, as required in regulation 25, is made of the time of the last closing of the doors specified in paragraph 2 and the time of any opening of particular doors in accordance with paragraph 3.

---

* Refer to the Recommendation on strength and securing and locking arrangements of shell doors on ro–ro passenger ships adopted by the Organization by resolution A.793(19).

† Refer to MSC/Circ.541 (as may be amended): Guidance notes on the integrity of flooding boundaries above the bulkhead deck of passenger ships for proper application of regulations II-1/8 and 20, paragraph 1, of SOLAS 1974, as amended.

Regulation 20-2
Watertight integrity from the ro–ro deck (bulkhead deck)
to spaces below

1 In ro–ro passenger ships constructed on or after 1 July 1997:

.1 subject to the provisions of subparagraphs .2 and .3, all accesses that lead to spaces below the bulkhead deck shall have a lowest point which is not less than 2.5 m above the bulkhead deck;

.2 where vehicle ramps are installed to give access to spaces below the bulkhead deck, their openings shall be able to be closed weathertight to prevent ingress of water below, alarmed and indicated to the navigation bridge;

.3 the Administration may permit the fitting of particular accesses to spaces below the bulkhead deck provided they are necessary for the essential working of the ship, e.g. the movement of machinery and stores, subject to such accesses being made watertight, alarmed and indicated to the navigation bridge;

.4 the accesses referred to in subparagraphs .2 and .3 shall be closed before the ship leaves the berth on any voyage and shall remain closed until the ship is at its next berth;

.5 the master shall ensure that an effective system of supervision and reporting of the closing and opening of such accesses referred to in subparagraphs .2 and .3 is implemented; and

.6 the master shall ensure, before the ship leaves the berth on any voyage, that an entry in the log-book, as required by regulation 25, is made of the time of the last closing of the accesses referred to in subparagraphs .2 and .3.

2 In ro–ro passenger ships constructed before 1 July 1997:

.1 all accesses from the ro–ro deck that lead to spaces below the bulkhead deck shall be made weathertight and means shall be provided on the navigation bridge, indicating whether the access is open or closed;

.2 all such accesses shall be closed before the ship leaves the berth on any voyage and shall remain closed until the ship is at its next berth;

.3 notwithstanding the requirements of subparagraph .2, the Administration may permit some accesses to be opened during the voyage but only for a period sufficient to permit through passage and, if required, for the essential working of the ship; and

.4 the requirements of subparagraph .1 shall apply not later than the date of the first periodical survey after 1 July 1997.

Regulation 20-3
Access to ro–ro decks

In all ro–ro passenger ships, the master or the designated officer shall ensure that, without the expressed consent of the master or the designated officer, no passengers are allowed access to an enclosed ro–ro deck when the ship is under way.

Regulation 20-4
Closure of bulkheads on the ro–ro deck

1 All transverse or longitudinal bulkheads which are taken into account as effective to confine the seawater accumulated on the ro–ro deck shall be in place and secured before the ship leaves the berth and remain in place and secured until the ship is at its next berth.

2 Notwithstanding the requirements of paragraph 1, the Administration may permit some accesses within such bulkheads to be opened during the voyage but only for sufficient time to permit through passage and, if required, for the essential working of the ship.

Regulation 21
Bilge pumping arrangements

(Paragraphs 1.6 and 2.9 of this regulation apply to ships constructed on or after 1 February 1992)

1 Passenger ships and cargo ships

1.1 An efficient bilge pumping system shall be provided, capable of pumping from and draining any watertight compartment other than a space permanently appropriated for the carriage of fresh water, water ballast, oil fuel or liquid cargo and for which other efficient means of pumping are provided, under all practical conditions. Efficient means shall be provided for draining water from insulated holds.

1.2 Sanitary, ballast and general service pumps may be accepted as independent power bilge pumps if fitted with the necessary connections to the bilge pumping system.

1.3 All bilge pipes used in or under coal bunkers or fuel storage tanks or in boiler or machinery spaces, including spaces in which oil-settling tanks or oil fuel pumping units are situated, shall be of steel or other suitable material.

1.4 The arrangement of the bilge and ballast pumping system shall be such as to prevent the possibility of water passing from the sea and from water ballast spaces into the cargo and machinery spaces, or from one compartment to another. Provision shall be made to prevent any deep tank having bilge and ballast connections being inadvertently flooded from the sea when containing cargo, or being discharged through a bilge pump when containing water ballast.

1.5   All distribution boxes and manually operated valves in connection with the bilge pumping arrangements shall be in positions which are accessible under ordinary circumstances.

1.6   Provision shall be made for the drainage of enclosed cargo spaces situated on the bulkhead deck of a passenger ship and on the freeboard deck of a cargo ship, provided that the Administration may permit the means of drainage to be dispensed with in any particular compartment of any ship or class of ship if it is satisfied that by reason of size or internal subdivision of those spaces the safety of the ship is not thereby impaired.

1.6.1   Where the freeboard to the bulkhead deck or the freeboard deck, respectively, is such that the deck edge is immersed when the ship heels more than 5°, the drainage shall be by means of a sufficient number of scuppers of suitable size discharging directly overboard, fitted in accordance with the requirements of regulation 17 in the case of a passenger ship and the requirements for scuppers, inlets and discharges of the International Convention on Load Lines in force in the case of a cargo ship.

1.6.2   Where the freeboard is such that the edge of the bulkhead deck or the edge of the freeboard deck, respectively, is immersed when the ship heels 5° or less, the drainage of the enclosed cargo spaces on the bulkhead deck or on the freeboard deck, respectively, shall be led to a suitable space, or spaces, of adequate capacity, having a high water level alarm and provided with suitable arrangements for discharge overboard. In addition it shall be ensured that:

.1   the number, size and disposition of the scuppers are such as to prevent unreasonable accumulation of free water;

.2   the pumping arrangements required by this regulation for passenger ships or cargo ships, as applicable, take account of the requirements for any fixed pressure water-spraying fire-extinguishing system;

.3   water contaminated with petrol or other dangerous substances is not drained to machinery spaces or other spaces where sources of ignition may be present; and

.4   where the enclosed cargo space is protected by a carbon dioxide fire-extinguishing system the deck scuppers are fitted with means to prevent the escape of the smothering gas.

2   Passenger ships

2.1   The bilge pumping system required by paragraph 1.1 shall be capable of operation under all practicable conditions after a casualty whether the ship is upright or listed. For this purpose wing suctions shall generally be fitted except in narrow compartments at the end of the ship where one suction may be sufficient. In compartments of unusual form, additional suctions may be required. Arrangements shall be made whereby water in the compartment may find its way to the suction pipes. Where, for particular compartments, the Administration is satisfied that the provision of drainage may be undesirable, it may allow such provision to be dispensed with if calculations made in accordance with the conditions laid down in regulations 8.2.1 to 8.2.3 show that the survival capability of the ship will not be impaired.

2.2   At least three power pumps shall be fitted connected to the bilge main, one of which may be driven by the propulsion machinery. Where the criterion numeral is 30 or more, one additional independent power pump shall be provided.

2.3   Where practicable, the power bilge pumps shall be placed in separate watertight compartments and so arranged or situated that these compartments will not be flooded by the same damage. If the main propulsion machinery, auxiliary machinery and boilers are in two or more watertight compartments, the pumps available for bilge service shall be distributed as far as is possible throughout these compartments.

2.4   On a ship of 91.5 m in length and upwards or having a criterion numeral of 30 or more, the arrangements shall be such that at least one power bilge pump shall be available for use in all flooding conditions which the ship is required to withstand, as follows:

> **.1**   one of the required bilge pumps shall be an emergency pump of a reliable submersible type having a source of power situated above the bulkhead deck; or

> **.2**   the bilge pumps and their sources of power shall be so distributed throughout the length of the ship that at least one pump in an undamaged compartment will be available.

2.5   With the exception of additional pumps which may be provided for peak compartments only, each required bilge pump shall be so arranged as to draw water from any space required to be drained by paragraph 1.1.

2.6   Each power bilge pump shall be capable of pumping water through the required main bilge pipe at a speed of not less than 2 m/s. Independent power bilge pumps situated in machinery spaces shall have direct suctions from these spaces, except that not more than two such suctions shall be required in any one space. Where two or more such suctions are provided, there shall be at least one on each side of the ship. The Administration may require independent power bilge pumps situated in other spaces to have separate direct suctions. Direct suctions shall be suitably arranged and those in a machinery space shall be of a diameter not less than that required for the bilge main.

2.7.1 In addition to the direct bilge suction or suctions required by paragraph 2.6 a direct suction from the main circulating pump leading to the drainage level of the machinery space and fitted with a non-return valve shall be provided in the machinery space. The diameter of this direct suction pipe shall be at least two thirds of the diameter of the pump inlet in the case of steamships, and of the same diameter as the pump inlet in the case of motorships.

2.7.2 Where in the opinion of the Administration the main circulating pump is not suitable for this purpose, a direct emergency bilge suction shall be led from the largest available independent power driven pump to the drainage level of the machinery space; the suction shall be of the same diameter as the main inlet of the pump used. The capacity of the pump so connected shall exceed that of a required bilge pump by an amount deemed satisfactory by the Administration.

2.7.3 The spindles of the sea inlet and direct suction valves shall extend well above the engine-room platform.

2.8 All bilge suction piping up to the connection to the pumps shall be independent of other piping.

2.9 The diameter d of the bilge main shall be calculated according to the following formula. However, the actual internal diameter of the bilge main may be rounded off to the nearest standard size acceptable to the Administration:

$$d = 25 + 1.68\sqrt{L(B+D)}$$

where:

d is the internal diameter of the bilge main (millimetres);

L and B are the length and the breadth of the ship (metres) as defined in regulation 2; and

D is the moulded depth of the ship to the bulkhead deck (metres) provided that, in a ship having an enclosed cargo space on the bulkhead deck which is internally drained in accordance with the requirements of paragraph 1.6.2 and which extends for the full length of the ship, D shall be measured to the next deck above the bulkhead deck. Where the enclosed cargo spaces cover a lesser length, D shall be taken as the moulded depth to the bulkhead deck plus lh/L where l and h are the aggregate length and height respectively of the enclosed cargo spaces (metres).

The diameter of the bilge branch pipes shall meet the requirements of the Administration.

2.10 Provision shall be made to prevent the compartment served by any bilge suction pipe being flooded in the event of the pipe being severed or otherwise damaged by collision or grounding in any other compartment. For this purpose, where the pipe is at any part situated nearer the side of the ship than one fifth of the breadth of the ship (as defined in regulation 2 and measured at right angles to the centreline at the level of the deepest subdivision load line), or is in a duct keel, a non-return valve shall be fitted to the pipe in the compartment containing the open end.

2.11 Distribution boxes, cocks and valves in connection with the bilge pumping system shall be so arranged that, in the event of flooding, one of the bilge pumps may be operative on any compartment; in addition, damage to a pump or its pipe connecting to the bilge main outboard of a line drawn at one fifth of the breadth of the ship shall not put the bilge system out of action. If there is only one system of pipes common to all the pumps, the necessary valves for controlling the bilge suctions must be capable of being operated from above the bulkhead deck. Where in addition to the main bilge pumping system an emergency bilge pumping system is provided, it shall be independent of the main system and so arranged that a pump is capable of operating on any compartment under flooding condition as specified in paragraph 2.1; in that case only the valves necessary for the operation of the emergency system need be capable of being operated from above the bulkhead deck.

2.12 All cocks and valves referred to in paragraph 2.11 which can be operated from above the bulkhead deck shall have their controls at their place of operation clearly marked and shall be provided with means to indicate whether they are open or closed.

3   Cargo ships

At least two power pumps connected to the main bilge system shall be provided, one of which may be driven by the propulsion machinery. If the Administration is satisfied that the safety of the ship is not impaired, bilge pumping arrangements may be dispensed with in particular compartments.

Regulation 22
*Stability information for passenger ships and cargo ships**

1   Every passenger ship regardless of size and every cargo ship having a length, as defined in the International Convention on Load Lines in force, of 24 m and upwards, shall be inclined upon its completion and the elements of its stability determined. The master shall be supplied with such

---

information satisfactory to the Administration as is necessary to enable him by rapid and simple processes to obtain accurate guidance as to the stability of the ship under varying conditions of service. A copy of the stability information shall be furnished to the Administration.

2 Where any alterations are made to a ship so as to materially affect the stability information supplied to the master, amended stability information shall be provided. If necessary the ship shall be re-inclined.

3 At periodical intervals not exceeding five years, a lightweight survey shall be carried out on all passenger ships to verify any changes in lightship displacement and longitudinal centre of gravity. The ship shall be re-inclined whenever, in comparison with the approved stability information, a deviation from the lightship displacement exceeding 2% or a deviation of the longitudinal centre of gravity exceeding 1% of L is found or anticipated.

4 The Administration may allow the inclining test of an individual ship to be dispensed with provided basic stability data are available from the inclining test of a sister ship and it is shown to the satisfaction of the Administration that reliable stability information for the exempted ship can be obtained from such basic data, as required by paragraph 1.

5 The Administration may also allow the inclining test of an individual ship or class of ships especially designed for the carriage of liquids or ore in bulk to be dispensed with when reference to existing data for similar ships clearly indicates that due to the ship's proportions and arrangements more than sufficient metacentric height will be available in all probable loading conditions.

Regulation 23
*Damage control plans in passenger ships**

There shall be permanently exhibited, for the guidance of the officer in charge of the ship, plans showing clearly for each deck and hold the boundaries of the watertight compartments, the openings therein with the means of closure and position of any controls thereof, and the arrangements for the correction of any list due to flooding. In addition, booklets containing the aforementioned information shall be made available to the officers of the ship.

Regulation 23-1
*Damage control in dry cargo ships**

(This regulation applies to ships constructed on or after 1 February 1992)

1 There shall be permanently exhibited or readily available on the navigation bridge, for the guidance of the officer in charge of the ship, a plan

---

* Refer to MSC/Circ. 919, Guidelines for damage control plans.

showing clearly for each deck and hold the boundaries of the watertight compartments, the openings therein with the means of closure and position of any controls thereof, and the arrangements for the correction of any list due to flooding. In addition, booklets containing the aforementioned information shall be made available to the officers of the ship.[*]

2   Indicators shall be provided for all sliding doors and for hinged doors in watertight bulkheads. Indication showing whether the doors are open or closed shall be given on the navigation bridge. In addition, shell doors and other openings which, in the opinion of the Administration, could lead to major flooding if left open or not properly secured, shall be provided with such indicators.

3.1   General precautions shall consist of a listing of equipment, conditions and operational procedures, considered by the Administration to be necessary to maintain watertight integrity under normal ship operations.

3.2   Specific precautions shall consist of a listing of elements (i.e. closures, security of cargo, sounding of alarms, etc.) considered by the Administration to be vital to the survival of the ship and its crew.

Regulation 23-2
Integrity of the hull and superstructure, damage prevention and control

(This regulation applies to all ro–ro passenger ships, except that for ships constructed before 1 July 1997, paragraph 2 shall apply not later than the date of the first periodical survey after 1 July 1997)

1   Indicators shall be provided on the navigation bridge for all shell doors, loading doors and other closing appliances which, if left open or not properly secured, could, in the opinion of the Administration, lead to flooding of a special category space or ro–ro cargo space. The indicator system shall be designed on the fail-safe principle and shall show by visual alarms if the door is not fully closed or if any of the securing arrangements are not in place and fully locked and by audible alarms if such door or closing appliances become open or the securing arrangements become unsecured. The indicator panel on the navigation bridge shall be equipped with a mode selection function "harbour/sea voyage" so arranged that an audible alarm is given on the navigation bridge if the ship leaves harbour with the bow doors, inner doors, stern ramp or any other side shell doors not closed or any closing device not in the correct position. The power supply for the indicator system shall be independent of the power supply for operating and securing the doors. The indicator systems, approved by the

---

[*] Refer to MSC/Circ.434, Guidelines for the preparation of information on the effect of flooding to be provided to masters of dry cargo ships.

Administration, which were installed on ships constructed before 1 July 1997 need not be changed.

2   Television surveillance and a water leakage detection system shall be arranged to provide an indication to the navigation bridge and to the engine control station of any leakage through inner and outer bow doors, stern doors or any other shell doors which could lead to flooding of special category spaces or ro–ro cargo spaces.

3   Special category spaces and ro–ro cargo spaces shall be continuously patrolled or monitored by effective means, such as television surveillance, so that any movement of vehicles in adverse weather conditions and unauthorized access by passengers thereto can be detected whilst the ship is under way.

4   Documented operating procedures for closing and securing all shell doors, loading doors and other closing appliances which, if left open or not properly secured, could, in the opinion of the Administration, lead to flooding of a special category space or ro–ro cargo space, shall be kept on board and posted at an appropriate place.

Regulation 24
Marking, periodical operation and inspection of watertight doors, etc., in passenger ships

1   This regulation applies to all ships.

2.1   Drills for the operating of watertight doors, sidescuttles, valves and closing mechanisms of scuppers, ash-chutes and rubbish-chutes shall take place weekly. In ships in which the voyage exceeds one week in duration a complete drill shall be held before leaving port, and others thereafter at least once a week during the voyage.

2.2   All watertight doors, both hinged and power operated, in main transverse bulkheads, in use at sea, shall be operated daily.

3.1   The watertight doors and all mechanisms and indicators connected therewith, all valves, the closing of which is necessary to make a compartment watertight, and all valves the operation of which is necessary for damage control cross-connections shall be periodically inspected at sea at least once a week.

3.2   Such valves, doors and mechanisms shall be suitably marked to ensure that they may be properly used to provide maximum safety.

Regulation 25
Entries in log of passenger ships

1   This regulation applies to all ships.

2   Hinged doors, portable plates, sidescuttles, gangway, cargo and coaling ports and other openings, which are required by these regulations to be kept closed during navigation, shall be closed before the ship leaves port. The time of closing and the time of opening (if permissible under these regulations) shall be recorded in such log-book as may be prescribed by the Administration.

3   A record of all drills and inspections required by regulation 24 shall be entered in the log-book with an explicit record of any defects which may be disclosed.

Part B-1
*Subdivision and damage stability of cargo ships**

(This part applies to cargo ships constructed
on or after 1 February 1992)

Regulation 25-1
Application

1   The requirements in this part shall apply to cargo ships over 100 m in length (L_s) but shall exclude those ships which are shown to comply with subdivision and damage stability regulations in other instruments[†] developed by the Organization. The requirements in this part shall also apply to cargo ships of 80 m in L_s and upwards but not exceeding 100 m in L_s constructed on or after 1 July 1998.

2   Any reference hereinafter to regulations refers to the set of regulations contained in this part.

3   The Administration may for a particular ship or group of ships accept alternative arrangements, if it is satisfied that at least the same degree of safety as represented by these regulations is achieved. Any Administration which allows such alternative arrangements shall communicate to the Organization particulars thereof.

---

* The Maritime Safety Committee, in adopting the regulations contained in part B-1, invited Administrations to note that the regulations should be applied in conjunction with the Explanatory notes to the SOLAS regulations on subdivision and damage stability of cargo ships of 100 metres in length and over, which were adopted by the Organization by resolution A.684(17), in order to ensure their uniform application. Refer also to resolution MSC.76(69) on Extended application of the Explanatory Notes to the SOLAS regulations on subdivision and damage stability of cargo ships of 100 metres in length and over (resolution A.684(17)).

[†]Ships shown to comply with the following regulations may be excluded from the application of part B-1:

   .1 Annex I to MARPOL 73/78;

   .2 International Bulk Chemical Code;

   .3 International Gas Carrier Code;

   .4 Guidelines for the design and construction of offshore supply vessels (resolution A.469(XII));

   .5 Code of Safety for Special Purpose Ships (resolution A.534(13), as amended);

   .6 Damage stability requirements of regulation 27 of the 1966 Load Line Convention as applied in compliance with resolutions A.320(IX) and A.514(13), provided that in the case of ships to which regulation 27(9) applies, main transverse watertight bulkheads, to be considered effective, are spaced according to paragraph (12)(f) of resolution A.320(IX).

Regulation 25-2
Definitions

For the purpose of these regulations, unless expressly provided otherwise:

1.1 *Subdivision load line* is a waterline used in determining the subdivision of the ship.

1.2 *Deepest subdivision load line* is the subdivision load line which corresponds to the summer draught to be assigned to the ship.

1.3 *Partial load line* is the light ship draught plus 60% of the difference between the light ship draught and deepest subdivision load line.

2.1 *Subdivision length of the ship* (L_s) is the greatest projected moulded length of that part of the ship at or below deck or decks limiting the vertical extent of flooding with the ship at the deepest subdivision load line.

2.2 *Mid-length* is the mid-point of the subdivision length of the ship.

2.3 *Aft terminal* is the aft limit of the subdivision length.

2.4 *Forward terminal* is the forward limit of the subdivision length.

3 *Breadth (B)* is the greatest moulded breadth of the ship at or below the deepest subdivision load line.

4 *Draught (d)* is the vertical distance from the moulded baseline at mid-length to the waterline in question.

5 *Permeability (μ)* of a space is the proportion of the immersed volume of that space which can be occupied by water.

Regulation 25-3
Required subdivision index R

1 These regulations are intended to provide ships with a minimum standard of subdivision.

2 The degree of subdivision to be provided shall be determined by the required subdivision index R, as follows:

.1 for ships over 100 m in L_s:

$$R = (0.002 + 0.0009L_s)^{\frac{1}{3}},$$

where L_s is in metres; and

.2 for ships of 80 m in L_s and upwards but not exceeding 100 m in length L_s:

$$R = 1 - [1/(1 + \frac{L_s}{100} \times \frac{R_o}{1 - R_o})],$$

where R_o is the value R as calculated in accordance with the formula in subparagraph .1.

Regulation 25-4
Attained subdivision index A

1   The attained subdivision index A, calculated in accordance with this regulation, shall not be less than the required subdivision index R, calculated in accordance with paragraph 2 of regulation 25-3.

2   The attained subdivision index A shall be calculated for the ship by the following formula:

$$A = \sum p_i s_i$$

where:

    i represents each compartment or group of compartments under consideration,

    p_i accounts for the probability that only the compartment or group of compartments under consideration may be flooded, disregarding any horizontal subdivision,

    s_i accounts for the probability of survival after flooding the compartment or group of compartments under consideration, including the effects of any horizontal subdivision.

3   In calculating A, level trim shall be used.

4   This summation covers only those cases of flooding which contribute to the value of the attained subdivision index A.

5   The summation indicated by the above formula shall be taken over the ship's length for all cases of flooding in which a single compartment or two or more adjacent compartments are involved.

6   Wherever wing compartments are fitted, contribution to the summation indicated by the formula shall be taken for all cases of flooding in which wing compartments are involved; and additionally, for all cases of simultaneous flooding of a wing compartment or compartments and the adjacent inboard compartment or compartments, assuming a rectangular penetration which extends to the ship's centreline, but excludes damage to any centreline bulkhead.

7   The assumed vertical extent of damage is to extend from the baseline upwards to any watertight horizontal subdivision above the waterline or higher. However, if a lesser extent will give a more severe result, such extent is to be assumed.

8   If pipes, ducts or tunnels are situated within assumed flooded compartments, arrangements are to be made to ensure that progressive flooding cannot thereby extend to compartments other than those assumed flooded. However, the Administration may permit minor progressive flooding if it is demonstrated that its effects can be easily controlled and the safety of the ship is not impaired.

9   In the flooding calculations carried out according to the regulations, only one breach of the hull need be assumed.

Regulation 25-5
Calculation of the factor p_i

1   The factor p_i shall be calculated according to paragraph 1.1 as appropriate, using the following notations:

x_1 = the distance from the aft terminal of L_s to the foremost portion of the aft end of the compartment being considered;

x_2 = the distance from the aft terminal of L_s to the aftermost portion of the forward end of the compartment being considered;

E_1 = $\dfrac{x_1}{L_s}$

E_2 = $\dfrac{x_2}{L_s}$

E = $E_1 + E_2 - 1$

J = $E_2 - E_1$

J' = $J - E$, if $E \geqslant 0$

J' = $J + E$, if $E < 0$

The maximum nondimensional damage length

$J_{\max}$ = $\dfrac{48}{L_s}$, but not more than 0.24.

The assumed distribution density of damage location along the ship's length

a = $1.2 + 0.8E$, but not more than 1.2.

The assumed distribution function of damage location along the ship's length

F = $0.4 + 0.25E\,(1.2 + a)$

γ = $\dfrac{J}{J_{\max}}$

p = $F_1 J_{\max}$

q = $0.4F_2(\,J_{\max})^2$

$$F_1 = \gamma^2 - \frac{\gamma^3}{3}, \qquad \text{if } \gamma < 1,$$

$$F_1 = \gamma - \frac{1}{3} \qquad \text{otherwise;}$$

$$F_2 = \frac{\gamma^3}{3} - \frac{\gamma^4}{12}, \qquad \text{if } \gamma < 1,$$

$$F_2 = \frac{\gamma^2}{2} - \frac{\gamma}{3} + \frac{1}{12} \qquad \text{otherwise.}$$

1.1 The factor p_i is determined for each single compartment:

1.1.1 Where the compartment considered extends over the entire ship length L_s:

$$p_i = 1$$

1.1.2 Where the aft limit of the compartment considered coincides with the aft terminal:

$$p_i = F + 0.5ap + q$$

1.1.3 Where the forward limit of the compartment considered coincides with the forward terminal:

$$p_i = 1 - F + 0.5ap$$

1.1.4 When both ends of the compartment considered are inside the aft and forward terminals of the ship length L_s:

$$p_i = ap$$

1.1.5 In applying the formulae of paragraphs 1.1.2, 1.1.3 and 1.1.4, where the compartment considered extends over the "mid-length", these formulae values shall be reduced by an amount determined according to the formula for q, in which F_2 is calculated taking γ to be J'/J_{max}.

2 Wherever wing compartments are fitted, the p_i-value for a wing compartment shall be obtained by multiplying the value, as determined in paragraph 3, by the reduction factor r according to paragraph 2.2, which represents the probability that the inboard spaces will not be flooded.

2.1 The p_i-value for the case of simultaneous flooding of a wing and adjacent inboard compartment shall be obtained by using the formulae of paragraph 3, multiplied by the factor $(1 - r)$.

2.2 The reduction factor r shall be determined by the following formulae:

For $J \geqslant 0.2 \dfrac{b}{B}$:

$$r = \frac{b}{B}(2.3 + \frac{0.08}{J + 0.02}) + 0.1, \quad \text{if } \frac{b}{B} \leqslant 0.2$$

$$r = (\frac{0.016}{J + 0.02} + \frac{b}{B} + 0.36), \qquad \text{if } \frac{b}{B} > 0.2$$

For $J < 0.2\frac{b}{B}$ the reduction factor r shall be determined by linear interpolation between:

$$r = 1, \quad \text{for } J = 0$$

and

$$r = \text{as for the case where } J \geqslant 0.2\frac{b}{B}, \quad \text{for } J = 0.2\frac{b}{B}$$

where:

b = the mean transverse distance in metres measured at right angles to the centreline at the deepest subdivision load line between the shell and a plane through the outermost portion of and parallel to that part of the longitudinal bulkhead which extends between the longitudinal limits used in calculating the factor p_i.

3   To evaluate p_i for compartments taken singly the formulae in paragraphs 1 and 2 shall be applied directly.

3.1   To evaluate the p_i-values attributable to groups of compartments the following applies:

for compartments taken by pairs:

$$p_i = p_{12} - p_1 - p_2$$
$$p_i = p_{23} - p_2 - p_3 \text{ , etc.}$$

for compartments taken by groups of three:

$$p_i = p_{123} - p_{12} - p_{23} + p_2$$
$$p_i = p_{234} - p_{23} - p_{34} + p_3 \text{ , etc.}$$

for compartments taken by groups of four:

$$p_i = p_{1234} - p_{123} - p_{234} + p_{23}$$
$$p_i = p_{2345} - p_{234} - p_{345} + p_{34} \text{ , etc.}$$

where:

p_{12}, p_{23}, p_{34}, etc.,
$p_{123}, p_{234}, p_{345}$, etc., and
$p_{1234}, p_{2345}, p_{3456}$, etc.

shall be calculated according to the formulae in paragraphs 1 and 2 for a single compartment whose nondimensional length J corresponds to that of a group consisting of the compartments indicated by the indices assigned to p.

3.2   The factor p_i for a group of three or more adjacent compartments equals zero if the nondimensional length of such a group minus the nondimensional length of the aftermost and foremost compartments in the group is greater than J_{max}.

Regulation 25-6
Calculation of the factor s_i

1   The factor s_i shall be determined for each compartment or group of compartments according to the following:

1.1   In general for any condition of flooding from any initial loading condition s shall be:

$$s = C\sqrt{0.5(GZ_{max})(\text{range})}$$

with:

$C = 1,$ if $\theta_e \leqslant 25°$,

$C = 0,$ if $\theta_e > 30°$,

$C = \sqrt{\dfrac{30 - \theta_e}{5}}$ otherwise;

GZ_{max} = maximum positive righting lever (metres) within the range as given below but not more than 0.1 m;

range = range of positive righting levers beyond the angle of equilibrium (degrees) but not more than 20°; however, the range shall be terminated at the angle where openings not capable of being closed weathertight are immersed;

θ_e = final equilibrium angle of heel (degrees).

1.2 $s = 0$ where the final waterline taking into account sinkage, heel and trim, immerses the lower edge of openings through which progressive flooding may take place. Such opening shall include air-pipes, ventilators and openings which are closed by means of weathertight doors or hatch covers, and may exclude those openings closed by means of watertight manhole covers and flush scuttles, small watertight hatch covers which maintain the high integrity of the deck, remotely operated sliding watertight doors, access doors and access hatch covers, of watertight integrity, normally closed at sea and sidescuttles of the non-opening type. However, if the compartments so flooded are taken into account in the calculations the requirements of this regulation shall be applied.

1.3   For each compartment or group of compartments s_i shall be weighted according to draught considerations as follows:

$$s_i = 0.5s_1 + 0.5s_p$$

where:

s_1 is the s-factor at the deepest subdivision load line

s_p is the s-factor at the partial load line.

2   For all compartments forward of the collision bulkhead, the *s*-value, calculated assuming the ship to be at its deepest subdivision load line and with assumed unlimited vertical extent of damage, is to be equal to 1.

3   Wherever a horizontal subdivision is fitted above the waterline in question the following applies.

3.1   The *s*-value for the lower compartment or group of compartments shall be obtained by multiplying the value as determined in paragraph 1.1 by the reduction factor *v* according to paragraph 3.3, which represents the probability that the spaces above the horizontal subdivision will not be flooded.

3.2   In cases of positive contribution to index *A* due to simultaneous flooding of the spaces above the horizontal subdivision, the resulting *s*-value for such a compartment or group of compartments shall be obtained by an increase of the value as determined by paragraph 3.1 by the *s*-value for simultaneous flooding according to paragraph 1.1, multiplied by the factor $(1 - v)$.

3.3   The probability factor v_i shall be calculated according to:

$$v_i = \frac{H - d}{H_{max} - d}$$

for the assumed flooding up to the horizontal subdivision above the subdivision load line, where *H* is to be restricted to a height of H_{max},

$$v_i = 1,$$

if the uppermost horizontal subdivision in way of the assumed damaged region is below H_{max},

where:

H   is the height of the horizontal subdivision above the baseline (in metres) which is assumed to limit the vertical extent of damage,

H_{max} is the maximum possible vertical extent of damage above the baseline (in metres), or

$$H_{max} = d + 0.056L_s \left(1 - \frac{L_s}{500}\right), \qquad \text{if } L_s \leqslant 250 \text{ m}$$

$$H_{max} = d + 7, \qquad \text{if } L_s > 250 \text{ m}$$

whichever is less.

Regulation 25-7
Permeability[*]

For the purpose of the subdivision and damage stability calculations of the regulations, the permeability of each space or part of a space shall be as follows:

Spaces	Permeability
Appropriated to stores	0.60
Occupied by accommodation	0.95
Occupied by machinery	0.85
Void spaces	0.95
Dry cargo spaces	0.70
Intended for liquid	0 or 0.95[†]

Regulation 25-8
Stability information

1   The master of the ship shall be supplied with such reliable information as is necessary to enable him by rapid and simple means to obtain accurate guidance as to the stability of the ship under varying conditions of service. The information shall include:

   .1   a curve of minimum operational metacentric height (GM) versus draught which assures compliance with the relevant intact stability requirements and the requirements of regulations 25-1 to 25-6, alternatively a corresponding curve of the maximum allowable vertical centre of gravity (KG) versus draught, or with the equivalents of either of these curves;

   .2   instructions concerning the operation of cross-flooding arrangements; and

   .3   all other data and aids which might be necessary to maintain stability after damage.

2   There shall be permanently exhibited, or readily available on the navigation bridge, for the guidance of the officer in charge of the ship, plans showing clearly for each deck and hold the boundaries of the watertight compartments, the openings therein with the means of closure and position of any controls thereof, and the arrangements for the correction of any list due to flooding. In addition, booklets containing the aforementioned information shall be made available to the officers of the ship.[‡]

---

[*] Refer to MSC/Circ.651, Interpretations of regulations of part B-1 of SOLAS chapter II-1.

[†] Whichever results in the more severe requirements.

[‡] Refer to MSC/Circ. 919, Guidelines for damage control plans.

3   In order to provide the information referred to in paragraph 1.1, the limiting GM (or KG) values to be used, if they have been determined from considerations related to the subdivision index, the limiting GM shall be varied linearly between the deepest subdivision load line and the partial load line.* In such cases, for draughts below the partial load line if the minimum GM requirement at this draught results from the calculation of the subdivision index, then this GM value shall be assumed for lesser draughts, unless the intact stability requirements apply.

Regulation 25-9
Openings in watertight bulkheads and internal decks
in cargo ships

1   The number of openings in watertight subdivisions is to be kept to a minimum compatible with the design and proper working of the ship. Where penetrations of watertight bulkheads and internal decks are necessary for access, piping, ventilation, electrical cables, etc., arrangements are to be made to maintain the watertight integrity. The Administration may permit relaxation in the watertightness of openings above the freeboard deck, provided that it is demonstrated that any progressive flooding can be easily controlled and that the safety of the ship is not impaired.

2   Doors provided to ensure the watertight integrity of internal openings which are used while at sea are to be sliding watertight doors capable of being remotely closed from the bridge and are also to be operable locally from each side of the bulkhead. Indicators are to be provided at the control position showing whether the doors are open or closed, and an audible alarm is to be provided at the door closure. The power, control and indicators are to be operable in the event of main power failure. Particular attention is to be paid to minimizing the effect of control system failure. Each power-operated sliding watertight door shall be provided with an individual hand-operated mechanism. It shall be possible to open and close the door by hand at the door itself from both sides.

3   Access doors and access hatch covers normally closed at sea, intended to ensure the watertight integrity of internal openings, shall be provided with means of indication locally and on the bridge showing whether these doors or hatch covers are open or closed. A notice is to be affixed to each such door or hatch cover to the effect that it is not to be left open. The use of such doors and hatch covers shall be authorized by the officer of the watch.

4   Watertight doors or ramps of satisfactory construction may be fitted to internally subdivide large cargo spaces, provided that the Administration is

---

* Refer to MSC/Circ.651, Interpretations of regulations of part B-1 of SOLAS chapter II-1.

satisfied that such doors or ramps are essential. These doors or ramps may be hinged, rolling or sliding doors or ramps, but shall not be remotely controlled.* Such doors or ramps shall be closed before the voyage commences and shall be kept closed during navigation; the time of opening such doors or ramps in port and of closing them before the ship leaves port shall be entered in the log-book. Should any of the doors or ramps be accessible during the voyage, they shall be fitted with a device which prevents unauthorized opening.

5   Other closing appliances which are kept permanently closed at sea to ensure the watertight integrity of internal openings shall be provided with a notice which is to be affixed to each such closing appliance to the effect that it is to be kept closed. Manholes fitted with closely bolted covers need not be so marked.

Regulation 25-10
External openings in cargo ships

1   All external openings leading to compartments assumed intact in the damage analysis, which are below the final damage waterline, are required to be watertight.

2   External openings required to be watertight in accordance with paragraph 1 shall be of sufficient strength and, except for cargo hatch covers, shall be fitted with indicators on the bridge.

3   Openings in the shell plating below the deck limiting the vertical extent of damage shall be kept permanently closed while at sea. Should any of these openings be accessible during the voyage, they shall be fitted with a device which prevents unauthorized opening.

4   Notwithstanding the requirements of paragraph 3, the Administration may authorize that particular doors may be opened at the discretion of the master, if necessary for the operation of the ship and provided that the safety of the ship is not impaired.

5   Other closing appliances which are kept permanently closed at sea to ensure the watertight integrity of external openings shall be provided with a notice affixed to each appliance to the effect that it is to be kept closed. Manholes fitted with closely bolted covers need not be so marked.

---

* Refer to MSC/Circ.651, Interpretations of regulations of part B-1 of SOLAS chapter II-1.

Part C
Machinery installations
(Except where expressly provided otherwise part C
applies to passenger ships and cargo ships)

Regulation 26
General

1   The machinery, boilers and other pressure vessels, associated piping
systems and fittings shall be of a design and construction adequate for the
service for which they are intended and shall be so installed and protected as
to reduce to a minimum any danger to persons on board, due regard being
paid to moving parts, hot surfaces and other hazards. The design shall have
regard to materials used in construction, the purpose for which the
equipment is intended, the working conditions to which it will be subjected
and the environmental conditions on board.[*]

2   The Administration shall give special consideration to the reliability of
single essential propulsion components and may require a separate source of
propulsion power sufficient to give the ship a navigable speed, especially in
the case of unconventional arrangements.

3   Means shall be provided whereby normal operation of propulsion
machinery can be sustained or restored even though one of the essential
auxiliaries becomes inoperative. Special consideration shall be given to the
malfunctioning of:

.1   a generating set which serves as a main source of electrical
power;

.2   the sources of steam supply;

.3   the boiler feedwater systems;

.4   the fuel oil supply systems for boilers or engines;[†]

.5   the sources of lubricating oil pressure;

.6   the sources of water pressure;

.7   a condensate pump and the arrangements to maintain vacuum in
condensers;

---

[*] Refer to MSC/Circ. 834, Guidelines for engine-room lay-out, design and arrangement.
[†] Refer to MSC/Circ.647, Guidelines to minimize leakage from flammable liquid systems, as
supplemented by MSC/Circ. 851, Guidelines on engine-room oil fuel systems.

.8 the mechanical air supply for boilers;

.9 an air compressor and receiver for starting or control purposes;

.10 the hydraulic, pneumatic or electrical means for control in main propulsion machinery including controllable pitch propellers.

However, the Administration, having regard to overall safety considerations, may accept a partial reduction in propulsion capability from normal operation.

4 Means shall be provided to ensure that the machinery can be brought into operation from the dead ship condition without external aid.

5 All boilers, all parts of machinery, all steam, hydraulic, pneumatic and other systems and their associated fittings which are under internal pressure shall be subjected to appropriate tests including a pressure test before being put into service for the first time.

6 Main propulsion machinery and all auxiliary machinery essential to the propulsion and the safety of the ship shall, as fitted in the ship, be designed to operate when the ship is upright and when inclined at any angle of list up to and including 15° either way under static conditions and 22.5° under dynamic conditions (rolling) either way and simultaneously inclined dynamically (pitching) 7.5° by bow or stern. The Administration may permit deviation from these angles, taking into consideration the type, size and service conditions of the ship.

7 Provision shall be made to facilitate cleaning, inspection and maintenance of main propulsion and auxiliary machinery including boilers and pressure vessels.

8 Special consideration shall be given to the design, construction and installation of propulsion machinery systems so that any mode of their vibrations shall not cause undue stresses in this machinery in the normal operating ranges.

9 Non-metallic expansion joints in piping systems, if located in a system which penetrates the ship's side and both the penetration and the non-metallic expansion joint are located below the deepest load waterline, shall be inspected as part of the surveys prescribed in regulation I/10(a) and replaced as necessary, or at an interval recommended by the manufacturer.

10 Operating and maintenance instructions and engineering drawings for ship machinery and equipment essential to the safe operation of the ship shall be written in a language understandable by those officers and crew members who are required to understand such information in the performance of their duties.

11 Location and arrangement of vent pipes for fuel oil service, settling and lubrication oil tanks shall be such that in the event of a broken vent pipe this shall not directly lead to the risk of ingress of seawater splashes or rainwater. Two fuel oil service tanks for each type of fuel used on board necessary for propulsion and vital systems or equivalent arrangements shall be provided on each new ship, with a capacity of at least 8 h at maximum continuous rating of the propulsion plant and normal operating load at sea of the generator plant.[*] This paragraph applies only to ships constructed on or after 1 July 1998.

Regulation 27
Machinery

1   Where risk from overspeeding of machinery exists, means shall be provided to ensure that the safe speed is not exceeded.

2   Where main or auxiliary machinery including pressure vessels or any parts of such machinery are subject to internal pressure and may be subject to dangerous overpressure, means shall be provided where practicable to protect against such excessive pressure.

3   All gearing and every shaft and coupling used for transmission of power to machinery essential for the propulsion and safety of the ship or for the safety of persons on board shall be so designed and constructed that they will withstand the maximum working stresses to which they may be subjected in all service conditions, and due consideration shall be given to the type of engines by which they are driven or of which they form part.

4   Internal combustion engines of a cylinder diameter of 200 mm or a crankcase volume of 0.6 m^3 and above shall be provided with crankcase explosion relief valves of a suitable type with sufficient relief area. The relief valves shall be arranged or provided with means to ensure that discharge from them is so directed as to minimize the possibility of injury to personnel.

5   Main turbine propulsion machinery and, where applicable, main internal combustion propulsion machinery and auxiliary machinery shall be provided with automatic shutoff arrangements in the case of failures such as lubricating oil supply failure which could lead rapidly to complete breakdown, serious damage or explosion. The Administration may permit provisions for overriding automatic shutoff devices.

---

[*] Refer to regulation II-2/4.2, "Arrangements for oil fuel, lubricating oil and other flammable oils".

Regulation 28
*Means of going astern**

1   Sufficient power for going astern shall be provided to secure proper control of the ship in all normal circumstances.

2   The ability of the machinery to reverse the direction of thrust of the propeller in sufficient time, and so to bring the ship to rest within a reasonable distance from maximum ahead service speed, shall be demonstrated and recorded.

3   The stopping times, ship headings and distances recorded on trials, together with the results of trials to determine the ability of ships having multiple propellers to navigate and manoeuvre with one or more propellers inoperative, shall be available on board for the use of the master or designated personnel.

4   Where the ship is provided with supplementary means for manoeuvring or stopping, the effectiveness of such means shall be demonstrated and recorded as referred to in paragraphs 2 and 3.

Regulation 29
Steering gear†

1   Unless expressly provided otherwise, every ship shall be provided with a main steering gear and an auxiliary steering gear to the satisfaction of the Administration. The main steering gear and the auxiliary steering gear shall be so arranged that the failure of one of them will not render the other one inoperative.

2.1   All the steering gear components and the rudder stock shall be of sound and reliable construction to the satisfaction of the Administration. Special consideration shall be given to the suitability of any essential component which is not duplicated. Any such essential component shall, where appropriate, utilize antifriction bearings such as ball-bearings, roller-bearings or sleeve-bearings which shall be permanently lubricated or provided with lubrication fittings.

2.2   The design pressure for calculations to determine the scantlings of piping and other steering gear components subjected to internal hydraulic pressure shall be at least 1.25 times the maximum working pressure to be

---

* Refer to the Recommendation on the provision and the display of manoeuvring information on board ships (resolution A.601(15)), the Standards for ship manoeuvrability (resolution MSC.137(76)), and the Explanatory notes to the standards for ship manoeuvrability (MSC/Circ.1053).

† Refer to resolution A.415(XI) on improved steering gear standards for passenger and cargo ships and resolution A.416(XI) on examination of steering gears on existing tankers.

expected under the operational conditions specified in paragraph 3.2, taking into account any pressure which may exist in the low-pressure side of the system. At the discretion of the Administration, fatigue criteria shall be applied for the design of piping and components, taking into account pulsating pressures due to dynamic loads.

2.3 Relief valves shall be fitted to any part of the hydraulic system which can be isolated and in which pressure can be generated from the power source or from external forces. The setting of the relief valves shall not exceed the design pressure. The valves shall be of adequate size and so arranged as to avoid an undue rise in pressure above the design pressure.

3 The main steering gear and rudder stock shall be:

.1 of adequate strength and capable of steering the ship at maximum ahead service speed which shall be demonstrated;

.2 capable of putting the rudder over from 35° on one side to 35° on the other side with the ship at its deepest seagoing draught and running ahead at maximum ahead service speed and, under the same conditions, from 35° on either side to 30° on the other side in not more than 28 s;

.3 operated by power where necessary to meet the requirements of paragraph 3.2 and in any case when the Administration requires a rudder stock of over 120 mm diameter in way of the tiller, excluding strengthening for navigation in ice; and

.4 so designed that they will not be damaged at maximum astern speed; however, this design requirement need not be proved by trials at maximum astern speed and maximum rudder angle.

4 The auxiliary steering gear shall be:

.1 of adequate strength and capable of steering the ship at navigable speed and of being brought speedily into action in an emergency;

.2 capable of putting the rudder over from 15° on one side to 15° on the other side in not more than 60 s with the ship at its deepest seagoing draught and running ahead at one half of the maximum ahead service speed or 7 knots, whichever is the greater; and

.3 operated by power where necessary to meet the requirements of paragraph 4.2 and in any case when the Administration requires a rudder stock of over 230 mm diameter in way of the tiller, excluding strengthening for navigation in ice.

5 Main and auxiliary steering gear power units shall be:

.1 arranged to restart automatically when power is restored after a power failure; and

.2   capable of being brought into operation from a position on the navigation bridge. In the event of a power failure to any one of the steering gear power units, an audible and visual alarm shall be given on the navigation bridge.

6.1   Where the main steering gear comprises two or more identical power units, an auxiliary steering gear need not be fitted, provided that:

.1   in a passenger ship, the main steering gear is capable of operating the rudder as required by paragraph 3.2 while any one of the power units is out of operation;

.2   in a cargo ship, the main steering gear is capable of operating the rudder as required by paragraph 3.2 while operating with all power units;

.3   the main steering gear is so arranged that after a single failure in its piping system or in one of the power units the defect can be isolated so that steering capability can be maintained or speedily regained.

6.2   The Administration may, until 1 September 1986, accept the fitting of a steering gear which has a proven record of reliability but does not comply with the requirements of paragraph 6.1.3 for a hydraulic system.

6.3   Steering gears, other than of the hydraulic type, shall achieve standards equivalent to the requirements of this paragraph to the satisfaction of the Administration.

7   Steering gear control shall be provided:

.1   for the main steering gear, both on the navigation bridge and in the steering gear compartment;

.2   where the main steering gear is arranged in accordance with paragraph 6, by two independent control systems, both operable from the navigation bridge. This does not require duplication of the steering wheel or steering lever. Where the control system consists of a hydraulic telemotor, a second independent system need not be fitted, except in a tanker, chemical tanker or gas carrier of 10,000 gross tonnage and upwards;

.3   for the auxiliary steering gear, in the steering gear compartment and, if power-operated, it shall also be operable from the navigation bridge and shall be independent of the control system for the main steering gear.

8   Any main and auxiliary steering gear control system operable from the navigation bridge shall comply with the following:

.1   if electric, it shall be served by its own separate circuit supplied from a steering gear power circuit from a point within the steering gear compartment, or directly from switchboard

> busbars supplying that steering gear power circuit at a point on the switchboard adjacent to the supply to the steering gear power circuit;

.2   means shall be provided in the steering gear compartment for disconnecting any control system operable from the navigation bridge from the steering gear it serves;

.3   the system shall be capable of being brought into operation from a position on the navigation bridge;

.4   in the event of a failure of electrical power supply to the control system, an audible and visual alarm shall be given on the navigation bridge; and

.5   short circuit protection only shall be provided for steering gear control supply circuits.

9   The electrical power circuits and the steering gear control systems with their associated components, cables and pipes required by this regulation and by regulation 30 shall be separated as far as is practicable throughout their length.

10   A means of communication shall be provided between the navigation bridge and the steering gear compartment.

11   The angular position of the rudder shall:

.1   if the main steering gear is power-operated, be indicated on the navigation bridge. The rudder angle indication shall be independent of the steering gear control system;

.2   be recognizable in the steering gear compartment.

12   Hydraulic power-operated steering gear shall be provided with the following:

.1   arrangements to maintain the cleanliness of the hydraulic fluid taking into consideration the type and design of the hydraulic system;

.2   a low-level alarm for each hydraulic fluid reservoir to give the earliest practicable indication of hydraulic fluid leakage. Audible and visual alarms shall be given on the navigation bridge and in the machinery space where they can be readily observed; and

.3   a fixed storage tank having sufficient capacity to recharge at least one power actuating system including the reservoir, where the main steering gear is required to be power-operated. The storage tank shall be permanently connected by piping in such a manner that the hydraulic systems can be readily recharged from a position within the steering gear compartment and shall be provided with a contents gauge.

13   The steering gear compartments shall be:

.1   readily accessible and, as far as practicable, separated from machinery spaces; and

.2   provided with suitable arrangements to ensure working access to steering gear machinery and controls. These arrangements shall include handrails and gratings or other nonslip surfaces to ensure suitable working conditions in the event of hydraulic fluid leakage.

14   Where the rudder stock is required to be over 230 mm diameter in way of the tiller, excluding strengthening for navigation in ice, an alternative power supply, sufficient at least to supply the steering gear power unit which complies with the requirements of paragraph 4.2 and also its associated control system and the rudder angle indicator, shall be provided automatically, within 45 s, either from the emergency source of electrical power or from an independent source of power located in the steering gear compartment. This independent source of power shall be used only for this purpose. In every ship of 10,000 gross tonnage and upwards, the alternative power supply shall have a capacity for at least 30 min of continuous operation and in any other ship for at least 10 min.

15   In every tanker, chemical tanker or gas carrier of 10,000 gross tonnage and upwards and in every other ship of 70,000 gross tonnage and upwards, the main steering gear shall comprise two or more identical power units complying with the provisions of paragraph 6.

16   Every tanker, chemical tanker or gas carrier of 10,000 gross tonnage and upwards shall, subject to paragraph 17, comply with the following:

.1   the main steering gear shall be so arranged that in the event of loss of steering capability due to a single failure in any part of one of the power actuating systems of the main steering gear, excluding the tiller, quadrant or components serving the same purpose, or seizure of the rudder actuators, steering capability shall be regained in not more than 45 s after the loss of one power actuating system;

.2   the main steering gear shall comprise either:

.2.1   two independent and separate power actuating systems, each capable of meeting the requirements of paragraph 3.2; or

.2.2   at least two identical power actuating systems which, acting simultaneously in normal operation, shall be capable of meeting the requirements of paragraph 3.2. Where necessary to comply with this requirement, interconnection of hydraulic power actuating systems shall be provided. Loss of hydraulic fluid from one system shall be capable of being detected and the defective system automatically isolated so that the other actuating system or systems shall remain fully operational;

.3   steering gears other than of the hydraulic type shall achieve equivalent standards.

17   For tankers, chemical tankers or gas carriers of 10,000 gross tonnage and upwards, but of less than 100,000 tonnes deadweight, solutions other than those set out in paragraph 16, which need not apply the single failure criterion to the rudder actuator or actuators, may be permitted provided that an equivalent safety standard is achieved and that:

.1   following loss of steering capability due to a single failure of any part of the piping system or in one of the power units, steering capability shall be regained within 45 s; and

.2   where the steering gear includes only a single rudder actuator, special consideration is given to stress analysis for the design including fatigue analysis and fracture mechanics analysis, as appropriate, to the material used, to the installation of sealing arrangements and to testing and inspection and to the provision of effective maintenance. In consideration of the foregoing, the Administration shall adopt regulations which include the provisions of the Guidelines for acceptance of non-duplicated rudder actuators for tankers, chemical tankers and gas carriers of 10,000 gross tonnage and above but less than 100,000 tonnes deadweight, adopted by the Organization.*

18   For a tanker, chemical tanker or gas carrier of 10,000 gross tonnage and upwards, but less than 70,000 tonnes deadweight, the Administration may, until 1 September 1986, accept a steering gear system with a proven record of reliability which does not comply with the single failure criterion required for a hydraulic system in paragraph 16.

19   Every tanker, chemical tanker or gas carrier of 10,000 gross tonnage and upwards, constructed before 1 September 1984, shall comply, not later than 1 September 1986, with the following:

.1   the requirements of paragraphs 7.1, 8.2, 8.4, 10, 11, 12.2, 12.3 and 13.2;

.2   two independent steering gear control systems shall be provided each of which can be operated from the navigation bridge. This does not require duplication of the steering wheel or steering lever;

---

* Adopted by the Organization by resolution A.467(XII).

.3 if the steering gear control system in operation fails, the second system shall be capable of being brought into immediate operation from the navigation bridge; and

.4 each steering gear control system, if electric, shall be served by its own separate circuit supplied from the steering gear power circuit or directly from switchboard busbars supplying that steering gear power circuit at a point on the switchboard adjacent to the supply to the steering gear power circuit.

20 In addition to the requirements of paragraph 19, in every tanker, chemical tanker or gas carrier of 40,000 gross tonnage and upwards, constructed before 1 September 1984, the steering gear shall, not later than 1 September 1988, be so arranged that, in the event of a single failure of the piping or of one of the power units, steering capability can be maintained or the rudder movement can be limited so that steering capability can be speedily regained. This shall be achieved by:

.1 an independent means of restraining the rudder; or

.2 fast-acting valves which may be manually operated to isolate the actuator or actuators from the external hydraulic piping together with a means of directly refilling the actuators by a fixed independent power-operated pump and piping system; or

.3 an arrangement such that, where hydraulic power systems are interconnected, loss of hydraulic fluid from one system shall be detected and the defective system isolated either automatically or from the navigation bridge so that the other system remains fully operational.

Regulation 30
Additional requirements for electric
and electrohydraulic steering gear

1 Means for indicating that the motors of electric and electrohydraulic steering gear are running shall be installed on the navigation bridge and at a suitable main machinery control position.

2 Each electric or electrohydraulic steering gear comprising one or more power units shall be served by at least two exclusive circuits fed directly from the main switchboard; however, one of the circuits may be supplied through the emergency switchboard. An auxiliary electric or electrohydraulic steering gear associated with a main electric or electrohydraulic steering gear may be connected to one of the circuits supplying this main steering gear. The circuits supplying an electric or electrohydraulic steering gear shall have adequate rating for supplying all motors which can be simultaneously connected to them and may be required to operate simultaneously.

3 Short circuit protection and an overload alarm shall be provided for such circuits and motors. Protection against excess current, including starting current, if provided, shall be for not less than twice the full load current of the motor or circuit so protected, and shall be arranged to permit the passage of the appropriate starting currents. Where a three-phase supply is used an alarm shall be provided that will indicate failure of any one of the supply phases. The alarms required in this paragraph shall be both audible and visual and shall be situated in a conspicuous position in the main machinery space or control room from which the main machinery is normally controlled and as may be required by regulation 51.

4 When in a ship of less than 1,600 gross tonnage an auxiliary steering gear which is required by regulation 29.4.3 to be operated by power is not electrically powered or is powered by an electric motor primarily intended for other services, the main steering gear may be fed by one circuit from the main switchboard. Where such an electric motor primarily intended for other services is arranged to power such an auxiliary steering gear, the requirement of paragraph 3 may be waived by the Administration if satisfied with the protection arrangement together with the requirements of regulation 29.5.1 and .2 and 29.7.3 applicable to auxiliary steering gear.

Regulation 31
Machinery controls

1 Main and auxiliary machinery essential for the propulsion and safety of the ship shall be provided with effective means for its operation and control.

2 Where remote control of propulsion machinery from the navigation bridge is provided and the machinery spaces are intended to be manned, the following shall apply:

.1 the speed, direction of thrust and, if applicable, the pitch of the propeller shall be fully controllable from the navigation bridge under all sailing conditions, including manoeuvring;

.2 the remote control shall be performed, for each independent propeller, by a control device so designed and constructed that its operation does not require particular attention to the operational details of the machinery. Where multiple propellers are designed to operate simultaneously, they may be controlled by one control device;

.3 the main propulsion machinery shall be provided with an emergency stopping device on the navigation bridge which shall be independent of the navigation bridge control system;

.4 propulsion machinery orders from the navigation bridge shall be indicated in the main machinery control room or at the manoeuvring platform as appropriate;

.5   remote control of the propulsion machinery shall be possible only from one location at a time; at such locations interconnected control positions are permitted. At each location there shall be an indicator showing which location is in control of the propulsion machinery. The transfer of control between the navigation bridge and machinery spaces shall be possible only in the main machinery space or the main machinery control room. This system shall include means to prevent the propelling thrust from altering significantly when transferring control from one location to another;

.6   it shall be possible to control the propulsion machinery locally, even in the case of failure in any part of the remote control system;

.7   the design of the remote control system shall be such that in case of its failure an alarm will be given. Unless the Administration considers it impracticable the preset speed and direction of thrust of the propellers shall be maintained until local control is in operation;

.8   indicators shall be fitted on the navigation bridge for:

.8.1   propeller speed and direction of rotation in the case of fixed pitch propellers;

.8.2   propeller speed and pitch position in the case of controllable pitch propellers;

.9   an alarm shall be provided on the navigation bridge and in the machinery space to indicate low starting air pressure which shall be set at a level to permit further main engine starting operations. If the remote control system of the propulsion machinery is designed for automatic starting, the number of automatic consecutive attempts which fail to produce a start shall be limited in order to safeguard sufficient starting air pressure for starting locally.

.10   automation systems shall be designed in a manner which ensures that threshold warning of impending or imminent slowdown or shutdown of the propulsion system is given to the officer in charge of the navigational watch in time to assess navigational circumstances in an emergency. In particular, the systems shall control, monitor, report, alert and take safety action to slow down or stop propulsion while providing the officer in charge of the navigational watch an opportunity to manually intervene, except for those cases where manual intervention will result in total failure of the engine and/or propulsion equipment within a short time, for example in the case of overspeed.

3   Where the main propulsion and associated machinery, including sources of main electrical supply, are provided with various degrees of automatic or remote control and are under continuous manual supervision from a control room the arrangements and controls shall be so designed, equipped and installed that the machinery operation will be as safe and effective as if it were under direct supervision; for this purpose regulations 46 to 50 shall apply as appropriate. Particular consideration shall be given to protect such spaces against fire and flooding.

4   In general, automatic starting, operational and control systems shall include provisions for manually overriding the automatic controls. Failure of any part of such systems shall not prevent the use of the manual override.

5   Ships constructed on or after 1 July 1998 shall comply with the requirements of paragraphs 1 to 4, as amended, as follows:

.1   paragraph 1 is replaced by the following:

"**1**   Main and auxiliary machinery essential for the propulsion, control and safety of the ship shall be provided with effective means for its operation and control. All control systems essential for the propulsion, control and safety of the ship shall be independent or designed such that failure of one system does not degrade the performance of another system.";

.2   in the second and third lines of paragraph 2, the words "and the machinery spaces are intended to be manned" are deleted;

.3   the first sentence of paragraph 2.2 is replaced by the following:

"**.2**   the control shall be performed by a single control device for each independent propeller, with automatic performance of all associated services, including, where necessary, means of preventing overload of the propulsion machinery.";

.4   paragraph 2.4 is replaced by the following:

"**.4**   propulsion machinery orders from the navigation bridge shall be indicated in the main machinery control room and at the manoeuvring platform;";

.5   a new sentence is added at the end of paragraph 2.6 to read as follows:

"It shall also be possible to control the auxiliary machinery, essential for the propulsion and safety of the ship, at or near the machinery concerned;" and

.6   paragraphs 2.8, 2.8.1 and 2.8.2 are replaced by the following:

"**.8**   indicators shall be fitted on the navigation bridge, the main machinery control room and at the manoeuvring platform, for:

.8.1 propeller speed and direction of rotation in the case of fixed pitch propellers; and

.8.2 propeller speed and pitch position in the case of controllable pitch propellers;"

Regulation 32
Steam boilers and boiler feed systems

1 Every steam boiler and every unfired steam generator shall be provided with not less than two safety valves of adequate capacity. However, having regard to the output or any other features of any boiler or unfired steam generator, the Administration may permit only one safety valve to be fitted if it is satisfied that adequate protection against overpressure is thereby provided.

2 Each oil-fired boiler which is intended to operate without manual supervision shall have safety arrangements which shut off the fuel supply and give an alarm in the case of low water level, air supply failure or flame failure.

3 Water tube boilers serving turbine propulsion machinery shall be fitted with a high-water-level alarm.

4 Every steam generating system which provides services essential for the safety of the ship, or which could be rendered dangerous by the failure of its feedwater supply, shall be provided with not less than two separate feedwater systems from and including the feed pumps, noting that a single penetration of the steam drum is acceptable. Unless overpressure is prevented by the pump characteristics, means shall be provided which will prevent overpressure in any part of the systems.

5 Boilers shall be provided with means to supervise and control the quality of the feedwater. Suitable arrangements shall be provided to preclude, as far as practicable, the entry of oil or other contaminants which may adversely affect the boiler.

6 Every boiler essential for the safety of the ship and designed to contain water at a specified level shall be provided with at least two means for indicating its water level, at least one of which shall be a direct reading gauge glass.

Regulation 33
Steam pipe systems

1 Every steam pipe and every fitting connected thereto through which steam may pass shall be so designed, constructed and installed as to withstand the maximum working stresses to which it may be subjected.

2   Means shall be provided for draining every steam pipe in which dangerous water hammer action might otherwise occur.

3   If a steam pipe or fitting may receive steam from any source at a higher pressure than that for which it is designed a suitable reducing valve, relief valve and pressure gauge shall be fitted.

Regulation 34
Air pressure systems

1   In every ship means shall be provided to prevent overpressure in any part of compressed air systems and wherever water jackets or casings of air compressors and coolers might be subjected to dangerous overpressure due to leakage into them from air pressure parts. Suitable pressure relief arrangements shall be provided for all systems.

2   The main starting air arrangements for main propulsion internal combustion engines shall be adequately protected against the effects of backfiring and internal explosion in the starting air pipes.

3   All discharge pipes from starting air compressors shall lead directly to the starting air receivers, and all starting pipes from the air receivers to main or auxiliary engines shall be entirely separate from the compressor discharge pipe system.

4   Provision shall be made to reduce to a minimum the entry of oil into the air pressure systems and to drain these systems.

Regulation 35
Ventilating systems in machinery spaces

Machinery spaces of category A shall be adequately ventilated so as to ensure that when machinery or boilers therein are operating at full power in all weather conditions including heavy weather, an adequate supply of air is maintained to the spaces for the safety and comfort of personnel and the operation of the machinery. Any other machinery space shall be adequately ventilated appropriate for the purpose of that machinery space.

Regulation 36
*Protection against noise**

Measures shall be taken to reduce machinery noise in machinery spaces to acceptable levels as determined by the Administration. If this noise cannot be sufficiently reduced the source of excessive noise shall be suitably

---

* Refer to the Code on Noise Levels on Board Ships adopted by the Organization by resolution A.468(XII).

insulated or isolated or a refuge from noise shall be provided if the space is required to be manned. Ear protectors shall be provided for personnel required to enter such spaces, if necessary.

Regulation 37
Communication between navigation bridge and machinery space

1   At least two independent means shall be provided for communicating orders from the navigation bridge to the position in the machinery space or in the control room from which the engines are normally controlled: one of these shall be an engine-room telegraph which provides visual indication of the orders and responses both in the machinery space and on the navigation bridge. Appropriate means of communication shall be provided to any other positions from which the engines may be controlled.

2   For ships constructed on or after 1 October 1994 the following requirements apply in lieu of the provisions of paragraph 1:

At least two independent means shall be provided for communicating orders from the navigation bridge to the position in the machinery space or in the control room from which the speed and direction of thrust of the propellers are normally controlled; one of these shall be an engine-room telegraph which provides visual indication of the orders and responses both in the machinery spaces and on the navigation bridge. Appropriate means of communication shall be provided from the navigation bridge and the engine-room to any other position from which the speed or direction of thrust of the propellers may be controlled.

Regulation 38
Engineers' alarm

An engineers' alarm shall be provided to be operated from the engine control room or at the manoeuvring platform as appropriate, and shall be clearly audible in the engineers' accommodation.

Regulation 39
Location of emergency installations in passenger ships

Emergency sources of electrical power, fire pumps, bilge pumps except those specifically serving the spaces forward of the collision bulkhead, any fixed fire-extinguishing system required by chapter II-2 and other emergency installations which are essential for the safety of the ship, except anchor windlasses, shall not be installed forward of the collision bulkhead.

Part D
Electrical installations

(Except where expressly provided otherwise part D
applies to passenger ships and cargo ships)

Regulation 40
General

1   Electrical installations shall be such that:

    .1   all electrical auxiliary services necessary for maintaining the ship in normal operational and habitable conditions will be ensured without recourse to the emergency source of electrical power;

    .2   electrical services essential for safety will be ensured under various emergency conditions; and

    .3   the safety of passengers, crew and ship from electrical hazards will be ensured.

2   The Administration shall take appropriate steps to ensure uniformity in the implementation and application of the provisions of this part in respect of electrical installations.[*]

Regulation 41
Main source of electrical power and lighting systems

1.1   A main source of electrical power of sufficient capacity to supply all those services mentioned in regulation 40.1.1 shall be provided. This main source of electrical power shall consist of at least two generating sets.

1.2   The capacity of these generating sets shall be such that in the event of any one generating set being stopped it will still be possible to supply those services necessary to provide normal operational conditions of propulsion and safety. Minimum comfortable conditions of habitability shall also be ensured which include at least adequate services for cooking, heating, domestic refrigeration, mechanical ventilation, sanitary and fresh water.

---

[*] Refer to the recommendations published by the International Electrotechnical Commission and, in particular, Publication 92 – *Electrical Installations in Ships*.

1.3   The arrangements of the ship's main source of electrical power shall be such that the services referred to in regulation 40.1.1 can be maintained regardless of the speed and direction of rotation of the propulsion machinery or shafting.

1.4   In addition, the generating sets shall be such as to ensure that with any one generator or its primary source of power out of operation, the remaining generating sets shall be capable of providing the electrical services necessary to start the main propulsion plant from a dead ship condition. The emergency source of electrical power may be used for the purpose of starting from a dead ship condition if its capability either alone or combined with that of any other source of electrical power is sufficient to provide at the same time those services required to be supplied by regulations 42.2.1 to 42.2.3 or 43.2.1 to 43.2.4.

1.5   Where transformers constitute an essential part of the electrical supply system required by this paragraph, the system shall be so arranged as to ensure the same continuity of the supply as is stated in this paragraph.

2.1   A main electric lighting system which shall provide illumination throughout those parts of the ship normally accessible to and used by passengers or crew shall be supplied from the main source of electrical power.

2.2   The arrangement of the main electric lighting system shall be such that a fire or other casualty in spaces containing the main source of electrical power, associated transforming equipment, if any, the main switchboard and the main lighting switchboard, will not render the emergency electric lighting system required by regulations 42.2.1 and 42.2.2 or 43.2.1, 43.2.2 and 43.2.3 inoperative.

2.3   The arrangement of the emergency electric lighting system shall be such that a fire or other casualty in spaces containing the emergency source of electrical power, associated transforming equipment, if any, the emergency switchboard and the emergency lighting switchboard will not render the main electric lighting system required by this regulation inoperative.

3   The main switchboard shall be so placed relative to one main generating station that, as far as is practicable, the integrity of the normal electrical supply may be affected only by a fire or other casualty in one space. An environmental enclosure for the main switchboard, such as may be provided by a machinery control room situated within the main boundaries of the space, is not to be considered as separating the switchboards from the generators.

4   Where the total installed electrical power of the main generating sets is in excess of 3 MW, the main busbars shall be subdivided into at least two parts which shall normally be connected by removable links or other approved means; so far as is practicable, the connection of generating sets and any other duplicated equipment shall be equally divided between the parts. Equivalent arrangements may be permitted to the satisfaction of the Administration.

5   Ships constructed on or after 1 July 1998:

   .1   in addition to paragraphs 1 to 3, shall comply with the following:

   .1.1   where the main source of electrical power is necessary for propulsion and steering of the ship, the system shall be so arranged that the electrical supply to equipment necessary for propulsion and steering and to ensure safety of the ship will be maintained or immediately restored in the case of loss of any one of the generators in service;

   .1.2   load shedding or other equivalent arrangements shall be provided to protect the generators required by this regulation against sustained overload;

   .1.3   where the main source of electrical power is necessary for propulsion of the ship, the main busbar shall be subdivided into at least two parts which shall normally be connected by circuit breakers or other approved means; so far as is practicable, the connection of generating sets and other duplicated equipment shall be equally divided between the parts; and

   .2   need not comply with paragraph 4.

Regulation 42
Emergency source of electrical power in passenger ships

(Paragraphs 2.6.1 and 4.2 of this regulation apply to ships constructed on or after 1 February 1992)

1.1   A self-contained emergency source of electrical power shall be provided.

1.2   The emergency source of electrical power, associated transforming equipment, if any, transitional source of emergency power, emergency switchboard and emergency lighting switchboard shall be located above the uppermost continuous deck and shall be readily accessible from the open deck. They shall not be located forward of the collision bulkhead.

1.3   The location of the emergency source of electrical power and associated transforming equipment, if any, the transitional source of emergency power, the emergency switchboard and the emergency electric lighting switchboards in relation to the main source of electrical power, associated transforming equipment, if any, and the main switchboard shall be such as to ensure to the satisfaction of the Administration that a fire or other casualty in spaces containing the main source of electrical power, associated transforming equipment, if any, and the main switchboard or in any machinery space of category A will not interfere with the supply, control and distribution of emergency electrical power. As far as practicable, the space containing the emergency source of electrical power, associated transforming equipment, if any, the transitional source of emergency electrical power and the emergency switchboard shall not be contiguous to the boundaries of machinery spaces of category A or those spaces containing the main source of electrical power, associated transforming equipment, if any, or the main switchboard.

1.4   Provided that suitable measures are taken for safeguarding independent emergency operation under all circumstances, the emergency generator may be used exceptionally, and for short periods, to supply non-emergency circuits.

2   The electrical power available shall be sufficient to supply all those services that are essential for safety in an emergency, due regard being paid to such services as may have to be operated simultaneously. The emergency source of electrical power shall be capable, having regard to starting currents and the transitory nature of certain loads, of supplying simultaneously at least the following services for the periods specified hereinafter, if they depend upon an electrical source for their operation:

2.1   For a period of 36 h, emergency lighting:

    .1   at every muster and embarkation station and over the sides as required by regulations III/11.4 and III/16.7;

    .2   in alleyways, stairways and exits giving access to the muster and embarkation stations, as required by regulation III/11.5;

    .3   in all service and accommodation alleyways, stairways and exits, personnel lift cars;

    .4   in the machinery spaces and main generating stations including their control positions;

    .5   in all control stations, machinery control rooms, and at each main and emergency switchboard;

    .6   at all stowage positions for firemen's outfits;

    .7   at the steering gear; and

    .8   at the fire pump, the sprinkler pump and the emergency bilge pump referred to in paragraph 2.4 and at the starting position of their motors.

2.2   For a period of 36 h:

    .1   the navigation lights and other lights required by the International Regulations for Preventing Collisions at Sea in force; and

.2 on ships constructed on or after 1 February 1995, the VHF radio installation required by regulation IV/7.1.1 and IV/7.1.2; and, if applicable:

.2.1 the MF radio installation required by regulations IV/9.1.1, IV/9.1.2, IV/10.1.2 and IV/10.1.3;

.2.2 the ship earth station required by regulation IV/10.1.1; and

.2.3 the MF/HF radio installation required by regulations IV/10.2.1, IV/10.2.2 and IV/11.1.

2.3 For a period of 36 h:

.1 all internal communication equipment required in an emergency;

.2 the shipborne navigational equipment as required by regulation V/12*; where such provision is unreasonable or impracticable the Administration may waive this requirement for ships of less than 5,000 gross tonnage;

.3 the fire detection and fire alarm system, and the fire door holding and release system; and

.4 for intermittent operation of the daylight signalling lamp, the ship's whistle, the manually operated call points, and all internal signals that are required in an emergency;

unless such services have an independent supply for the period of 36 h from an accumulator battery suitably located for use in an emergency.

2.4 For a period of 36 h:

.1 one of the fire pumps required by regulation II-2/4.3.1 and 4.3.3;†

.2 the automatic sprinkler pump, if any; and

.3 the emergency bilge pump and all the equipment essential for the operation of electrically powered remote controlled bilge valves.

2.5 For the period of time required by regulation 29.14 the steering gear if required to be so supplied by that regulation.

2.6 For a period of half an hour:

.1 any watertight doors required by regulation 15 to be power-operated together with their indicators and warning signals;

---

* This relates to the chapter V in force before 1 July 2002. The equivalent in the amended chapter V is regulation 19.

† These relate to the chapter II-2 in force before 1 July 2002. The equivalents in the amended chapter II-2 are 10.2.2.2 and 10.2.2.3.

> **.2** the emergency arrangements to bring the lift cars to deck level for the escape of persons. The passenger lift cars may be brought to deck level sequentially in an emergency.

2.7   In a ship engaged regularly on voyages of short duration, the Administration if satisfied that an adequate standard of safety would be attained may accept a lesser period than the 36 h period specified in paragraphs 2.1 to 2.5 but not less than 12 h.

3   The emergency source of electrical power may be either a generator or an accumulator battery, which shall comply with the following:

3.1   Where the emergency source of electrical power is a generator, it shall be:

> **.1** driven by a suitable prime mover with an independent supply of fuel having a flashpoint (closed cup test) of not less than 43°C;

> **.2** started automatically upon failure of the electrical supply from the main source of electrical power and shall be automatically connected to the emergency switchboard; those services referred to in paragraph 4 shall then be transferred automatically to the emergency generating set. The automatic starting system and the characteristic of the prime mover shall be such as to permit the emergency generator to carry its full rated load as quickly as is safe and practicable, subject to a maximum of 45 s; unless a second independent means of starting the emergency generating set is provided, the single source of stored energy shall be protected to preclude its complete depletion by the automatic starting system; and

> **.3** provided with a transitional source of emergency electrical power according to paragraph 4.

3.2   Where the emergency source of electrical power is an accumulator battery, it shall be capable of:

> **.1** carrying the emergency electrical load without recharging while maintaining the voltage of the battery throughout the discharge period within 12% above or below its nominal voltage;

> **.2** automatically connecting to the emergency switchboard in the event of failure of the main source of electrical power; and

> **.3** immediately supplying at least those services specified in paragraph 4.

3.3   The following provisions in paragraph 3.1.2 shall not apply to ships constructed on or after 1 October 1994:

> Unless a second independent means of starting the emergency generating set is provided, the single source of stored energy shall

be protected to preclude its complete depletion by the automatic starting system.

3.4 For ships constructed on or after 1 July 1998, where electrical power is necessary to restore propulsion, the capacity shall be sufficient to restore propulsion to the ship in conjunction with other machinery, as appropriate, from a dead ship condition within 30 min after blackout.

4 The transitional source of emergency electrical power required by paragraph 3.1.3 shall consist of an accumulator battery suitably located for use in an emergency which shall operate without recharging while maintaining the voltage of the battery throughout the discharge period within 12% above or below its nominal voltage and be of sufficient capacity and so arranged as to supply automatically in the event of failure of either the main or emergency source of electrical power at least the following services, if they depend upon an electrical source for their operation:

4.1 For half an hour:

  .1 the lighting required by paragraphs 2.1 and 2.2;

  .2 all services required by paragraphs 2.3.1, 2.3.3 and 2.3.4 unless such services have an independent supply for the period specified from an accumulator battery suitably located for use in an emergency.

4.2 Power to operate the watertight doors, as required by regulation 15.7.3.3, but not necessarily all of them simultaneously, unless an independent temporary source of stored energy is provided. Power to the control, indication and alarm circuits as required by regulation 15.7.2 for half an hour.

5.1 The emergency switchboard shall be installed as near as is practicable to the emergency source of electrical power.

5.2 Where the emergency source of electrical power is a generator, the emergency switchboard shall be located in the same space unless the operation of the emergency switchboard would thereby be impaired.

5.3 No accumulator battery fitted in accordance with this regulation shall be installed in the same space as the emergency switchboard. An indicator shall be mounted in a suitable place on the main switchboard or in the machinery control room to indicate when the batteries constituting either the emergency source of electrical power or the transitional source of emergency electrical power referred to in paragraph 3.1.3 or 4 are being discharged.

5.4 The emergency switchboard shall be supplied during normal operation from the main switchboard by an interconnector feeder which is to be adequately protected at the main switchboard against overload and short circuit and which is to be disconnected automatically at the emergency switchboard upon failure of the main source of electrical power. Where the system is arranged for feedback operation, the interconnector feeder is also to be protected at the emergency switchboard at least against short circuit.

5.5 In order to ensure ready availability of the emergency source of electrical power, arrangements shall be made where necessary to disconnect automatically non-emergency circuits from the emergency switchboard to ensure that power shall be available to the emergency circuits.

6 The emergency generator and its prime mover and any emergency accumulator battery shall be so designed and arranged as to ensure that they will function at full rated power when the ship is upright and when inclined at any angle of list up to 22.5° or when inclined up to 10° either in the fore or aft direction, or is in any combination of angles within those limits.

7 Provision shall be made for the periodic testing of the complete emergency system and shall include the testing of automatic starting arrangements.

Regulation 42-1
Supplementary emergency lighting for ro–ro passenger ships

(This regulation applies to all passenger ships with ro–ro cargo spaces or special category spaces as defined in regulation II-2/3, except that for ships constructed before 22 October 1989, this regulation shall apply not later than 22 October 1990)

1 In addition to the emergency lighting required by regulation 42.2, on every passenger ship with ro–ro cargo spaces or special category spaces as defined in regulation II-2/3:

    .1 all passenger public spaces and alleyways shall be provided with supplementary electric lighting that can operate for at least 3 h when all other sources of electrical power have failed and under any condition of heel. The illumination provided shall be such that the approach to the means of escape can be readily seen. The source of power for the supplementary lighting shall consist of accumulator batteries located within the lighting units that are continuously charged, where practicable, from the emergency switchboard. Alternatively, any other means of lighting which is at least as effective may be accepted by the Administration. The supplementary lighting shall be such that any failure of the lamp will be immediately apparent. Any accumulator battery provided shall be replaced at intervals having regard to the specified service life in the ambient conditions that they are subject to in service; and

.2 a portable rechargeable battery operated lamp shall be provided in every crew space alleyway, recreational space and every working space which is normally occupied unless supplementary emergency lighting, as required by subparagraph .1, is provided.

Regulation 43
Emergency source of electrical power in cargo ships

1.1 A self-contained emergency source of electrical power shall be provided.

1.2 The emergency source of electrical power, associated transforming equipment, if any, transitional source of emergency power, emergency switchboard and emergency lighting switchboard shall be located above the uppermost continuous deck and shall be readily accessible from the open deck. They shall not be located forward of the collision bulkhead, except where permitted by the Administration in exceptional circumstances.

1.3 The location of the emergency source of electrical power, associated transforming equipment, if any, the transitional source of emergency power, the emergency switchboard and the emergency lighting switchboard in relation to the main source of electrical power, associated transforming equipment, if any, and the main switchboard shall be such as to ensure to the satisfaction of the Administration that a fire or other casualty in the space containing the main source of electrical power, associated transforming equipment, if any, and the main switchboard, or in any machinery space of category A will not interfere with the supply, control and distribution of emergency electrical power. As far as practicable the space containing the emergency source of electrical power, associated transforming equipment, if any, the transitional source of emergency electrical power and the emergency switchboard shall not be contiguous to the boundaries of machinery spaces of category A or those spaces containing the main source of electrical power, associated transforming equipment, if any, and the main switchboard.

1.4 Provided that suitable measures are taken for safeguarding independent emergency operation under all circumstances, the emergency generator may be used, exceptionally, and for short periods, to supply non-emergency circuits.

2 The electrical power available shall be sufficient to supply all those services that are essential for safety in an emergency, due regard being paid to such services as may have to be operated simultaneously. The emergency source of electrical power shall be capable, having regard to starting currents and the transitory nature of certain loads, of supplying simultaneously at least the following services for the periods specified hereinafter, if they depend upon an electrical source for their operation:

2.1   For a period of 3 h, emergency lighting at every muster and embarkation station and over the sides as required by regulations III/11.4 and III/16.7.

2.2   For a period of 18 h, emergency lighting:

  .1   in all service and accommodation alleyways, stairways and exits, personnel lift cars and personnel lift trunks;

  .2   in the machinery spaces and main generating stations including their control positions;

  .3   in all control stations, machinery control rooms, and at each main and emergency switchboard;

  .4   at all stowage positions for firemen's outfits;

  .5   at the steering gear;

  .6   at the fire pump referred to in paragraph 2.5, at the sprinkler pump, if any, and at the emergency bilge pump, if any, and at the starting positions of their motors; and

  .7   in all cargo pump-rooms of tankers constructed on or after 1 July 2002.

2.3   For a period of 18 h:

  .1   the navigation lights and other lights required by the International Regulations for Preventing Collisions at Sea in force;

  .2   on ships constructed on or after 1 February 1995 the VHF radio installation required by regulation IV/7.1.1 and IV/7.1.2; and, if applicable:

  .2.1   the MF radio installation required by regulations IV/9.1.1, IV/9.1.2, IV/10.1.2 and IV/10.1.3;

  .2.2   the ship earth station required by regulation IV/10.1.1; and

  .2.3   the MF/HF radio installation required by regulations IV/10.2.1, IV/10.2.2 and IV/11.1.

2.4   For a period of 18 h:

  .1   all internal communication equipment as required in an emergency;

  .2   the shipborne navigational equipment as required by regulation V/12;* where such provision is unreasonable or impracticable the Administration may waive this requirement for ships of less than 5,000 gross tonnage;

  .3   the fire detection and fire alarm system; and

  .4   intermittent operation of the daylight signalling lamp, the ship's whistle, the manually operated call points and all internal signals that are required in an emergency;

---

* This relates to the chapter V in force before 1 July 2002. The equivalent in the amended chapter V is regulation 19.

unless such services have an independent supply for the period of 18 h from an accumulator battery suitably located for use in an emergency.

2.5 For a period of 18 h one of the fire pumps required by regulation II-2/4.3.1 and 4.3.3* if dependent upon the emergency generator for its source of power.

2.6.1 For the period of time required by regulation 29.14 the steering gear where it is required to be so supplied by that regulation.

2.6.2 In a ship engaged regularly in voyages of short duration, the Administration if satisfied that an adequate standard of safety would be attained may accept a lesser period than the 18 h period specified in paragraphs 2.2 to 2.5 but not less than 12 h.

3 The emergency source of electrical power may be either a generator or an accumulator battery, which shall comply with the following:

3.1 Where the emergency source of electrical power is a generator, it shall be:

.1 driven by a suitable prime mover with an independent supply of fuel, having a flashpoint (closed cup test) of not less than 43°C;

.2 started automatically upon failure of the main source of electrical power supply unless a transitional source of emergency electrical power in accordance with paragraph 3.1.3 is provided; where the emergency generator is automatically started, it shall be automatically connected to the emergency switchboard; those services referred to in paragraph 4 shall then be connected automatically to the emergency generator; and unless a second independent means of starting the emergency generator is provided the single source of stored energy shall be protected to preclude its complete depletion by the automatic starting system; and

.3 provided with a transitional source of emergency electrical power as specified in paragraph 4 unless an emergency generator is provided capable both of supplying the services mentioned in that paragraph and of being automatically started and supplying the required load as quickly as is safe and practicable subject to a maximum of 45 s.

3.2 Where the emergency source of electrical power is an accumulator battery it shall be capable of:

.1 carrying the emergency electrical load without recharging while maintaining the voltage of the battery throughout the discharge period within 12% above or below its nominal voltage;

---

* These relate to the chapter II-2 in force before 1 July 2002. The equivalents in the amended chapter II-2 are 10.2.2.2 and 10.2.2.3.

.2   automatically connecting to the emergency switchboard in the event of failure of the main source of electrical power; and

.3   immediately supplying at least those services specified in paragraph 4.

3.3   The following provision in paragraph 3.1.2 shall not apply to ships constructed on or after 1 October 1994:

Unless a second independent means of starting the emergency generating set is provided, the single source of stored energy shall be protected to preclude its complete depletion by the automatic starting system.

3.4   For ships constructed on or after 1 July 1998, where electrical power is necessary to restore propulsion, the capacity shall be sufficient to restore propulsion to the ship in conjunction with other machinery, as appropriate, from a dead ship condition within 30 min after blackout.

4   The transitional source of emergency electrical power where required by paragraph 3.1.3 shall consist of an accumulator battery suitably located for use in an emergency which shall operate without recharging while maintaining the voltage of the battery throughout the discharge period within 12% above or below its nominal voltage and be of sufficient capacity and shall be so arranged as to supply automatically in the event of failure of either the main or the emergency source of electrical power for half an hour at least the following services if they depend upon an electrical source for their operation:

.1   the lighting required by paragraphs 2.1, 2.2 and 2.3.1. For this transitional phase, the required emergency electric lighting, in respect of the machinery space and accommodation and service spaces may be provided by permanently fixed, individual, automatically charged, relay operated accumulator lamps; and

.2   all services required by paragraphs 2.4.1, 2.4.3 and 2.4.4 unless such services have an independent supply for the period specified from an accumulator battery suitably located for use in an emergency.

5.1   The emergency switchboard shall be installed as near as is practicable to the emergency source of electrical power.

5.2   Where the emergency source of electrical power is a generator, the emergency switchboard shall be located in the same space unless the operation of the emergency switchboard would thereby be impaired.

5.3   No accumulator battery fitted in accordance with this regulation shall be installed in the same space as the emergency switchboard. An indicator shall be mounted in a suitable place on the main switchboard or in the machinery control room to indicate when the batteries constituting either the emergency source of electrical power or the transitional source of electrical power referred to in paragraph 3.2 or 4 are being discharged.

5.4 The emergency switchboard shall be supplied during normal operation from the main switchboard by an interconnector feeder which is to be adequately protected at the main switchboard against overload and short circuit and which is to be disconnected automatically at the emergency switchboard upon failure of the main source of electrical power. Where the system is arranged for feedback operation, the interconnector feeder is also to be protected at the emergency switchboard at least against short circuit.

5.5 In order to ensure ready availability of the emergency source of electrical power, arrangements shall be made where necessary to disconnect automatically non-emergency circuits from the emergency switchboard to ensure that electrical power shall be available automatically to the emergency circuits.

6 The emergency generator and its prime mover and any emergency accumulator battery shall be so designed and arranged as to ensure that they will function at full rated power when the ship is upright and when inclined at any angle of list up to 22.5° or when inclined up to 10° either in the fore or aft direction, or is in any combination of angles within those limits.

7 Provision shall be made for the periodic testing of the complete emergency system and shall include the testing of automatic starting arrangements.

Regulation 44
Starting arrangements for emergency generating sets

1 Emergency generating sets shall be capable of being readily started in their cold condition at a temperature of 0°C. If this is impracticable, or if lower temperatures are likely to be encountered, provision acceptable to the Administration shall be made for the maintenance of heating arrangements, to ensure ready starting of the generating sets.

2 Each emergency generating set arranged to be automatically started shall be equipped with starting devices approved by the Administration with a stored energy capability of at least three consecutive starts. A second source of energy shall be provided for an additional three starts within 30 min unless manual starting can be demonstrated to be effective.

2.1 Ships constructed on or after 1 October 1994, in lieu of the provision of the second sentence of paragraph 2, shall comply with the following requirements:

The source of stored energy shall be protected to preclude critical depletion by the automatic starting system, unless a second independent means of starting is provided. In addition, a second source of energy shall be provided for an additional three starts within 30 min unless manual starting can be demonstrated to be effective.

3   The stored energy shall be maintained at all times, as follows:

.1   electrical and hydraulic starting systems shall be maintained from the emergency switchboard;

.2   compressed air starting systems may be maintained by the main or auxiliary compressed air receivers through a suitable non-return valve or by an emergency air compressor which, if electrically driven, is supplied from the emergency switchboard;

.3   all of these starting, charging and energy storing devices shall be located in the emergency generator space; these devices are not to be used for any purpose other than the operation of the emergency generating set. This does not preclude the supply to the air receiver of the emergency generating set from the main or auxiliary compressed air system through the non-return valve fitted in the emergency generator space.

4.1   Where automatic starting is not required, manual starting is permissible, such as manual cranking, inertia starters, manually charged hydraulic accumulators, or powder charge cartridges, where they can be demonstrated as being effective.

4.2   When manual starting is not practicable, the requirements of paragraphs 2 and 3 shall be complied with except that starting may be manually initiated.

Regulation 45
Precautions against shock, fire and other hazards of electrical origin

1.1   Exposed metal parts of electrical machines or equipment which are not intended to be live but which are liable under fault conditions to become live shall be earthed unless the machines or equipment are:

.1   supplied at a voltage not exceeding 50 V direct current or 50 V root mean square between conductors; auto-transformers shall not be used for the purpose of achieving this voltage; or

.2   supplied at a voltage not exceeding 250 V by safety isolating transformers supplying only one consuming device; or

.3   constructed in accordance with the principle of double insulation.

1.2   The Administration may require additional precautions for portable electrical equipment for use in confined or exceptionally damp spaces where particular risks due to conductivity may exist.

1.3 All electrical apparatus shall be so constructed and so installed as not to cause injury when handled or touched in the normal manner.

2 Main and emergency switchboards shall be so arranged as to give easy access as may be needed to apparatus and equipment, without danger to personnel. The sides and the rear and, where necessary, the front of switchboards shall be suitably guarded. Exposed live parts having voltages to earth exceeding a voltage to be specified by the Administration shall not be installed on the front of such switchboards. Where necessary, nonconducting mats or gratings shall be provided at the front and rear of the switchboard.

3.1 The hull return system of distribution shall not be used for any purpose in a tanker, or for power, heating, or lighting in any other ship of 1,600 gross tonnage and upwards.

3.2 The requirement of paragraph 3.1 does not preclude under conditions approved by the Administration the use of:

.1 impressed current cathodic protective systems;

.2 limited and locally earthed systems; or

.3 insulation level monitoring devices provided the circulation current does not exceed 30 mA under the most unfavourable conditions.

3.2-1 For ships constructed on or after 1 October 1994, the requirement of paragraph 3.1 does not preclude the use of limited and locally earthed systems, provided that any possible resulting current does not flow directly through any dangerous spaces.

3.3 Where the hull return system is used, all final subcircuits, i.e. all circuits fitted after the last protective device, shall be two-wire and special precautions shall be taken to the satisfaction of the Administration.

4.1 Earthed distribution systems shall not be used in a tanker. The Administration may exceptionally permit in a tanker the earthing of the neutral for alternating current power networks of 3,000 V (line to line) and over, provided that any possible resulting current does not flow directly through any of the dangerous spaces.

4.2 When a distribution system, whether primary or secondary, for power, heating or lighting, with no connection to earth is used, a device capable of continuously monitoring the insulation level to earth and of giving an audible or visual indication of abnormally low insulation values shall be provided.

4.3   Ships constructed on or after 1 October 1994, in lieu of the provisions of paragraph 4.1, shall comply with the following requirements:

.1   Except as permitted by paragraph 4.3.2, earthed distribution systems shall not be used in a tanker.

.2   The requirement of paragraph 4.3.1 does not preclude the use of earthed intrinsically safe circuits and in addition, under conditions approved by the Administration, the use of the following earthed systems:

.2.1   power-supplied control circuits and instrumentation circuits where technical or safety reasons preclude the use of a system with no connection to earth, provided the current in the hull is limited to not more than 5 A in both normal and fault conditions; or

.2.2   limited and locally earthed systems, provided that any possible resulting current does not flow directly through any of the dangerous spaces; or

.2.3   alternating current power networks of 1,000 V root mean square (line to line) and over, provided that any possible resulting current does not flow directly through any of the dangerous spaces.

5.1   Except as permitted by the Administration in exceptional circumstances, all metal sheaths and armour of cables shall be electrically continuous and shall be earthed.

5.2   All electric cables and wiring external to equipment shall be at least of a flame-retardant type and shall be so installed as not to impair their original flame-retarding properties. Where necessary for particular applications the Administration may permit the use of special types of cables such as radio frequency cables, which do not comply with the foregoing.

5.3   Cables and wiring serving essential or emergency power, lighting, internal communications or signals shall so far as practicable be routed clear of galleys, laundries, machinery spaces of category A and their casings and other high fire risk areas. In ro–ro passenger ships, cabling for emergency alarms and public address systems installed on or after 1 July 1998 shall be approved by the Administration having regard to the recommendations developed by the Organization.* Cables connecting fire pumps to the emergency switchboard shall be of a fire-resistant type where they pass through high fire risk areas. Where practicable all such cables should be run in such a manner as to preclude their being rendered unserviceable by heating of the bulkheads that may be caused by a fire in an adjacent space.

---

* Refer to MSC/Circ.808, Recommendation on performance standards for public address systems on passenger ships, including cabling.

5.4   Where cables which are installed in hazardous areas introduce the risk of fire or explosion in the event of an electrical fault in such areas, special precautions against such risks shall be taken to the satisfaction of the Administration.

5.5   Cables and wiring shall be installed and supported in such a manner as to avoid chafing or other damage.

5.6   Terminations and joints in all conductors shall be so made as to retain the original electrical, mechanical, flame-retarding and, where necessary, fire-resisting properties of the cable.

6.1   Each separate circuit shall be protected against short circuit and against overload, except as permitted in regulations 29 and 30 or where the Administration may exceptionally otherwise permit.

6.2   The rating or appropriate setting of the overload protective device for each circuit shall be permanently indicated at the location of the protective device.

7   Lighting fittings shall be so arranged as to prevent temperature rises which could damage the cables and wiring, and to prevent surrounding material from becoming excessively hot.

8   All lighting and power circuits terminating in a bunker or cargo space shall be provided with a multiple-pole switch outside the space for disconnecting such circuits.

9.1   Accumulator batteries shall be suitably housed, and compartments used primarily for their accommodation shall be properly constructed and efficiently ventilated.

9.2   Electrical or other equipment which may constitute a source of ignition of flammable vapours shall not be permitted in these compartments except as permitted in paragraph 10.

9.3   Accumulator batteries shall not be located in sleeping quarters except where hermetically sealed to the satisfaction of the Administration.

10   No electrical equipment shall be installed in any space where flammable mixtures are liable to collect including those on board tankers or in compartments assigned principally to accumulator batteries, in paint lockers, acetylene stores or similar spaces, unless the Administration is satisfied that such equipment is:

    .1   essential for operational purposes;

    .2   of a type which will not ignite the mixture concerned;

    .3   appropriate to the space concerned; and

    .4   appropriately certified for safe usage in the dusts, vapours or gases likely to be encountered.

11   In a passenger ship, distribution systems shall be so arranged that fire in any main vertical zone as is defined in regulation II-2/3.9* will not interfere with services essential for safety in any other such zone. This requirement will be met if main and emergency feeders passing through any such zone are separated both vertically and horizontally as widely as is practicable.

---

* This relates to the chapter II-2 in force before 1 July 2002. The equivalent in the amended chapter II-2 is 3.32.

Part E

Additional requirements for periodically unattended machinery spaces

(Part E applies to cargo ships except that regulation 54
refers to passenger ships)

Regulation 46
General

1   The arrangements provided shall be such as to ensure that the safety of
the ship in all sailing conditions, including manoeuvring, is equivalent to
that of a ship having the machinery spaces manned.

2   Measures shall be taken to the satisfaction of the Administration to
ensure that the equipment is functioning in a reliable manner and that
satisfactory arrangements are made for regular inspections and routine tests
to ensure continuous reliable operation.

3   Every ship shall be provided with documentary evidence, to the
satisfaction of the Administration, of its fitness to operate with periodically
unattended machinery spaces.

Regulation 47
Fire precautions

1   Means shall be provided to detect and give alarms at an early stage in
case of fires:

> **.1**   in boiler air supply casings and exhausts (uptakes); and
>
> **.2**   in scavenging air belts of propulsion machinery,

unless the Administration considers this to be unnecessary in a particular
case.

2   Internal combustion engines of 2,250 kW and above or having
cylinders of more than 300 mm bore shall be provided with crankcase oil
mist detectors or engine bearing temperature monitors or equivalent
devices.

Regulation 48
Protection against flooding

1   Bilge wells in periodically unattended machinery spaces shall be located and monitored in such a way that the accumulation of liquids is detected at normal angles of trim and heel, and shall be large enough to accommodate easily the normal drainage during the unattended period.

2   Where the bilge pumps are capable of being started automatically, means shall be provided to indicate when the influx of liquid is greater than the pump capacity or when the pump is operating more frequently than would normally be expected. In these cases, smaller bilge wells to cover a reasonable period of time may be permitted. Where automatically controlled bilge pumps are provided, special attention shall be given to oil pollution prevention requirements.

3   The location of the controls of any valve serving a sea inlet, a discharge below the waterline or a bilge injection system shall be so sited as to allow adequate time for operation in case of influx of water to the space, having regard to the time likely to be required in order to reach and operate such controls. If the level to which the space could become flooded with the ship in the fully loaded condition so requires, arrangements shall be made to operate the controls from a position above such level.

Regulation 49
Control of propulsion machinery
from the navigation bridge

1   Under all sailing conditions, including manoeuvring, the speed, direction of thrust and, if applicable, the pitch of the propeller shall be fully controllable from the navigation bridge.

1.1   Such remote control shall be performed by a single control device for each independent propeller, with automatic performance of all associated services, including, where necessary, means of preventing overload of the propulsion machinery.

1.2   The main propulsion machinery shall be provided with an emergency stopping device on the navigation bridge which shall be independent of the navigation bridge control system.

2   Propulsion machinery orders from the navigation bridge shall be indicated in the main machinery control room or at the propulsion machinery control position as appropriate.

3   Remote control of the propulsion machinery shall be possible only from one location at a time; at such locations interconnected control positions are permitted. At each location there shall be an indicator showing which location is in control of the propulsion machinery. The transfer of control between the navigation bridge and machinery spaces shall be possible only in the main machinery space or in the main machinery control room. The system shall include means to prevent the propelling thrust from altering significantly when transferring control from one location to another.

4   It shall be possible for all machinery essential for the safe operation of the ship to be controlled from a local position, even in the case of failure in any part of the automatic or remote control systems.

5   The design of the remote automatic control system shall be such that in case of its failure an alarm will be given. Unless the Administration considers it impracticable, the preset speed and direction of thrust of the propeller shall be maintained until local control is in operation.

6   Indicators shall be fitted on the navigation bridge for:

> .1   propeller speed and direction of rotation in the case of fixed pitch propellers; or
>
> .2   propeller speed and pitch position in the case of controllable pitch propellers.

7   The number of consecutive automatic attempts which fail to produce a start shall be limited to safeguard sufficient starting air pressure. An alarm shall be provided to indicate low starting air pressure set at a level which still permits starting operations of the propulsion machinery.

Regulation 50
Communication

A reliable means of vocal communication shall be provided between the main machinery control room or the propulsion machinery control position as appropriate, the navigation bridge and the engineer officers' accommodation.

Regulation 51
Alarm system

1   An alarm system shall be provided indicating any fault requiring attention and shall:

> .1   be capable of sounding an audible alarm in the main machinery control room or at the propulsion machinery control position, and indicate visually each separate alarm function at a suitable position;
>
> .2   have a connection to the engineers' public rooms and to each of the engineers' cabins through a selector switch, to ensure

connection to at least one of those cabins. Administrations may permit equivalent arrangements;

.3   activate an audible and visual alarm on the navigation bridge for any situation which requires action by or attention of the officer on watch;

.4   as far as is practicable be designed on the fail-to-safety principle; and

.5   activate the engineers' alarm required by regulation 38 if an alarm function has not received attention locally within a limited time.

2.1   The alarm system shall be continuously powered and shall have an automatic change-over to a stand-by power supply in case of loss of normal power supply.

2.2   Failure of the normal power supply of the alarm system shall be indicated by an alarm.

3.1   The alarm system shall be able to indicate at the same time more than one fault and the acceptance of any alarm shall not inhibit another alarm.

3.2   Acceptance at the position referred to in paragraph 1 of any alarm condition shall be indicated at the positions where it was shown. Alarms shall be maintained until they are accepted and the visual indications of individual alarms shall remain until the fault has been corrected, when the alarm system shall automatically reset to the normal operating condition.

Regulation 52
Safety systems

A safety system shall be provided to ensure that serious malfunction in machinery or boiler operations, which presents an immediate danger, shall initiate the automatic shutdown of that part of the plant and that an alarm shall be given. Shutdown of the propulsion system shall not be automatically activated except in cases which could lead to serious damage, complete breakdown, or explosion. Where arrangements for overriding the shutdown of the main propelling machinery are fitted, these shall be such as to preclude inadvertent operation. Visual means shall be provided to indicate when the override has been activated.

Regulation 53
Special requirements for machinery, boiler and electrical installations

1   The special requirements for the machinery, boiler and electrical installations shall be to the satisfaction of the Administration and shall include at least the requirements of this regulation.

2   The main source of electrical power shall comply with the following:

2.1   Where the electrical power can normally be supplied by one generator, suitable load-shedding arrangements shall be provided to ensure the integrity of supplies to services required for propulsion and steering as well as the safety of the ship. In the case of loss of the generator in operation, adequate provision shall be made for automatic starting and connecting to the main switchboard of a stand-by generator of sufficient capacity to permit propulsion and steering and to ensure the safety of the ship with automatic restarting of the essential auxiliaries including, where necessary, sequential operations. The Administration may dispense with this requirement for a ship of less than 1,600 gross tonnage, if it is considered impracticable.

2.2   If the electrical power is normally supplied by more than one generator simultaneously in parallel operation, provision shall be made, for instance by load shedding, to ensure that, in case of loss of one of these generating sets, the remaining ones are kept in operation without overload to permit propulsion and steering, and to ensure the safety of the ship.

3   Where stand-by machines are required for other auxiliary machinery essential to propulsion, automatic change-over devices shall be provided.

4   **Automatic control and alarm system**

4.1   The control system shall be such that the services needed for the operation of the main propulsion machinery and its auxiliaries are ensured through the necessary automatic arrangements.

4.2   An alarm shall be given on the automatic change-over.

4.3   An alarm system complying with regulation 51 shall be provided for all important pressures, temperatures and fluid levels and other essential parameters.

4.4   A centralized control position shall be arranged with the necessary alarm panels and instrumentation indicating any alarm.

5   Means shall be provided to keep the starting air pressure at the required level where internal combustion engines are used for main propulsion.

Regulation 54
Special consideration in respect of passenger ships

Passenger ships shall be specially considered by the Administration as to whether or not their machinery spaces may be periodically unattended and if so whether additional requirements to those stipulated in these regulations are necessary to achieve equivalent safety to that of normally attended machinery spaces.

CHAPTER II-2
Construction – Fire protection, fire detection and fire extinction

Part E – *Operational requirements*

Part F – *Alternative design and arrangements*

Part G – *Special requirements*

Part A
General

Regulation 1
Application

1   Application

1.1   Unless expressly provided otherwise, this chapter shall apply to ships constructed on or after 1 July 2002.

1.2   For the purpose of this chapter:

.1   the expression *ships constructed* means ships the keels of which are laid or which are at a similar stage of construction;

.2   the expression *all ships* means ships, irrespective of type, constructed before, on or after 1 July 2002; and

.3   a cargo ship, whenever built, which is converted to a passenger ship shall be treated as a passenger ship constructed on the date on which such a conversion commences.

1.3   For the purpose of this chapter, the expression *a similar stage of construction* means the stage at which:

.1   construction identifiable with a specific ship begins; and

.2   assembly of that ship has commenced comprising at least 50 tonnes or 1% of the estimated mass of all structural material, whichever is less.

2   Applicable requirements to existing ships

2.1   Unless expressly provided otherwise, for ships constructed before 1 July 2002 the Administration shall ensure that the requirements which are applicable under chapter II-2 of the International Convention for the Safety of Life at Sea, 1974, as amended by resolutions MSC.1(XLV), MSC.6(48), MSC.13(57), MSC.22(59), MSC.24(60), MSC.27(61), MSC.31(63) and MSC.57(67), are complied with.

2.2   Ships constructed before 1 July 2002 shall also comply with:

.1   paragraphs 3, 6.5 and 6.7 as appropriate;

.2   regulations 13.3.4.2 to 13.3.4.5, 13.4.3 and part E, except regulations 16.3.2.2 and 16.3.2.3 thereof, as appropriate, not later than the date of the first survey after 1 July 2002;

.3   regulations 10.4.1.3 and 10.6.4 for new installations only; and

.4   regulation 10.5.6 not later than 1 October 2005 for passenger ships of 2,000 gross tonnage and above.

3   Repairs, alterations, modifications and outfitting

3.1   All ships which undergo repairs, alterations, modifications and outfitting related thereto shall continue to comply with at least the requirements previously applicable to these ships. Such ships, if constructed before 1 July 2002, shall, as a rule, comply with the requirements for ships constructed on or after that date to at least the same extent as they did before undergoing such repairs, alterations, modifications or outfitting.

3.2   Repairs, alterations and modifications which substantially alter the dimensions of a ship or the passenger accommodation spaces, or substantially increase a ship's service life and outfitting related thereto, shall meet the requirements for ships constructed on or after 1 July 2002 in so far as the Administration deems reasonable and practicable.

4   Exemptions

4.1   The Administration may, if it considers that the sheltered nature and conditions of the voyage are such as to render the application of any specific requirements of this chapter unreasonable or unnecessary, exempt[*] from those requirements individual ships or classes of ships entitled to fly the flag of its State, provided that such ships, in the course of their voyage, do not sail at distances of more than 20 miles from the nearest land.

4.2   In the case of passenger ships which are employed in special trades for the carriage of large numbers of special trade passengers, such as the pilgrim trade, the Administration, if satisfied that it is impracticable to enforce compliance with the requirements of this chapter, may exempt such ships from those requirements, provided that they comply fully with the provisions of:

.1   the rules annexed to the Special Trade Passenger Ships Agreement, 1971; and

.2   the rules annexed to the Protocol on Space Requirements for Special Trade Passenger Ships, 1973.

---

[*] Refer to port State concurrence with SOLAS exemptions (MSC/Circ.606).

5   Applicable requirements depending on ship type

Unless expressly provided otherwise:

.1   requirements not referring to a specific ship type shall apply to ships of all types; and

.2   requirements referring to "tankers" shall apply to tankers subject to the requirements specified in paragraph 6 below.

6   Application of requirements for tankers

6.1   Requirements for tankers in this chapter shall apply to tankers carrying crude oil or petroleum products having a flashpoint not exceeding 60°C (closed cup test), as determined by an approved flashpoint apparatus, and a Reid vapour pressure which is below the atmospheric pressure or other liquid products having a similar fire hazard.

6.2   Where liquid cargoes other than those referred to in paragraph 6.1 or liquefied gases which introduce additional fire hazards are intended to be carried, additional safety measures shall be required, having due regard to the provisions of the International Bulk Chemical Code, as defined in regulation VII/8.1, the Bulk Chemical Code, the International Gas Carrier Code, as defined in regulation VII/11.1, and the Gas Carrier Code, as appropriate.

6.2.1   A liquid cargo with a flashpoint of less than 60°C for which a regular foam fire-fighting system complying with the Fire Safety Systems Code is not effective, is considered to be a cargo introducing additional fire hazards in this context. The following additional measures are required:

.1   the foam shall be of alcohol-resistant type;

.2   the type of foam concentrates for use in chemical tankers shall be to the satisfaction of the Administration, taking into account the guidelines developed by the Organization;* and

.3   the capacity and application rates of the foam extinguishing system shall comply with chapter 11 of the International Bulk Chemical Code, except that lower application rates may be accepted based on performance tests. For tankers fitted with inert gas systems, a quantity of foam concentrate sufficient for 20 min of foam generation may be accepted.†

6.2.2   For the purpose of this regulation, a liquid cargo with a vapour pressure greater than 1.013 bar absolute at 37.8°C is considered to be a cargo introducing additional fire hazards. Ships carrying such substances

---

* Refer to the Guidelines for performance and testing criteria and surveys of expansion foam concentrates for fire-extinguishing systems for chemical tankers (MSC/Circ.799).

† Refer to the Information on flashpoint and recommended fire-fighting media for chemicals to which neither the IBC nor BCH Codes apply (MSC/Circ.553).

shall comply with paragraph 15.14 of the International Bulk Chemical Code. When ships operate in restricted areas and at restricted times, the Administration concerned may agree to waive the requirements for refrigeration systems in accordance with paragraph 15.14.3 of the International Bulk Chemical Code.

6.3   Liquid cargoes with a flashpoint exceeding 60°C other than oil products or liquid cargoes subject to the requirements of the International Bulk Chemical Code are considered to constitute a low fire risk, not requiring the protection of a fixed foam extinguishing system.

6.4   Tankers carrying petroleum products with a flashpoint exceeding 60°C (closed cup test), as determined by an approved flashpoint apparatus, shall comply with the requirements provided in regulations 10.2.1.4.4 and 10.10.2.3 and the requirements for cargo ships other than tankers, except that, in lieu of the fixed fire-extinguishing system required in regulation 10.7, they shall be fitted with a fixed deck foam system which shall comply with the provisions of the Fire Safety Systems Code.

6.5   Combination carriers constructed before, on or after 1 July 2002 shall not carry cargoes other than oil unless all cargo spaces are empty of oil and gas-freed or unless the arrangements provided in each case have been approved by the Administration taking into account the guidelines developed by the Organization.*

6.6   Chemical tankers and gas carriers shall comply with the requirements for tankers, except where alternative and supplementary arrangements are provided to the satisfaction of the Administration, having due regard to the provisions of the International Bulk Chemical Code and the International Gas Carrier Code, as appropriate.

6.7   The requirements of regulations 4.5.10.1.1 and 4.5.10.1.4 and a system for continuous monitoring of the concentration of hydrocarbon gases shall be fitted on all tankers constructed before 1 July 2002 by the date of the first scheduled dry-docking after 1 July 2002, but not later than 1 July 2005. Sampling points or detector heads shall be located in suitable positions in order that potentially dangerous leakages are readily detected. When the hydrocarbon gas concentration reaches a pre-set level which shall not be higher than 10% of the lower flammable limit, a continuous audible and visual alarm signal shall be automatically effected in the pump-room and cargo control room to alert personnel to the potential hazard. However, existing monitoring systems already fitted having a pre-set level not greater than 30% of the lower flammable limit may be accepted.

---

* Refer to the Guidelines for inert gas systems (MSC/Circ.353), as amended by MSC/Circ.387.

Regulation 2
Fire safety objectives and functional requirements

1   Fire safety objectives

1.1   The fire safety objectives of this chapter are to:

.1   prevent the occurrence of fire and explosion;

.2   reduce the risk to life caused by fire;

.3   reduce the risk of damage caused by fire to the ship, its cargo and the environment;

.4   contain, control and suppress fire and explosion in the compartment of origin; and

.5   provide adequate and readily accessible means of escape for passengers and crew.

2   Functional requirements

2.1   In order to achieve the fire safety objectives set out in paragraph 1, the following functional requirements are embodied in the regulations of this chapter as appropriate:

.1   division of the ship into main vertical and horizontal zones by thermal and structural boundaries;

.2   separation of accommodation spaces from the remainder of the ship by thermal and structural boundaries;

.3   restricted use of combustible materials;

.4   detection of any fire in the zone of origin;

.5   containment and extinction of any fire in the space of origin;

.6   protection of means of escape and access for fire fighting;

.7   ready availability of fire-extinguishing appliances; and

.8   minimization of possibility of ignition of flammable cargo vapour.

3   Achievement of the fire safety objectives

The fire safety objectives set out in paragraph 1 shall be achieved by ensuring compliance with the prescriptive requirements specified in parts B, C, D, E or G, or by alternative design and arrangements which comply with part F. A ship shall be considered to meet the functional requirements set out in paragraph 2 and to achieve the fire safety objectives set out in paragraph 1 when either:

.1   the ship's design and arrangements, as a whole, comply with the relevant prescriptive requirements in parts B, C, D, E or G;

.2   the ship's design and arrangements, as a whole, have been reviewed and approved in accordance with part F; or

.3   part(s) of the ship's design and arrangements have been reviewed and approved in accordance with part F and the remaining parts of the ship comply with the relevant prescriptive requirements in parts B, C, D, E or G.

Regulation 3
Definitions

For the purpose of this chapter, unless expressly provided otherwise, the following definitions shall apply:

1   *Accommodation spaces* are those spaces used for public spaces, corridors, lavatories, cabins, offices, hospitals, cinemas, game and hobby rooms, barber shops, pantries containing no cooking appliances and similar spaces.

2   *"A" class divisions* are those divisions formed by bulkheads and decks which comply with the following criteria:

.1   they are constructed of steel or other equivalent material;

.2   they are suitably stiffened;

.3   they are insulated with approved non-combustible materials such that the average temperature of the unexposed side will not rise more than 140°C above the original temperature, nor will the temperature, at any one point, including any joint, rise more than 180°C above the original temperature, within the time listed below:

class "A-60"	60 min
class "A-30"	30 min
class "A-15"	15 min
class "A-0"	0 min

.4   they are so constructed as to be capable of preventing the passage of smoke and flame to the end of the one-hour standard fire test; and

.5   the Administration required a test of a prototype bulkhead or deck in accordance with the Fire Test Procedures Code to ensure that it meets the above requirements for integrity and temperature rise.

3   *Atriums* are public spaces within a single main vertical zone spanning three or more open decks.

4   *"B" class divisions* are those divisions formed by bulkheads, decks, ceilings or linings which comply with the following criteria:

.1   they are constructed of approved non-combustible materials and all materials used in the construction and erection of "B" class divisions are non-combustible, with the exception that combustible veneers may be permitted provided they meet other appropriate requirements of this chapter;

.2   they have an insulation value such that the average temperature of the unexposed side will not rise more than 140°C above the original temperature, nor will the temperature at any one point, including any joint, rise more than 225°C above the original temperature, within the time listed below:

> class "B-15"   15 min
>
> class "B-0"   0 min

.3   they are so constructed as to be capable of preventing the passage of flame to the end of the first half hour of the standard fire test; and

.4   the Administration required a test of a prototype division in accordance with the Fire Test Procedures Code to ensure that it meets the above requirements for integrity and temperature rise.

5   *Bulkhead deck* is the uppermost deck up to which the transverse watertight bulkheads are carried.

6   *Cargo area* is that part of the ship that contains cargo holds, cargo tanks, slop tanks and cargo pump-rooms including pump-rooms, cofferdams, ballast and void spaces adjacent to cargo tanks and also deck areas throughout the entire length and breadth of the part of the ship over the aforementioned spaces.

7   *Cargo ship* is a ship as defined in regulation I/2(g).

8   *Cargo spaces* are spaces used for cargo, cargo oil tanks, tanks for other liquid cargo and trunks to such spaces.

9   *Central control station* is a control station in which the following control and indicator functions are centralized:

.1   fixed fire detection and fire alarm systems;

.2   automatic sprinkler, fire detection and fire alarm systems;

.3   fire door indicator panels;

.4   fire door closure;

.5   watertight door indicator panels;

.6   watertight door closures;

.7   ventilation fans;

.8   general/fire alarms;

.9   communication systems including telephones; and

.10   microphones to public address systems.

10   *"C" class divisions* are divisions constructed of approved non-combustible materials. They need meet neither requirements relative to the passage of smoke and flame nor limitations relative to the temperature rise. Combustible veneers are permitted provided they meet the requirements of this chapter.

11   *Chemical tanker* is a cargo ship constructed or adapted and used for the carriage in bulk of any liquid product of a flammable nature listed in chapter 17 of the International Bulk Chemical Code, as defined in regulation VII/8.1.

12   *Closed ro–ro spaces* are ro–ro spaces which are neither open ro–ro spaces nor weather decks.

13   *Closed vehicle spaces* are vehicle spaces which are neither open vehicle spaces nor weather decks.

14   *Combination carrier* is a cargo ship designed to carry both oil and solid cargoes in bulk.

15   *Combustible material* is any material other than a non-combustible material.

16   *Continuous "B" class ceilings or linings* are those "B" class ceilings or linings which terminate at an "A" or "B" class division.

17   *Continuously manned central control station* is a central control station which is continuously manned by a responsible member of the crew.

18   *Control stations* are those spaces in which the ship's radio or main navigating equipment or the emergency source of power is located or where the fire recording or fire control equipment is centralized. Spaces where the fire recording or fire control equipment is centralized are also considered to be a fire control station.

19   *Crude oil* is any oil occurring naturally in the earth, whether or not treated to render it suitable for transportation, and includes crude oil where certain distillate fractions may have been removed from or added to.

20   *Dangerous goods* are those goods referred to in the IMDG Code, as defined in regulation VII/1.1.

21   *Deadweight* is the difference in tonnes between the displacement of a ship in water of a specific gravity of 1.025 at the load waterline corresponding to the assigned summer freeboard and the lightweight of the ship.

22   *Fire Safety Systems Code* means the International Code for Fire Safety Systems as adopted by the Maritime Safety Committee of the Organization by resolution MSC.98(73), as may be amended by the Organization, provided that such amendments are adopted, brought into force and take effect in accordance with the provisions of article VIII of the present Convention concerning the amendment procedures applicable to the annex other than chapter I thereof.

23   *Fire Test Procedures Code* means the International Code for Application of Fire Test Procedures as adopted by the Maritime Safety Committee of the Organization by resolution MSC.61(67), as may be amended by the Organization, provided that such amendments are adopted, brought into force and take effect in accordance with the provisions of article VIII of the present Convention concerning the amendment procedures applicable to the annex other than chapter I thereof.

24   *Flashpoint* is the temperature in degrees Celsius (closed cup test) at which a product will give off enough flammable vapour to be ignited, as determined by an approved flashpoint apparatus.

25   *Gas carrier* is a cargo ship constructed or adapted and used for the carriage in bulk of any liquefied gas or other products of a flammable nature listed in chapter 19 of the International Gas Carrier Code, as defined in regulation VII/11.1.

26   *Helideck* is a purpose-built helicopter landing area located on a ship including all structure, fire-fighting appliances and other equipment necessary for the safe operation of helicopters.

27   *Helicopter facility* is a helideck including any refuelling and hangar facilities.

28   *Lightweight* is the displacement of a ship in tonnes without cargo, fuel, lubricating oil, ballast water, fresh water and feedwater in tanks, consumable stores, and passengers and crew and their effects.

29   *Low flame-spread* means that the surface thus described will adequately restrict the spread of flame, this being determined in accordance with the Fire Test Procedures Code.

30   *Machinery spaces* are machinery spaces of category A and other spaces containing propulsion machinery, boilers, oil fuel units, steam and internal combustion engines, generators and major electrical machinery, oil filling stations, refrigerating, stabilizing, ventilation and air conditioning machinery, and similar spaces, and trunks to such spaces.

31   *Machinery spaces of category A* are those spaces and trunks to such spaces which contain either:

    .1   internal combustion machinery used for main propulsion;

.2   internal combustion machinery used for purposes other than main propulsion where such machinery has in the aggregate a total power output of not less than 375 kW; or

.3   any oil-fired boiler or oil fuel unit, or any oil-fired equipment other than boilers, such as inert gas generators, incinerators, etc.

32   *Main vertical zones* are those sections into which the hull, super-structure and deckhouses are divided by "A" class divisions, the mean length and width of which on any deck does not in general exceed 40 m.

33   *Non-combustible material* is a material which neither burns nor gives off flammable vapours in sufficient quantity for self-ignition when heated to approximately 750°C, this being determined in accordance with the Fire Test Procedures Code.

34   *Oil fuel unit* is the equipment used for the preparation of oil fuel for delivery to an oil-fired boiler, or equipment used for the preparation for delivery of heated oil to an internal combustion engine, and includes any oil pressure pumps, filters and heaters dealing with oil at a pressure of more than 0.18 N/mm^2.

35   *Open ro–ro spaces* are those ro–ro spaces which are either open at both ends or have an opening at one end, and are provided with adequate natural ventilation effective over their entire length through permanent openings distributed in the side plating or deckhead or from above, having a total area of at least 10% of the total area of the space sides.

36   *Open vehicle spaces* are those vehicle spaces which are either open at both ends or have an opening at one end and are provided with adequate natural ventilation effective over their entire length through permanent openings distributed in the side plating or deckhead or from above, having a total area of at least 10% of the total area of the space sides.

37   *Passenger ship* is a ship as defined in regulation I/2(f).

38   *Prescriptive requirements* means the construction characteristics, limiting dimensions, or fire safety systems specified in parts B, C, D, E or G.

39   *Public spaces* are those portions of the accommodation which are used for halls, dining rooms, lounges and similar permanently enclosed spaces.

40   *Rooms containing furniture and furnishings of restricted fire risk,* for the purpose of regulation 9, are those rooms containing furniture and furnishings of restricted fire risk (whether cabins, public spaces, offices or other types of accommodation) in which:

.1   case furniture such as desks, wardrobes, dressing tables, bureaux, or dressers are constructed entirely of approved non-combustible materials, except that a combustible veneer not exceeding 2 mm may be used on the working surface of such articles;

.2   free-standing furniture such as chairs, sofas, or tables are constructed with frames of non-combustible materials;

.3   draperies, curtains and other suspended textile materials have qualities of resistance to the propagation of flame not inferior to those of wool having a mass of 0.8 kg/m^2, this being determined in accordance with the Fire Test Procedures Code;

.4   floor coverings have low flame-spread characteristics;

.5   exposed surfaces of bulkheads, linings and ceilings have low flame-spread characteristics;

.6   upholstered furniture has qualities of resistance to the ignition and propagation of flame, this being determined in accordance with the Fire Test Procedures Code; and

.7   bedding components have qualities of resistance to the ignition and propagation of flame, this being determined in accordance with the Fire Test Procedures Code.

41   *Ro–ro spaces* are spaces not normally subdivided in any way and normally extending to either a substantial length or the entire length of the ship in which motor vehicles with fuel in their tanks for their own propulsion and/or goods (packaged or in bulk, in or on rail or road cars, vehicles (including road or rail tankers), trailers, containers, pallets, demountable tanks or in or on similar stowage units or other receptacles) can be loaded and unloaded normally in a horizontal direction.

42   *Ro–ro passenger ship* means a passenger ship with ro–ro spaces or special category spaces.

43   *Steel or other equivalent material* means any non-combustible material which, by itself or due to insulation provided, has structural and integrity properties equivalent to steel at the end of the applicable exposure to the standard fire test (e.g., aluminium alloy with appropriate insulation).

44   *Sauna* is a hot room with temperatures normally varying between 80°C and 120°C where the heat is provided by a hot surface (e.g., by an electrically heated oven). The hot room may also include the space where the oven is located and adjacent bathrooms.

45   *Service spaces* are those spaces used for galleys, pantries containing cooking appliances, lockers, mail and specie rooms, store-rooms, work-shops other than those forming part of the machinery spaces, and similar spaces and trunks to such spaces.

46   *Special category spaces* are those enclosed vehicle spaces above and below the bulkhead deck, into and from which vehicles can be driven and to which passengers have access. Special category spaces may be accommodated on more than one deck provided that the total overall clear height for vehicles does not exceed 10 m.

47 *A standard fire test* is a test in which specimens of the relevant bulkheads or decks are exposed in a test furnace to temperatures corresponding approximately to the standard time–temperature curve in accordance with the test method specified in the Fire Test Procedures Code.

48 *Tanker* is a ship as defined in regulation I/2(h).

49 *Vehicle spaces* are cargo spaces intended for carriage of motor vehicles with fuel in their tanks for their own propulsion.

50 *Weather deck* is a deck which is completely exposed to the weather from above and from at least two sides.

Part B
Prevention of fire and explosion

Regulation 4
Probability of ignition

1   Purpose

The purpose of this regulation is to prevent the ignition of combustible materials or flammable liquids. For this purpose, the following functional requirements shall be met:

.1   means shall be provided to control leaks of flammable liquids;

.2   means shall be provided to limit the accumulation of flammable vapours;

.3   the ignitability of combustible materials shall be restricted;

.4   ignition sources shall be restricted;

.5   ignition sources shall be separated from combustible materials and flammable liquids; and

.6   the atmosphere in cargo tanks shall be maintained out of the explosive range.

2   Arrangements for oil fuel, lubrication oil and other flammable oils

2.1   *Limitations in the use of oils as fuel*

The following limitations shall apply to the use of oil as fuel:

.1   except as otherwise permitted by this paragraph, no oil fuel with a flashpoint of less than 60°C shall be used;*

.2   in emergency generators, oil fuel with a flashpoint of not less than 43°C may be used;

.3   the use of oil fuel having a flashpoint of less than 60°C but not less than 43°C may be permitted (e.g., for feeding the

---

* Refer to the *Recommended procedures to prevent the illegal or accidental use of low flashpoint cargo oil as fuel* adopted by the Organization by resolution A.565(14).

emergency fire pump's engines and the auxiliary machines which are not located in the machinery spaces of category A) subject to the following:

.3.1 fuel oil tanks except those arranged in double bottom compartments shall be located outside of machinery spaces of category A;

.3.2 provisions for the measurement of oil temperature are provided on the suction pipe of the oil fuel pump;

.3.3 stop valves and/or cocks are provided on the inlet side and outlet side of the oil fuel strainers; and

.3.4 pipe joints of welded construction or of circular cone type or spherical type union joint are applied as much as possible; and

.4 in cargo ships the use of fuel having a lower flashpoint than otherwise specified in paragraph 2.1, for example crude oil, may be permitted provided that such fuel is not stored in any machinery space and subject to the approval by the Administration of the complete installation.

2.2 *Arrangements for oil fuel*

In a ship in which oil fuel is used, the arrangements for the storage, distribution and utilization of the oil fuel shall be such as to ensure the safety of the ship and persons on board and shall at least comply with the following provisions.

2.2.1 *Location of oil fuel systems*

As far as practicable, parts of the oil fuel system containing heated oil under pressure exceeding 0.18 N/mm^2 shall not be placed in a concealed position such that defects and leakage cannot readily be observed. The machinery spaces in way of such parts of the oil fuel system shall be adequately illuminated.

2.2.2 *Ventilation of machinery spaces*

The ventilation of machinery spaces shall be sufficient under normal conditions to prevent accumulation of oil vapour.

2.2.3 *Oil fuel tanks*

2.2.3.1 Fuel oil, lubrication oil and other flammable oils shall not be carried in forepeak tanks.

2.2.3.2 As far as practicable, oil fuel tanks shall be part of the ship's structure and shall be located outside machinery spaces of category A. Where oil fuel tanks, other than double bottom tanks, are necessarily located adjacent to or within machinery spaces of category A, at least one of their vertical sides shall be contiguous to the machinery space boundaries, and shall preferably have a common boundary with the double bottom tanks, and the area of the tank boundary common with the machinery spaces shall be kept to a minimum. Where such tanks are situated within the boundaries of machinery spaces of category A they shall not contain oil fuel having a flashpoint of less than 60°C. In general, the use of free-standing oil fuel tanks shall be avoided. When such tanks are employed their use shall be prohibited in category A machinery spaces on passenger ships. Where permitted, they shall be placed in an oil-tight spill tray of ample size having a suitable drain pipe leading to a suitably sized spill oil tank.

2.2.3.3 No oil fuel tank shall be situated where spillage or leakage therefrom can constitute a fire or explosion hazard by falling on heated surfaces.

2.2.3.4 Oil fuel pipes, which, if damaged, would allow oil to escape from a storage, settling or daily service tank having a capacity of 500 *l* and above situated above the double bottom, shall be fitted with a cock or valve directly on the tank capable of being closed from a safe position outside the space concerned in the event of a fire occurring in the space in which such tanks are situated. In the special case of deep tanks situated in any shaft or pipe tunnel or similar space, valves on the tank shall be fitted, but control in the event of fire may be effected by means of an additional valve on the pipe or pipes outside the tunnel or similar space. If such an additional valve is fitted in the machinery space, it shall be operated from a position outside this space. The controls for remote operation of the valve for the emergency generator fuel tank shall be in a separate location from the controls for remote operation of other valves for tanks located in machinery spaces.

2.2.3.5 Safe and efficient means of ascertaining the amount of oil fuel contained in any oil fuel tank shall be provided.

2.2.3.5.1 Where sounding pipes are used, they shall not terminate in any space where the risk of ignition of spillage from the sounding pipe might arise. In particular, they shall not terminate in passenger or crew spaces. As a general rule, they shall not terminate in machinery spaces. However, where the Administration considers that these latter requirements are impracticable, it may permit termination of sounding pipes in machinery spaces on condition that all of the following requirements are met:

.1 an oil-level gauge is provided meeting the requirements of paragraph 2.2.3.5.2;

.2 the sounding pipes terminate in locations remote from ignition hazards unless precautions are taken, such as the fitting of effective screens, to prevent the oil fuel in the case of spillage through the terminations of the sounding pipes from coming into contact with a source of ignition; and

.3 the terminations of sounding pipes are fitted with self-closing blanking devices and with a small-diameter self-closing control cock located below the blanking device for the purpose of ascertaining before the blanking device is opened that oil fuel is not present. Provisions shall be made so as to ensure that any spillage of oil fuel through the control cock involves no ignition hazard.

2.2.3.5.2 Other oil-level gauges may be used in place of sounding pipes subject to the following conditions:

.1   in passenger ships, such gauges shall not require penetration below the top of the tank and their failure or overfilling of the tanks shall not permit release of fuel; and

.2   in cargo ships, the failure of such gauges or overfilling of the tank shall not permit release of fuel into the space. The use of cylindrical gauge glasses is prohibited. The Administration may permit the use of oil-level gauges with flat glasses and self-closing valves between the gauges and fuel tanks.

2.2.3.5.3 The means prescribed in paragraph 2.2.3.5.2 which are acceptable to the Administration shall be maintained in the proper condition to ensure their continued accurate functioning in service.

2.2.4 *Prevention of overpressure*

Provisions shall be made to prevent overpressure in any oil tank or in any part of the oil fuel system, including the filling pipes served by pumps on board. Air and overflow pipes and relief valves shall discharge to a position where there is no risk of fire or explosion from the emergence of oils and vapour and shall not lead into crew spaces, passenger spaces nor into special category spaces, closed ro–ro cargo spaces, machinery spaces or similar spaces.

2.2.5 *Oil fuel piping*

2.2.5.1   Oil fuel pipes and their valves and fittings shall be of steel or other approved material, except that restricted use of flexible pipes shall be permissible in positions where the Administration is satisfied that they are necessary.* Such flexible pipes and end attachments shall be of approved fire-resisting materials of adequate strength and shall be constructed to the satisfaction of the Administration. For valves fitted to oil fuel tanks and under static pressure, steel or spheroidal-graphite cast iron may be accepted. However, ordinary cast iron valves may be used in piping systems where the design pressure is lower than 7 bar and the design temperature is below 60°C.

---

* Refer to recommendations published by the International Organization for Standardization, in particular publications ISO 15540:1999, *Fire resistance of hose assemblies – test methods* and ISO 15541:1999, *Fire resistance of hose assemblies – requirements for the test bench*.

2.2.5.2   External high-pressure fuel delivery lines between the high-pressure fuel pumps and fuel injectors shall be protected with a jacketed piping system capable of containing fuel from a high-pressure line failure. A jacketed pipe incorporates an outer pipe into which the high-pressure fuel pipe is placed, forming a permanent assembly. The jacketed piping system shall include a means for collection of leakages and arrangements shall be provided with an alarm in case of a fuel line failure.

2.2.5.3   Oil fuel lines shall not be located immediately above or near units of high temperature, including boilers, steam pipelines, exhaust manifolds, silencers or other equipment required to be insulated by paragraph 2.2.6. As far as practicable, oil fuel lines shall be arranged far apart from hot surfaces, electrical installations or other sources of ignition and shall be screened or otherwise suitably protected to avoid oil spray or oil leakage onto the sources of ignition. The number of joints in such piping systems shall be kept to a minimum.

2.2.5.4   Components of a diesel engine fuel system shall be designed considering the maximum peak pressure which will be experienced in service, including any high-pressure pulses which are generated and transmitted back into the fuel supply and spill lines by the action of fuel injection pumps. Connections within the fuel supply and spill lines shall be constructed having regard to their ability to prevent pressurized oil fuel leaks while in service and after maintenance.

2.2.5.5   In multi-engine installations which are supplied from the same fuel source, means of isolating the fuel supply and spill piping to individual engines shall be provided. The means of isolation shall not affect the operation of the other engines and shall be operable from a position not rendered inaccessible by a fire on any of the engines.

2.2.5.6   Where the Administration may permit the conveying of oil and combustible liquids through accommodation and service spaces, the pipes conveying oil or combustible liquids shall be of a material approved by the Administration having regard to the fire risk.

2.2.6 *Protection of high-temperature surfaces*

2.2.6.1   Surfaces with temperatures above 220°C which may be impinged as a result of a fuel system failure shall be properly insulated.

2.2.6.2   Precautions shall be taken to prevent any oil that may escape under pressure from any pump, filter or heater from coming into contact with heated surfaces.

2.3 *Arrangements for lubricating oil*

2.3.1 The arrangements for the storage, distribution and utilization of oil used in pressure lubrication systems shall be such as to ensure the safety of the ship and persons on board. The arrangements made in machinery spaces

167

of category A, and whenever practicable in other machinery spaces, shall at least comply with the provisions of paragraphs 2.2.1, 2.2.3.3, 2.2.3.4, 2.2.3.5, 2.2.4, 2.2.5.1, 2.2.5.3 and 2.2.6, except that:

.1 this does not preclude the use of sight-flow glasses in lubricating systems provided that they are shown by testing to have a suitable degree of fire resistance; and

.2 sounding pipes may be authorized in machinery spaces; however, the requirements of paragraphs 2.2.3.5.1.1 and 2.2.3.5.1.3 need not be applied on condition that the sounding pipes are fitted with appropriate means of closure.

2.3.2 The provisions of paragraph 2.2.3.4 shall also apply to lubricating oil tanks except those having a capacity less than 500 *l*, storage tanks on which valves are closed during the normal operation mode of the ship, or where it is determined that an unintended operation of a quick-closing valve on the oil lubricating tank would endanger the safe operation of the main propulsion and essential auxiliary machinery.

2.4 *Arrangements for other flammable oils*

The arrangements for the storage, distribution and utilization of other flammable oils employed under pressure in power transmission systems, control and activating systems and heating systems shall be such as to ensure the safety of the ship and persons on board. Suitable oil collecting arrangements for leaks shall be fitted below hydraulic valves and cylinders. In locations where means of ignition are present, such arrangements shall at least comply with the provisions of paragraphs 2.2.3.3, 2.2.3.5, 2.2.5.3 and 2.2.6 and with the provisions of paragraphs 2.2.4 and 2.2.5.1 in respect of strength and construction.

2.5 *Arrangements for oil fuel in periodically unattended machinery spaces*

In addition to the requirements of paragraphs 2.1 to 2.4, the oil fuel and lubricating oil systems in a periodically unattended machinery space shall comply with the following:

.1 where daily service oil fuel tanks are filled automatically, or by remote control, means shall be provided to prevent overflow spillages. Other equipment which treats flammable liquids automatically (e.g., oil fuel purifiers) which, whenever practicable, shall be installed in a special space reserved for purifiers and their heaters, shall have arrangements to prevent overflow spillages; and

.2 where daily service oil fuel tanks or settling tanks are fitted with heating arrangements, a high temperature alarm shall be provided if the flashpoint of the oil fuel can be exceeded.

3   Arrangements for gaseous fuel for domestic purposes

Gaseous fuel systems used for domestic purposes shall be approved by the Administration. Storage of gas bottles shall be located on the open deck or in a well ventilated space which opens only to the open deck.

4   Miscellaneous items of ignition sources and ignitability

4.1   *Electric radiators*

Electric radiators, if used, shall be fixed in position and so constructed as to reduce fire risks to a minimum. No such radiators shall be fitted with an element so exposed that clothing, curtains, or other similar materials can be scorched or set on fire by heat from the element.

4.2   *Waste receptacles*

Waste receptacles shall be constructed of non-combustible materials with no openings in the sides or bottom.

4.3   *Insulation surfaces protected against oil penetration*

In spaces where penetration of oil products is possible, the surface of insulation shall be impervious to oil or oil vapours.

4.4   *Primary deck coverings*

Primary deck coverings, if applied within accommodation and service spaces and control stations, shall be of approved material which will not readily ignite, this being determined in accordance with the Fire Test Procedures Code.

5   Cargo areas of tankers

5.1   *Separation of cargo oil tanks*

5.1.1 Cargo pump-rooms, cargo tanks, slop tanks and cofferdams shall be positioned forward of machinery spaces. However, oil fuel bunker tanks need not be forward of machinery spaces. Cargo tanks and slop tanks shall be isolated from machinery spaces by cofferdams, cargo pump-rooms, oil bunker tanks or ballast tanks. Pump-rooms containing pumps and their accessories for ballasting those spaces situated adjacent to cargo tanks and slop tanks and pumps for oil fuel transfer shall be considered as equivalent to a cargo pump-room within the context of this regulation provided that such pump-rooms have the same safety standard as that required for cargo pump-rooms. Pump-rooms intended solely for ballast or oil fuel transfer, however, need not comply with the requirements of regulation 10.9. The lower portion of the pump-room may be recessed into machinery spaces of category A to accommodate pumps, provided that the deck head of the recess is in general not more than one third of the moulded depth above the keel, except that in the case of ships of not more than 25,000 tonnes deadweight, where it can be demonstrated that for reasons of access and satisfactory piping arrangements this is impracticable, the Administration may permit a recess in excess of such height, but not exceeding one half of the moulded depth above the keel.

5.1.2 Main cargo control stations, control stations, accommodation and service spaces (excluding isolated cargo handling gear lockers) shall be positioned aft of cargo tanks, slop tanks, and spaces which isolate cargo or slop tanks from machinery spaces, but not necessarily aft of the oil fuel bunker tanks and ballast tanks, and shall be arranged in such a way that a single failure of a deck or bulkhead shall not permit the entry of gas or fumes from the cargo tanks into main cargo control stations, control stations, or accommodation and service spaces. A recess provided in accordance with paragraph 5.1.1 need not be taken into account when the position of these spaces is being determined.

5.1.3 However, where deemed necessary, the Administration may permit main cargo control stations, control stations, accommodation and service spaces forward of the cargo tanks, slop tanks and spaces which isolate cargo and slop tanks from machinery spaces, but not necessarily forward of oil fuel bunker tanks or ballast tanks. Machinery spaces, other than those of category A, may be permitted forward of the cargo tanks and slop tanks provided they are isolated from the cargo tanks and slop tanks by cofferdams, cargo pump-rooms, oil fuel bunker tanks or ballast tanks, and have at least one portable fire extinguisher. In cases where they contain internal combustion machinery, one approved foam-type extinguisher of at least 45 *l* capacity or equivalent shall be arranged in addition to portable fire extinguishers. If operation of a semi-portable fire extinguisher is impracticable, this fire extinguisher may be replaced by two additional portable fire extinguishers. Main cargo control stations, control stations and accommodation and service spaces shall be arranged in such a way that a single failure of a deck or bulkhead shall not permit the entry of gas or fumes from the cargo tanks into such spaces. In addition, where deemed necessary for the safety or navigation of the ship, the Administration may permit machinery spaces containing internal combustion machinery not being main propulsion machinery having an output greater than 375 kW to be located forward of the cargo area provided the arrangements are in accordance with the provisions of this paragraph.

5.1.4 In combination carriers only:

 .1 The slop tanks shall be surrounded by cofferdams except where the boundaries of the slop tanks are part of the hull, main cargo deck, cargo pump-room bulkhead or oil fuel bunker tank. These cofferdams shall not be open to a double bottom, pipe tunnel, pump-room or other enclosed space, nor shall they be used for cargo or ballast and shall not be connected to piping systems serving oil cargo or ballast. Means shall be provided for filling the cofferdams with water and for draining them. Where the boundary of a slop tank is part of the cargo pump-room bulkhead, the pump-room shall not be open to the double bottom, pipe tunnel or other enclosed space; however, openings provided with gastight bolted covers may be permitted;

.2   Means shall be provided for isolating the piping connecting the pump-room with the slop tanks referred to in paragraph 5.1.4.1. The means of isolation shall consist of a valve followed by a spectacle flange or a spool piece with appropriate blank flanges. This arrangement shall be located adjacent to the slop tanks, but where this is unreasonable or impracticable, it may be located within the pump-room directly after the piping penetrates the bulkhead. A separate permanently installed pumping and piping arrangement incorporating a manifold, provided with a shut-off valve and a blank flange, shall be provided for discharging the contents of the slop tanks directly to the open deck for disposal to shore reception facilities when the ship is in the dry cargo mode. When the transfer system is used for slop transfer in the dry cargo mode, it shall have no connection to other systems. Separation from other systems by means of removal of spool pieces may be accepted;

.3   Hatches and tank cleaning openings to slop tanks shall only be permitted on the open deck and shall be fitted with closing arrangements. Except where they consist of bolted plates with bolts at watertight spacing, these closing arrangements shall be provided with locking arrangements under the control of the responsible ship's officer; and

.4   Where cargo wing tanks are provided, cargo oil lines below deck shall be installed inside these tanks. However, the Administration may permit cargo oil lines to be placed in special ducts provided these are capable of being adequately cleaned and ventilated to the satisfaction of the Administration. Where cargo wing tanks are not provided, cargo oil lines below deck shall be placed in special ducts.

5.1.5 Where the fitting of a navigation position above the cargo area is shown to be necessary, it shall be for navigation purposes only and it shall be separated from the cargo tank deck by means of an open space with a height of at least 2 m. The fire protection requirements for such a navigation position shall be those required for control stations, as specified in regulation 9.2.4.2 and other provisions for tankers, as applicable.

5.1.6 Means shall be provided to keep deck spills away from the accommodation and service areas. This may be accomplished by provision of a permanent continuous coaming of a height of at least 300 mm, extending from side to side. Special consideration shall be given to the arrangements associated with stern loading.

5.2 *Restriction on boundary openings*

5.2.1 Except as permitted in paragraph 5.2.2, access doors, air inlets and openings to accommodation spaces, service spaces, control stations and machinery spaces shall not face the cargo area. They shall be located on the transverse bulkhead not facing the cargo area or on the outboard side of the superstructure or deckhouse at a distance of at least 4% of the length of the ship, but not less than 3 m from the end of the superstructure or deckhouse facing the cargo area. This distance need not exceed 5 m.

5.2.2 The Administration may permit access doors in boundary bulkheads facing the cargo area or within the 5 m limits specified in paragraph 5.2.1, to main cargo control stations and to such service spaces used as provision rooms, store-rooms and lockers, provided they do not give access directly or indirectly to any other space containing or providing for accommodation, control stations or service spaces such as galleys, pantries or workshops, or similar spaces containing sources of vapour ignition. The boundary of such a space shall be insulated to "A-60" class standard, with the exception of the boundary facing the cargo area. Bolted plates for the removal of machinery may be fitted within the limits specified in paragraph 5.2.1. Wheelhouse doors and windows may be located within the limits specified in paragraph 5.2.1 so long as they are designed to ensure that the wheelhouse can be made rapidly and efficiently gastight and vapourtight.

5.2.3 Windows and sidescuttles facing the cargo area and on the sides of the superstructures and deckhouses within the limits specified in paragraph 5.2.1 shall be of the fixed (non-opening) type. Such windows and sidescuttles, except wheelhouse windows, shall be constructed to "A-60" class standard.

5.2.4 Where there is permanent access from a pipe tunnel to the main pump-room, a watertight door shall be fitted complying with the requirements of regulation II-1/25-9.2 and, in addition, with the following:

    .1   in addition to the bridge operation, the watertight door shall be capable of being manually closed from outside the main pump-room entrance; and

    .2   the watertight door shall be kept closed during normal operations of the ship except when access to the pipe tunnel is required.

5.2.5 Permanent approved gastight lighting enclosures for illuminating cargo pump-rooms may be permitted in bulkheads and decks separating cargo pump-rooms and other spaces provided they are of adequate strength and the integrity and gastightness of the bulkhead or deck is maintained.

5.2.6 The arrangement of ventilation inlets and outlets and other deckhouse and superstructure boundary space openings shall be such as to complement the provisions of paragraph 5.3 and regulation 11.6. Such vents, especially for machinery spaces, shall be situated as far aft as practicable. Due consideration in this regard shall be given when the ship is equipped to load or discharge at the stern. Sources of ignition such as electrical equipment shall be so arranged as to avoid an explosion hazard.

5.3 *Cargo tank venting*

5.3.1 *General requirements*

The venting systems of cargo tanks shall be entirely distinct from the air pipes of the other compartments of the ship. The arrangements and position of openings in the cargo tank deck from which emission of flammable vapours can occur shall be such as to minimize the possibility of flammable vapours being admitted to enclosed spaces containing a source of ignition, or collecting in the vicinity of deck machinery and equipment which may constitute an ignition hazard. In accordance with this general principle, the criteria in paragraphs 5.3.2 to 5.3.5 and regulation 11.6 will apply.

5.3.2 *Venting arrangements*

5.3.2.1 The venting arrangements in each cargo tank may be independent or combined with other cargo tanks and may be incorporated into the inert gas piping.

5.3.2.2 Where the arrangements are combined with other cargo tanks, either stop valves or other acceptable means shall be provided to isolate each cargo tank. Where stop valves are fitted, they shall be provided with locking arrangements which shall be under the control of the responsible ship's officer. There shall be a clear visual indication of the operational status of the valves or other acceptable means. Where tanks have been isolated, it shall be ensured that relevant isolating valves are opened before cargo loading or ballasting or discharging of those tanks is commenced. Any isolation must continue to permit the flow caused by thermal variations in a cargo tank in accordance with regulation 11.6.1.1.

5.3.2.3 If cargo loading and ballasting or discharging of a cargo tank or cargo tank group which is isolated from a common venting system is intended, that cargo tank or cargo tank group shall be fitted with a means for over-pressure or under-pressure protection as required in regulation 11.6.3.2.

5.3.2.4 The venting arrangements shall be connected to the top of each cargo tank and shall be self-draining to the cargo tanks under all normal conditions of trim and list of the ship. Where it may not be possible to provide self-draining lines, permanent arrangements shall be provided to drain the vent lines to a cargo tank.

5.3.3 *Safety devices in venting systems*

The venting system shall be provided with devices to prevent the passage of flame into the cargo tanks. The design, testing and locating of these devices shall comply with the requirements established by the Administration based on the guidelines developed by the Organization.* Ullage openings shall not be used for pressure equalization. They shall be provided with self-closing and tightly sealing covers. Flame arresters and screens are not permitted in these openings.

5.3.4 *Vent outlets for cargo handling and ballasting*

5.3.4.1 Vent outlets for cargo loading, discharging and ballasting required by regulation 11.6.1.2 shall:

.1.1 permit the free flow of vapour mixtures; or

.1.2 permit the throttling of the discharge of the vapour mixtures to achieve a velocity of not less than 30 m/s;

.2 be so arranged that the vapour mixture is discharged vertically upwards;

.3 where the method is by free flow of vapour mixtures, be such that the outlet shall be not less than 6 m above the cargo tank deck or fore and aft gangway if situated within 4 m of the gangway and located not less than 10 m measured horizontally from the nearest air intakes and openings to enclosed spaces containing a source of ignition and from deck machinery, which may include anchor windlass and chain locker openings, and equipment which may constitute an ignition hazard; and

.4 where the method is by high-velocity discharge, be located at a height not less than 2 m above the cargo tank deck and not less than 10 m measured horizontally from the nearest air intakes and openings to enclosed spaces containing a source of ignition and from deck machinery, which may include anchor windlass and chain locker openings, and equipment which may constitute an ignition hazard. These outlets shall be provided with high-velocity devices of an approved type.

5.3.4.2 The arrangements for the venting of vapours displaced from the cargo tanks during loading and ballasting shall comply with paragraph 5.3 and regulation 11.6 and shall consist of either one or more mast risers, or a

---

* Refer to the Revised standards for the design, testing and locating of devices to prevent the passage of flame into cargo tanks in tankers (MSC/Circ.677), as amended by MSC/Circ.1009, and to the Revised factors to be taken into consideration when designing cargo tank venting and gas-freeing arrangements (MSC/Circ.731).

number of high-velocity vents. The inert gas supply main may be used for such venting.

5.3.5 *Isolation of slop tanks in combination carriers*

In combination carriers, the arrangements for isolating slop tanks containing oil or oil residues from other cargo tanks shall consist of blank flanges which will remain in position at all times when cargoes other than liquid cargoes referred to in regulation 1.6.1 are carried.

5.4 Ventilation

5.4.1 *Ventilation systems in cargo pump-rooms*

Cargo pump-rooms shall be mechanically ventilated and discharges from the exhaust fans shall be led to a safe place on the open deck. The ventilation of these rooms shall have sufficient capacity to minimize the possibility of accumulation of flammable vapours. The number of air changes shall be at least 20 per hour, based upon the gross volume of the space. The air ducts shall be arranged so that all of the space is effectively ventilated. The ventilation shall be of the suction type using fans of the non-sparking type.

5.4.2 *Ventilation systems in combination carriers*

In combination carriers, cargo spaces and any enclosed spaces adjacent to cargo spaces shall be capable of being mechanically ventilated. The mechanical ventilation may be provided by portable fans. An approved fixed gas warning system capable of monitoring flammable vapours shall be provided in cargo pump-rooms, pipe ducts and cofferdams, as referred to in paragraph 5.1.4, adjacent to slop tanks. Suitable arrangements shall be made to facilitate measurement of flammable vapours in all other spaces within the cargo area. Such measurements shall be made possible from the open deck or easily accessible positions.

5.5 Inert gas systems

5.5.1 *Application*

5.5.1.1 For tankers of 20,000 tonnes deadweight and upwards, the protection of the cargo tanks shall be achieved by a fixed inert gas system in accordance with the requirements of the Fire Safety Systems Code, except that, in lieu of the above, the Administration, after having given consideration to the ship's arrangement and equipment, may accept other fixed installations if they afford protection equivalent to the above, in accordance with regulation I/5. The requirements for alternative fixed installations shall comply with the requirements in paragraph 5.5.4.

5.5.1.2 Tankers operating with a cargo tank cleaning procedure using crude oil washing shall be fitted with an inert gas system complying with the Fire Safety Systems Code and with fixed tank washing machines.

5.5.1.3 Tankers required to be fitted with inert gas systems shall comply with the following provisions:

.1 double hull spaces shall be fitted with suitable connections for the supply of inert gas;

.2 where hull spaces are connected to a permanently fitted inert gas distribution system, means shall be provided to prevent hydrocarbon gases from the cargo tanks entering the double hull spaces through the system; and

.3 where such spaces are not permanently connected to an inert gas distribution system, appropriate means shall be provided to allow connection to the inert gas main.

5.5.2 *Inert gas systems of chemical tankers and gas carriers*

The requirements for inert gas systems contained in the Fire Safety Systems Code need not be applied to:

.1 chemical tankers and gas carriers when carrying cargoes described in regulation 1.6.1, provided that they comply with the requirements for inert gas systems on chemical tankers established by the Administration, based on the guidelines developed by the Organization;* or

.2 chemical tankers and gas carriers when carrying flammable cargoes other than crude oil or petroleum products such as cargoes listed in chapters 17 and 18 of the International Bulk Chemical Code, provided that the capacity of tanks used for their carriage does not exceed 3,000 m^3 and the individual nozzle capacities of tank washing machines do not exceed 17.5 m^3/h and the total combined throughput from the number of machines in use in a cargo tank at any one time does not exceed 110 m^3/h.

5.5.3 *General requirements for inert gas systems*

5.5.3.1 The inert gas system shall be capable of inerting, purging and gas-freeing empty tanks and maintaining the atmosphere in cargo tanks with the required oxygen content.

5.5.3.2 The inert gas system referred to in paragraph 5.5.3.1 shall be designed, constructed and tested in accordance with the Fire Safety Systems Code.

5.5.3.3 Tankers fitted with a fixed inert gas system shall be provided with a closed ullage system.

---

* Refer to the Regulation for inert gas systems on chemical tankers adopted by the Organization by resolution A.567(14).

5.5.4 *Requirements for equivalent systems*

5.5.4.1 Where an installation equivalent to a fixed inert gas system is installed, it shall:

.1 be capable of preventing dangerous accumulations of explosive mixtures in intact cargo tanks during normal service throughout the ballast voyage and necessary in-tank operations; and

.2 be so designed as to minimize the risk of ignition from the generation of static electricity by the system itself.

5.6 Inerting, purging and gas-freeing

5.6.1 Arrangements for purging and/or gas-freeing shall be such as to minimize the hazards due to dispersal of flammable vapours in the atmosphere and to flammable mixtures in a cargo tank.

5.6.2 The procedure for cargo tank purging and/or gas-freeing shall be carried out in accordance with regulation 16.3.2.

5.6.3 The arrangements for inerting, purging or gas-freeing of empty tanks as required in paragraph 5.5.3.1 shall be to the satisfaction of the Administration and shall be such that the accumulation of hydrocarbon vapours in pockets formed by the internal structural members in a tank is minimized and that:

.1 on individual cargo tanks, the gas outlet pipe, if fitted, shall be positioned as far as practicable from the inert gas/air inlet and in accordance with paragraph 5.3 and regulation 11.6. The inlet of such outlet pipes may be located either at deck level or at not more than 1 m above the bottom of the tank;

.2 the cross-sectional area of such gas outlet pipe referred to in paragraph 5.6.3.1 shall be such that an exit velocity of at least 20 m/s can be maintained when any three tanks are being simultaneously supplied with inert gas. Their outlets shall extend not less than 2 m above deck level; and

.3 each gas outlet referred to in paragraph 5.6.3.2 shall be fitted with suitable blanking arrangements.

5.7 Gas measurement

5.7.1 *Portable instrument*

Tankers shall be equipped with at least one portable instrument for measuring flammable vapour concentrations, together with a sufficient set of spares. Suitable means shall be provided for the calibration of such instruments.

5.7.2 *Arrangements for gas measurement in double hull spaces
and double bottom spaces*

5.7.2.1   Suitable portable instruments for measuring oxygen and flammable vapour concentrations shall be provided. In selecting these instruments, due attention shall be given to their use in combination with the fixed gas sampling line systems referred to in paragraph 5.7.2.2.

5.7.2.2   Where the atmosphere in double hull spaces cannot be reliably measured using flexible gas sampling hoses, such spaces shall be fitted with permanent gas sampling lines. The configuration of gas sampling lines shall be adapted to the design of such spaces.

5.7.2.3   The materials of construction and the dimensions of gas sampling lines shall be such as to prevent restriction. Where plastic materials are used, they shall be electrically conductive.

5.8   *Air supply to double hull spaces and double bottom spaces*

Double hull spaces and double bottom spaces shall be fitted with suitable connections for the supply of air.

5.9   *Protection of cargo area*

Drip pans for collecting cargo residues in cargo lines and hoses shall be provided in the area of pipe and hose connections under the manifold area. Cargo hoses and tank washing hoses shall have electrical continuity over their entire lengths, including couplings and flanges (except shore connections), and shall be earthed for removal of electrostatic charges.

5.10   *Protection of cargo pump-rooms*

5.10.1   In tankers:

.1   cargo pumps, ballast pumps and stripping pumps, installed in cargo pump-rooms and driven by shafts passing through pump-room bulkheads shall be fitted with temperature sensing devices for bulkhead shaft glands, bearings and pump casings. A continuous audible and visual alarm signal shall be automatically effected in the cargo control room or the pump control station;

.2   lighting in cargo pump-rooms, except emergency lighting, shall be interlocked with ventilation such that the ventilation shall be in operation when switching on the lighting. Failure of the ventilation system shall not cause the lighting to go out;

.3   a system for continuous monitoring of the concentration of hydrocarbon gases shall be fitted. Sampling points or detector heads shall be located in suitable positions in order that potentially dangerous leakages are readily detected. When the hydrocarbon gas concentration reaches a pre-set level, which shall not be higher than 10% of the lower flammable limit, a continuous audible and visual alarm signal shall be automatically effected in the pump-room, engine control room, cargo control room and navigation bridge to alert personnel to the potential hazard; and

.4   all pump-rooms shall be provided with bilge level monitoring devices together with appropriately located alarms.

Regulation 5
Fire growth potential

1   Purpose

The purpose of this regulation is to limit the fire growth potential in every space of the ship. For this purpose, the following functional requirements shall be met:

.1   means of control for the air supply to the space shall be provided;

.2   means of control for flammable liquids in the space shall be provided; and

.3   the use of combustible materials shall be restricted.

2   Control of air supply and flammable liquid to the space

2.1   *Closing appliances and stopping devices of ventilation*

2.1.1 The main inlets and outlets of all ventilation systems shall be capable of being closed from outside the spaces being ventilated. The means of closing shall be easily accessible as well as prominently and permanently marked and shall indicate whether the shut-off is open or closed.

2.1.2 Power ventilation of accommodation spaces, service spaces, cargo spaces, control stations and machinery spaces shall be capable of being stopped from an easily accessible position outside the space being served. This position shall not be readily cut off in the event of a fire in the spaces served.

2.1.3 In passenger ships carrying more than 36 passengers, power ventilation, except machinery space and cargo space ventilation and any alternative system which may be required under regulation 8.2, shall be fitted with controls so grouped that all fans may be stopped from either of two separate positions which shall be situated as far apart as practicable. Fans serving power ventilation systems to cargo spaces shall be capable of being stopped from a safe position outside such spaces.

2.2 *Means of control in machinery spaces*

2.2.1 Means of control shall be provided for opening and closure of skylights, closure of openings in funnels which normally allow exhaust ventilation and closure of ventilator dampers.

2.2.2 Means of control shall be provided for stopping ventilating fans. Controls provided for the power ventilation serving machinery spaces shall be grouped so as to be operable from two positions, one of which shall be outside such spaces. The means provided for stopping the power ventilation of the machinery spaces shall be entirely separate from the means provided for stopping ventilation of other spaces.

2.2.3 Means of control shall be provided for stopping forced and induced draught fans, oil fuel transfer pumps, oil fuel unit pumps, lubricating oil service pumps, thermal oil circulating pumps and oil separators (purifiers). However, paragraphs 2.2.4 and 2.2.5 need not apply to oily water separators.

2.2.4 The controls required in paragraphs 2.2.1 to 2.2.3 and in regulation 4.2.2.3.4 shall be located outside the space concerned so they will not be cut off in the event of fire in the space they serve.

2.2.5 In passenger ships, the controls required in paragraphs 2.2.1 to 2.2.4 and in regulations 8.3.3 and 9.5.2.3 and the controls for any required fire-extinguishing system shall be situated at one control position or grouped in as few positions as possible to the satisfaction of the Administration. Such positions shall have a safe access from the open deck.

2.3 *Additional requirements for means of control in periodically unattended machinery spaces*

2.3.1 For periodically unattended machinery spaces, the Administration shall give special consideration to maintaining the fire integrity of the machinery spaces, the location and centralization of the fire-extinguishing system controls, the required shutdown arrangements (e.g., ventilation, fuel pumps, etc.) and that additional fire-extinguishing appliances and other fire-fighting equipment and breathing apparatus may be required.

2.3.2 In passenger ships, these requirements shall be at least equivalent to those of machinery spaces normally attended.

3   Fire protection materials

3.1   *Use of non-combustible materials*

3.1.1 *Insulating materials*

Insulating materials shall be non-combustible, except in cargo spaces, mail rooms, baggage rooms and refrigerated compartments of service spaces. Vapour barriers and adhesives used in conjunction with insulation, as well as the insulation of pipe fittings for cold service systems, need not be of non-combustible materials, but they shall be kept to the minimum quantity practicable and their exposed surfaces shall have low flame-spread characteristics.

3.1.2 *Ceilings and linings*

3.1.2.1 In passenger ships, except in cargo spaces, all linings, grounds, draught stops and ceilings shall be of non-combustible material except in mail rooms, baggage rooms, saunas or refrigerated compartments of service spaces. Partial bulkheads or decks used to subdivide a space for utility or artistic treatment shall also be of non-combustible materials.

3.1.2.2 In cargo ships, all linings, ceilings, draught stops and their associated grounds shall be of non-combustible materials in the following spaces:

.1 in accommodation and service spaces and control stations for ships where method IC is specified as referred to in regulation 9.2.3.1; and

.2 in corridors and stairway enclosures serving accommodation and service spaces and control stations for ships where methods IIC or IIIC are specified as referred to in regulation 9.2.3.1.

3.2 *Use of combustible materials*

3.2.1 *General*

3.2.1.1 In passenger ships, "A", "B" or "C" class divisions in accommodation and service spaces which are faced with combustible materials, facings, mouldings, decorations and veneers shall comply with the provisions of paragraphs 3.2.2 to 3.2.4 and regulation 6. However, traditional wooden benches and wooden linings on bulkheads and ceilings are permitted in saunas and such materials need not be subject to the calculations prescribed in paragraphs 3.2.2 and 3.2.3.

3.2.1.2 In cargo ships, non-combustible bulkheads, ceilings and linings fitted in accommodation and service spaces may be faced with combustible materials, facings, mouldings, decorations and veneers provided such spaces are bounded by non-combustible bulkheads, ceilings and linings in accordance with the provisions of paragraphs 3.2.2 to 3.2.4 and regulation 6.

3.2.2 *Maximum calorific value of combustible materials*

Combustible materials used on the surfaces and linings specified in paragraph 3.2.1 shall have a calorific value[*] not exceeding 45 MJ/m^2 of

---

[*] Refer to the recommendations published by the International Organization for Standardization, in particular publication ISO 1716:2002, *Determination of calorific potential.*

the area for the thickness used. The requirements of this paragraph are not applicable to the surfaces of furniture fixed to linings or bulkheads.

3.2.3 *Total volume of combustible materials*

Where combustible materials are used in accordance with paragraph 3.2.1, they shall comply with the following requirements:

.1 The total volume of combustible facings, mouldings, decorations and veneers in accommodation and service spaces shall not exceed a volume equivalent to 2.5 mm veneer on the combined area of the walls and ceiling linings. Furniture fixed to linings, bulkheads or decks need not be included in the calculation of the total volume of combustible materials; and

.2 in the case of ships fitted with an automatic sprinkler system complying with the provisions of the Fire Safety Systems Code, the above volume may include some combustible material used for erection of "C" class divisions.

3.2.4 *Low flame-spread characteristics of exposed surfaces*

The following surfaces shall have low flame-spread characteristics in accordance with the Fire Test Procedures Code:

3.2.4.1 In passenger ships:

.1 exposed surfaces in corridors and stairway enclosures and of bulkhead and ceiling linings in accommodation and service spaces (except saunas) and control stations; and

.2 surfaces and grounds in concealed or inaccessible spaces in accommodation and service spaces and control stations.

3.2.4.2 In cargo ships:

.1 exposed surfaces in corridors and stairway enclosures and of ceilings in accommodation and service spaces (except saunas) and control stations; and

.2 surfaces and grounds in concealed or inaccessible spaces in accommodation and service spaces and control stations.

3.3 *Furniture in stairway enclosures of passenger ships*

Furniture in stairway enclosures shall be limited to seating. It shall be fixed, limited to six seats on each deck in each stairway enclosure, be of restricted fire risk determined in accordance with the Fire Test Procedures Code, and shall not restrict the passenger escape route. The Administration may permit additional seating in the main reception area within a stairway enclosure if it is fixed, non-combustible and does not restrict the passenger escape route. Furniture shall not be permitted in passenger and crew corridors forming escape routes in cabin areas. In addition to the above, lockers of non-combustible material, providing storage for non-hazardous safety equipment required by these regulations, may be permitted. Drinking water dispensers and ice cube machines may be permitted in corridors provided they are fixed and do not restrict the width of the escape routes. This applies as well to decorative flower or plant arrangements, statues or other objects of art such as paintings and tapestries in corridors and stairways.

Regulation 6
Smoke generation potential and toxicity

1   Purpose

The purpose of this regulation is to reduce the hazard to life from smoke and toxic products generated during a fire in spaces where persons normally work or live. For this purpose, the quantity of smoke and toxic products released from combustible materials, including surface finishes, during fire shall be limited.

2   Paints, varnishes and other finishes

Paints, varnishes and other finishes used on exposed interior surfaces shall not be capable of producing excessive quantities of smoke and toxic products, this being determined in accordance with the Fire Test Procedures Code.

3   Primary deck coverings

Primary deck coverings, if applied within accommodation and service spaces and control stations, shall be of approved material which will not give rise to smoke or toxic or explosive hazards at elevated temperatures, this being determined in accordance with the Fire Test Procedures Code.

Part C
Suppression of fire

Regulation 7
Detection and alarm

1   Purpose

The purpose of this regulation is to detect a fire in the space of origin and to provide for alarm for safe escape and fire-fighting activity. For this purpose, the following functional requirements shall be met:

.1   fixed fire detection and fire alarm system installations shall be suitable for the nature of the space, fire growth potential and potential generation of smoke and gases;

.2   manually operated call points shall be placed effectively to ensure a readily accessible means of notification; and

.3   fire patrols shall provide an effective means of detecting and locating fires and alerting the navigation bridge and fire teams.

2   General requirements

2.1   A fixed fire detection and fire alarm system shall be provided in accordance with the provisions of this regulation.

2.2   A fixed fire detection and fire alarm system and a sample extraction smoke detection system required in this regulation and other regulations in this part shall be of an approved type and comply with the Fire Safety Systems Code.

2.3   Where a fixed fire detection and fire alarm system is required for the protection of spaces other than those specified in paragraph 5.1, at least one detector complying with the Fire Safety Systems Code shall be installed in each such space.

3   Initial and periodical tests

3.1   The function of fixed fire detection and fire alarm systems required by the relevant regulations of this chapter shall be tested under varying conditions of ventilation after installation.

3.2   The function of fixed fire detection and fire alarm systems shall be periodically tested to the satisfaction of the Administration by means of equipment producing hot air at the appropriate temperature, or smoke or aerosol particles having the appropriate range of density or particle size, or other phenomena associated with incipient fires to which the detector is designed to respond.

4 Protection of machinery spaces

4.1 *Installation*

A fixed fire detection and fire alarm system shall be installed in:

.1   periodically unattended machinery spaces; and

.2   machinery spaces where:

.2.1   the installation of automatic and remote control systems and equipment has been approved in lieu of continuous manning of the space; and

.2.2   the main propulsion and associated machinery, including the main sources of electrical power, are provided with various degrees of automatic or remote control and are under continuous manned supervision from a control room.

4.2 *Design*

The fixed fire detection and fire alarm system required in paragraph 4.1.1 shall be so designed and the detectors so positioned as to detect rapidly the onset of fire in any part of those spaces and under any normal conditions of operation of the machinery and variations of ventilation as required by the possible range of ambient temperatures. Except in spaces of restricted height and where their use is specially appropriate, detection systems using only thermal detectors shall not be permitted. The detection system shall initiate audible and visual alarms distinct in both respects from the alarms of any other system not indicating fire, in sufficient places to ensure that the alarms are heard and observed on the navigation bridge and by a responsible engineer officer. When the navigation bridge is unmanned, the alarm shall sound in a place where a responsible member of the crew is on duty.

5 Protection of accommodation and service spaces and control stations

5.1 *Smoke detectors in accommodation spaces*

Smoke detectors shall be installed in all stairways, corridors and escape routes within accommodation spaces as provided in paragraphs 5.2, 5.3 and 5.4. Consideration shall be given to the installation of special purpose smoke detectors within ventilation ducting.

5.2   *Requirements for passenger ships carrying more than 36 passengers*

A fixed fire detection and fire alarm system shall be so installed and arranged as to provide smoke detection in service spaces, control stations and accommodation spaces, including corridors, stairways and escape routes within accommodation spaces. Smoke detectors need not be fitted in private bathrooms and galleys. Spaces having little or no fire risk such as voids, public toilets, carbon dioxide rooms and similar spaces need not be fitted with a fixed fire detection and alarm system.

5.3   *Requirements for passenger ships carrying not more than 36 passengers*

There shall be installed throughout each separate zone, whether vertical or horizontal, in all accommodation and service spaces and, where it is considered necessary by the Administration, in control stations, except spaces which afford no substantial fire risk such as void spaces, sanitary spaces, etc., either:

.1   a fixed fire detection and fire alarm system so installed and arranged as to detect the presence of fire in such spaces and providing smoke detection in corridors, stairways and escape routes within accommodation spaces; or

.2   an automatic sprinkler, fire detection and fire alarm system of an approved type complying with the relevant requirements of the Fire Safety Systems Code and so installed and arranged as to protect such spaces and, in addition, a fixed fire detection and fire alarm system and so installed and arranged as to provide smoke detection in corridors, stairways and escape routes within accommodation spaces.

5.4   *Protection of atriums in passenger ships*

The entire main vertical zone containing the atrium shall be protected throughout with a smoke detection system.

5.5   *Cargo ships*

Accommodation and service spaces and control stations of cargo ships shall be protected by a fixed fire detection and fire alarm system and/or an automatic sprinkler, fire detection and fire alarm system as follows, depending on a protection method adopted in accordance with regulation 9.2.3.1.

5.5.1   *Method IC* – A fixed fire detection and fire alarm system shall be so installed and arranged as to provide smoke detection in all corridors, stairways and escape routes within accommodation spaces.

5.5.2   *Method IIC* – An automatic sprinkler, fire detection and fire alarm system of an approved type complying with the relevant requirements of the

Fire Safety Systems Code shall be so installed and arranged as to protect accommodation spaces, galleys and other service spaces, except spaces which afford no substantial fire risk such as void spaces, sanitary spaces, etc. In addition, a fixed fire detection and fire alarm system shall be so installed and arranged as to provide smoke detection in all corridors, stairways and escape routes within accommodation spaces.

5.5.3 *Method IIIC* – A fixed fire detection and fire alarm system shall be so installed and arranged as to detect the presence of fire in all accommodation spaces and service spaces, providing smoke detection in corridors, stairways and escape routes within accommodation spaces, except spaces which afford no substantial fire risk such as void spaces, sanitary spaces, etc. In addition, a fixed fire detection and fire alarm system shall be so installed and arranged as to provide smoke detection in all corridors, stairways and escape routes within accommodation spaces.

6   Protection of cargo spaces in passenger ships

A fixed fire detection and fire alarm system or a sample extraction smoke detection system shall be provided in any cargo space which, in the opinion of the Administration, is not accessible, except where it is shown to the satisfaction of the Administration that the ship is engaged on voyages of such short duration that it would be unreasonable to apply this requirement.

7   Manually operated call points

Manually operated call points complying with the Fire Safety Systems Code shall be installed throughout the accommodation spaces, service spaces and control stations. One manually operated call point shall be located at each exit. Manually operated call points shall be readily accessible in the corridors of each deck such that no part of the corridor is more than 20 m from a manually operated call point.

8   Fire patrols in passenger ships

8.1   *Fire patrols*

For ships carrying more than 36 passengers, an efficient patrol system shall be maintained so that an outbreak of fire may be promptly detected. Each member of the fire patrol shall be trained to be familiar with the arrangements of the ship as well as the location and operation of any equipment he may be called upon to use.

8.2   *Inspection hatches*

The construction of ceilings and bulkheads shall be such that it will be possible, without impairing the efficiency of the fire protection, for the fire patrols to detect any smoke originating in concealed and inaccessible places, except where in the opinion of the Administration there is no risk of fire originating in such places.

8.3 *Two-way portable radiotelephone apparatus*

Each member of the fire patrol shall be provided with a two-way portable radiotelephone apparatus.

9 Fire alarm signalling systems in passenger ships[*]

9.1 Passenger ships shall at all times when at sea, or in port (except when out of service), be so manned or equipped as to ensure that any initial fire alarm is immediately received by a responsible member of the crew.

9.2 The control panel of fixed fire detection and fire alarm systems shall be designed on the fail-safe principle (e.g., an open detector circuit shall cause an alarm condition).

9.3 Passenger ships carrying more than 36 passengers shall have the fire detection alarms for the systems required by paragraph 5.2 centralized in a continuously manned central control station. In addition, controls for remote closing of the fire doors and shutting down the ventilation fans shall be centralized in the same location. The ventilation fans shall be capable of reactivation by the crew at the continuously manned control station. The control panels in the central control station shall be capable of indicating open or closed positions of fire doors and closed or off status of the detectors, alarms and fans. The control panel shall be continuously powered and shall have an automatic change-over to standby power supply in case of loss of normal power supply. The control panel shall be powered from the main source of electrical power and the emergency source of electrical power defined by regulation II-1/42 unless other arrangements are permitted by the regulations, as applicable.

9.4 A special alarm, operated from the navigation bridge or fire control station, shall be fitted to summon the crew. This alarm may be part of the ship's general alarm system and shall be capable of being sounded independently of the alarm to the passenger spaces.

Regulation 8
Control of smoke spread

1 Purpose

The purpose of this regulation is to control the spread of smoke in order to minimize the hazards from smoke. For this purpose, means for controlling

---

[*] Refer to the Code on Alarms and Indicators adopted by the Organization by resolution A.830(19).

smoke in atriums, control stations, machinery spaces and concealed spaces shall be provided.

2   Protection of control stations outside machinery spaces

Practicable measures shall be taken for control stations outside machinery spaces in order to ensure that ventilation, visibility and freedom from smoke are maintained so that, in the event of fire, the machinery and equipment contained therein may be supervised and continue to function effectively. Alternative and separate means of air supply shall be provided and air inlets of the two sources of supply shall be so disposed that the risk of both inlets drawing in smoke simultaneously is minimized. At the discretion of the Administration, such requirements need not apply to control stations situated on, and opening onto, an open deck or where local closing arrangements would be equally effective.

3   Release of smoke from machinery spaces

3.1   The provisions of this paragraph shall apply to machinery spaces of category A and, where the Administration considers it desirable, to other machinery spaces.

3.2   Suitable arrangements shall be made to permit the release of smoke, in the event of fire, from the space to be protected, subject to the provisions of regulation 9.5.2.1 The normal ventilation systems may be acceptable for this purpose.

3.3   Means of control shall be provided for permitting the release of smoke and such controls shall be located outside the space concerned so that they will not be cut off in the event of fire in the space they serve.

3.4   In passenger ships, the controls required by paragraph 3.3 shall be situated at one control position or grouped in as few positions as possible to the satisfaction of the Administration. Such positions shall have a safe access from the open deck.

4   Draught stops

Air spaces enclosed behind ceilings, panelling or linings shall be divided by close-fitting draught stops spaced not more than 14 m apart. In the vertical direction, such enclosed air spaces, including those behind linings of stairways, trunks, etc., shall be closed at each deck.

5   Smoke extraction systems in atriums of passenger ships

Atriums shall be equipped with a smoke extraction system. The smoke extraction system shall be activated by the required smoke detection system and be capable of manual control. The fans shall be sized such that the entire volume within the space can be exhausted in 10 min or less.

Regulation 9
Containment of fire

1 Purpose

The purpose of this regulation is to contain a fire in the space of origin. For this purpose, the following functional requirements shall be met:

.1   the ship shall be subdivided by thermal and structural boundaries;

.2   thermal insulation of boundaries shall have due regard to the fire risk of the space and adjacent spaces; and

.3   the fire integrity of the divisions shall be maintained at openings and penetrations.

2 Thermal and structural boundaries

2.1 *Thermal and structural subdivision*

Ships of all types shall be subdivided into spaces by thermal and structural divisions having regard to the fire risks of the spaces.

2.2 *Passenger ships*

2.2.1 *Main vertical zones and horizontal zones*

2.2.1.1.1 In ships carrying more than 36 passengers, the hull, superstructure and deckhouses shall be subdivided into main vertical zones by "A-60" class divisions. Steps and recesses shall be kept to a minimum, but where they are necessary they shall also be "A-60" class divisions. Where a category (5), (9) or (10) space defined in paragraph 2.2.3.2.2 is on one side or where fuel oil tanks are on both sides of the division the standard may be reduced to "A-0".

2.2.1.1.2 In ships carrying not more than 36 passengers, the hull, superstructure and deckhouses in way of accommodation and service spaces shall be subdivided into main vertical zones by "A" class divisions. These divisions shall have insulation values in accordance with tables in paragraph 2.2.4.

2.2.1.2 As far as practicable, the bulkheads forming the boundaries of the main vertical zones above the bulkhead deck shall be in line with watertight subdivision bulkheads situated immediately below the bulkhead deck. The length and width of main vertical zones may be extended to a maximum of 48 m in order to bring the ends of main vertical zones to coincide with watertight subdivision bulkheads or in order to accommodate a large public space extending for the whole length of the main vertical zone provided that the total area of the main vertical zone is not greater than 1,600 m^2 on any deck. The length or width of a main vertical zone is the maximum distance between the furthermost points of the bulkheads bounding it.

2.2.1.3   Such bulkheads shall extend from deck to deck and to the shell or other boundaries.

2.2.1.4   Where a main vertical zone is subdivided by horizontal "A" class divisions into horizontal zones for the purpose of providing an appropriate barrier between a zone with sprinklers and a zone without sprinklers, the divisions shall extend between adjacent main vertical zone bulkheads and to the shell or exterior boundaries of the ship and shall be insulated in accordance with the fire insulation and integrity values given in table 9.4.

2.2.1.5.1   On ships designed for special purposes, such as automobile or railroad car ferries, where the provision of main vertical zone bulkheads would defeat the purpose for which the ship is intended, equivalent means for controlling and limiting a fire shall be substituted and specifically approved by the Administration. Service spaces and ship stores shall not be located on ro–ro decks unless protected in accordance with the applicable regulations.

2.2.1.5.2   However, in a ship with special category spaces, such spaces shall comply with the applicable provisions of regulation 20 and, where such compliance would be inconsistent with other requirements for passenger ships specified in this chapter, the requirements of regulation 20 shall prevail.

2.2.2   *Bulkheads within a main vertical zone*

2.2.2.1   For ships carrying more than 36 passengers, bulkheads which are not required to be "A" class divisions shall be at least "B" class or "C" class divisions as prescribed in the tables in paragraph 2.2.3.

2.2.2.2   For ships carrying not more than 36 passengers, bulkheads within accommodation and service spaces which are not required to be "A" class divisions shall be at least "B" class or "C" class divisions as prescribed in the tables in paragraph 2.2.4. In addition, corridor bulkheads, where not required to be "A" class, shall be "B" class divisions which shall extend from deck to deck except:

> .1   when continuous "B" class ceilings or linings are fitted on both sides of the bulkhead, the portion of the bulkhead behind the continuous ceiling or lining shall be of material which, in thickness and composition, is acceptable in the construction of "B" class divisions, but which shall be required to meet "B" class integrity standards only in so far as is reasonable and practicable in the opinion of the Administration; and

    .2   in the case of a ship protected by an automatic sprinkler system complying with the provisions of the Fire Safety Systems Code, the corridor bulkheads may terminate at a ceiling in the corridor provided such bulkheads and ceilings are of "B" class standard in compliance with paragraph 2.2.4. All doors and frames in such bulkheads shall be of non-combustible materials and shall have the same fire integrity as the bulkhead in which they are fitted.

2.2.2.3 Bulkheads required to be "B" class divisions, except corridor bulkheads as prescribed in paragraph 2.2.2.2, shall extend from deck to deck and to the shell or other boundaries. However, where a continuous "B" class ceiling or lining is fitted on both sides of a bulkhead which is at least of the same fire resistance as the adjoining bulkhead, the bulkhead may terminate at the continuous ceiling or lining.

2.2.3 *Fire integrity of bulkheads and decks in ships carrying more than 36 passengers*

2.2.3.1 In addition to complying with the specific provisions for fire integrity of bulkheads and decks of passenger ships, the minimum fire integrity of all bulkheads and decks shall be as prescribed in tables 9.1 and 9.2. Where, due to any particular structural arrangements in the ship, difficulty is experienced in determining from the tables the minimum fire integrity value of any divisions, such values shall be determined to the satisfaction of the Administration.

2.2.3.2 The following requirements shall govern application of the tables:

    .1   Table 9.1 shall apply to bulkheads not bounding either main vertical zones or horizontal zones. Table 9.2 shall apply to decks not forming steps in main vertical zones nor bounding horizontal zones.

    .2   For determining the appropriate fire integrity standards to be applied to boundaries between adjacent spaces, such spaces are classified according to their fire risk as shown in categories (1) to (14) below. Where the contents and use of a space are such that there is a doubt as to its classification for the purpose of this regulation, or where it is possible to assign two or more classifications to a space, it shall be treated as a space within the relevant category having the most stringent boundary requirements. Smaller, enclosed rooms within a space that have less than 30% communicating openings to that space are considered separate spaces. The fire integrity of the boundary bulkheads and decks of such smaller rooms shall be as prescribed in tables 9.1 and 9.2. The title of each category is intended to be typical rather than restrictive. The number in parentheses preceding each category refers to the applicable column or row in the tables.

(1) *Control stations*

Spaces containing emergency sources of power and lighting.

Wheelhouse and chartroom.

Spaces containing the ship's radio equipment.

Fire control stations.

Control room for propulsion machinery when located outside the propulsion machinery space.

Spaces containing centralized fire alarm equipment.

Spaces containing centralized emergency public address system stations and equipment.

(2) *Stairways*

Interior stairways, lifts, totally enclosed emergency escape trunks, and escalators (other than those wholly contained within the machinery spaces) for passengers and crew and enclosures thereto.

In this connection, a stairway which is enclosed at only one level shall be regarded as part of the space from which it is not separated by a fire door.

(3) *Corridors*

Passenger and crew corridors and lobbies.

(4) *Evacuation stations and external escape routes*

Survival craft stowage area.

Open deck spaces and enclosed promenades forming lifeboat and liferaft embarkation and lowering stations.

Assembly stations, internal and external.

External stairs and open decks used for escape routes.

The ship's side to the waterline in the lightest seagoing condition, superstructure and deckhouse sides situated below and adjacent to the liferaft and evacuation slide embarkation areas.

(5) *Open deck spaces*

Open deck spaces and enclosed promenades clear of lifeboat and liferaft embarkation and lowering stations. To be considered in this category, enclosed promenades shall have no significant fire risk, meaning that furnishings shall be restricted to deck furniture. In addition, such spaces shall be naturally ventilated by permanent openings.

Air spaces (the space outside superstructures and deckhouses).

Table 9.1 – Bulkheads not bounding either main vertical zones or horizontal zones

Spaces		(1)	(2)	(3)	(4)	(5)	(6)	(7)	(8)	(9)	(10)	(11)	(12)	(13)	(14)
Control stations	(1)	B-0[a]	A-0	A-0	A-0	A-0	A-60	A-60	A-60	A-0	A-0	A-60	A-60	A-60	A-60
Stairways	(2)		A-0[a]	A-0	A-0	A-0	A-0	A-15	A-15	A-0[c]	A-0	A-15	A-30	A-15	A-30
Corridors	(3)			B-15	A-60	A-0	B-15	B-15	B-15	B-15	A-0	A-15	A-30	A-0	A-30
Evacuation stations and external escape routes	(4)					A-0	A-60[b,d]	A-60[b,d]	A-60[b,d]	A-0[d]	A-0	A-60[b]	A-60[b]	A-60[b]	A-60[b]
Open deck spaces	(5)						A-0	A-0	A-0	A-0	A-0	A-0	A-0	A-0	A-0
Accommodation spaces of minor fire risk	(6)						B-0	B-0	B-0	C	A-0	A-0	A-30	A-0	A-30
Accommodation spaces of moderate fire risk	(7)							B-0	B-0	C	A-0	A-15	A-60	A-15	A-60
Accommodation spaces of greater fire risk	(8)								B-0	C	A-0	A-30	A-60	A-15	A-60
Sanitary and similar spaces	(9)									C	A-0	A-0	A-0	A-0	A-0
Tanks, voids and auxiliary machinery spaces having little or no fire risk	(10)										A-0[a]	A-0	A-0	A-0	A-0
Auxiliary machinery spaces, cargo spaces, cargo and other oil tanks and other similar spaces of moderate fire risk	(11)											A-0[a]	A-0	A-0	A-15
Machinery spaces and main galleys	(12)												A-0[a]	A-0	A-60
Store-rooms, workshops, pantries, etc.	(13)													A-0[a]	A-0
Other spaces in which flammable liquids are stowed	(14)														A-30

See notes following table 9.2.

194

Table 9.2 – Decks not forming steps in main vertical zones nor bounding horizontal zones

Space below ↓ \ Space above →	(1)	(2)	(3)	(4)	(5)	(6)	(7)	(8)	(9)	(10)	(11)	(12)	(13)	(14)
Control stations (1)	A-30	A-30	A-15	A-0	A-0	A-0	A-15	A-30	A-0	A-0	A-0	A-60	A-0	A-60
Stairways (2)	A-0	A-0	A-0	A-0	A-0	A-0	A-0	A-0	A-0	A-0	A-0	A-30	A-0	A-30
Corridors (3)	A-15	A-0	A-0ᵃ	A-60	A-0	A-0	A-15	A-15	A-0	A-0	A-0	A-30	A-0	A-30
Evacuation stations and external escape routes (4)	A-0	A-0	A-0	A-0	–	A-0	A-0	A-0	A-0	A-0	A-0	A-0	A-0	A-0
Open deck spaces (5)	A-0	A-0	A-0	A-0	–	A-0	A-0	A-0	A-0	A-0	A-0	A-0	A-0	A-0
Accommodation spaces of minor fire risk (6)	A-0	A-15	A-0	A-60	A-0	A-0	A-0	A-0	A-0	A-0	A-0	A-0	A-0	A-0
Accommodation spaces of moderate fire risk (7)	A-60	A-15	A-15	A-60	A-0	A-0	A-15	A-15	A-0	A-0	A-0	A-0	A-0	A-0
Accommodation spaces of greater fire risk (8)	A-60	A-15	A-15	A-60	A-0	A-15	A-15	A-30	A-0	A-0	A-0	A-0	A-0	A-0
Sanitary and similar spaces (9)	A-0	A-0	A-0	A-0	A-0	A-0	A-0	A-0	A-0	A-0	A-0	A-0	A-0	A-0
Tanks, voids and auxiliary machinery spaces having little or no fire risk (10)	A-0	A-0	A-0	A-0	A-0	A-0	A-0	A-0	A-0	A-0ᵃ	A-0	A-0	A-0	A-0
Auxiliary machinery spaces, cargo spaces, cargo and other oil tanks and other similar spaces of moderate fire risk (11)	A-60	A-60	A-60	A-60	A-0	A-0	A-15	A-30	A-0	A-0	A-0ᵃ	A-0	A-0	A-30
Machinery spaces and main galleys (12)	A-60	A-60	A-60	A-60	A-0	A-60	A-60	A-60	A-0	A-0	A-30	A-30ᵃ	A-0	A-60
Store-rooms, workshops, pantries, etc. (13)	A-60	A-30	A-15	A-60	A-0	A-15	A-30	A-30	A-0	A-0	A-0	A-0	A-0	A-0
Other spaces in which flammable liquids are stowed (14)	A-60	A-60	A-60	A-60	A-0	A-30	A-60	A-60	A-0	A-0	A-0	A-0	A-0	A-0

Notes: To be applied to tables 9.1 and 9.2, as appropriate.

a   Where adjacent spaces are in the same numerical category and superscript "a" appears, a bulkhead or deck between such spaces need not be fitted if deemed unnecessary by the Administration. For example, in category (12) a bulkhead need not be required between a galley and its annexed pantries provided the pantry bulkhead and decks maintain the integrity of the galley boundaries. A bulkhead is, however, required between a galley and machinery space even though both spaces are in category (12).

b   The ship's side, to the waterline in the lightest seagoing condition, superstructure and deckhouse sides situated below and adjacent to liferafts and evacuation slides may be reduced to "A-30".

c   Where public toilets are installed completely within the stairway enclosure, the public toilet bulkhead within the stairway enclosure can be of "B" class integrity.

d   Where spaces of categories (6), (7), (8) and (9) are located completely within the outer perimeter of the assembly station, the bulkheads of these spaces are allowed to be of "B-0" class integrity. Control positions for audio, video and light installations may be considered as part of the assembly station.

(6)   *Accommodation spaces of minor fire risk*

Cabins containing furniture and furnishings of restricted fire risk.

Offices and dispensaries containing furniture and furnishings of restricted fire risk.

Public spaces containing furniture and furnishings of restricted fire risk and having a deck area of less than 50 m^2.

(7)   *Accommodation spaces of moderate fire risk*

Spaces as in category (6) above but containing furniture and furnishings of other than restricted fire risk.

Public spaces containing furniture and furnishings of restricted fire risk and having a deck area of 50 m^2 or more.

Isolated lockers and small store-rooms in accommodation spaces having areas less than 4 m^2 (in which flammable liquids are not stowed).

Sale shops. Motion picture projection and film stowage rooms. Diet kitchens (containing no open flame).

Cleaning gear lockers (in which flammable liquids are not stowed).

Laboratories (in which flammable liquids are not stowed).

Pharmacies.

Small drying rooms (having a deck area of 4 m^2 or less).

Specie rooms.

Operating rooms.

(8)   *Accommodation spaces of greater fire risk*

Public spaces containing furniture and furnishings of other than restricted fire risk and having a deck area of 50 m^2 or more.

Barber shops and beauty parlours.

Saunas.

(9)   *Sanitary and similar spaces*

Communal sanitary facilities, showers, baths, water closets, etc.

Small laundry rooms.

Indoor swimming pool area.

Isolated pantries containing no cooking appliances in accommodation spaces.

Private sanitary facilities shall be considered a portion of the space in which they are located.

(10) *Tanks, voids and auxiliary machinery spaces having little or no fire risk*

Water tanks forming part of the ship's structure.

Voids and cofferdams.

Auxiliary machinery spaces which do not contain machinery having a pressure lubrication system and where storage of combustibles is prohibited, such as:

ventilation and air-conditioning rooms; windlass room; steering gear room; stabilizer equipment room; electrical propulsion motor room; rooms containing section switchboards and purely electrical equipment other than oil-filled electrical transformers (above 10 kVA); shaft alleys and pipe tunnels; and spaces for pumps and refrigeration machinery (not handling or using flammable liquids).

Closed trunks serving the spaces listed above.

Other closed trunks such as pipe and cable trunks.

(11) *Auxiliary machinery spaces, cargo spaces, cargo and other oil tanks and other similar spaces of moderate fire risk*

Cargo oil tanks.

Cargo holds, trunkways and hatchways.

Refrigerated chambers.

Oil fuel tanks (where installed in a separate space with no machinery).

Shaft alleys and pipe tunnels allowing storage of combustibles.

Auxiliary machinery spaces as in category (10) which contain machinery having a pressure lubrication system or where storage of combustibles is permitted.

Oil fuel filling stations.

Spaces containing oil-filled electrical transformers (above 10 kVA).

Spaces containing turbine and reciprocating steam engine driven auxiliary generators and small internal combustion engines of power output up to 110 kW driving generators, sprinkler, drencher or fire pumps, bilge pumps, etc.

Closed trunks serving the spaces listed above.

(12) *Machinery spaces and main galleys*

Main propulsion machinery rooms (other than electric propulsion motor rooms) and boiler rooms.

Auxiliary machinery spaces other than those in categories (10) and (11) which contain internal combustion machinery or other oil-burning, heating or pumping units.

Main galleys and annexes.

Trunks and casings to the spaces listed above.

(13) *Store-rooms, workshops, pantries, etc.*

Main pantries not annexed to galleys.

Main laundry.

Large drying rooms (having a deck area of more than 4 m^2).

Miscellaneous stores.

Mail and baggage rooms.

Garbage rooms.

Workshops (not part of machinery spaces, galleys, etc.).

Lockers and store-rooms having areas greater than 4 m^2, other than those spaces that have provisions for the storage of flammable liquids.

(14) *Other spaces in which flammable liquids are stowed*

Paint lockers.

Store-rooms containing flammable liquids (including dyes, medicines, etc.).

Laboratories (in which flammable liquids are stowed).

.3 Where a single value is shown for the fire integrity of a boundary between two spaces, that value shall apply in all cases.

.4 Notwithstanding the provisions of paragraph 2.2.2, there are no special requirements for material or integrity of boundaries where only a dash appears in the tables.

.5 The Administration shall determine in respect of category (5) spaces whether the insulation values in table 9.1 shall apply to ends of deckhouses and superstructures, and whether the insulation values in table 9.2 shall apply to weather decks. In no case shall the requirements of category (5) of tables 9.1 or 9.2 necessitate enclosure of spaces which in the opinion of the Administration need not be enclosed.

2.2.3.3 Continuous ''B'' class ceilings or linings, in association with the relevant decks or bulkheads, may be accepted as contributing, wholly or in part, to the required insulation and integrity of a division.

2.2.3.4 *Construction and arrangement of saunas*

2.2.3.4.1 The perimeter of the sauna shall be of "A" class boundaries and may include changing rooms, showers and toilets. The sauna shall be insulated to "A-60" standard against other spaces except those inside of the perimeter and spaces of categories (5), (9) and (10).

2.2.3.4.2 Bathrooms with direct access to saunas may be considered as part of them. In such cases, the door between sauna and the bathroom need not comply with fire safety requirements.

2.2.3.4.3 The traditional wooden lining on the bulkheads and ceiling are permitted in the sauna. The ceiling above the oven shall be lined with a non-combustible plate with an air gap of at least 30 mm. The distance from the hot surfaces to combustible materials shall be at least 500 mm or the combustible materials shall be protected (e.g., non-combustible plate with an air gap of at least 30 mm).

2.2.3.4.4 The traditional wooden benches are permitted to be used in the sauna.

2.2.3.4.5 The sauna door shall open outwards by pushing.

2.2.3.4.6 Electrically heated ovens shall be provided with a timer.

2.2.4 *Fire integrity of bulkheads and decks in ships carrying not more than 36 passengers*

2.2.4.1 In addition to complying with the specific provisions for fire integrity of bulkheads and decks of passenger ships, the minimum fire integrity of bulkheads and decks shall be as prescribed in tables 9.3 and 9.4.

2.2.4.2 The following requirements shall govern application of the tables:

.1 Tables 9.3 and 9.4 shall apply respectively to the bulkheads and decks separating adjacent spaces.

.2 For determining the appropriate fire integrity standards to be applied to divisions between adjacent spaces, such spaces are classified according to their fire risk as shown in categories (1) to (11) below. Where the contents and use of a space are such that there is a doubt as to its classification for the purpose of this regulation, or where it is possible to assign two or more classifications to a space, it shall be treated as a space within the relevant category having the most stringent boundary requirements. Smaller, enclosed rooms within a space that have less than 30% communicating openings to that space are considered separate spaces. The fire integrity of the boundary bulkheads and decks of such smaller rooms shall be as prescribed in tables 9.3 and 9.4. The title of each category is intended to be typical rather than restrictive. The number in parentheses preceding each category refers to the applicable column or row in the tables.

Table 9.3 – Fire integrity of bulkheads separating adjacent spaces

Spaces		(1)	(2)	(3)	(4)	(5)	(6)	(7)	(8)	(9)	(10)	(11)
Control stations	(1)	A-0^c	A-0	A-60	A-0	A-15	A-60	A-15	A-60	A-60	*	A-60
Corridors	(2)		C^c	B-0^c	A-0^a B-0^c	B-0^c	A-60	A-0	A-0	A-15 A-0^d	*	A-15
Accommodation spaces	(3)			C^c	A-0^a B-0^c	B-0^c	A-60	A-0	A-0	A-15 A-0^d	*	A-30 A-0^d
Stairways	(4)				A-0^a B-0^c	A-0^a B-0^c	A-60	A-0	A-0	A-15 A-0^d	*	A-15
Service spaces (low risk)	(5)					C^c	A-60	A-0	A-0	A-0	*	A-0
Machinery spaces of category A	(6)						*	A-0	A-0	A-60	*	A-60
Other machinery spaces	(7)							A-0^b	A-0	A-0	*	A-0
Cargo spaces	(8)								*	A-0	*	A-0
Service spaces (high risk)	(9)									A-0^b	*	A-30
Open decks	(10)											A-0
Special category and ro-ro spaces	(11)											A-0

See notes following table 9.4.

Table 9.4 – Fire integrity of decks separating adjacent spaces

Space below ↓ \ Space above →	(1)	(2)	(3)	(4)	(5)	(6)	(7)	(8)	(9)	(10)	(11)
Control stations	(1)	A-0	A-0	A-0	A-0	A-0	A-60	A-0	A-0	A-0	*	A-30
Corridors	(2)	A-0	*	*	A-0	*	A-60	A-0	A-0	A-0	*	A-0
Accommodation spaces	(3)	A-60	A-0	*	A-0	*	A-60	A-0	A-0	A-0	*	A-30 A-0^d
Stairways	(4)	A-0	A-0	A-0	*	A-0	A-60	A-0	A-0	A-0	*	A-0
Service spaces (low risk)	(5)	A-15	A-0	A-0	A-0	*	A-60	A-0	A-0	A-0	*	A-0
Machinery spaces of category A	(6)	A-60	A-60	A-60	A-60	A-60	*	A-60^f	A-30	A-60	*	A-60
Other machinery spaces	(7)	A-15	A-0	A-0	A-0	A-0	A-0	*	A-0	A-0	*	A-0
Cargo spaces	(8)	A-60	A-0	A-0	A-0	A-0	A-60	A-0	*	A-0	*	A-0
Service spaces (high risk)	(9)	A-60	A-30 A-0^d	A-30 A-0^d	A-30 A-0^d	A-0	A-60	A-0	A-0	A-0	*	A-30
Open decks	(10)	*	*	*	*	*	*	*	*	*	–	A-0
Special category and ro-ro spaces	(11)	A-60	A-15	A-30 A-0d	A-15	A-0	A-30	A-0	A-0	A-30	A-0	A-0

Notes: To be applied to both tables 9.3 and 9.4 as appropriate.

a   For clarification as to which applies, see paragraphs 2.2.2 and 2.2.5.

b   Where spaces are of the same numerical category and superscript "b" appears, a bulkhead or deck of the rating shown in the tables is only required when the adjacent spaces are for a different purpose (e.g., in category (9)). A galley next to a galley does not require a bulkhead, but a galley next to a paint room requires an "A-0" bulkhead.

c   Bulkheads separating the wheelhouse and chartroom from each other may have a "B-0" rating.

d   See paragraphs 2.2.4.2.3 and 2.2.4.2.4.

e   For the application of paragraph 2.2.1.1.2, "B-0" and "C", where appearing in table 9.3, shall be read as "A-0".

f   Fire insulation need not be fitted if the machinery space in category (7), in the opinion of the Administration, has little or no fire risk.

*   Where an asterisk appears in the tables, the division is required to be of steel or other equivalent material, but is not required to be of "A" class standard. However, where a deck, except in a category (10) space, is penetrated for the passage of electric cables, pipes and vent ducts, such penetrations shall be made tight to prevent the passage of flame and smoke. Divisions between control stations (emergency generators) and open decks may have air intake openings without means for closure, unless a fixed gas fire-extinguishing system is fitted.
    For the application of paragraph 2.2.1.1.2, an asterisk, where appearing in table 9.4, except for categories (8) and (10), shall be read as "A-0".

(1) **Control stations**

Spaces containing emergency sources of power and lighting.

Wheelhouse and chartroom.

Spaces containing the ship's radio equipment.

Fire control stations.

Control room for propulsion machinery when located outside the machinery space.

Spaces containing centralized fire alarm equipment.

(2) *Corridors*

Passenger and crew corridors and lobbies.

(3) *Accommodation spaces*

Spaces as defined in regulation 3.1 excluding corridors.

(4) *Stairways*

Interior stairways, lifts, totally enclosed emergency escape trunks, and escalators (other than those wholly contained within the machinery spaces) and enclosures thereto.

In this connection, a stairway which is enclosed only at one level shall be regarded as part of the space from which it is not separated by a fire door.

(5) *Service spaces (low risk)*

Lockers and store-rooms not having provisions for the storage of flammable liquids and having areas less than 4 m^2 and drying rooms and laundries.

(6) *Machinery spaces of category A*

Spaces as defined in regulation 3.31.

(7) *Other machinery spaces*

Electrical equipment rooms (auto-telephone exchange, air-conditioning duct spaces).

Spaces as defined in regulation 3.30 excluding machinery spaces of category A.

(8) *Cargo spaces*

All spaces used for cargo (including cargo oil tanks) and trunkways and hatchways to such spaces, other than special category spaces.

(9) *Service spaces (high risk)*

Galleys, pantries containing cooking appliances, paint lockers, lockers and store-rooms having areas of 4 m^2 or more, spaces for the storage of flammable liquids, saunas and workshops other than those forming part of the machinery spaces.

(10) *Open decks*

Open deck spaces and enclosed promenades having little or no fire risk. To be considered in this category, enclosed promenades shall have no significant fire risk, meaning that furnishing shall be restricted to deck furniture. In addition, such spaces shall be naturally ventilated by permanent openings.

Air spaces (the space outside superstructures and deckhouses).

(11) *Special category and ro–ro spaces*

Spaces as defined in regulations 3.41 and 3.46.

.3 In determining the applicable fire integrity standard of a boundary between two spaces within a main vertical zone or horizontal zone which is not protected by an automatic sprinkler system complying with the provisions of the Fire Safety Systems Code or between such zones neither of which is so protected, the higher of the two values given in the tables shall apply.

.4 In determining the applicable fire integrity standard of a boundary between two spaces within a main vertical zone or horizontal zone which is protected by an automatic sprinkler system complying with the provisions of the Fire Safety Systems Code or between such zones both of which are so protected, the lesser of the two values given in the tables shall apply. Where a zone with sprinklers and a zone without sprinklers meet within accommodation and service spaces, the higher of the two values given in the tables shall apply to the division between the zones.

2.2.4.3 Continuous "B" class ceilings or linings, in association with the relevant decks or bulkheads, may be accepted as contributing, wholly or in part, to the required insulation and integrity of a division.

2.2.4.4 External boundaries which are required in regulation 11.2 to be of steel or other equivalent material may be pierced for the fitting of windows and sidescuttles provided that there is no requirement for such boundaries of passenger ships to have "A" class integrity. Similarly, in such boundaries which are not required to have "A" class integrity, doors may be constructed of materials which are to the satisfaction of the Administration.

2.2.4.5 Saunas shall comply with paragraph 2.2.3.4.

2.2.5 *Protection of stairways and lifts in accommodation area*

2.2.5.1 Stairways shall be within enclosures formed of "A" class divisions, with positive means of closure at all openings, except that:

.1 a stairway connecting only two decks need not be enclosed, provided the integrity of the deck is maintained by proper bulkheads or self-closing doors in one 'tween-deck space. When a stairway is closed in one 'tween-deck space, the stairway enclosure shall be protected in accordance with the tables for decks in paragraphs 2.2.3 or 2.2.4; and

.2 stairways may be fitted in the open in a public space, provided they lie wholly within the public space.

2.2.5.2 Lift trunks shall be so fitted as to prevent the passage of smoke and flame from one 'tween-deck to another and shall be provided with means of closing so as to permit the control of draught and smoke. Machinery for lifts located within stairway enclosures shall be arranged in a separate room, surrounded by steel boundaries, except that small passages for lift cables are permitted. Lifts which open into spaces other than corridors, public spaces, special category spaces, stairways and external areas shall not open into stairways included in the means of escape.

2.3 *Cargo ships except tankers*

2.3.1 *Methods of protection in accommodation area*

2.3.1.1 One of the following methods of protection shall be adopted in accommodation and service spaces and control stations:

.1 *Method IC* – The construction of internal divisional bulkheads of non-combustible "B" or "C" class divisions generally without the installation of an automatic sprinkler, fire detection and fire alarm system in the accommodation and service spaces, except as required by regulation 7.5.5.1; or

.2 *Method IIC* – The fitting of an automatic sprinkler, fire detection and fire alarm system as required by regulation 7.5.5.2 for the detection and extinction of fire in all spaces in which fire might be expected to originate, generally with no restriction on the type of internal divisional bulkheads; or

.3 *Method IIIC* – The fitting of a fixed fire detection and fire alarm system as required by regulation 7.5.5.3 in spaces in which a fire might be expected to originate, generally with no restriction on the type of internal divisional bulkheads, except that in no case shall the area of any accommodation space or spaces bounded by an "A" or "B" class division exceed 50 m^2. However, consideration may be given by the Administration to increasing this area for public spaces.

2.3.1.2 The requirements for the use of non-combustible materials in the construction and insulation of boundary bulkheads of machinery spaces, control stations, service spaces, etc., and the protection of the above stairway enclosures and corridors will be common to all three methods outlined in paragraph 2.3.1.1.

2.3.2 *Bulkheads within accommodation area*

2.3.2.1   Bulkheads required to be "B" class divisions shall extend from deck to deck and to the shell or other boundaries. However, where a continuous "B" class ceiling or lining is fitted on both sides of the bulkhead, the bulkhead may terminate at the continuous ceiling or lining.

2.3.2.2   *Method IC* – Bulkheads not required by this or other regulations for cargo ships to be "A" or "B" class divisions shall be of at least "C" class construction.

2.3.2.3   *Method IIC* – There shall be no restriction on the construction of bulkheads not required by this or other regulations for cargo ships to be "A" or "B" class divisions except in individual cases where "C" class bulkheads are required in accordance with table 9.5.

2.3.2.4   *Method IIIC* – There shall be no restriction on the construction of bulkheads not required for cargo ships to be "A" or "B" class divisions except that the area of any accommodation space or spaces bounded by a continuous "A" or "B" class division shall in no case exceed 50 m^2, except in individual cases where "C" class bulkheads are required in accordance with table 9.5. However, consideration may be given by the Administration to increasing this area for public spaces.

2.3.3 *Fire integrity of bulkheads and decks*

2.3.3.1   In addition to complying with the specific provisions for fire integrity of bulkheads and decks of cargo ships, the minimum fire integrity of bulkheads and decks shall be as prescribed in tables 9.5 and 9.6.

2.3.3.2   The following requirements shall govern application of the tables:

.1   Tables 9.5 and 9.6 shall apply respectively to the bulkheads and decks separating adjacent spaces.

.2   For determining the appropriate fire integrity standards to be applied to divisions between adjacent spaces, such spaces are classified according to their fire risk as shown in categories (1) to (11) below. Where the contents and use of a space are such that there is a doubt as to its classification for the purpose of this regulation, or where it is possible to assign two or more classifications to a space, it shall be treated as a space within the relevant category having the most stringent boundary requirements. Smaller, enclosed rooms within a space that have less than 30% communicating openings to that space are considered separate spaces. The fire integrity of the boundary bulkheads and decks of such smaller rooms shall be as prescribed in tables 9.5 and 9.6. The title of each category is intended to be typical rather than restrictive. The number in parentheses preceding each category refers to the applicable column or row in the tables.

Table 9.5 – Fire integrity of bulkheads separating adjacent spaces

Spaces		(1)	(2)	(3)	(4)	(5)	(6)	(7)	(8)	(9)	(10)	(11)
Control stations	(1)	A-0c	A-0	A-60	A-0	A-15	A-60	A-15	A-60	A-60	*	A-60
Corridors	(2)		C	B-0	B-0 A-0c	B-0	A-60	A-0	A-0	A-0	*	A-30
Accommodation spaces	(3)			C a, b	B-0 A-0c	B-0	A-60	A-0	A-0	A-0	*	A-30
Stairways	(4)				B-0 A-0c	B-0 A-0c	A-60	A-0	A-0	A-0	*	A-30
Service spaces (low risk)	(5)					C	A-60	A-0	A-0	A-0	*	A-0
Machinery spaces of category A	(6)						*	A-0	A-0g	A-60	*	A-60f
Other machinery spaces	(7)							A-0d	A-0	A-0	*	A-0
Cargo spaces	(8)								*	A-0	*	A-0
Service spaces (high risk)	(9)									A-0d	*	A-30
Open decks	(10)										-	A-0
Ro-ro and vehicle spaces	(11)											*h

See notes following table 9.6.

206

Table 9.6 – Fire integrity of decks separating adjacent spaces

Space below↓ / Space above→	(1)	(2)	(3)	(4)	(5)	(6)	(7)	(8)	(9)	(10)	(11)
Control stations (1)	A-0	A-0	A-0	A-0	A-0	A-60	A-0	A-0	A-0	*	A-60
Corridors (2)	A-0	*	*	A-0	A-0	A-60	A-0	A-0	A-0	*	A-30
Accommodation spaces (3)	A-60	A-0	*	A-0	A-0	A-60	A-0	A-0	A-0	*	A-30
Stairways (4)	A-0	A-0	A-0	*	A-0	A-60	A-0	A-0	A-0	*	A-30
Service spaces (low risk) (5)	A-15	A-0	A-0	A-0	*	A-60	A-0	A-0	A-0	*	A-0
Machinery spaces of category A (6)	A-60	A-60	A-60	A-60	A-60	*	A-60^i	A-30	A-60	*	A-60
Other machinery spaces (7)	A-15	A-0	A-0	A-0	A-0	A-0	*	A-0	A-0	*	A-0
Cargo spaces (8)	A-60	A-0	A-0	A-0	A-0	A-60	A-0	*	A-0	*	A-0
Service spaces (high risk) (9)	A-60	A-0	A-0	A-0	A-0	A-60	A-0	A-0	A-0^d	*	A-30
Open decks (10)	*	*	*	*	*	*	*	*	*	–	*
Ro-ro and vehicle spaces (11)	A-60	A-30	A-30	A-30	A-0	A-60	A-0	A-0	A-30	*	*^{h}

Notes: To be applied to tables 9.5 and 9.6, as appropriate.

a No special requirements are imposed upon bulkheads in methods IIC and IIIC fire protection.

b In case of method IIIC, "B" class bulkheads of "B-0" rating shall be provided between spaces or groups of spaces of 50 m^2 and over in area.

c For clarification as to which applies, see paragraphs 2.3.2 and 2.3.4.

d Where spaces are of the same numerical category and superscript "d" appears, a bulkhead or deck of the rating shown in the tables is only required when the adjacent spaces are for a different purpose (e.g., in category (9)). A galley next to a galley does not require a bulkhead, but a galley next to a paint room requires an "A-0" bulkhead.

e Bulkheads separating the wheelhouse, chartroom and radio room from each other may have a "B-0" rating.

f An "A-0" rating may be used if no dangerous goods are intended to be carried or if such goods are stowed not less than 3 m horizontally from such a bulkhead.

g For cargo spaces in which dangerous goods are intended to be carried, regulation 19.3.8 applies.

h Bulkheads and decks separating ro–ro spaces shall be capable of being closed reasonably gastight and such divisions shall have "A" class integrity in so far as reasonable and practicable, if in the opinion of the Administration it has little or no fire risk.

i Fire insulation need not be fitted in the machinery space in category (7) if, in the opinion of the Administration, it has little or no fire risk.

* Where an asterisk appears in the tables, the division is required to be of steel or other equivalent material but is not required to be of "A" class standard. However, where a deck, except an open deck, is penetrated for the passage of electric cables, pipes and vent ducts, such penetrations shall be made tight to prevent the passage of flame and smoke. Divisions between control stations (emergency generators) and open decks may have air intake openings without means for closure, unless a fixed gas fire-extinguishing system is fitted.

(1) *Control stations*

Spaces containing emergency sources of power and lighting.

Wheelhouse and chartroom.

Spaces containing the ship's radio equipment.

Fire control stations.

Control room for propulsion machinery when located outside the machinery space.

Spaces containing centralized fire alarm equipment.

(2) *Corridors*

Corridors and lobbies.

(3) *Accommodation spaces*

Spaces as defined in regulation 3.1, excluding corridors.

(4) *Stairways*

Interior stairway, lifts, totally enclosed emergency escape trunks, and escalators (other than those wholly contained within the machinery spaces) and enclosures thereto.

In this connection, a stairway which is enclosed only at one level shall be regarded as part of the space from which it is not separated by a fire door.

(5) *Service spaces (low risk)*

Lockers and store-rooms not having provisions for the storage of flammable liquids and having areas less than 4 m^2 and drying rooms and laundries.

(6) *Machinery spaces of category A*

Spaces as defined in regulation 3.31.

(7) *Other machinery spaces*

Electrical equipment rooms (auto-telephone exchange, air-conditioning duct spaces).

Spaces as defined in regulation 3.30, excluding machinery spaces of category A.

(8) *Cargo spaces*

All spaces used for cargo (including cargo oil tanks) and trunkways and hatchways to such spaces.

(9) *Service spaces (high risk)*

Galleys, pantries containing cooking appliances, saunas, paint lockers and store-rooms having areas of 4 m^2 or more, spaces for the storage of flammable liquids, and workshops other than those forming part of the machinery spaces.

(10) *Open decks*

Open deck spaces and enclosed promenades having little or no fire risk. To be considered in this category, enclosed promenades shall have no significant fire risk, meaning that furnishings shall be restricted to deck furniture. In addition, such spaces shall be naturally ventilated by permanent openings.

Air spaces (the space outside superstructures and deck-houses).

(11) *Ro–ro and vehicle spaces*

Ro–ro spaces as defined in regulation 3.41.

Vehicle spaces as defined in regulation 3.49.

2.3.3.3 Continuous "B" class ceilings or linings, in association with the relevant decks or bulkheads, may be accepted as contributing, wholly or in part, to the required insulation and integrity of a division.

2.3.3.4 External boundaries which are required in regulation 11.2 to be of steel or other equivalent material may be pierced for the fitting of windows and sidescuttles provided that there is no requirement for such boundaries of cargo ships to have "A" class integrity. Similarly, in such boundaries which are not required to have "A" class integrity, doors may be constructed of materials which are to the satisfaction of the Administration.

2.3.3.5 Saunas shall comply with paragraph 2.2.3.4.

2.3.4 *Protection of stairways and lift trunks in accommodation spaces, service spaces and control stations*

2.3.4.1 Stairways which penetrate only a single deck shall be protected, at a minimum, at one level by at least "B-0" class divisions and self-closing doors. Lifts which penetrate only a single deck shall be surrounded by "A-0" class divisions with steel doors at both levels. Stairways and lift trunks which penetrate more than a single deck shall be surrounded by at least "A-0" class divisions and be protected by self-closing doors at all levels.

2.3.4.2 On ships having accommodation for 12 persons or less, where stairways penetrate more than a single deck and where there are at least two escape routes direct to the open deck at every accommodation level, the "A-0" requirements of paragraph 2.3.4.1 may be reduced to "B-0".

2.4 *Tankers*

2.4.1 *Application*

For tankers, only method IC as defined in paragraph 2.3.1.1 shall be used.

2.4.2 *Fire integrity of bulkheads and decks*

2.4.2.1 In lieu of paragraph 2.3 and in addition to complying with the specific provisions for fire integrity of bulkheads and decks of tankers, the minimum fire integrity of bulkheads and decks shall be as prescribed in tables 9.7 and 9.8.

2.4.2.2 The following requirements shall govern application of the tables:

.1   Tables 9.7 and 9.8 shall apply respectively to the bulkhead and decks separating adjacent spaces.

.2   For determining the appropriate fire integrity standards to be applied to divisions between adjacent spaces, such spaces are classified according to their fire risk as shown in categories (1) to (10) below. Where the contents and use of a space are such that there is a doubt as to its classification for the purpose of this regulation, or where it is possible to assign two or more classifications to a space, it shall be treated as a space within the relevant category having the most stringent boundary requirements. Smaller, enclosed areas within a space that have less than 30% communicating openings to that space are considered separate areas. The fire integrity of the boundary bulkheads and decks of such smaller spaces shall be as prescribed in tables 9.7 and 9.8. The title of each category is intended to be typical rather than restrictive. The number in parentheses preceding each category refers to the applicable column or row in the tables.

(1)   *Control stations*

Spaces containing emergency sources of power and lighting.

Wheelhouse and chartroom.

Spaces containing the ship's radio equipment.

Fire control stations.

Control room for propulsion machinery when located outside the machinery space.

Spaces containing centralized fire alarm equipment.

(2)   *Corridors*

Corridors and lobbies.

(3)   *Accommodation spaces*

Spaces as defined in regulation 3.1, excluding corridors.

(4)   *Stairways*

Interior stairways, lifts, totally enclosed emergency escape trunks, and escalators (other than those wholly contained within the machinery spaces) and enclosures thereto.

In this connection, a stairway which is enclosed only at one level shall be regarded as part of the space from which it is not separated by a fire door.

(5)   *Service spaces (low risk)*

Lockers and store-rooms not having provisions for the storage of flammable liquids and having areas less than 4 m^2 and drying rooms and laundries.

(6)   *Machinery spaces of category A*

Spaces as defined in regulation 3.31.

(7)   *Other machinery spaces*

Electrical equipment rooms (auto-telephone exchange and air-conditioning duct spaces).

Spaces as defined in regulation 3.30, excluding machinery spaces of category A.

(8)   *Cargo pump-rooms*

Spaces containing cargo pumps and entrances and trunks to such spaces.

(9)   *Service spaces (high risk)*

Galleys, pantries containing cooking appliances, saunas, paint lockers and store-rooms having areas of 4 m^2 or more, spaces for the storage of flammable liquids and workshops other than those forming part of the machinery spaces.

(10) *Open decks*

Open deck spaces and enclosed promenades having little or no fire risk. To be considered in this category, enclosed promenades shall have no significant fire risk, meaning that furnishings shall be restricted to deck furniture. In addition, such spaces shall be naturally ventilated by permanent openings.

Air spaces (the space outside superstructures and deck-houses).

2.4.2.3   Continuous "B" class ceilings or linings, in association with the relevant decks or bulkheads, may be accepted as contributing, wholly or in part, to the required insulation and integrity of a division.

2.4.2.4   External boundaries which are required in regulation 11.2 to be of steel or other equivalent material may be pierced for the fitting of windows

Table 9.7 – Fire integrity of bulkheads separating adjacent spaces

Spaces		(1)	(2)	(3)	(4)	(5)	(6)	(7)	(8)	(9)	(10)
Control stations	(1)	A-0[c]	A-0	A-60	A-0	A-15	A-60	A-15	A-60	A-60	*
Corridors	(2)		C	B-0	B-0 A-0[a]	B-0	A-60	A-0	A-60	A-0	*
Accommodation spaces	(3)			C	B-0 A-0[a]	B-0	A-60	A-0	A-60	A-0	*
Stairways	(4)				B-0 A-0[a]	B-0 A-0[a]	A-60	A-0	A-60	A-0	*
Service spaces (low risk)	(5)					C	A-60	A-0	A-60	A-0	*
Machinery spaces of category A	(6)						*	A-0	A-0[d]	A-60	*
Other machinery spaces	(7)							A-0[b]	A-0	A-0	*
Cargo pump-rooms	(8)								*	A-60	*
Service spaces (high risk)	(9)									A-0[b]	*
Open decks	(10)										–

See notes following table 9.8.

Table 9.8 – Fire integrity of decks separating adjacent spaces

Space below ↓ / Space above →	(1)	(2)	(3)	(4)	(5)	(6)	(7)	(8)	(9)	(10)
Control stations (1)	A-0	A-0	A-0	A-0	A-0	A-60	A-0	-	A-0	*
Corridors (2)	A-0	*	*	A-0	*	A-60	A-0	-	A-0	*
Accommodation spaces (3)	A-60	A-0	*	A-0	*	A-60	A-0	-	A-0	*
Stairways (4)	A-0	A-0	A-0	*	A-0	A-60	A-0	-	A-0	*
Service spaces (low risk) (5)	A-15	A-0	A-0	A-0	*	A-60	A-0	-	A-0	*
Machinery spaces of category A (6)	A-60	A-60	A-60	A-60	A-60	*	A-60c	A-0	A-60	*
Other machinery spaces (7)	A-15	A-0	A-0	A-0	A-0	A-0d	*	A-0	A-0	*
Cargo pump-rooms (8)	-	-	-	-	-	A-0d	A-0	*	-	*
Service spaces (high risk) (9)	A-60	A-0	A-0	A-0	A-0	A-60	A-0	-	A-0b	*
Open decks (10)	*	*	*	*	*	*	*	*	*	-

Notes: To be applied to tables 9.7 and 9.8 as appropriate.

a For clarification as to which applies, see paragraphs 2.3.2 and 2.3.4.

b Where spaces are of the same numerical category and superscript "b" appears, a bulkhead or deck of the rating shown in the tables is only required when the adjacent spaces are for a different purpose (e.g., in category (9)). A galley next to a galley does not require a bulkhead but a galley next to a paint room requires an "A-0" bulkhead.

c Bulkheads separating the wheelhouse, chartroom and radio room from each other may have a "B-0" rating.

d Bulkheads and decks between cargo pump-rooms and machinery spaces of category A may be penetrated by cargo pump shaft glands and similar gland penetrations, provided that gastight seals with efficient lubrication or other means of ensuring the permanence of the gas seal are fitted in way of the bulkheads or deck.

e Fire insulation need not be fitted in the machinery space in category (7) if, in the opinion of the Administration, it has little or no fire risk.

* Where an asterisk appears in the table, the division is required to be of steel or other equivalent material, but is not required to be of "A" class standard. However, where a deck, except an open deck, is penetrated for the passage of electric cables, pipes and vent ducts, such penetrations shall be made tight to prevent the passage of flame and smoke. Divisions between control stations (emergency generators) and open decks may have air intake openings without means for closure, unless a fixed gas fire-extinguishing system is fitted.

213

and sidescuttles provided that there is no requirement for such boundaries of tankers to have "A" class integrity. Similarly, in such boundaries which are not required to have "A" class integrity, doors may be constructed of materials which are to the satisfaction of the Administration.

2.4.2.5   Exterior boundaries of superstructures and deckhouses enclosing accommodation and including any overhanging decks which support such accommodation shall be constructed of steel and insulated to "A-60" standard for the whole of the portions which face the cargo area and on the outward sides for a distance of 3 m from the end boundary facing the cargo area. The distance of 3 m shall be measured horizontally and parallel to the middle line of the ship from the boundary which faces the cargo area at each deck level. In the case of the sides of those superstructures and deckhouses, such insulation shall be carried up to the underside of the deck of the navigation bridge.

2.4.2.6   Skylights to cargo pump-rooms shall be of steel, shall not contain any glass and shall be capable of being closed from outside the pump-room.

2.4.2.7   Construction and arrangement of saunas shall comply with paragraph 2.2.3.4.

3   Penetrations in fire-resisting divisions and prevention of heat transmission

3.1   Where "A" class divisions are penetrated, such penetrations shall be tested in accordance with the Fire Test Procedures Code, subject to the provisions of paragraph 4.1.1.5. In the case of ventilation ducts, paragraphs 7.1.2 and 7.3.1 apply. However, where a pipe penetration is made of steel or equivalent material having a thickness of 3 mm or greater and a length of not less than 900 mm (preferably 450 mm on each side of the division), and there are no openings, testing is not required. Such penetrations shall be suitably insulated by extension of the insulation at the same level of the division.

3.2   Where "B" class divisions are penetrated for the passage of electric cables, pipes, trunks, ducts, etc., or for the fitting of ventilation terminals, lighting fixtures and similar devices, arrangements shall be made to ensure that the fire resistance is not impaired, subject to the provisions of paragraph 7.3.2. Pipes other than steel or copper that penetrate "B" class divisions shall be protected by either:

.1   a fire-tested penetration device suitable for the fire resistance of the division pierced and the type of pipe used; or

.2   a steel sleeve, having a thickness of not less than 1.8 mm and a length of not less than 900 mm for pipe diameters of 150 mm or more and not less than 600 mm for pipe diameters of less than 150 mm (preferably equally divided to each side of the division).

The pipe shall be connected to the ends of the sleeve by flanges or couplings; or the clearance between the sleeve and the pipe shall not exceed 2.5 mm; or any clearance between pipe and sleeve shall be made tight by means of non-combustible or other suitable material.

3.3 Uninsulated metallic pipes penetrating "A" or "B" class divisions shall be of materials having a melting temperature which exceeds 950°C for "A-0" and 850°C for "B-0" class divisions.

3.4 In approving structural fire protection details, the Administration shall have regard to the risk of heat transmission at intersections and terminal points of required thermal barriers. The insulation of a deck or bulkhead shall be carried past the penetration, intersection or terminal point for a distance of at least 450 mm in the case of steel and aluminium structures. If a space is divided with a deck or a bulkhead of "A" class standard having insulation of different values, the insulation with the higher value shall continue on the deck or bulkhead with the insulation of the lesser value for a distance of at least 450 mm.

4   Protection of openings in fire-resisting divisions

4.1 *Openings in bulkheads and decks in passenger ships*

4.1.1 *Openings in "A" class divisions*

4.1.1.1 Except for hatches between cargo, special category, store, and baggage spaces, and between such spaces and the weather decks, openings shall be provided with permanently attached means of closing which shall be at least as effective for resisting fires as the divisions in which they are fitted.

4.1.1.2 The construction of doors and door frames in "A" class divisions, with the means of securing them when closed, shall provide resistance to fire as well as to the passage of smoke and flame equivalent to that of the bulkheads in which the doors are situated, this being determined in accordance with the Fire Test Procedures Code. Such doors and door frames shall be constructed of steel or other equivalent material. Watertight doors need not be insulated.

4.1.1.3 It shall be possible for each door to be opened and closed from each side of the bulkhead by one person only.

4.1.1.4 Fire doors in main vertical zone bulkheads, galley boundaries and stairway enclosures other than power-operated watertight doors and those which are normally locked shall satisfy the following requirements:

.1   the doors shall be self-closing and be capable of closing with an angle of inclination of up to 3.5° opposing closure;

.2 the approximate time of closure for hinged fire doors shall be no more than 40 s and no less than 10 s from the beginning of their movement with the ship in upright position. The approximate uniform rate of closure for sliding doors shall be of no more than 0.2 m/s and no less than 0.1 m/s with the ship in upright position;

.3 the doors, except those for emergency escape trunks, shall be capable of remote release from the continuously manned central control station, either simultaneously or in groups, and shall be capable of release also individually from a position at both sides of the door. Release switches shall have an on–off function to prevent automatic resetting of the system;

.4 hold-back hooks not subject to central control station release are prohibited;

.5 a door closed remotely from the central control station shall be capable of being re-opened from both sides of the door by local control. After such local opening, the door shall automatically close again;

.6 indication shall be provided at the fire door indicator panel in the continuously manned central control station whether each door is closed;

.7 the release mechanism shall be so designed that the door will automatically close in the event of disruption of the control system or central power supply;

.8 local power accumulators for power-operated doors shall be provided in the immediate vicinity of the doors to enable the doors to be operated at least ten times (fully opened and closed) after disruption of the control system or central power supply using the local controls;

.9 disruption of the control system or central power supply at one door shall not impair the safe functioning of the other doors;

.10 remote-released sliding or power-operated doors shall be equipped with an alarm that sounds at least 5 s but no more than 10 s, after the door is released from the central control station and before the door begins to move and continues sounding until the door is completely closed;

.11 a door designed to re-open upon contacting an object in its path shall re-open not more than 1 m from the point of contact;

.12 double-leaf doors equipped with a latch necessary for their fire integrity shall have a latch that is automatically activated by the operation of the doors when released by the system;

.13 doors giving direct access to special category spaces which are power-operated and automatically closed need not be equipped with the alarms and remote-release mechanisms required in paragraphs 4.1.1.4.3 and 4.1.1.4.10;

.14 the components of the local control system shall be accessible for maintenance and adjusting;

.15 power-operated doors shall be provided with a control system of an approved type which shall be able to operate in case of fire and be in accordance with the Fire Test Procedures Code. This system shall satisfy the following requirements:

.15.1 the control system shall be able to operate the door at the temperature of at least 200°C for at least 60 min, served by the power supply;

.15.2 the power supply for all other doors not subject to fire shall not be impaired; and

.15.3 at temperatures exceeding 200°C, the control system shall be automatically isolated from the power supply and shall be capable of keeping the door closed up to at least 945°C.

4.1.1.5 In ships carrying not more than 36 passengers, where a space is protected by an automatic sprinkler fire detection and fire alarm system complying with the provisions of the Fire Safety Systems Code or fitted with a continuous "B" class ceiling, openings in decks not forming steps in main vertical zones nor bounding horizontal zones shall be closed reasonably tight and such decks shall meet the "A" class integrity requirements in so far as is reasonable and practicable in the opinion of the Administration.

4.1.1.6 The requirements for "A" class integrity of the outer boundaries of a ship shall not apply to glass partitions, windows and sidescuttles, provided that there is no requirement for such boundaries to have "A" class integrity in paragraph 4.1.3.3. The requirements for "A" class integrity of the outer boundaries of the ship shall not apply to exterior doors, except for those in superstructures and deckhouses facing life-saving appliances, embarkation and external assembly station areas, external stairs and open decks used for escape routes. Stairway enclosure doors need not meet this requirement.

4.1.1.7 Except for watertight doors, weathertight doors (semi-watertight doors), doors leading to the open deck and doors which need to be reasonably gastight, all "A" class doors located in stairways, public spaces and main vertical zone bulkheads in escape routes shall be equipped with a self-closing hose port. The material, construction and fire resistance of the hose port shall be equivalent to the door into which it is fitted, and shall be a 150 mm square clear opening with the door closed and shall be inset into the lower edge of the door, opposite the door hinges or, in the case of sliding doors, nearest the opening.

4.1.1.8   Where it is necessary that a ventilation duct passes through a main vertical zone division, a fail-safe automatic closing fire damper shall be fitted adjacent to the division. The damper shall also be capable of being manually closed from each side of the division. The operating position shall be readily accessible and be marked in red light-reflecting colour. The duct between the division and the damper shall be of steel or other equivalent material and, if necessary, insulated to comply with the requirements of paragraph 3.1. The damper shall be fitted on at least one side of the division with a visible indicator showing whether the damper is in the open position.

4.1.2   *Openings in "B" class divisions*

4.1.2.1   Doors and door frames in "B" class divisions and means of securing them shall provide a method of closure which shall have resistance to fire equivalent to that of the divisions, this being determined in accordance with the Fire Test Procedures Code except that ventilation openings may be permitted in the lower portion of such doors. Where such opening is in or under a door, the total net area of any such opening or openings shall not exceed 0.05 m^2. Alternatively, a non-combustible air balance duct routed between the cabin and the corridor, and located below the sanitary unit, is permitted where the cross-sectional area of the duct does not exceed 0.05 m^2. All ventilation openings shall be fitted with a grill made of non-combustible material. Doors shall be non-combustible.

4.1.2.2   Cabin doors in "B" class divisions shall be of a self-closing type. Hold-back hooks are not permitted.

4.1.2.3   The requirements for "B" class integrity of the outer boundaries of a ship shall not apply to glass partitions, windows and sidescuttles. Similarly, the requirements for "B" class integrity shall not apply to exterior doors in superstructures and deckhouses. For ships carrying not more than 36 passengers, the Administration may permit the use of combustible materials in doors separating cabins from the individual interior sanitary spaces such as showers.

4.1.2.4   In ships carrying not more than 36 passengers, where an automatic sprinkler system complying with the provisions of the Fire Safety Systems Code is fitted:

.1   openings in decks not forming steps in main vertical zones nor bounding horizontal zones shall be closed reasonably tight and such decks shall meet the "B" class integrity requirements in so far as is reasonable and practicable in the opinion of the Administration; and

.2   openings in corridor bulkheads of "B" class materials shall be protected in accordance with the provisions of paragraph 2.2.2.

4.1.3 *Windows and sidescuttles*

4.1.3.1   Windows and sidescuttles in bulkheads within accommodation and service spaces and control stations other than those to which the provisions of paragraphs 4.1.1.6 and 4.1.2.3 apply shall be so constructed as to preserve the integrity requirements of the type of bulkheads in which they are fitted, this being determined in accordance with the Fire Test Procedures Code.

4.1.3.2   Notwithstanding the requirements of tables 9.1 to 9.4, windows and sidescuttles in bulkheads separating accommodation and service spaces and control stations from weather shall be constructed with frames of steel or other suitable material. The glass shall be retained by a metal glazing bead or angle.

4.1.3.3   Windows facing life-saving appliances, embarkation and assembly stations, external stairs and open decks used for escape routes, and windows situated below liferaft and escape slide embarkation areas shall have fire integrity as required in table 9.1. Where automatic dedicated sprinkler heads are provided for windows, "A-0" windows may be accepted as equivalent. To be considered under this paragraph, the sprinkler heads shall either be:

.1   dedicated heads located above the windows, and installed in addition to the conventional ceiling sprinklers; or

.2   conventional ceiling sprinkler heads arranged such that the window is protected by an average application rate of at least 5 $l/\mathrm{min}/\mathrm{m}^2$ and the additional window area is included in the calculation of the area of coverage.

Windows located in the ship's side below the lifeboat embarkation area shall have fire integrity at least equal to "A-0" class.

4.2   *Doors in fire-resisting divisions in cargo ships*

4.2.1 The fire resistance of doors shall be equivalent to that of the division in which they are fitted, this being determined in accordance with the Fire Test Procedures Code. Doors and door frames in "A" class divisions shall be constructed of steel. Doors in "B" class divisions shall be non-combustible. Doors fitted in boundary bulkheads of machinery spaces of category A shall be reasonably gastight and self-closing. In ships constructed according to method IC, the Administration may permit the use of combustible materials in doors separating cabins from individual interior sanitary accommodation such as showers.

4.2.2 Doors required to be self-closing shall not be fitted with hold-back hooks. However, hold-back arrangements fitted with remote release devices of the fail-safe type may be utilized.

4.2.3 In corridor bulkheads, ventilation openings may be permitted in and under the doors of cabins and public spaces. Ventilation openings are also permitted in "B" class doors leading to lavatories, offices, pantries, lockers and store-rooms. Except as permitted below, the openings shall be provided only in the lower half of a door. Where such an opening is in or under a door, the total net area of any such opening or openings shall not exceed 0.05 m². Alternatively, a non-combustible air balance duct routed between the cabin and the corridor, and located below the sanitary unit, is permitted where the cross-sectional area of the duct does not exceed 0.05 m². Ventilation openings, except those under the door, shall be fitted with a grill made of non-combustible material.

4.2.4 Watertight doors need not be insulated.

5 Protection of openings in machinery spaces boundaries

5.1 *Application*

5.1.1 The provision of this paragraph shall apply to machinery spaces of category A and, where the Administration considers it desirable, to other machinery spaces.

5.2 *Protection of openings in machinery space boundaries*

5.2.1 The number of skylights, doors, ventilators, openings in funnels to permit exhaust ventilation and other openings to machinery spaces shall be reduced to a minimum consistent with the needs of ventilation and the proper and safe working of the ship.

5.2.2 Skylights shall be of steel and shall not contain glass panels.

5.2.3 Means of control shall be provided for closing power-operated doors or actuating release mechanisms on doors other than power-operated watertight doors. The controls shall be located outside the space concerned, where they will not be cut off in the event of fire in the space it serves.

5.2.4 In passenger ships, the means of control required in paragraph 5.2.3 shall be situated at one control position or grouped in as few positions as possible, to the satisfaction of the Administration. Such positions shall have safe access from the open deck.

5.2.5 In passenger ships, doors, other than power-operated watertight doors, shall be so arranged that positive closure is assured in case of fire in the space by power-operated closing arrangements or by the provision of self-closing doors capable of closing against an inclination of 3.5° opposing closure, and having a fail-safe hold-back arrangement, provided with a remotely operated release device. Doors for emergency escape trunks need not be fitted with a fail-safe hold-back facility and a remotely operated release device.

5.2.6 Windows shall not be fitted in machinery space boundaries. However, this does not preclude the use of glass in control rooms within the machinery spaces.

6   Protection of cargo space boundaries

6.1   In passenger ships carrying more than 36 passengers, the boundary bulkheads and decks of special category and ro–ro spaces shall be insulated to "A-60" class standard. However, where a category (5), (9) or (10) space, as defined in paragraph 2.2.3, is on one side of the division, the standard may be reduced to "A-0". Where fuel oil tanks are below a special category space, the integrity of the deck between such spaces may be reduced to "A-0" standard.

6.2   In passenger ships carrying not more than 36 passengers, the boundary bulkheads of special category spaces shall be insulated as required for category (11) spaces in table 9.3 and the horizontal boundaries as required for category (11) spaces in table 9.4.

6.3   In passenger ships carrying not more than 36 passengers, the boundary bulkheads and decks of closed and open ro–ro spaces shall have a fire integrity as required for category (8) spaces in table 9.3 and the horizontal boundaries as required for category (8) spaces in table 9.4.

6.4   In passenger ships, indicators shall be provided on the navigation bridge which shall indicate when any fire door leading to or from the special category spaces is closed.

6.5   In tankers, for the protection of cargo tanks carrying crude oil and petroleum products having a flashpoint not exceeding 60°C, materials readily rendered ineffective by heat shall not be used for valves, fittings, tank opening covers, cargo vent piping, and cargo piping so as to prevent the spread of fire to the cargo.

7   Ventilation systems

7.1   *Ducts and dampers*

7.1.1   Ventilation ducts shall be of non-combustible material. However, short ducts, not generally exceeding 2 m in length and with a free cross-sectional area* not exceeding 0.02 m^2, need not be non-combustible, subject to the following conditions:

    .1   the ducts are made of a material which has low flame-spread characteristics;

    .2   the ducts are only used at the end of the ventilation device; and

    .3   the ducts are not situated less than 600 mm, measured along the duct, from an opening in an "A" or "B" class division, including continuous "B" class ceiling.

---

* The term *free cross-sectional area* means, even in the case of a pre-insulated duct, the area calculated on the basis of the inner diameter of the duct.

7.1.2 The following arrangements shall be tested in accordance with the Fire Test Procedures Code:

   .1   fire dampers, including their relevant means of operation; and

   .2   duct penetrations through "A" class divisions. However, the test is not required where steel sleeves are directly joined to ventilation ducts by means of riveted or screwed flanges or by welding.

7.2   *Arrangement of ducts*

7.2.1 The ventilation systems for machinery spaces of category A, vehicle spaces, ro–ro spaces, galleys, special category spaces and cargo spaces shall, in general, be separated from each other and from the ventilation systems serving other spaces, except that the galley ventilation systems on cargo ships of less than 4,000 gross tonnage and in passenger ships carrying not more than 36 passengers need not be completely separated, but may be served by separate ducts from a ventilation unit serving other spaces. In any case, an automatic fire damper shall be fitted in the galley ventilation duct near the ventilation unit. Ducts provided for the ventilation of machinery spaces of category A, galleys, vehicle spaces, ro–ro spaces or special category spaces shall not pass through accommodation spaces, service spaces or control stations unless they comply with the conditions specified in paragraphs 7.2.1.1.1 to 7.2.1.1.4 or 7.2.1.2.1 and 7.2.1.2.2 below:

   .1.1   the ducts are constructed of steel having a thickness of at least 3 mm and 5 mm for ducts the widths or diameters of which are up to and including 300 mm and 760 mm and over respectively and, in the case of such ducts, the widths or diameters of which are between 300 mm and 760 mm, having a thickness obtained by interpolation;

   .1.2   the ducts are suitably supported and stiffened;

   .1.3   the ducts are fitted with automatic fire dampers close to the boundaries penetrated; and

   .1.4   the ducts are insulated to "A-60" class standard from the machinery spaces, galleys, vehicle spaces, ro–ro spaces or special category spaces to a point at least 5 m beyond each fire damper;

or

   .2.1   the ducts are constructed of steel in accordance with paragraphs 7.2.1.1.1 and 7.2.1.1.2; and

   .2.2   the ducts are insulated to "A-60" class standard throughout the accommodation spaces, service spaces or control stations;

except that penetrations of main zone divisions shall also comply with the requirements of paragraph 4.1.1.8.

7.2.2 Ducts provided for ventilation to accommodation spaces, service spaces or control stations shall not pass through machinery spaces of category A, galleys, vehicle spaces, ro–ro spaces or special category spaces unless they comply with the conditions specified in paragraphs 7.2.2.1.1 to 7.2.2.1.3 or 7.2.2.2.1 and 7.2.2.2.2 below:

    .1.1   the ducts, where they pass through a machinery space of category A, galley, vehicle space, ro–ro space or special category space, are constructed of steel in accordance with paragraphs 7.2.1.1.1 and 7.2.1.1.2;

    .1.2   automatic fire dampers are fitted close to the boundaries penetrated; and

    .1.3   the integrity of the machinery space, galley, vehicle space, ro–ro space or special category space boundaries is maintained at the penetrations;

or

    .2.1   the ducts, where they pass through a machinery space of category A, galley, vehicle space, ro–ro space or special category space, are constructed of steel in accordance with paragraphs 7.2.1.1.1 and 7.2.1.1.2; and

    .2.2   the ducts are insulated to "A-60" standard within the machinery space, galley, vehicle space, ro–ro space or special category space;

except that penetrations of main zone divisions shall also comply with the requirements of paragraph 4.1.1.8.

7.3   *Details of duct penetrations*

7.3.1 Where a thin plated duct with a free cross-sectional area equal to, or less than, 0.02 m^2 passes through "A" class bulkheads or decks, the opening shall be lined with a steel sheet sleeve having a thickness of at least 3 mm and a length of at least 200 mm, divided preferably into 100 mm on each side of the bulkhead or, in the case of the deck, wholly laid on the lower side of the decks pierced. Where ventilation ducts with a free cross-sectional area exceeding 0.02 m^2 pass through "A" class bulkheads or decks, the opening shall be lined with a steel sheet sleeve. However, where such ducts are of steel construction and pass through a deck or bulkhead, the ducts and sleeves shall comply with the following:

    .1   The sleeves shall have a thickness of at least 3 mm and a length of at least 900 mm. When passing through bulkheads, this length shall be divided preferably into 450 mm on each side of the bulkhead. These ducts, or sleeves lining such ducts, shall be provided with fire insulation. The insulation shall have at least the same fire integrity as the bulkhead or deck through which the duct passes; and

.2   Ducts with a free cross-sectional area exceeding 0.075 m² shall be fitted with fire dampers in addition to the requirements of paragraph 7.3.1.1. The fire damper shall operate automatically, but shall also be capable of being closed manually from both sides of the bulkhead or deck. The damper shall be provided with an indicator which shows whether the damper is open or closed. Fire dampers are not required, however, where ducts pass through spaces surrounded by "A" class divisions, without serving those spaces, provided those ducts have the same fire integrity as the divisions which they pierce. Fire dampers shall be easily accessible. Where they are placed behind ceilings or linings, these ceilings or linings shall be provided with an inspection door on which a plate reporting the identification number of the fire damper is provided. The fire damper identification number shall also be placed on any remote controls required.

7.3.2 Ventilation ducts with a free cross-sectional area exceeding 0.02 m² passing through "B" class bulkheads shall be lined with steel sheet sleeves of 900 mm in length, divided preferably into 450 mm on each side of the bulkheads unless the duct is of steel for this length.

7.4   *Ventilation systems for passenger ships carrying more than 36 passengers*

7.4.1 The ventilation system of a passenger ship carrying more than 36 passengers shall be in compliance with the following additional requirements.

7.4.2 In general, the ventilation fans shall be so disposed that the ducts reaching the various spaces remain within the main vertical zone.

7.4.3 Where ventilation systems penetrate decks, precautions shall be taken, in addition to those relating to the fire integrity of the deck required by paragraphs 3.1 and 4.1.1.5, to reduce the likelihood of smoke and hot gases passing from one 'tween-deck space to another through the system. In addition to insulation requirements contained in paragraph 7.4, vertical ducts shall, if necessary, be insulated as required by the appropriate tables 9.1 and 9.2.

7.4.4 Except in cargo spaces, ventilation ducts shall be constructed of the following materials:

.1   ducts not less than 0.075 m² in free cross-sectional area and all vertical ducts serving more than a single 'tween-deck space shall be constructed of steel or other equivalent material;

.2   ducts less than 0.075 m² in free cross-sectional area, other than the vertical ducts referred to in paragraph 7.4.4.1, shall be constructed of non-combustible materials. Where such ducts penetrate "A" or "B" class divisions, due regard shall be given to ensuring the fire integrity of the division; and

.3   short lengths of duct, not in general exceeding 0.02 m^2 in free cross-sectional area nor 2 m in length, need not be non-combustible provided that all of the following conditions are met:

.3.1   the duct is constructed of a material which has low flame-spread characteristics;

.3.2   the duct is used only at the terminal end of the ventilation system; and

.3.3   the duct is not located closer than 600 mm measured along its length to a penetration of an "A" or "B" class division, including continuous "B" class ceilings.

7.4.5 Stairway enclosures shall be ventilated and served by an independent fan and duct system which shall not serve any other spaces in the ventilation systems.

7.4.6 Exhaust ducts shall be provided with hatches for inspection and cleaning. The hatches shall be located near the fire dampers.

7.5   *Exhaust ducts from galley ranges*

7.5.1   *Requirements for passenger ships carrying more than 36 passengers*

Exhaust ducts from galley ranges shall meet the requirements of paragraphs 7.2.1.2.1 and 7.2.1.2.2 and shall be fitted with:

.1   a grease trap readily removable for cleaning unless an alternative approved grease removal system is fitted;

.2   a fire damper located in the lower end of the duct which is automatically and remotely operated and, in addition, a remotely operated fire damper located in the upper end of the duct;

.3   a fixed means for extinguishing a fire within the duct;

.4   remote-control arrangements for shutting off the exhaust fans and supply fans, for operating the fire dampers mentioned in paragraph 7.5.1.2 and for operating the fire-extinguishing system, which shall be placed in a position close to the entrance to the galley. Where a multi-branch system is installed, a remote means located with the above controls shall be provided to close all branches exhausting through the same main duct before an extinguishing medium is released into the system; and

.5   suitably located hatches for inspection and cleaning.

7.5.2 *Requirements for cargo ships and passenger ships carrying not more than 36 passengers*

7.5.2.1 Where they pass through accommodation spaces or spaces containing combustible materials, the exhaust ducts from galley ranges shall be constructed of "A" class divisions. Each exhaust duct shall be fitted with:

.1 a grease trap readily removable for cleaning;

.2 a fire damper located in the lower end of the duct;

.3 arrangements, operable from within the galley, for shutting off the exhaust fans; and

.4 fixed means for extinguishing a fire within the duct.

Regulation 10
Fire fighting

1 Purpose

The purpose of this regulation is to suppress and swiftly extinguish a fire in the space of origin. For this purpose, the following functional requirements shall be met:

.1 fixed fire-extinguishing systems shall be installed, having due regard to the fire growth potential of the protected spaces; and

.2 fire-extinguishing appliances shall be readily available.

2 Water supply systems

Ships shall be provided with fire pumps, fire mains, hydrants and hoses complying with the applicable requirements of this regulation.

2.1 *Fire mains and hydrants*

2.1.1 *General*

Materials readily rendered ineffective by heat shall not be used for fire mains and hydrants unless adequately protected. The pipes and hydrants shall be so placed that the fire hoses may be easily coupled to them. The arrangement of pipes and hydrants shall be such as to avoid the possibility of freezing. Suitable drainage provisions shall be provided for fire main piping. Isolation valves shall be installed for all open deck fire main branches used for purposes other than fire fighting. In ships where deck cargo may be carried, the positions of the hydrants shall be such that they are always readily accessible and the pipes shall be arranged as far as practicable to avoid risk of damage by such cargo.

2.1.2 *Ready availability of water supply*

The arrangements for the ready availability of water supply shall be:

.1 in passenger ships:

.1.1   of 1,000 gross tonnage and upwards such that at least one effective jet of water is immediately available from any hydrant in an interior location and so as to ensure the continuation of the output of water by the automatic starting of one required fire pump;

.1.2   of less than 1,000 gross tonnage by automatic start of at least one fire pump or by remote starting from the navigation bridge of at least one fire pump. If the pump starts automatically or if the bottom valve cannot be opened from where the pump is remotely started, the bottom valve shall always be kept open; and

.1.3   if fitted with periodically unattended machinery spaces in accordance with regulation II-1/54, the Administration shall determine provisions for fixed water fire-extinguishing arrangements for such spaces equivalent to those required for normally attended machinery spaces;

.2   in cargo ships:

.2.1   to the satisfaction of the Administration; and

.2.2   with a periodically unattended machinery space or when only one person is required on watch, there shall be immediate water delivery from the fire main system at a suitable pressure, either by remote starting of one of the main fire pumps with remote starting from the navigation bridge and fire control station, if any, or permanent pressurization of the fire main system by one of the main fire pumps, except that the Administration may waive this requirement for cargo ships of less than 1,600 gross tonnage if the fire pump starting arrangement in the machinery space is in an easily accessible position.

2.1.3 *Diameter of fire mains*

The diameter of the fire main and water service pipes shall be sufficient for the effective distribution of the maximum required discharge from two fire pumps operating simultaneously, except that in the case of cargo ships the diameter need only be sufficient for the discharge of 140 m³/h.

2.1.4 *Isolating valves and relief valves*

2.1.4.1 Isolating valves to separate the section of the fire main within the machinery space containing the main fire pump or pumps from the rest of the fire main shall be fitted in an easily accessible and tenable position outside the machinery spaces. The fire main shall be so arranged that when the isolating valves are shut all the hydrants on the ship, except those in the machinery space referred to above, can be supplied with water by another fire pump or an emergency fire pump. The emergency fire pump, its seawater inlet, and suction and delivery pipes and isolating valves shall be located outside the machinery space. If this arrangement cannot be made, the sea-chest may be fitted in the machinery space if the valve is remotely controlled from a position in the same compartment as the emergency fire pump and the suction pipe is as short as practicable. Short lengths of suction or discharge piping may penetrate the machinery space, provided they are enclosed in a substantial steel casing or are insulated to "A-60" class standards. The pipes shall have substantial wall thickness, but in no case less than 11 mm, and shall be welded except for the flanged connection to the sea inlet valve.

2.1.4.2 A valve shall be fitted to serve each fire hydrant so that any fire hose may be removed while the fire pumps are in operation.

2.1.4.3 Relief valves shall be provided in conjunction with fire pumps if the pumps are capable of developing a pressure exceeding the design pressure of the water service pipes, hydrants and hoses. These valves shall be so placed and adjusted as to prevent excessive pressure in any part of the fire main system.

2.1.4.4 In tankers, isolation valves shall be fitted in the fire main at the poop front in a protected position and on the tank deck at intervals of not more than 40 m to preserve the integrity of the fire main system in case of fire or explosion.

2.1.5 *Number and position of hydrants*

2.1.5.1 The number and position of hydrants shall be such that at least two jets of water not emanating from the same hydrant, one of which shall be from a single length of hose, may reach any part of the ship normally accessible to the passengers or crew while the ship is being navigated and any part of any cargo space when empty, any ro–ro space or any vehicle space, in which latter case the two jets shall reach any part of the space, each from a single length of hose. Furthermore, such hydrants shall be positioned near the accesses to the protected spaces.

2.1.5.2 In addition to the requirements in paragraph 2.1.5.1, passenger ships shall comply with the following:

.1 in the accommodation, service and machinery spaces, the number and position of hydrants shall be such that the requirements of paragraph 2.1.5.1 may be complied with when all watertight doors and all doors in main vertical zone bulkheads are closed; and

.2 where access is provided to a machinery space of category A at a low level from an adjacent shaft tunnel, two hydrants shall be provided external to, but near the entrance to, that machinery space. Where such access is provided from other spaces, in one of those spaces two hydrants shall be provided near the entrance to the machinery space of category A. Such provision need not be made where the tunnel or adjacent spaces are not part of the escape route.

2.1.6 *Pressure at hydrants*

With the two pumps simultaneously delivering water through the nozzles specified in paragraph 2.3.3, with the quantity of water as specified in paragraph 2.1.3, through any adjacent hydrants, the following minimum pressures shall be maintained at all hydrants:

.1 for passenger ships:
4,000 gross tonnage and upwards 0.40 N/mm^2
less than 4,000 gross tonnage 0.30 N/mm^2

.2 for cargo ships:
6,000 gross tonnage and upwards 0.27 N/mm^2
less than 6,000 gross tonnage 0.25 N/mm^2

and

.3 the maximum pressure at any hydrant shall not exceed that at which the effective control of a fire hose can be demonstrated.

2.1.7 *International shore connection*

2.1.7.1 Ships of 500 gross tonnage and upwards shall be provided with at least one international shore connection complying with the Fire Safety Systems Code.

2.1.7.2 Facilities shall be available enabling such a connection to be used on either side of the ship.

2.2 *Fire pumps*

2.2.1 *Pumps accepted as fire pumps*

Sanitary, ballast, bilge or general service pumps may be accepted as fire pumps, provided that they are not normally used for pumping oil and that if they are subject to occasional duty for the transfer or pumping of oil fuel, suitable change-over arrangements are fitted.

2.2.2 *Number of fire pumps*

Ships shall be provided with independently driven fire pumps as follows:

.1 in passenger ships of:
4,000 gross tonnage and upwards at least three
less than 4,000 gross tonnage at least two

.2 in cargo ships of:
1,000 gross tonnage and upwards at least two
less than 1,000 gross tonnage at least two power-driven pumps, one of which shall be independently driven

2.2.3 *Arrangement of fire pumps and fire mains*

2.2.3.1 Fire pumps

The arrangement of sea connections, fire pumps and their sources of power shall be as to ensure that:

> .1   in passenger ships of 1,000 gross tonnage and upwards, in the event of a fire in any one compartment, all the fire pumps will not be put out of action; and

> .2   in passenger ships of less than 1,000 gross tonnage and in cargo ships, if a fire in any one compartment could put all the pumps out of action, there shall be an alternative means consisting of an emergency fire pump complying with the provisions of the Fire Safety Systems Code with its source of power and sea connection located outside the space where the main fire pumps or their sources of power are located.

2.2.3.2   Requirements for the space containing the emergency fire pump

2.2.3.2.1 Location of the space

The space containing the fire pump shall not be contiguous to the boundaries of machinery spaces of category A or those spaces containing main fire pumps. Where this is not practicable, the common bulkhead between the two spaces shall be insulated to a standard of structural fire protection equivalent to that required for a control station.

2.2.3.2.2 Access to the emergency fire pump

No direct access shall be permitted between the machinery space and the space containing the emergency fire pump and its source of power. When this is impracticable, the Administration may accept an arrangement where the access is by means of an airlock with the door of the machinery space being of "A-60" class standard and the other door being at least steel, both reasonably gastight, self-closing and without any hold-back arrangements. Alternatively, the access may be through a watertight door capable of being operated from a space remote from the machinery space and the space containing the emergency fire pump and unlikely to be cut off in the event of fire in those spaces. In such cases, a second means of access to the space containing the emergency fire pump and its source of power shall be provided.

2.2.3.2.3 Ventilation of the emergency fire pump space

Ventilation arrangements to the space containing the independent source of power for the emergency fire pump shall be such as to preclude, as far as practicable, the possibility of smoke from a machinery space fire entering or being drawn into that space.

2.2.3.3 Additional pumps for cargo ships

In addition, in cargo ships where other pumps, such as general service, bilge and ballast, etc., are fitted in a machinery space, arrangements shall be made to ensure that at least one of these pumps, having the capacity and pressure required by paragraphs 2.1.6.2 and 2.2.4.2, is capable of providing water to the fire main.

2.2.4 *Capacity of fire pumps*

2.2.4.1 Total capacity of required fire pumps

The required fire pumps shall be capable of delivering for fire-fighting purposes a quantity of water, at the pressure specified in paragraph 2.1.6, as follows:

.1   pumps in passenger ships: the quantity of water is not less than two thirds of the quantity required to be dealt with by the bilge pumps when employed for bilge pumping; and

.2   pumps in cargo ships, other than any emergency pump: the quantity of water is not less than four thirds of the quantity required under regulation II-1/21 to be dealt with by each of the independent bilge pumps in a passenger ship of the same dimension when employed in bilge pumping, provided that in no cargo ship need the total required capacity of the fire pumps exceed 180 m³/h.

2.2.4.2 Capacity of each fire pump

Each of the required fire pumps (other than any emergency pump required in paragraph 2.2.3.1.2 for cargo ships) shall have a capacity not less than 80% of the total required capacity divided by the minimum number of required fire pumps, but in any case not less than 25 m³/h, and each such pump shall in any event be capable of delivering at least the two required jets of water. These fire pumps shall be capable of supplying the fire main system under the required conditions. Where more pumps than the minimum of required pumps are installed, such additional pumps shall have a capacity of at least 25 m³/h and shall be capable of delivering at least the two jets of water required in paragraph 2.1.5.1.

2.3 *Fire hoses and nozzles*

2.3.1 *General specifications*

2.3.1.1 Fire hoses shall be of non-perishable material approved by the Administration and shall be sufficient in length to project a jet of water to any of the spaces in which they may be required to be used. Each hose shall be provided with a nozzle and the necessary couplings. Hoses specified in this chapter as "fire hoses" shall, together with any necessary fittings and tools, be kept ready for use in conspicuous positions near the water service hydrants or connections. Additionally, in interior locations in passenger ships carrying more than 36 passengers, fire hoses shall be connected to the hydrants at all times. Fire hoses shall have a length of at least 10 m, but not more than:

.1   15 m in machinery spaces;

.2   20 m in other spaces and open decks; and

.3   25 m for open decks on ships with a maximum breadth in excess of 30 m.

2.3.1.2   Unless one hose and nozzle is provided for each hydrant in the ship, there shall be complete interchangeability of hose couplings and nozzles.

2.3.2 *Number and diameter of fire hoses*

2.3.2.1   Ships shall be provided with fire hoses, the number and diameter of which shall be to the satisfaction of the Administration.

2.3.2.2   In passenger ships, there shall be at least one fire hose for each of the hydrants required by paragraph 2.1.5 and these hoses shall be used only for the purposes of extinguishing fires or testing the fire-extinguishing apparatus at fire drills and surveys.

2.3.2.3   In cargo ships:

.1   of 1,000 gross tonnage and upwards, the number of fire hoses to be provided shall be one for each 30 m length of the ship and one spare, but in no case less than five in all. This number does not include any hoses required in any engine-room or boiler room. The Administration may increase the number of hoses required so as to ensure that hoses in sufficient number are available and accessible at all times, having regard to the type of ship and the nature of trade in which the ship is employed. Ships carrying dangerous goods in accordance with regulation 19 shall be provided with three hoses and nozzles, in addition to those required above; and

.2   of less than 1,000 gross tonnage, the number of fire hoses to be provided shall be calculated in accordance with the provisions of paragraph 2.3.2.3.1. However, the number of hoses shall in no case be less than three.

2.3.3 *Size and types of nozzles*

2.3.3.1   For the purposes of this chapter, standard nozzle sizes shall be 12 mm, 16 mm and 19 mm or as near thereto as possible. Larger diameter nozzles may be permitted at the discretion of the Administration.

2.3.3.2   For accommodation and service spaces, a nozzle size greater than 12 mm need not be used.

2.3.3.3   For machinery spaces and exterior locations, the nozzle size shall be such as to obtain the maximum discharge possible from two jets at the pressure mentioned in paragraph 2.1.6 from the smallest pump, provided that a nozzle size greater than 19 mm need not be used.

2.3.3.4   Nozzles shall be of an approved dual-purpose type (i.e. spray/jet type) incorporating a shutoff.

3   Portable fire extinguishers[*]

3.1   *Type and design*

Portable fire extinguishers shall comply with the requirements of the Fire Safety Systems Code.

3.2   *Arrangement of fire extinguishers*

3.2.1 Accommodation spaces, service spaces and control stations shall be provided with portable fire extinguishers of appropriate types and in sufficient number to the satisfaction of the Administration. Ships of 1,000 gross tonnage and upwards shall carry at least five portable fire extinguishers.

3.2.2 One of the portable fire extinguishers intended for use in any space shall be stowed near the entrance to that space.

3.2.3 Carbon dioxide fire extinguishers shall not be placed in accommodation spaces. In control stations and other spaces containing electrical or electronic equipment or appliances necessary for the safety of the ship, fire extinguishers shall be provided whose extinguishing media are neither electrically conductive nor harmful to the equipment and appliances.

3.2.4 Fire extinguishers shall be situated ready for use at easily visible places, which can be reached quickly and easily at any time in the event of a fire, and in such a way that their serviceability is not impaired by the weather, vibration or other external factors. Portable fire extinguishers shall be provided with devices which indicate whether they have been used.

3.3   *Spare charges*

3.3.1 Spare charges shall be provided for 100% of the first ten extinguishers and 50% of the remaining fire extinguishers capable of being recharged on board. Not more than sixty total spare charges are required. Instructions for recharging shall be carried on board.

---

[*] Refer to the Improved Guidelines for Marine Portable Fire Extinguishers adopted by the Organization by resolution A.951(23).

3.3.2 For fire extinguishers which cannot be recharged on board, additional portable fire extinguishers of the same quantity, type, capacity and number as determined in paragraph 3.3.1 above shall be provided in lieu of spare charges.

4 Fixed fire-extinguishing systems

4.1 *Types of fixed fire-extinguishing systems*

4.1.1 A fixed fire-extinguishing system required by paragraph 5 below may be any of the following systems:

.1 a fixed gas fire-extinguishing system complying with the provisions of the Fire Safety Systems Code;

.2 a fixed high-expansion foam fire-extinguishing system complying with the provisions of the Fire Safety Systems Code; and

.3 a fixed pressure water-spraying fire-extinguishing system complying with the provisions of the Fire Safety Systems Code.

4.1.2 Where a fixed fire-extinguishing system not required by this chapter is installed, it shall meet the requirements of the relevant regulations of this chapter and the Fire Safety Systems Code.

4.1.3 Fire-extinguishing systems using Halon 1211, 1301, and 2402 and perfluorocarbons shall be prohibited.

4.1.4 In general, the Administration shall not permit the use of steam as a fire-extinguishing medium in fixed fire-extinguishing systems. Where the use of steam is permitted by the Administration, it shall be used only in restricted areas as an addition to the required fire-extinguishing system and shall comply with the requirements of the Fire Safety System Code.

4.2 *Closing appliances for fixed gas fire-extinguishing systems*

Where a fixed gas fire-extinguishing system is used, openings which may admit air to, or allow gas to escape from, a protected space shall be capable of being closed from outside the protected space.

4.3 *Storage rooms of fire-extinguishing medium*

When the fire-extinguishing medium is stored outside a protected space, it shall be stored in a room which is located behind the forward collision bulkhead, and is used for no other purposes. Any entrance to such a storage room shall preferably be from the open deck and shall be independent of the protected space. If the storage space is located below deck, it shall be located no more than one deck below the open deck and shall be directly accessible by a stairway or ladder from the open deck. Spaces which are located below deck or spaces where access from the open deck is not provided shall be fitted with a mechanical ventilation system designed to take exhaust air from the bottom of the space and shall be sized to provide at least 6 air changes per hour. Access doors shall open outwards, and bulkheads and decks, including doors and other means of closing any opening therein, which form the boundaries between such rooms and adjacent enclosed spaces shall be gastight. For the purpose of the application of tables 9.1 to 9.8, such storage rooms shall be treated as fire control stations.

4.4 *Water pumps for other fire-extinguishing systems*

Pumps, other than those serving the fire main, required for the provision of water for fire-extinguishing systems required by this chapter, their sources of power and their controls shall be installed outside the space or spaces protected by such systems and shall be so arranged that a fire in the space or spaces protected will not put any such system out of action.

5 Fire-extinguishing arrangements in machinery spaces

5.1 *Machinery spaces containing oil-fired boilers or oil fuel units*

5.1.1 *Fixed fire-extinguishing systems*

Machinery spaces of category A containing oil-fired boilers or oil fuel units shall be provided with any one of the fixed fire-extinguishing systems in paragraph 4.1. In each case, if the engine-room and boiler room are not entirely separate, or if fuel oil can drain from the boiler room into the engine-room, the combined engine and boiler rooms shall be considered as one compartment.

5.1.2 *Additional fire-extinguishing arrangements*

5.1.2.1 There shall be in each boiler room or at an entrance outside of the boiler room at least one portable foam applicator unit complying with the provisions of the Fire Safety Systems Code.

5.1.2.2 There shall be at least two portable foam extinguishers or equivalent in each firing space in each boiler room and in each space in which a part of the oil fuel installation is situated. There shall be not less than one approved foam-type extinguisher of at least 135 *l* capacity or equivalent in each boiler room. These extinguishers shall be provided with hoses on reels suitable for reaching any part of the boiler room. In the case of domestic boilers of less than 175 kW an approved foam-type extinguisher of at least 135 *l* capacity is not required.

5.1.2.3 In each firing space there shall be a receptacle containing at least 0.1 m^3 sand, sawdust impregnated with soda, or other approved dry material, along with a suitable shovel for spreading the material. An approved portable extinguisher may be substituted as an alternative.

5.2   *Machinery spaces containing internal combustion machinery*

5.2.1 *Fixed fire-extinguishing systems*

Machinery spaces of category A containing internal combustion machinery shall be provided with one of the fixed fire-extinguishing systems in paragraph 4.1.

5.2.2 *Additional fire-extinguishing arrangements*

5.2.2.1   There shall be at least one portable foam applicator unit complying with the provisions of the Fire Safety Systems Code.

5.2.2.2   There shall be in each such space approved foam-type fire extinguishers, each of at least 45 *l* capacity or equivalent, sufficient in number to enable foam or its equivalent to be directed onto any part of the fuel and lubricating oil pressure systems, gearing and other fire hazards. In addition, there shall be provided a sufficient number of portable foam extinguishers or equivalent which shall be so located that no point in the space is more than 10 m walking distance from an extinguisher and that there are at least two such extinguishers in each such space. For smaller spaces of cargo ships the Administration may consider relaxing this requirement.

5.3   *Machinery spaces containing steam turbines or enclosed steam engines*

5.3.1 *Fixed fire-extinguishing systems*

In spaces containing steam turbines or enclosed steam engines used for main propulsion or other purposes having in the aggregate a total output of not less than 375 kW, one of the fire-extinguishing systems specified in paragraph 4.1 shall be provided if such spaces are periodically unattended.

5.3.2 *Additional fire-extinguishing arrangements*

5.3.2.1   There shall be approved foam fire extinguishers, each of at least 45 *l* capacity or equivalent, sufficient in number to enable foam or its equivalent to be directed on to any part of the pressure lubrication system, on to any part of the casings enclosing pressure-lubricated parts of the turbines, engines or associated gearing, and any other fire hazards. However, such extinguishers shall not be required if protection, at least equivalent to that required by this subparagraph, is provided in such spaces by a fixed fire-extinguishing system fitted in compliance with paragraph 4.1.

5.3.2.2   There shall be a sufficient number of portable foam extinguishers or equivalent which shall be so located that no point in the space is more than 10 m walking distance from an extinguisher and that there are at least two such extinguishers in each such space, except that such extinguishers shall not be required in addition to any provided in compliance with paragraph 5.1.2.2.

5.4   *Other machinery spaces*

Where, in the opinion of the Administration, a fire hazard exists in any machinery space for which no specific provisions for fire-extinguishing appliances are prescribed in paragraphs 5.1, 5.2 and 5.3, there shall be provided in, or adjacent to, that space such a number of approved portable fire extinguishers or other means of fire extinction as the Administration may deem sufficient.

5.5   *Additional requirements for passenger ships*

In passenger ships carrying more than 36 passengers, each machinery space of category A shall be provided with at least two suitable water fog applicators.[*]

5.6   *Fixed local application fire-extinguishing systems*

5.6.1   Paragraph 5.6 shall apply to passenger ships of 500 gross tonnage and above and cargo ships of 2,000 gross tonnage and above.

5.6.2   Machinery spaces of category A above 500 m^3 in volume shall, in addition to the fixed fire-extinguishing system required in paragraph 5.1.1, be protected by an approved type of fixed water-based or equivalent local application fire-extinguishing system, based on the guidelines developed by the Organization.[†] In the case of periodically unattended machinery spaces, the fire-extinguishing system shall have both automatic and manual release capabilities. In the case of continuously manned machinery spaces, the fire-extinguishing system is only required to have a manual release capability.

5.6.3   Fixed local application fire-extinguishing systems are to protect areas such as the following without the necessity of engine shutdown, personnel evacuation, or sealing of the spaces:

> **.1**   the fire hazard portions of internal combustion machinery used for the ship's main propulsion and power generation;
>
> **.2**   boiler fronts;
>
> **.3**   the fire hazard portions of incinerators; and
>
> **.4**   purifiers for heated fuel oil.

5.6.4   Activation of any local application system shall give a visual and distinct audible alarm in the protected space and at continuously manned stations. The alarm shall indicate the specific system activated. The system alarm requirements described within this paragraph are in addition to, and not a substitute for, the detection and fire alarm system required elsewhere in this chapter.

---

[*] A water fog applicator might consist of a metal L-shaped pipe, the long limb being about 2 m in length, capable of being fitted to a fire hose, and the short limb being about 250 mm in length, fitted with a fixed water fog nozzle or capable of being fitted with a water spray nozzle.

[†] Refer to the Guidelines for the approval of fixed water-based local application fire-fighting systems for use in category A machinery spaces (MSC/Circ.913).

6 Fire-extinguishing arrangements in control stations, accommodation and service spaces

6.1 *Sprinkler systems in passenger ships*

6.1.1 Passenger ships carrying more than 36 passengers shall be equipped with an automatic sprinkler, fire detection and fire alarm system of an approved type complying with the requirements of the Fire Safety Systems Code in all control stations, accommodation and service spaces, including corridors and stairways. Alternatively, control stations, where water may cause damage to essential equipment, may be fitted with an approved fixed fire-extinguishing system of another type. Spaces having little or no fire risk such as voids, public toilets, carbon dioxide rooms and similar spaces need not be fitted with an automatic sprinkler system.

6.1.2 In passenger ships carrying not more than 36 passengers, when a fixed smoke detection and fire alarm system complying with the provisions of the Fire Safety Systems Code is provided only in corridors, stairways and escape routes within accommodation spaces, an automatic sprinkler system shall be installed in accordance with regulation 7.5.3.2.

6.2 *Sprinkler systems for cargo ships*

In cargo ships in which method IIC specified in regulation 9.2.3.1.1.2 is adopted, an automatic sprinkler, fire detection and fire alarm system shall be fitted in accordance with the requirements in regulation 7.5.5.2.

6.3 *Spaces containing flammable liquid*

6.3.1 Paint lockers shall be protected by:

- .1 a carbon dioxide system, designed to give a minimum volume of free gas equal to 40% of the gross volume of the protected space;
- .2 a dry powder system, designed for at least 0.5 kg powder/m^3;
- .3 a water spraying or sprinkler system, designed for 5 l/m^2 min. Water spraying systems may be connected to the fire main of the ship; or
- .4 a system providing equivalent protection, as determined by the Administration.

In all cases, the system shall be operable from outside the protected space.

6.3.2 Flammable liquid lockers shall be protected by an appropriate fire-extinguishing arrangement approved by the Administration.

6.3.3 For lockers of a deck area of less than 4 m^2, which do not give access to accommodation spaces, a portable carbon dioxide fire extinguisher sized to provide a minimum volume of free gas equal to 40% of the gross volume of the space may be accepted in lieu of a fixed system. A discharge port shall be arranged in the locker to allow the discharge of the extinguisher without having to enter into the protected space. The required portable fire extinguisher shall be stowed adjacent to the port. Alternatively, a port or hose connection may be provided to facilitate the use of fire main water.

6.4   *Deep-fat cooking equipment*

Deep-fat cooking equipment shall be fitted with the following:

.1   an automatic or manual fire-extinguishing system tested to an international standard acceptable to the Organization;*

.2   a primary and backup thermostat with an alarm to alert the operator in the event of failure of either thermostat;

.3   arrangements for automatically shutting off the electrical power upon activation of the fire-extinguishing system;

.4   an alarm for indicating operation of the fire-extinguishing system in the galley where the equipment is installed; and

.5   controls for manual operation of the fire-extinguishing system which are clearly labelled for ready use by the crew.

7   **Fire-extinguishing arrangements in cargo spaces**

7.1   *Fixed gas fire-extinguishing systems for general cargo*

7.1.1   Except as provided for in paragraph 7.2, the cargo spaces of passenger ships of 1,000 gross tonnage and upwards shall be protected by a fixed carbon dioxide or inert gas fire-extinguishing system complying with the provisions of the Fire Safety Systems Code or by a fixed high-expansion foam fire-extinguishing system which gives equivalent protection.

7.1.2   Where it is shown to the satisfaction of the Administration that a passenger ship is engaged on voyages of such short duration that it would be unreasonable to apply the requirements of paragraph 7.1.1 and also in ships of less than 1,000 gross tonnage, the arrangements in cargo spaces shall be to the satisfaction of the Administration, provided that the ship is fitted with steel hatch covers and effective means of closing all ventilators and other openings leading to the cargo spaces.

7.1.3   Except for ro–ro and vehicle spaces, cargo spaces on cargo ships of 2,000 gross tonnage and upwards shall be protected by a fixed carbon dioxide or inert gas fire-extinguishing system complying with the provisions of the Fire Safety Systems Code, or by a fire-extinguishing system which gives equivalent protection.

---

* Refer to the recommendations by the International Organization for Standardization, in particular publication ISO 15371:2000, *Fire-extinguishing systems for protection of galley deep-fat cooking equipment – fire tests*.

7.1.4 The Administration may exempt from the requirements of paragraphs 7.1.3 and 7.2 cargo spaces of any cargo ship if constructed, and solely intended, for the carriage of ore, coal, grain, unseasoned timber, non-combustible cargoes or cargoes which, in the opinion of the Administration, constitute a low fire risk.* Such exemptions may be granted only if the ship is fitted with steel hatch covers and effective means of closing all ventilators and other openings leading to the cargo spaces. When such exemptions are granted, the Administration shall issue an Exemption Certificate, irrespective of the date of construction of the ship concerned, in accordance with regulation I/12(a)(vi), and shall ensure that the list of cargoes the ship is permitted to carry is attached to the Exemption Certificate.

7.2 *Fixed gas fire-extinguishing systems for dangerous goods*

A ship engaged in the carriage of dangerous goods in any cargo spaces shall be provided with a fixed carbon dioxide or inert gas fire-extinguishing system complying with the provisions of the Fire Safety Systems Code or with a fire-extinguishing system which, in the opinion of the Administration, gives equivalent protection for the cargoes carried.

8   Cargo tank protection

8.1   *Fixed deck foam fire-extinguishing systems*

8.1.1 For tankers of 20,000 tonnes deadweight and upwards, a fixed deck foam fire-extinguishing system shall be provided complying with the provisions of the Fire Safety Systems Code, except that, in lieu of the above, the Administration, after having given consideration to the ship's arrangement and equipment, may accept other fixed installations if they afford protection equivalent to the above, in accordance with regulation I/5. The requirements for alternative fixed installations shall comply with the requirements in paragraph 8.1.2.

8.1.2 In accordance with paragraph 8.1.1, where the Administration accepts an equivalent fixed installation in lieu of the fixed deck foam fire-extinguishing system, the installation shall:

.1   be capable of extinguishing spill fires and also preclude ignition of spilled oil not yet ignited; and

.2   be capable of combating fires in ruptured tanks.

8.1.3 Tankers of less than 20,000 tonnes deadweight shall be provided with a deck foam fire-extinguishing system complying with the requirements of the Fire Safety Systems Code.

---

* Refer to the Code of Safe Practice for Solid Bulk Cargoes, emergency schedule B14, entry for coal, and to the List of solid bulk cargoes which are non-combustible or constitute a low fire risk or for which a fixed gas fire-extinguishing system is ineffective (MSC/Circ.671).

9   Protection of cargo pump-rooms in tankers

9.1   *Fixed fire-extinguishing systems*

Each cargo pump-room shall be provided with one of the following fixed fire-extinguishing systems operated from a readily accessible position outside the pump-room. Cargo pump-rooms shall be provided with a system suitable for machinery spaces of category A.

9.1.1 A carbon dioxide fire-extinguishing system complying with the provisions of the Fire Safety Systems Code and with the following:

.1   the alarms giving audible warning of the release of fire-extinguishing medium shall be safe for use in a flammable cargo vapour/air mixture; and

.2   a notice shall be exhibited at the controls stating that, due to the electrostatic ignition hazard, the system is to be used only for fire extinguishing and not for inerting purposes.

9.1.2 A high-expansion foam fire-extinguishing system complying with the provisions of the Fire Safety Systems Code, provided that the foam concentrate supply is suitable for extinguishing fires involving the cargoes carried.

9.1.3 A fixed pressure water-spraying fire-extinguishing system complying with the provisions of the Fire Safety Systems Code.

9.2   *Quantity of fire-extinguishing medium*

Where the fire-extinguishing medium used in the cargo pump-room system is also used in systems serving other spaces, the quantity of medium provided or its delivery rate need not be more than the maximum required for the largest compartment.

10   Fire-fighter's outfits

10.1   *Types of fire-fighter's outfits*

Fire-fighter's outfits shall comply with the Fire Safety Systems Code.

10.2   *Number of fire-fighter's outfits*

10.2.1 Ships shall carry at least two fire-fighter's outfits.

10.2.2 In addition, in passenger ships there shall be provided:

.1   for every 80 m, or part thereof, of the aggregate of the lengths of all passenger spaces and service spaces on the deck which carries such spaces or, if there is more than one such deck, on the deck which has the largest aggregate of such lengths, two fire-fighter's outfits and, in addition, two sets of personal equipment, each set comprising the items stipulated in the Fire Safety Systems Code. In passenger ships carrying more than 36 passengers, two additional fire-fighter's outfits shall be provided for each main vertical zone. However, for stairway enclosures which constitute individual main vertical zones and for the main vertical zones in the fore or aft end of a ship which do not contain spaces of categories (6), (7), (8) or (12) defined in regulation 9.2.2.3, no additional fire-fighter's outfits are required; and

.2   on ships carrying more than 36 passengers, for each pair of breathing apparatus, one water fog applicator which shall be stored adjacent to such apparatus.

10.2.3 In addition, in tankers, two fire-fighter's outfits shall be provided.

10.2.4 The Administration may require additional sets of personal equipment and breathing apparatus, having due regard to the size and type of the ship.

10.2.5 Two spare charges shall be provided for each required breathing apparatus. Passenger ships carrying not more than 36 passengers and cargo ships that are equipped with suitably located means for fully recharging the air cylinders free from contamination need carry only one spare charge for each required apparatus. In passenger ships carrying more than 36 passengers, at least two spare charges for each breathing apparatus shall be provided.

10.3   *Storage of fire-fighter's outfits*

10.3.1 The fire-fighter's outfits or sets of personal equipment shall be kept ready for use in an easily accessible location that is permanently and clearly marked and, where more than one fire-fighter's outfit or more than one set of personal equipment is carried, they shall be stored in widely separated positions.

10.3.2 In passenger ships, at least two fire-fighter's outfits and, in addition, one set of personal equipment shall be available at any one position. At least two fire-fighter's outfits shall be stored in each main vertical zone.

Regulation 11
Structural integrity

1   **Purpose**

The purpose of this regulation is to maintain structural integrity of the ship, preventing partial or whole collapse of the ship structures due to strength deterioration by heat. For this purpose, materials used in the ships' structure shall ensure that the structural integrity is not degraded due to fire.

2   Material of hull, superstructures, structural bulkheads, decks and deckhouses

The hull, superstructures, structural bulkheads, decks and deckhouses shall be constructed of steel or other equivalent material. For the purpose of applying the definition of steel or other equivalent material as given in regulation 3.43, the "applicable fire exposure" shall be according to the integrity and insulation standards given in tables 9.1 to 9.4. For example, where divisions such as decks or sides and ends of deckhouses are permitted to have "B-0" fire integrity, the "applicable fire exposure" shall be half an hour.

3   Structure of aluminium alloy

Unless otherwise specified in paragraph 2, in cases where any part of the structure is of aluminium alloy, the following shall apply:

.1   the insulation of aluminium alloy components of "A" or "B" class divisions, except structure which, in the opinion of the Administration, is non-load-bearing, shall be such that the temperature of the structural core does not rise more than 200°C above the ambient temperature at any time during the applicable fire exposure to the standard fire test; and

.2   special attention shall be given to the insulation of aluminium alloy components of columns, stanchions and other structural members required to support lifeboat and liferaft stowage, launching and embarkation areas, and "A" and "B" class divisions to ensure:

.2.1   that for such members supporting lifeboat and liferaft areas and "A" class divisions, the temperature rise limitation specified in paragraph 3.1 shall apply at the end of one hour; and

.2.2   that for such members required to support "B" class divisions, the temperature rise limitation specified in paragraph 3.1 shall apply at the end of half an hour.

4   Machinery spaces of category A

4.1   *Crowns and casings*

Crowns and casings of machinery spaces of category A shall be of steel construction and shall be insulated as required by tables 9.5 and 9.7, as appropriate.

4.2   *Floor plating*

The floor plating of normal passageways in machinery spaces of category A shall be made of steel.

5   Materials of overboard fittings

Materials readily rendered ineffective by heat shall not be used for overboard scuppers, sanitary discharges, and other outlets which are close to the waterline and where the failure of the material in the event of fire would give rise to danger of flooding.

6   Protection of cargo tank structure against pressure or vacuum in tankers

6.1   *General*

The venting arrangements shall be so designed and operated as to ensure that neither pressure nor vacuum in cargo tanks shall exceed design parameters and be such as to provide for:

   .1   the flow of the small volumes of vapour, air or inert gas mixtures caused by thermal variations in a cargo tank in all cases through pressure/vacuum valves; and

   .2   the passage of large volumes of vapour, air or inert gas mixtures during cargo loading and ballasting, or during discharging.

6.2   *Openings for small flow by thermal variations*

Openings for pressure release required by paragraph 6.1.1 shall:

   .1   have as great a height as is practicable above the cargo tank deck to obtain maximum dispersal of flammable vapours, but in no case less than 2 m above the cargo tank deck; and

   .2   be arranged at the furthest distance practicable, but not less than 5 m, from the nearest air intakes and openings to enclosed spaces containing a source of ignition and from deck machinery and equipment which may constitute an ignition hazard. Anchor windlass and chain locker openings constitute an ignition hazard.

6.3   *Safety measures in cargo tanks*

6.3.1   *Preventive measures against liquid rising in the venting system*

Provisions shall be made to guard against liquid rising in the venting system to a height which would exceed the design head of cargo tanks. This shall be accomplished by high-level alarms or overflow control systems or other equivalent means, together with independent gauging devices and cargo tank filling procedures. For the purposes of this regulation, spill valves are not considered equivalent to an overflow system.

6.3.2   *Secondary means for pressure/vacuum relief*

A secondary means of allowing full flow relief of vapour, air or inert gas mixtures shall be provided to prevent over-pressure or under-pressure in the event of failure of the arrangements in paragraph 6.1.2. Alternatively, pressure sensors may be fitted in each tank protected by the arrangement required in paragraph 6.1.2, with a monitoring system in the ship's cargo control room or the position from which cargo operations are normally carried out. Such monitoring equipment shall also provide an alarm facility which is activated by detection of over-pressure or under-pressure conditions within a tank.

6.3.3 *Bypasses in vent mains*

Pressure/vacuum valves required by paragraph 6.1.1 may be provided with a bypass arrangement when they are located in a vent main or masthead riser. Where such an arrangement is provided there shall be suitable indicators to show whether the bypass is open or closed.

6.3.4 *Pressure/vacuum-breaking devices*

One or more pressure/vacuum-breaking devices shall be provided to prevent the cargo tanks from being subject to:

　　.1　　a positive pressure, in excess of the test pressure of the cargo tank, if the cargo were to be loaded at the maximum rated capacity and all other outlets are left shut; and

　　.2　　a negative pressure in excess of 700 mm water gauge if the cargo were to be discharged at the maximum rated capacity of the cargo pumps and the inert gas blowers were to fail.

Such devices shall be installed on the inert gas main unless they are installed in the venting system required by regulation 4.5.3.1 or on individual cargo tanks. The location and design of the devices shall be in accordance with regulation 4.5.3 and paragraph 6.

6.4　　*Size of vent outlets*

Vent outlets for cargo loading, discharging and ballasting required by paragraph 6.1.2 shall be designed on the basis of the maximum designed loading rate multiplied by a factor of at least 1.25 to take account of gas evolution, in order to prevent the pressure in any cargo tank from exceeding the design pressure. The master shall be provided with information regarding the maximum permissible loading rate for each cargo tank and, in the case of combined venting systems, for each group of cargo tanks.

Part D

Escape

Regulation 12
Notification of crew and passengers

1   Purpose

The purpose of this regulation is to notify crew and passengers of a fire for safe evacuation. For this purpose, a general emergency alarm system and a public address system shall be provided.

2   General emergency alarm system

A general emergency alarm system required by regulation III/6.4.2 shall be used for notifying crew and passengers of a fire.

3   Public address systems in passenger ships

A public address system or other effective means of communication complying with the requirements of regulation III/6.5 shall be available throughout the accommodation and service spaces and control stations and open decks.

Regulation 13
Means of escape

1   Purpose

The purpose of this regulation is to provide means of escape so that persons on board can safely and swiftly escape to the lifeboat and liferaft embarkation deck. For this purpose, the following functional requirements shall be met:

   .1   safe escape routes shall be provided;

   .2   escape routes shall be maintained in a safe condition, clear of obstacles; and

   .3   additional aids for escape shall be provided as necessary to ensure accessibility, clear marking, and adequate design for emergency situations.

2   General requirements

2.1   Unless expressly provided otherwise in this regulation, at least two widely separated and ready means of escape shall be provided from all spaces or groups of spaces.

2.2   Lifts shall not be considered as forming one of the means of escape as required by this regulation.

3   Means of escape from control stations, accommodation spaces and service spaces

3.1   *General requirements*

3.1.1   Stairways and ladders shall be so arranged as to provide ready means of escape to the lifeboat and liferaft embarkation deck from passenger and crew accommodation spaces and from spaces in which the crew is normally employed, other than machinery spaces.

3.1.2   Unless expressly provided otherwise in this regulation, a corridor, lobby, or part of a corridor from which there is only one route of escape shall be prohibited. Dead-end corridors used in service areas which are necessary for the practical utility of the ship, such as fuel oil stations and athwartship supply corridors, shall be permitted, provided such dead-end corridors are separated from crew accommodation areas and are inaccessible from passenger accommodation areas. Also, a part of a corridor that has a depth not exceeding its width is considered a recess or local extension and is permitted.

3.1.3   All stairways in accommodation and service spaces and control stations shall be of steel frame construction except where the Administration sanctions the use of other equivalent material.

3.1.4   If a radiotelegraph station has no direct access to the open deck, two means of escape from, or access to, the station shall be provided, one of which may be a porthole or window of sufficient size or other means to the satisfaction of the Administration.

3.1.5   Doors in escape routes shall, in general, open in way of the direction of escape, except that:

    .1   individual cabin doors may open into the cabins in order to avoid injury to persons in the corridor when the door is opened; and

    .2   doors in vertical emergency escape trunks may open out of the trunk in order to permit the trunk to be used both for escape and for access.

3.2   *Means of escape in passenger ships* *

3.2.1 *Escape from spaces below the bulkhead deck*

3.2.1.1   Below the bulkhead deck, two means of escape, at least one of which shall be independent of watertight doors, shall be provided from each watertight compartment or similarly restricted space or group of spaces. Exceptionally, the Administration may dispense with one of the means of escape for crew spaces that are entered only occasionally, if the required escape route is independent of watertight doors.

3.2.1.2   Where the Administration has granted dispensation under the provisions of paragraph 3.2.1.1, this sole means of escape shall provide safe escape. However, stairways shall not be less than 800 mm in clear width with handrails on both sides.

3.2.2 *Escape from spaces above the bulkhead deck*

Above the bulkhead deck there shall be at least two means of escape from each main vertical zone or similarly restricted space or group of spaces, at least one of which shall give access to a stairway forming a vertical escape.

3.2.3 *Direct access to stairway enclosures*

Stairway enclosures in accommodation and service spaces shall have direct access from the corridors and be of a sufficient area to prevent congestion, having in view the number of persons likely to use them in an emergency. Within the perimeter of such stairway enclosures, only public toilets, lockers of non-combustible material providing storage for non-hazardous safety equipment and open information counters are permitted. Only public spaces, corridors, lifts, public toilets, special category spaces and open ro-ro spaces to which any passengers carried can have access, other escape stairways required by paragraph 3.2.4.1 and external areas are permitted to have direct access to these stairway enclosures. Small corridors or "lobbies" used to separate an enclosed stairway from galleys or main laundries may have direct access to the stairway provided they have a minimum deck area of 4.5 m², a width of no less than 900 mm and contain a fire hose station.

3.2.4 *Details of means of escape*

3.2.4.1   At least one of the means of escape required by paragraphs 3.2.1.1 and 3.2.2 shall consist of a readily accessible enclosed stairway, which shall provide continuous fire shelter from the level of its origin to the appropriate lifeboat and liferaft embarkation decks, or to the uppermost weather deck if the embarkation deck does not extend to the main vertical zone being considered. In the latter case, direct access to the embarkation deck by way of external open stairways and passageways shall be provided and shall have

---

* Refer to the Interim Guidelines for evacuation analysis for new and existing passenger ships (MSC/Circ. 1033)

emergency lighting in accordance with regulation III/11.5 and slip-free surfaces underfoot. Boundaries facing external open stairways and passageways forming part of an escape route and boundaries in such a position that their failure during a fire would impede escape to the embarkation deck shall have fire integrity, including insulation values, in accordance with tables 9.1 to 9.4, as appropriate.

3.2.4.2   Protection of access from the stairway enclosures to the lifeboat and liferaft embarkation areas shall be provided either directly or through protected internal routes which have fire integrity and insulation values for stairway enclosures as determined by tables 9.1 to 9.4, as appropriate.

3.2.4.3   Stairways serving only a space and a balcony in that space shall not be considered as forming one of the required means of escape.

3.2.4.4   Each level within an atrium shall have two means of escape, one of which shall give direct access to an enclosed vertical means of escape meeting the requirements of paragraph 3.2.4.1.

3.2.4.5   The widths, number and continuity of escapes shall be in accordance with the requirements in the Fire Safety Systems Code.

3.2.5   *Marking of escape routes*

3.2.5.1   In addition to the emergency lighting required by regulations II-1/42 and III/11.5, the means of escape, including stairways and exits, shall be marked by lighting or photoluminescent strip indicators placed not more than 300 mm above the deck at all points of the escape route, including angles and intersections. The marking must enable passengers to identify the routes of escape and readily identify the escape exits. If electric illumination is used, it shall be supplied by the emergency source of power and it shall be so arranged that the failure of any single light or cut in a lighting strip will not result in the marking being ineffective. Additionally, escape route signs and fire equipment location markings shall be of photoluminescent material or marked by lighting. The Administration shall ensure that such lighting or photoluminescent equipment has been evaluated, tested and applied in accordance with the Fire Safety Systems Code.

3.2.5.2   In passenger ships carrying more than 36 passengers, the requirements of the paragraph 3.2.5.1 shall also apply to the crew accommodation areas.

3.2.6   *Normally locked doors that form part of an escape route*

3.2.6.1   Cabin and stateroom doors shall not require keys to unlock them from inside the room. Neither shall there be any doors along any designated escape route which require keys to unlock them when moving in the direction of escape.

3.2.6.2   Escape doors from public spaces that are normally latched shall be fitted with a means of quick release. Such means shall consist of a door-latching mechanism incorporating a device that releases the latch upon the application of a force in the direction of escape flow. Quick release mechanisms shall be designed and installed to the satisfaction of the Administration and, in particular:

.1   consist of bars or panels, the actuating portion of which extends across at least one half of the width of the door leaf, at least 760 mm and not more than 1,120 mm above the deck;

.2   cause the latch to release when a force not exceeding 67 N is applied; and

.3   not be equipped with any locking device, set screw or other arrangement that prevents the release of the latch when pressure is applied to the releasing device.

3.3   *Means of escape in cargo ships*

3.3.1 *General*

At all levels of accommodation there shall be provided at least two widely separated means of escape from each restricted space or group of spaces.

3.3.2 *Escape from spaces below the lowest open deck*

Below the lowest open deck the main means of escape shall be a stairway and the second escape may be a trunk or a stairway.

3.3.3 *Escape from spaces above the lowest open deck*

Above the lowest open deck the means of escape shall be stairways or doors to an open deck or a combination thereof.

3.3.4 *Dead-end corridors*

No dead-end corridors having a length of more than 7 m shall be accepted.

3.3.5 *Width and continuity of escape routes*

The width, number and continuity of escape routes shall be in accordance with the requirements in the Fire Safety Systems Code.

3.3.6 *Dispensation from two means of escape*

Exceptionally, the Administration may dispense with one of the means of escape, for crew spaces that are entered only occasionally, if the required escape route is independent of watertight doors.

3.4 *Emergency escape breathing devices*

3.4.1 Emergency escape breathing devices shall comply with the Fire Safety Systems Code. Spare emergency escape breathing devices shall be kept on board.

3.4.2 All ships shall carry at least two emergency escape breathing devices within accommodation spaces.

3.4.3 In all passenger ships, at least two emergency escape breathing devices shall be carried in each main vertical zone.

3.4.4 In all passenger ships carrying more than 36 passengers, two emergency escape breathing devices, in addition to those required in paragraph 3.4.3 above, shall be carried in each main vertical zone.

3.4.5 However, paragraphs 3.4.3 and 3.4.4 do not apply to stairway enclosures which constitute individual main vertical zones and to the main vertical zones in the fore or aft end of a ship which do not contain spaces of categories (6), (7), (8) or (12) as defined in regulation 9.2.2.3.

4   Means of escape from machinery spaces

4.1 *Means of escape on passenger ships*

Means of escape from each machinery space in passenger ships shall comply with the following provisions.

4.1.1 *Escape from spaces below the bulkhead deck*

Where the space is below the bulkhead deck, the two means of escape shall consist of either:

.1   two sets of steel ladders, as widely separated as possible, leading to doors in the upper part of the space, similarly separated and from which access is provided to the appropriate lifeboat and liferaft embarkation decks. One of these ladders shall be located within a protected enclosure that satisfies regulation 9.2.2.3, category (2), or regulation 9.2.2.4, category (4), as appropriate, from the lower part of the space it serves to a safe position outside the space. Self-closing fire doors of the same fire integrity standards shall be fitted in the enclosure. The ladder shall be fixed in such a way that heat is not transferred into the enclosure through non-insulated fixing points. The protected enclosure shall have minimum internal dimensions of at least 800 mm × 800 mm, and shall have emergency lighting provisions; or

.2   one steel ladder leading to a door in the upper part of the space from which access is provided to the embarkation deck and additionally, in the lower part of the space and in a position well separated from the ladder referred to, a steel door capable of being operated from each side and which provides access to a safe escape route from the lower part of the space to the embarkation deck.

4.1.2 *Escape from spaces above the bulkhead deck*

Where the space is above the bulkhead deck, the two means of escape shall be as widely separated as possible and the doors leading from such means of escape shall be in a position from which access is provided to the appropriate lifeboat and liferaft embarkation decks. Where such means of escape require the use of ladders, these shall be of steel.

4.1.3 *Dispensation from two means of escape*

In a ship of less than 1,000 gross tonnage, the Administration may dispense with one of the means of escape, due regard being paid to the width and disposition of the upper part of the space. In a ship of 1,000 gross tonnage and above, the Administration may dispense with one means of escape from any such space, including a normally unattended auxiliary machinery space, so long as either a door or a steel ladder provides a safe escape route to the embarkation deck, due regard being paid to the nature and location of the space and whether persons are normally employed in that space. In the steering gear space, a second means of escape shall be provided when the emergency steering position is located in that space unless there is direct access to the open deck.

4.1.4 *Escape from machinery control rooms*

Two means of escape shall be provided from a machinery control room located within a machinery space, at least one of which will provide continuous fire shelter to a safe position outside the machinery space.

4.2 *Means of escape on cargo ships*

Means of escape from each machinery space in cargo ships shall comply with the following provisions.

4.2.1 *Escape from machinery spaces of category A*

Except as provided in paragraph 4.2.2, two means of escape shall be provided from each machinery space of category A. In particular, one of the following provisions shall be complied with:

.1 two sets of steel ladders, as widely separated as possible, leading to doors in the upper part of the space, similarly separated and from which access is provided to the open deck. One of these ladders shall be located within a protected enclosure that satisfies regulation 9.2.3.3, category (4), from the lower part of the space it serves to a safe position outside the space. Self-closing fire doors of the same fire integrity standards shall be fitted in the enclosure. The ladder shall be fixed in such a way that heat is not transferred into the enclosure through non-insulated fixing points. The enclosure shall have minimum internal dimensions of at least 800 mm × 800 mm, and shall have emergency lighting provisions; or

.2 one steel ladder leading to a door in the upper part of the space from which access is provided to the open deck and, additionally, in the lower part of the space and in a position well separated from the ladder referred to, a steel door capable of being operated from each side and which provides access to a safe escape route from the lower part of the space to the open deck.

4.2.2 *Dispensation from two means of escape*

In a ship of less than 1,000 gross tonnage, the Administration may dispense with one of the means of escape required under paragraph 4.2.1, due regard being paid to the dimension and disposition of the upper part of the space. In addition, the means of escape from machinery spaces of category A need not comply with the requirement for an enclosed fire shelter listed in paragraph 4.2.1.1. In the steering gear space, a second means of escape shall be provided when the emergency steering position is located in that space unless there is direct access to the open deck.

4.2.3 *Escape from machinery spaces other than those of category A*

From machinery spaces other than those of category A, two escape routes shall be provided except that a single escape route may be accepted for spaces that are entered only occasionally and for spaces where the maximum travel distance to the door is 5 m or less.

4.3 *Emergency escape breathing devices*

4.3.1 On all ships, within the machinery spaces, emergency escape breathing devices shall be situated ready for use at easily visible places, which can be reached quickly and easily at any time in the event of fire. The location of emergency escape breathing devices shall take into account the layout of the machinery space and the number of persons normally working in the spaces.*

4.3.2 The number and location of these devices shall be indicated in the fire control plan required in regulation 15.2.4.

---

* Refer to the Guidelines for the performance, location, use and care of emergency escape breathing devices (MSC/Circ.849).

4.3.3 Emergency escape breathing devices shall comply with the Fire Safety Systems Code.

5 Means of escape on passenger ships from special category and open ro–ro spaces to which any passengers carried can have access

5.1 In special category and open ro–ro spaces to which any passengers carried can have access, the number and locations of the means of escape both below and above the bulkhead deck shall be to the satisfaction of the Administration and, in general, the safety of access to the embarkation deck shall be at least equivalent to that provided for under paragraphs 3.2.1.1, 3.2.2, 3.2.4.1 and 3.2.4.2. Such spaces shall be provided with designated walkways to the means of escape with a breadth of at least 600 mm. The parking arrangements for the vehicles shall maintain the walkways clear at all times.

5.2 One of the escape routes from the machinery spaces where the crew is normally employed shall avoid direct access to any special category space.

6 Means of escape from ro–ro spaces

At least two means of escape shall be provided in ro–ro spaces where the crew are normally employed. The escape routes shall provide a safe escape to the lifeboat and liferaft embarkation decks and shall be located at the fore and aft ends of the space.

7 Additional requirements for ro–ro passenger ships

7.1 *General*

7.1.1 Escape routes shall be provided from every normally occupied space on the ship to an assembly station. These escape routes shall be arranged so as to provide the most direct route possible to the assembly station,[*] and shall be marked with symbols based on the guidelines developed by the Organization.[†]

7.1.2 The escape route from cabins to stairway enclosures shall be as direct as possible, with a minimum number of changes in direction. It shall not be necessary to cross from one side of the ship to the other to reach an escape route. It shall not be necessary to climb more than two decks up or down in order to reach an assembly station or open deck from any passenger space.

---

[*] Refer to Indication of the assembly stations in passenger ships (MSC/Circ.777).
[†] Refer to Symbols related to life-saving appliances and arrangements adopted by the Organization by resolution A.760(18).

7.1.3 External routes shall be provided from open decks, as referred to in paragraph 7.1.2, to the survival craft embarkation stations.

7.1.4 Where enclosed spaces adjoin an open deck, openings from the enclosed space to the open deck shall, where practicable, be capable of being used as an emergency exit.

7.1.5 Escape routes shall not be obstructed by furniture and other obstructions. With the exception of tables and chairs which may be cleared to provide open space, cabinets and other heavy furnishings in public spaces and along escape routes shall be secured in place to prevent shifting if the ship rolls or lists. Floor coverings shall also be secured in place. When the ship is under way, escape routes shall be kept clear of obstructions such as cleaning carts, bedding, luggage and boxes of goods.

7.2 *Instruction for safe escape*

7.2.1 Decks shall be sequentially numbered, starting with "1" at the tank top or lowest deck. The numbers shall be prominently displayed at stair landings and lift lobbies. Decks may also be named, but the deck number shall always be displayed with the name.

7.2.2 Simple "mimic" plans showing the "you are here" position and escape routes marked by arrows shall be prominently displayed on the inside of each cabin door and in public spaces. The plan shall show the directions of escape and shall be properly oriented in relation to its position on the ship.

7.3 *Strength of handrails and corridors*

7.3.1 Handrails or other handholds shall be provided in corridors along the entire escape route so that a firm handhold is available at every step of the way, where possible, to the assembly stations and embarkation stations. Such handrails shall be provided on both sides of longitudinal corridors more than 1.8 m in width and transverse corridors more than 1 m in width. Particular attention shall be paid to the need to be able to cross lobbies, atriums and other large open spaces along escape routes. Handrails and other handholds shall be of such strength as to withstand a distributed horizontal load of 750 N/m applied in the direction of the centre of the corridor or space, and a distributed vertical load of 750 N/m applied in the downward direction. The two loads need not be applied simultaneously.

7.3.2 The lowest 0.5 m of bulkheads and other partitions forming vertical divisions along escape routes shall be able to sustain a load of 750 N/m to allow them to be used as walking surfaces from the side of the escape route with the ship at large angles of heel.

7.4 *Evacuation analysis**

Escape routes shall be evaluated by an evacuation analysis early in the design process. The analysis shall be used to identify and eliminate, as far as practicable, congestion which may develop during an abandonment, due to normal movement of passengers and crew along escape routes, including the possibility that crew may need to move along these routes in a direction opposite to the movement of passengers. In addition, the analysis shall be used to demonstrate that escape arrangements are sufficiently flexible to provide for the possibility that certain escape routes, assembly stations, embarkation stations or survival craft may not be available as a result of a casualty.

---

* Refer to the Interim Guidelines for evacuation analysis for new and existing passenger ships (MSC/Circ.1033).

Part E
Operational requirements

Regulation 14
Operational readiness and maintenance

1   Purpose

The purpose of this regulation is to maintain and monitor the effectiveness of the fire safety measures the ship is provided with. For this purpose, the following functional requirements shall be met:

.1   fire protection systems and fire-fighting systems and appliances shall be maintained ready for use; and

.2   fire protection systems and fire-fighting systems and appliances shall be properly tested and inspected.

2   General requirements

At all times while the ship is in service, the requirements of paragraph 1.1 shall be complied with. A ship is not in service when:

.1   it is in for repairs or lay-up (either at anchor or in port) or in dry-dock;

.2   it is declared not in service by the owner or the owner's representative; and

.3   in the case of passenger ships, there are no passengers on board.

2.1   *Operational readiness*

2.1.1 The following fire protection systems shall be kept in good order so as to ensure their required performance if a fire occurs:

.1   structural fire protection, including fire-resisting divisions, and protection of openings and penetrations in these divisions;

.2   fire detection and fire alarm systems; and

.3   means of escape systems and appliances.

2.1.2 Fire-fighting systems and appliances shall be kept in good working order and readily available for immediate use. Portable extinguishers which have been discharged shall be immediately recharged or replaced with an equivalent unit.

2.2 *Maintenance, testing and inspections*

2.2.1 Maintenance, testing and inspections shall be carried out based on the guidelines developed by the Organization* and in a manner having due regard to ensuring the reliability of fire-fighting systems and appliances.

2.2.2 The maintenance plan shall be kept on board the ship and shall be available for inspection whenever required by the Administration.

2.2.3 The maintenance plan shall include at least the following fire protection systems and fire-fighting systems and appliances, where installed:

- .1 fire mains, fire pumps and hydrants, including hoses, nozzles and international shore connections;
- .2 fixed fire detection and fire alarm systems;
- .3 fixed fire-extinguishing systems and other fire-extinguishing appliances;
- .4 automatic sprinkler, fire detection and fire alarm systems;
- .5 ventilation systems, including fire and smoke dampers, fans and their controls;
- .6 emergency shutdown of fuel supply;
- .7 fire doors, including their controls;
- .8 general emergency alarm systems;
- .9 emergency escape breathing devices;
- .10 portable fire extinguishers, including spare charges; and
- .11 fire-fighter's outfits.

2.2.4 The maintenance programme may be computer-based.

3 Additional requirements for passenger ships

In addition to the fire protection systems and appliances listed in paragraph 2.2.3, ships carrying more than 36 passengers shall develop a maintenance plan for low-location lighting and public address systems.

4 Additional requirements for tankers

In addition to the fire protection systems and appliances listed in paragraph 2.2.3, tankers shall have a maintenance plan for:

- .1 inert gas systems;
- .2 deck foam systems;

---

* Refer to the Guidelines on maintenance and inspection of fire protection systems and appliances (MSC/Circ.850).

> **.3** fire safety arrangements in cargo pump-rooms; and
>
> **.4** flammable gas detectors.

Regulation 15
Instructions, on-board training and drills

1 Purpose

The purpose of this regulation is to mitigate the consequences of fire by means of proper instructions for training and drills of persons on board in correct procedures under emergency conditions. For this purpose, the crew shall have the necessary knowledge and skills to handle fire emergency cases, including passenger care.

2 General requirements

2.1 *Instructions, duties and organization*

2.1.1 Crew members shall receive instruction on fire safety on board the ship.

2.1.2 Crew members shall receive instructions on their assigned duties.

2.1.3 Parties responsible for fire extinguishing shall be organized. These parties shall have the capability to complete their duties at all times while the ship is in service.

2.2 *On-board training and drills*

2.2.1 Crew members shall be trained to be familiar with the arrangements of the ship as well as the location and operation of any fire-fighting systems and appliances that they may be called upon to use.

2.2.2 Training in the use of the emergency escape breathing devices shall be considered as part of on-board training.

2.2.3 Performance of crew members assigned fire-fighting duties shall be periodically evaluated by conducting on-board training and drills to identify areas in need of improvement, to ensure competency in fire-fighting skills is maintained, and to ensure the operational readiness of the fire-fighting organization.

2.2.4 On-board training in the use of the ship's fire-extinguishing systems and appliances shall be planned and conducted in accordance with the provisions of regulation III/19.4.1.

2.2.5 Fire drills shall be conducted and recorded in accordance with the provisions of regulations III/19.3 and III/19.5.

2.3 *Training manuals*

2.3.1 A training manual shall be provided in each crew mess room and recreation room or in each crew cabin.

2.3.2 The training manual shall be written in the working language of the ship.

2.3.3 The training manual, which may comprise several volumes, shall contain the instructions and information required in paragraph 2.3.4 in easily understood terms and illustrated wherever possible. Any part of such information may be provided in the form of audio-visual aids in lieu of the manual.

2.3.4 The training manual shall explain the following in detail:

.1 general fire safety practice and precautions related to the dangers of smoking, electrical hazards, flammable liquids and similar common shipboard hazards;

.2 general instructions on fire-fighting activities and fire-fighting procedures, including procedures for notification of a fire and use of manually operated call points;

.3 meanings of the ship's alarms;

.4 operation and use of fire-fighting systems and appliances;

.5 operation and use of fire doors;

.6 operation and use of fire and smoke dampers; and

.7 escape systems and appliances.

2.4 *Fire control plans**

2.4.1 General arrangement plans shall be permanently exhibited for the guidance of the ship's officers, showing clearly for each deck the control stations, the various fire sections enclosed by "A" class divisions, the sections enclosed by "B" class divisions together with particulars of the fire detection and fire alarm systems, the sprinkler installation, the fire-extinguishing appliances, means of access to different compartments, decks, etc., and the ventilating system, including particulars of the fan control positions, the position of dampers and identification numbers of the ventilating fans serving each section. Alternatively, at the discretion of the Administration, the aforementioned details may be set out in a booklet, a copy of which shall be supplied to each officer, and one copy shall at all times be available on board in an accessible position. Plans and booklets shall be kept up to date; any alterations thereto shall be recorded as soon as practicable. Description in such plans and booklets shall be in the language

---

* Refer to Graphical symbols for fire control plans, adopted by the Organization by resolution A.952(23).

or languages required by the Administration. If the language is neither English nor French, a translation into one of those languages shall be included.

2.4.2 A duplicate set of fire control plans or a booklet containing such plans shall be permanently stored in a prominently marked weathertight enclosure outside the deckhouse for the assistance of shore-side fire-fighting personnel.[*]

3   Additional requirements for passenger ships

3.1   *Fire drills*

In addition to the requirement of paragraph 2.2.3, fire drills shall be conducted in accordance with the provisions of regulation III/30, having due regard to notification of passengers and movement of passengers to assembly stations and embarkation decks.

3.2   *Fire control plans*

In ships carrying more than 36 passengers, plans and booklets required by this regulation shall provide information regarding fire protection, fire detection and fire extinction based on the guidelines developed by the Organization.[†]

Regulation 16
Operations

1   Purpose

The purpose of this regulation is to provide information and instructions for proper ship and cargo handling operations in relation to fire safety. For this purpose, the following functional requirements shall be met:

    .1   fire safety operational booklets shall be provided on board; and

    .2   flammable vapour releases from cargo tank venting shall be controlled.

2   Fire safety operational booklets

2.1   The required fire safety operational booklet shall contain the necessary information and instructions for the safe operation of the ship and cargo handling operations in relation to fire safety. The booklet shall include

---

[*] Refer to the Guidance concerning the location of fire control plans for assistance of shoreside fire-fighting personnel (MSC/Circ.451).

[†] Refer to the Guidelines on the information to be provided with fire control plans and booklets required by SOLAS regulations II-2/20 and 41-2, adopted by the Organization by resolution A.756(18).

information concerning the crew's responsibilities for the general fire safety of the ship while loading and discharging cargo and while under way. Necessary fire safety precautions for handling general cargoes shall be explained. For ships carrying dangerous goods and flammable bulk cargoes, the fire safety operational booklet shall also provide reference to the pertinent fire-fighting and emergency cargo handling instructions contained in the Code of Safe Practice for Solid Bulk Cargoes, the International Bulk Chemical Code, the International Gas Carrier Code and the International Maritime Dangerous Goods Code, as appropriate.

2.2   The fire safety operational booklet shall be provided in each crew mess room and recreation room or in each crew cabin.

2.3   The fire safety operational booklet shall be written in the working language of the ship.

2.4   The fire safety operational booklet may be combined with the training manuals required in regulation 15.2.3.

3   Additional requirements for tankers

3.1   *General*

The fire safety operational booklet referred to in paragraph 2 shall include provisions for preventing fire spread to the cargo area due to ignition of flammable vapours and include procedures of cargo tank gas-purging and/or gas-freeing, taking into account the provisions in paragraph 3.2.

3.2   *Procedures for cargo tank purging and/or gas-freeing*

3.2.1 When the ship is provided with an inert gas system, the cargo tanks shall first be purged in accordance with the provisions of regulation 4.5.6 until the concentration of hydrocarbon vapours in the cargo tanks has been reduced to less than 2% by volume. Thereafter, gas-freeing may take place at the cargo tank deck level.

3.2.2 When the ship is not provided with an inert gas system, the operation shall be such that the flammable vapour is discharged initially through:

- .1   the vent outlets as specified in regulation 4.5.3.4;

- .2   outlets at least 2 m above the cargo tank deck level with a vertical efflux velocity of at least 30 m/s maintained during the gas-freeing operation; or

- .3   outlets at least 2 m above the cargo tank deck level with a vertical efflux velocity of at least 20 m/s and which are protected by suitable devices to prevent the passage of flame.

3.2.3 The above outlets shall be located not less than 10 m, measured horizontally, from the nearest air intakes and openings to enclosed spaces containing a source of ignition and from deck machinery, which may include anchor windlass and chain locker openings, and equipment which may constitute an ignition hazard.

3.2.4 When the flammable vapour concentration at the outlet has been reduced to 30% of the lower flammable limit, gas-freeing may be continued at cargo tank deck level.

Part F
Alternative design and arrangements

Regulation 17
Alternative design and arrangements

1   Purpose

The purpose of this regulation is to provide a methodology for alternative design and arrangements for fire safety.

2   General

2.1   Fire safety design and arrangements may deviate from the prescriptive requirements set out in parts B, C, D, E or G, provided that the design and arrangements meet the fire safety objectives and the functional requirements.

2.2   When fire safety design or arrangements deviate from the prescriptive requirements of this chapter, engineering analysis, evaluation and approval of the alternative design and arrangements shall be carried out in accordance with this regulation.

3   Engineering analysis

The engineering analysis shall be prepared and submitted to the Administration, based on the guidelines developed by the Organization,[*] and shall include, as a minimum, the following elements:

    .1   determination of the ship type and space(s) concerned;

    .2   identification of prescriptive requirement(s) with which the ship or the space(s) will not comply;

    .3   identification of the fire and explosion hazards of the ship or the space(s) concerned, including:

    .3.1   identification of the possible ignition sources;

    .3.2   identification of the fire growth potential of each space concerned;

---

[*] Refer to the Guidelines on alternative design and arrangements for fire safety (MSC/Circ.1002).

.3.3   identification of the smoke and toxic effluent generation potential for each space concerned;

.3.4   identification of the potential for the spread of fire, smoke or of toxic effluents from the space(s) concerned to other spaces;

.4   determination of the required fire safety performance criteria for the ships or the space(s) concerned addressed by the prescriptive requirement(s), in particular:

.4.1   performance criteria shall be based on the fire safety objectives and on the functional requirements of this chapter;

.4.2   performance criteria shall provide a degree of safety not less than that achieved by using the prescriptive requirements; and

.4.3   performance criteria shall be quantifiable and measurable;

.5   detailed description of the alternative design and arrangements, including a list of the assumptions used in the design and any proposed operational restrictions or conditions; and

.6   technical justification demonstrating that the alternative design and arrangements meet the required fire safety performance criteria.

4   Evaluation of the alternative design and arrangements

4.1   The engineering analysis required in paragraph 3 shall be evaluated and approved by the Administration, taking into account the guidelines developed by the Organization.*

4.2   A copy of the documentation, as approved by the Administration, indicating that the alternative design and arrangements comply with this regulation shall be carried on board the ship.

5   Exchange of information

The Administration shall communicate to the Organization pertinent information concerning alternative design and arrangements approved by them for circulation to all Contracting Governments.

6   Re-evaluation due to change of conditions

If the assumptions, and operational restrictions that were stipulated in the alternative design and arrangements are changed, the engineering analysis shall be carried out under the changed condition and shall be approved by the Administration.

---

* Refer to the Guidelines on alternative design and arrangements for fire safety (MSC/Circ.1002).

Part G
Special requirements

Regulation 18
Helicopter facilities

1   Purpose

The purpose of this regulation is to provide additional measures in order to address the fire safety objectives of this chapter for ships fitted with special facilities for helicopters. For this purpose, the following functional requirements shall be met:

.1   helideck structure shall be adequate to protect the ship from the fire hazards associated with helicopter operations;

.2   fire-fighting appliances shall be provided to adequately protect the ship from the fire hazards associated with helicopter operations;

.3   refuelling and hangar facilities and operations shall provide the necessary measures to protect the ship from the fire hazards associated with helicopter operations; and

.4   operation manuals and training shall be provided.

2   Application

2.1   In addition to complying with the requirements of regulations in parts B, C, D and E, as appropriate, ships equipped with helidecks shall comply with the requirements of this regulation.

2.2   Where helicopters land or conduct winching operations on an occasional or emergency basis on ships without helidecks, fire-fighting equipment fitted in accordance with the requirements in part C may be used. This equipment shall be made readily available in close proximity to the landing or winching areas during helicopter operations.

2.3   Notwithstanding the requirements of paragraph 2.2 above, ro–ro passenger ships without helidecks shall comply with regulation III/28.

3 Structure

3.1 *Construction of steel or other equivalent material*

In general, the construction of the helidecks shall be of steel or other equivalent materials. If the helideck forms the deckhead of a deckhouse or superstructure, it shall be insulated to "A-60" class standard.

3.2 *Construction of aluminium or other low melting point metals*

If the Administration permits aluminium or other low melting point metal construction that is not made equivalent to steel, the following provisions shall be satisfied:

.1   if the platform is cantilevered over the side of the ship, after each fire on the ship or on the platform, the platform shall undergo a structural analysis to determine its suitability for further use; and

.2   if the platform is located above the ship's deckhouse or similar structure, the following conditions shall be satisfied:

.2.1   the deckhouse top and bulkheads under the platform shall have no openings;

.2.2   windows under the platform shall be provided with steel shutters; and

.2.3   after each fire on the platform or in close proximity, the platform shall undergo a structural analysis to determine its suitability for further use.

4 Means of escape

A helideck shall be provided with both a main and an emergency means of escape and access for fire fighting and rescue personnel. These shall be located as far apart from each other as is practicable and preferably on opposite sides of the helideck.

5 Fire-fighting appliances

5.1   In close proximity to the helideck, the following fire-fighting appliances shall be provided and stored near the means of access to that helideck:

.1   at least two dry powder extinguishers having a total capacity of not less than 45 kg;

.2   carbon dioxide extinguishers of a total capacity of not less than 18 kg or equivalent;

.3   a suitable foam application system consisting of monitors or foam-making branch pipes capable of delivering foam to all parts of the helideck in all weather conditions in which helicopters can operate. The system shall be capable of delivering a discharge rate as required in table 18.1 for at least five minutes;

Table 18.1 – Foam discharge rates

Category	Helicopter overall length	Discharge rate foam solution (l/min)
H1	up to but not including 15 m	250
H2	from 15 m up to but not including 24 m	500
H3	from 24 m up to but not including 35 m	800

.4   the principal agent shall be suitable for use with salt water and conform to performance standards not inferior to those acceptable to the Organization;[*]

.5   at least two nozzles of an approved dual-purpose type (jet/spray) and hoses sufficient to reach any part of the helideck;

.6   in addition to the requirements of regulation 10.10, two sets of fire-fighter's outfits; and

.7   at least the following equipment shall be stored in a manner that provides for immediate use and protection from the elements:

    .1   adjustable wrench;

    .2   blanket, fire-resistant;

    .3   cutters, bolt, 60 cm;

    .4   hook, grab or salving;

    .5   hacksaw, heavy duty complete with 6 spare blades;

    .6   ladder;

    .7   lift line 5 mm diameter and 15 m in length;

    .8   pliers, side-cutting;

    .9   set of assorted screwdrivers; and

    .10   harness knife complete with sheath.

6   Drainage facilities

Drainage facilities in way of helidecks shall be constructed of steel and shall lead directly overboard independent of any other system and shall be designed so that drainage does not fall onto any part of the ship.

---

[*] Refer to the *International Civil Aviation Organization Airport Services Manual*, part 1, Rescue and Fire Fighting, chapter 8, Extinguishing Agent Characteristics, paragraph 8.1.5, Foam Specifications table 8-1, level 'B'.

7   Helicopter refuelling and hangar facilities

Where the ship has helicopter refuelling and hangar facilities, the following requirements shall be complied with:

.1   a designated area shall be provided for the storage of fuel tanks which shall be:

.1.1   as remote as is practicable from accommodation spaces, escape routes and embarkation stations; and

.1.2   isolated from areas containing a source of vapour ignition;

.2   the fuel storage area shall be provided with arrangements whereby fuel spillage may be collected and drained to a safe location;

.3   tanks and associated equipment shall be protected against physical damage and from a fire in an adjacent space or area;

.4   where portable fuel storage tanks are used, special attention shall be given to:

.4.1   design of the tank for its intended purpose;

.4.2   mounting and securing arrangements;

.4.3   electric bonding; and

.4.4   inspection procedures;

.5   storage tank fuel pumps shall be provided with means which permit shutdown from a safe remote location in the event of a fire. Where a gravity fuelling system is installed, equivalent closing arrangements shall be provided to isolate the fuel source;

.6   the fuel pumping unit shall be connected to one tank at a time. The piping between the tank and the pumping unit shall be of steel or equivalent material, as short as possible, and protected against damage;

.7   electrical fuel pumping units and associated control equipment shall be of a type suitable for the location and potential hazards;

.8   fuel pumping units shall incorporate a device which will prevent over-pressurization of the delivery or filling hose;

.9   equipment used in refuelling operations shall be electrically bonded;

.10   "NO SMOKING" signs shall be displayed at appropriate locations;

.11   hangar, refuelling and maintenance facilities shall be treated as category A machinery spaces with regard to structural fire protection, fixed fire-extinguishing and detection system requirements;

.12   enclosed hangar facilities or enclosed spaces containing refuelling installations shall be provided with mechanical ventilation, as required by regulation 20.3 for closed ro–ro spaces of cargo ships. Ventilation fans shall be of non-sparking type; and

.13   electric equipment and wiring in enclosed hangars or enclosed spaces containing refuelling installations shall comply with regulations 20.3.2, 20.3.3 and 20.3.4.

8   Operations manual and fire-fighting arrangements

8.1   Each helicopter facility shall have an operations manual, including a description and a checklist of safety precautions, procedures and equipment requirements. This manual may be part of the ship's emergency response procedures.

8.2   The procedures and precautions to be followed during refuelling operations shall be in accordance with recognized safe practices and contained in the operations manual.

8.3   Fire-fighting personnel, consisting of at least two persons trained for rescue and fire-fighting duties, and fire-fighting equipment shall be immediately available at all times when helicopter operations are expected.

8.4   Fire-fighting personnel shall be present during refuelling operations. However, the fire-fighting personnel shall not be involved with refuelling activities.

8.5   On-board refresher training shall be carried out and additional supplies of fire-fighting media shall be provided for training and testing of the equipment.

Regulation 19
*Carriage of dangerous goods**

1   Purpose

The purpose of this regulation is to provide additional safety measures in order to address the fire safety objectives of this chapter for ships carrying dangerous goods. For this purpose, the following functional requirements shall be met:

.1   fire protection systems shall be provided to protect the ship from the added fire hazards associated with carriage of dangerous goods;

---

* Refer to the Interim guidelines for open-top containerships (MSC/Circ.608/Rev.1).

.2   dangerous goods shall be adequately separated from ignition sources; and

.3   appropriate personnel protective equipment shall be provided for the hazards associated with the carriage of dangerous goods.

2   General requirements

2.1   In addition to complying with the requirements of regulations in parts B, C, D, E and regulations 18 and 20,[*] as appropriate, ship types and cargo spaces, referred to in paragraph 2.2, intended for the carriage of dangerous goods shall comply with the requirements of this regulation, as appropriate, except when carrying dangerous goods in limited quantities[†] unless such requirements have already been met by compliance with the requirements elsewhere in this chapter. The types of ships and modes of carriage of dangerous goods are referred to in paragraph 2.2 and in table 19.1. Cargo ships of less than 500 gross tonnage shall comply with this regulation, but Administrations may reduce the requirements and such reduced requirements shall be recorded in the document of compliance referred to in paragraph 4.

2.2   The following ship types and cargo spaces shall govern the application of tables 19.1 and 19.2:

.1   ships and cargo spaces not specifically designed for the carriage of freight containers, but intended for the carriage of dangerous goods in packaged form, including goods in freight containers and portable tanks;

.2   purpose-built containerships and cargo spaces intended for the carriage of dangerous goods in freight containers and portable tanks;

.3   ro–ro ships and ro–ro spaces intended for the carriage of dangerous goods;

.4   ships and cargo spaces intended for the carriage of solid dangerous goods in bulk; and

.5   ships and cargo spaces intended for carriage of dangerous goods other than liquids and gases in bulk in shipborne barges.

3   Special requirements

Unless otherwise specified, the following requirements shall govern the application of tables 19.1, 19.2 and 19.3 to both "on-deck" and "under-

---

[*] Refer to part 7 of the International Maritime Dangerous Goods Code.

[†] Refer to chapter 3.4 of the International Maritime Dangerous Goods Code.

deck" stowage of dangerous goods where the numbers of the following paragraphs are indicated in the first column of the tables.

3.1 *Water supplies*

3.1.1 Arrangements shall be made to ensure immediate availability of a supply of water from the fire main at the required pressure either by permanent pressurization or by suitably placed remote arrangements for the fire pumps.

3.1.2 The quantity of water delivered shall be capable of supplying four nozzles of a size and at pressures as specified in regulation 10.2, capable of being trained on any part of the cargo space when empty. This amount of water may be applied by equivalent means to the satisfaction of the Administration.

3.1.3 Means shall be provided for effectively cooling the designated under-deck cargo space by at least 5 *l*/min per square metre of the horizontal area of cargo spaces, either by a fixed arrangement of spraying nozzles or by flooding the cargo space with water. Hoses may be used for this purpose in small cargo spaces and in small areas of larger cargo spaces at the discretion of the Administration. However, the drainage and pumping arrangements shall be such as to prevent the build-up of free surfaces. The drainage system shall be sized to remove no less than 125% of the combined capacity of both the water spraying system pumps and the required number of fire hose nozzles. The drainage system valves shall be operable from outside the protected space at a position in the vicinity of the extinguishing system controls. Bilge wells shall be of sufficient holding capacity and shall be arranged at the side shell of the ship at a distance from each other of not more than 40 m in each watertight compartment. If this is not possible, the adverse effect upon stability of the added weight and free surface of water shall be taken into account to the extent deemed necessary by the Administration in its approval of the stability information.*

3.1.4 Provision to flood a designated under-deck cargo space with suitable specified media may be substituted for the requirements in paragraph 3.1.3.

3.1.5 The total required capacity of the water supply shall satisfy paragraphs 3.1.2 and 3.1.3, if applicable, simultaneously calculated for the largest designated cargo space. The capacity requirements of paragraph 3.1.2 shall be met by the total capacity of the main fire pump(s), not including the capacity of the emergency fire pump, if fitted. If a drencher system is used to satisfy paragraph 3.1.3, the drencher pump shall also be taken into account in this total capacity calculation.

---

* Refer to the Recommendation on fixed fire-extinguishing systems for special category spaces adopted by the Organization by resolution A.123(V).

3.2   *Sources of ignition*

Electrical equipment and wiring shall not be fitted in enclosed cargo spaces or vehicle spaces unless it is essential for operational purposes in the opinion of the Administration. However, if electrical equipment is fitted in such spaces, it shall be of a certified safe type* for use in the dangerous environments to which it may be exposed unless it is possible to completely isolate the electrical system (e.g. by removal of links in the system, other than fuses). Cable penetrations of the decks and bulkheads shall be sealed against the passage of gas or vapour. Through runs of cables and cables within the cargo spaces shall be protected against damage from impact. Any other equipment which may constitute a source of ignition of flammable vapour shall not be permitted.

3.3   *Detection system*

Ro–ro spaces shall be fitted with a fixed fire detection and fire alarm system complying with the requirements of the Fire Safety Systems Code. All other types of cargo spaces shall be fitted with either a fixed fire detection and fire alarm system or a sample extraction smoke detection system complying with the requirements of the Fire Safety Systems Code. If a sample extraction smoke detection system is fitted, particular attention shall be given to paragraph 2.1.3 in chapter 10 of the Fire Safety Systems Code in order to prevent the leakage of toxic fumes into occupied areas.

3.4   *Ventilation*

3.4.1 Adequate power ventilation shall be provided in enclosed cargo spaces. The arrangement shall be such as to provide for at least six air changes per hour in the cargo space, based on an empty cargo space, and for removal of vapours from the upper or lower parts of the cargo space, as appropriate.

3.4.2 The fans shall be such as to avoid the possibility of ignition of flammable gas/air mixtures. Suitable wire mesh guards shall be fitted over inlet and outlet ventilation openings.

3.4.3 Natural ventilation shall be provided in enclosed cargo spaces intended for the carriage of solid dangerous goods in bulk, where there is no provision for mechanical ventilation.

3.5   *Bilge pumping*

3.5.1 Where it is intended to carry flammable or toxic liquids in enclosed cargo spaces, the bilge pumping system shall be designed to protect against inadvertent pumping of such liquids through machinery space piping or

---

* Refer to the recommendations of the International Electrotechnical Commission, in particular publication IEC 60092, *Electrical installations in ships*.

pumps. Where large quantities of such liquids are carried, consideration shall be given to the provision of additional means of draining those cargo spaces.

3.5.2 If the bilge drainage system is additional to the system served by pumps in the machinery space, the capacity of the system shall be not less than 10 m^3/h per cargo space served. If the additional system is common, the capacity need not exceed 25 m^3/h. The additional bilge system need not be arranged with redundancy.

3.5.3 Whenever flammable or toxic liquids are carried, the bilge line into the machinery space shall be isolated either by fitting a blank flange or by a closed lockable valve.

3.5.4 Enclosed spaces outside machinery spaces containing bilge pumps serving cargo spaces intended for carriage of flammable or toxic liquids shall be fitted with separate mechanical ventilation giving at least six air changes per hour. If the space has access from another enclosed space, the door shall be self-closing.

3.5.5 If bilge drainage of cargo spaces is arranged by gravity drainage, the drainage shall be either led directly overboard or to a closed drain tank located outside the machinery spaces. The tank shall be provided with a vent pipe to a safe location on the open deck. Drainage from a cargo space into bilge wells in a lower space is only permitted if that space satisfies the same requirements as the cargo space above.

3.6   *Personnel protection*

3.6.1 Four sets of full protective clothing, resistant to chemical attack, shall be provided in addition to the fire-fighter's outfits required by regulation 10.10. The protective clothing shall cover all skin, so that no part of the body is unprotected.

3.6.2 At least two self-contained breathing apparatuses additional to those required by regulation 10.10 shall be provided. Two spare charges suitable for use with the breathing apparatus shall be provided for each required apparatus. Passenger ships carrying not more than 36 passengers and cargo ships that are equipped with suitably located means for fully recharging the air cylinders free from contamination need carry only one spare charge for each required apparatus.

3.7   *Portable fire extinguishers*

Portable fire extinguishers with a total capacity of at least 12 kg of dry powder or equivalent shall be provided for the cargo spaces. These extinguishers shall be in addition to any portable fire extinguishers required elsewhere in this chapter.

3.8   *Insulation of machinery space boundaries*

Bulkheads forming boundaries between cargo spaces and machinery spaces of category A shall be insulated to "A-60" class standard, unless the dangerous goods are stowed at least 3 m horizontally away from such bulkheads. Other boundaries between such spaces shall be insulated to "A-60" class standard.

3.9   *Water-spray system*

Each open ro–ro space having a deck above it and each space deemed to be a closed ro–ro space not capable of being sealed shall be fitted with an approved fixed pressure water-spraying system for manual operation which shall protect all parts of any deck and vehicle platform in the space, except that the Administration may permit the use of any other fixed fire-extinguishing system that has been shown by full-scale test to be no less effective. However, the drainage and pumping arrangements shall be such as to prevent the build-up of free surfaces. The drainage system shall be sized to remove no less than 125% of the combined capacity of both the water-spraying system pumps and the required number of fire hose nozzles. The drainage system valves shall be operable from outside the protected space at a position in the vicinity of the extinguishing system controls. Bilge wells shall be of sufficient holding capacity and shall be arranged at the side shell of the ship at a distance from each other of not more than 40 m in each watertight compartment. If this is not possible, the adverse effect upon stability of the added weight and free surface of water shall be taken into account to the extent deemed necessary by the Administration in its approval of the stability information.*

3.10   *Separation of ro–ro spaces*

3.10.1   In ships having ro–ro spaces, a separation shall be provided between a closed ro–ro space and an adjacent open ro–ro space. The separation shall be such as to minimize the passage of dangerous vapours and liquids between such spaces. Alternatively, such separation need not be provided if the ro–ro space is considered to be a closed cargo space over its entire length and fully complies with the relevant special requirements of this regulation.

3.10.2   In ships having ro–ro spaces, a separation shall be provided between a closed ro–ro space and the adjacent weather deck. The separation shall be such as to minimize the passage of dangerous vapours and liquids between such spaces. Alternatively, a separation need not be provided if the arrangements of the closed ro–ro spaces are in accordance with those required for the dangerous goods carried on adjacent weather decks.

---

* Refer to the Recommendation on fixed fire-extinguishing systems for special category spaces adopted by the Organization by resolution A.123(V).

Table 19.1 – Application of the requirements to different modes of carriage of dangerous goods in ships and cargo spaces

Where X appears in table 19.1, it means this requirement is applicable to all classes of dangerous goods as given in the appropriate line of table 19.3, except as indicated by the notes.

Regulation 19 / Regulation 19.2.2	Weather decks (.1 to .5 inclusive)	.1 Not specifically designed	.2 Container cargo spaces	.3 Closed ro–ro spaces[5]	.3 Open ro–ro spaces	.4 Solid dangerous goods in bulk	.5 Shipborne barges
.3.1.1	X	X	X	X	X		X
.3.1.2	X	X	X	X	X		–
.3.1.3	–	X	X	X	X		X
.3.1.4	–	X	X	X	X		X
.3.2	–	X	X	X	X		X[4]
.3.3	–	X	X	X	–		X[4]
.3.4.1	–	X	X[1]	X	–		X[4]
.3.4.2	–	X	X[1]	X	–		X[4]
.3.5	–	X	X	X	–	For application of requirements of regulation 19 to different classes of dangerous goods, see table 19.2	–
.3.6.1	X	X	X	X	X		–
.3.6.2	X	X	X	X	X		–
.3.7	X	X	–	–	X		–
.3.8	X	X	X[2]	X	X		–
.3.9	–	–	–	X[3]	X		–
.3.10.1	–	–	–	X	–		–
.3.10.2	–	–	–	X	–		–

Notes:

1 For classes 4 and 5.1 not applicable to closed freight containers.
  For classes 2, 3, 6.1 and 8 when carried in closed freight containers, the ventilation rate may be reduced to not less than two air changes. For the purpose of this requirement a portable tank is a closed freight container.

2 Applicable to decks only.

3 Applies only to closed ro–ro spaces, not capable of being sealed.

4 In the special case where the barges are capable of containing flammable vapours or alternatively if they are capable of discharging flammable vapours to a safe space outside the barge carrier compartment by means of ventilation ducts connected to the barges, these requirements may be reduced or waived to the satisfaction of the Administration.

5 Special category spaces shall be treated as closed ro–ro spaces when dangerous goods are carried.

Table 19.2 – Application of the requirements to different classes
of dangerous goods for ships and cargo spaces carrying
solid dangerous goods in bulk

Class / Regulation 19	4.1	4.2	4.3[6]	5.1	6.1	8	9
.3.1.1	X	X	–	X	–	–	X
.3.1.2	X	X	–	X	–	–	X
.3.2	X	X[7]	X	X[8]	–	–	X[8]
.3.4.1	–	X[7]	X	–	–	–	–
.3.4.2	X[9]	X[7]	X	X[7,9]	–	–	X[7,9]
.3.4.3	X	X	X	X	X	X	X
.3.6	X	X	X	X	X	X	X
.3.8	X	X	X	X[7]	–	–	X[10]

Notes:

6 The hazards of substances in this class which may be carried in bulk are such that special consideration shall be given by the Administration to the construction and equipment of the ship involved in addition to meeting the requirements enumerated in this table.

7 Only applicable to Seedcake containing solvent extractions, to Ammonium nitrate and to Ammonium nitrate fertilizers.

8 Only applicable to Ammonium nitrate and to Ammonium nitrate fertilizers. However, a degree of protection in accordance with standards contained in the International Electrotechnical Commission publication 60079, *Electrical apparatus for explosive gas atmospheres*, is sufficient.

9 Only suitable wire mesh guards are required.

10 The requirements of the Code of Safe Practice for Solid Bulk Cargoes, adopted by resolution A.434(XI), as amended, are sufficient.

Table 19.3 – Application of the requirements to different classes of dangerous goods except solid dangerous goods in bulk

Class / Regulation 19	1.1 to 1.6	1.4S	2.1	2.2	2.3	3 liquids ≤23°C¹⁵	3 liquids >23C¹⁵ ≤61°C	4.1	4.2	4.3	5.1	5.2	6.1 liquids	6.1 liquids ≤23 C¹⁵	6.1 liquids >23 C¹⁵ ≤61°C	6.1 solids	8 liquids	8 liquids ≤23 C¹⁵	8 liquids >23 C¹⁵ ≤61°C	8 solids	9
.3.1.1	×	×	×	×	×	×	×	×	×	×	×	×	×	×	×	×	×	×	×	×	×
.3.1.2	×	×	×	×	×	×	×	×	×	×	×	×	×	×	×	×	×	×	×	×	–
.3.1.3	×	–	–	–	–	–	–	–	–	–	–	–	–	–	–	–	–	–	–	–	–
.3.1.4	×	–	–	–	–	×	–	–	–	–	–	–	–	–	–	–	–	×	–	–	–
.3.2	×	×	×	–	–	×	–	–	–	–	–	–	×	×	–	–	×	×	×	–	–
.3.3	×	×	×	–	×	×	–	×	×	×	×	–	×	×	×	×	×	×	×	×	–
.3.4.1	–	–	×	–	–	×	–	×¹¹	×¹¹	×	×¹¹	–	–	×	×	×¹¹	–	×	×	–	×¹¹
.3.4.2	–	–	×	–	–	×	–	–	–	–	–	–	–	×	×	–	–	×	×	–	–
.3.5	–	–	–	–	–	×	×	–	–	–	–	–	×	×	×	–	–	×	–	–	–
.3.6	–	–	×	×	×	×	×	×	×	×	×	×	×	×	×	×	×	×	×	×	×¹⁴
.3.7	–	–	–	–	–	×	×	×	×	×	×	–	–	×	×	–	–	×	×	–	–
.3.8	×¹²	–	×	×	×	×	×	×	×	×	×¹³	–	–	×	×	–	–	×	×	–	–
.3.9	×	×	×	×	×	×	×	×	×	×	×	×	×	×	×	×	×	×	×	×	×
.3.10.1	×	×	×	×	×	×	×	×	×	×	×	×¹⁶	×	×	×	×	×	×	×	×	×
.3.10.2	×	×	×	×	×	×	×	×	×	×	×	×¹⁶	×	×	×	×	×	×	×	×	×

Notes:
11 When "mechanically-ventilated spaces" are required by the International Maritime Dangerous Goods Code, as amended.
12 Stow 3 m horizontally away from the machinery space boundaries in all cases.
13 Refer to the International Maritime Dangerous Goods Code, as amended.
14 As appropriate to the goods to be carried.
15 Refers to flashpoint.
16 Under the provisions of the IMDG Code, as amended, stowage of class 5.2 dangerous goods under deck or in enclosed ro-ro spaces is prohibited.

4   Document of compliance[*]

The Administration shall provide the ship with an appropriate document as evidence of compliance of construction and equipment with the requirements of this regulation. Certification for dangerous goods, except solid dangerous goods in bulk, is not required for those cargoes specified as class 6.2 and 7, as defined in regulation VII/2, and dangerous goods in limited quantities.

Regulation 20
Protection of vehicle, special category and ro–ro spaces

1   Purpose

The purpose of this regulation is to provide additional safety measures in order to address the fire safety objectives of this chapter for ships fitted with vehicle, special category and ro–ro spaces. For this purpose, the following functional requirements shall be met:

   .1   fire protection systems shall be provided to adequately protect the ship from the fire hazards associated with vehicle, special category and ro–ro spaces;

   .2   ignition sources shall be separated from vehicle, special category and ro–ro spaces; and

   .3   vehicle, special category and ro–ro spaces shall be adequately ventilated.

2   General requirements

2.1   *Application*

In addition to complying with the requirements of regulations in parts B, C, D and E, as appropriate, vehicle, special category and ro–ro spaces shall comply with the requirements of this regulation.

2.2   *Basic principles for passenger ships*

2.2.1 The basic principle underlying the provisions of this regulation is that the main vertical zoning required by regulation 9.2 may not be practicable in vehicle spaces of passenger ships and, therefore, equivalent protection must be obtained in such spaces on the basis of a horizontal zone concept and by the provision of an efficient fixed fire-extinguishing system. Based

---

[*] Refer to the Document of compliance with the special requirements for ships carrying dangerous goods under the provisions of regulation II-2/19 of SOLAS 74, as amended (MSC/Circ.1027).

on this concept, a horizontal zone for the purpose of this regulation may include special category spaces on more than one deck provided that the total overall clear height for vehicles does not exceed 10 m.

2.2.2 The basic principle underlying the provisions of paragraph 2.2.1 is also applicable to ro–ro spaces.

2.2.3 The requirements of ventilation systems, openings in "A" class divisions and penetrations in "A" class divisions for maintaining the integrity of vertical zones in this chapter shall be applied equally to decks and bulkheads forming the boundaries separating horizontal zones from each other and from the remainder of the ship.

3   Precaution against ignition of flammable vapours in closed vehicle spaces, closed ro–ro spaces and special category spaces

3.1   *Ventilation systems**

3.1.1 *Capacity of ventilation systems*

There shall be provided an effective power ventilation system sufficient to give at least the following air changes:

.1   Passenger ships:

Special category spaces	10 air changes per hour
Closed ro–ro and vehicle spaces other than special category spaces for ships carrying more than 36 passengers	10 air changes per hour
Closed ro–ro and vehicle spaces other than special category spaces for ships carrying not more than 36 passengers	6 air changes per hour

.2   Cargo ships: 6 air changes per hour

The Administration may require an increased number of air changes when vehicles are being loaded and unloaded.

3.1.2 *Performance of ventilation systems*

3.1.2.1   In passenger ships, the power ventilation system required in paragraph 3.1.1 shall be separate from other ventilation systems and shall be in operation at all times when vehicles are in such spaces. Ventilation ducts serving such cargo spaces capable of being effectively sealed shall be separated for each such space. The system shall be capable of being controlled from a position outside such spaces.

---

* Refer to the Design Guidelines and operational recommendations for ventilation systems in ro–ro cargo spaces (MSC/Circ.729).

3.1.2.2 In cargo ships, ventilation fans shall normally be run continuously whenever vehicles are on board. Where this is impracticable, they shall be operated for a limited period daily as weather permits and in any case for a reasonable period prior to discharge, after which period the ro–ro or vehicle space shall be proved gas-free. One or more portable combustible gas detecting instruments shall be carried for this purpose. The system shall be entirely separate from other ventilating systems. Ventilation ducts serving ro–ro or vehicle spaces shall be capable of being effectively sealed for each cargo space. The system shall be capable of being controlled from a position outside such spaces.

3.1.2.3 The ventilation system shall be such as to prevent air stratification and the formation of air pockets.

3.1.3 *Indication of ventilation systems*

Means shall be provided on the navigation bridge to indicate any loss of the required ventilating capacity.

3.1.4 *Closing appliances and ducts*

3.1.4.1 Arrangements shall be provided to permit a rapid shutdown and effective closure of the ventilation system from outside of the space in case of fire, taking into account the weather and sea conditions.

3.1.4.2 Ventilation ducts, including dampers, within a common horizontal zone shall be made of steel. In passenger ships, ventilation ducts that pass through other horizontal zones or machinery spaces shall be "A-60" class steel ducts constructed in accordance with regulations 9.7.2.1.1 and 9.7.2.1.2.

3.1.5 *Permanent openings*

Permanent openings in the side plating, the ends or deckhead of the space shall be so situated that a fire in the cargo space does not endanger stowage areas and embarkation stations for survival craft and accommodation spaces, service spaces and control stations in superstructures and deckhouses above the cargo spaces.

3.2 *Electrical equipment and wiring*

3.2.1 Except as provided in paragraph 3.2.2, electrical equipment and wiring shall be of a type suitable for use in an explosive petrol and air mixture.[*]

3.2.2 In case of other than special category spaces below the bulkhead deck, notwithstanding the provisions in paragraph 3.2.1, above a height of

---

[*] Refer to the recommendations of the International Electrotechnical Commission, in particular publication 60079.

450 mm from the deck and from each platform for vehicles, if fitted, except platforms with openings of sufficient size permitting penetration of petrol gases downwards, electrical equipment of a type so enclosed and protected as to prevent the escape of sparks shall be permitted as an alternative, on condition that the ventilation system is so designed and operated as to provide continuous ventilation of the cargo spaces at the rate of at least ten air changes per hour whenever vehicles are on board.

3.3   *Electrical equipment and wiring in exhaust ventilation ducts*

Electrical equipment and wiring, if installed in an exhaust ventilation duct, shall be of a type approved for use in explosive petrol and air mixtures and the outlet from any exhaust duct shall be sited in a safe position, having regard to other possible sources of ignition.

3.4   *Other ignition sources*

Other equipment which may constitute a source of ignition of flammable vapours shall not be permitted.

3.5   *Scuppers and discharges*

Scuppers shall not be led to machinery or other spaces where sources of ignition may be present.

4   Detection and alarm

4.1   *Fixed fire detection and fire alarm systems*

Except as provided in paragraph 4.3.1, there shall be provided a fixed fire detection and fire alarm system complying with the requirements of the Fire Safety Systems Code. The fixed fire detection system shall be capable of rapidly detecting the onset of fire. The type of detectors and their spacing and location shall be to the satisfaction of the Administration, taking into account the effects of ventilation and other relevant factors. After being installed, the system shall be tested under normal ventilation conditions and shall give an overall response time to the satisfaction of the Administration.

4.2   *Sample extraction smoke detection systems*

Except open ro–ro spaces, open vehicle spaces and special category spaces, a sample extraction smoke detection system complying with the requirements of the Fire Safety Systems Code may be used as an alternative for the fixed fire detection and fire alarm system required in paragraph 4.1.

4.3   *Special category spaces*

4.3.1 An efficient fire patrol system shall be maintained in special category spaces. If an efficient fire patrol system is maintained by a continuous fire watch at all times during the voyage, a fixed fire detection and fire alarm system is not required.

4.3.2 Manually operated call points shall be spaced so that no part of the space is more than 20 m from a manually operated call point, and one shall be placed close to each exit from such spaces.

5   Structural fire protection

Notwithstanding the provisions of regulation 9.2.2, in passenger ships carrying more than 36 passengers, the boundary bulkheads and decks of special category spaces and ro–ro spaces shall be insulated to "A-60" class standard. However, where a category (5), (9) or (10) space, as defined in regulation 9.2.2.3, is on one side of the division, the standard may be reduced to "A-0". Where fuel oil tanks are below a special category space or a ro–ro space, the integrity of the deck between such spaces may be reduced to "A-0" standard.

6   Fire extinction

6.1   *Fixed fire-extinguishing systems**

6.1.1 Vehicle spaces and ro–ro spaces which are not special category spaces and are capable of being sealed from a location outside of the cargo spaces shall be fitted with a fixed gas fire-extinguishing system which shall comply with the provisions of the Fire Safety Systems Code, except that:

.1   if a carbon dioxide fire-extinguishing system is fitted, the quantity of gas available shall be at least sufficient to give a minimum volume of free gas equal to 45% of the gross volume of the largest such cargo space which is capable of being sealed, and the arrangements shall be such as to ensure that at least two thirds of the gas required for the relevant space shall be introduced within 10 min;

.2   any other fixed inert gas fire-extinguishing system or fixed high-expansion foam fire-extinguishing system may be fitted provided the Administration is satisfied that an equivalent protection is achieved; and

.3   as an alternative, a fire-extinguishing system meeting the requirements of paragraph 6.1.2 may be fitted.

6.1.2 Ro–ro and vehicle spaces not capable of being sealed and special category spaces shall be fitted with an approved fixed pressure water-spraying system† for manual operation which shall protect all parts of any deck and vehicle platform in such spaces. Such water-spray systems shall have:

---

* Refer to the Guidelines for the approval of alternative fixed water-based fire-fighting systems for special category spaces (MSC/Circ.914).
† Refer to the Recommendation on fixed fire-extinguishing systems for special category spaces adopted by the Organization by resolution A.123(V).

.1 a pressure gauge on the valve manifold;

.2 clear marking on each manifold valve indicating the spaces served;

.3 instructions for maintenance and operation located in the valve room; and

.4 a sufficient number of drainage valves.

6.1.3 The Administration may permit the use of any other fixed fire-extinguishing system[*] that has been shown, by a full-scale test in conditions simulating a flowing petrol fire in a vehicle space or a ro–ro space, to be not less effective in controlling fires likely to occur in such a space.

6.1.4 When fixed pressure water-spraying fire-extinguishing systems are provided, in view of the serious loss of stability which could arise due to large quantities of water accumulating on the deck or decks during the operation of the water-spraying system, the following arrangements shall be provided:

.1 in passenger ships:

.1.1 in the spaces above the bulkhead deck, scuppers shall be fitted so as to ensure that such water is rapidly discharged directly overboard;

.1.2.1 in ro–ro passenger ships, discharge valves for scuppers, fitted with positive means of closing operable from a position above the bulkhead deck in accordance with the requirements of the International Convention on Load Lines in force, shall be kept open while the ships are at sea;

.1.2.2 any operation of valves referred to in paragraph 6.1.4.1.2.1 shall be recorded in the log-book;

.1.3 in the spaces below the bulkhead deck, the Administration may require pumping and drainage facilities to be provided additional to the requirements of regulation II-1/21. In such case, the drainage system shall be sized to remove no less than 125% of the combined capacity of both the water-spraying system pumps and the required number of fire hose nozzles. The drainage system valves shall be operable from outside the protected space at a position in the vicinity of the extinguishing system controls. Bilge wells shall be of sufficient holding capacity and shall be arranged at the side shell of the ship at a distance from each other of not more than 40 m in each watertight compartment;

---

[*] Refer to the Guidelines for the approval of alternative fixed water-based fire-fighting systems for special category spaces (MSC/Circ.914).

   .2   in cargo ships, the drainage and pumping arrangements shall be such as to prevent the build-up of free surfaces. In such case, the drainage system shall be sized to remove no less than 125% of the combined capacity of both the water-spraying system pumps and the required number of fire hose nozzles. The drainage system valves shall be operable from outside the protected space at a position in the vicinity of the extinguishing system controls. Bilge wells shall be of sufficient holding capacity and shall be arranged at the side shell of the ship at a distance from each other of not more than 40 m in each watertight compartment. If this is not possible, the adverse effect upon stability of the added weight and free surface of water shall be taken into account to the extent deemed necessary by the Administration in its approval of the stability information.* Such information shall be included in the stability information supplied to the master as required by regulation II-1/22.

6.2   *Portable fire extinguishers*

6.2.1 Portable fire extinguishers shall be provided at each deck level in each hold or compartment where vehicles are carried, spaced not more than 20 m apart on both sides of the space. At least one portable fire extinguisher shall be located at each access to such a cargo space.

6.2.2 In addition to the provision of paragraph 6.2.1, the following fire-extinguishing appliances shall be provided in vehicle, ro–ro and special category spaces intended for the carriage of motor vehicles with fuel in their tanks for their own propulsion:

   .1   at least three water-fog applicators; and

   .2   one portable foam applicator unit complying with the provisions of the Fire Safety Systems Code, provided that at least two such units are available in the ship for use in such spaces.

---

* Refer to the Recommendation on fixed fire-extinguishing systems for special category spaces adopted by the Organization by resolution A.123(V).

Part A
General

Regulation 1
Application

1   Unless expressly provided otherwise, this chapter shall apply to ships the keels of which are laid or which are at a similar stage of construction on or after 1 July 1998.

2   For the purpose of this chapter the term *a similar stage of construction* means the stage at which:

    .1   construction identifiable with a specific ship begins; and

    .2   assembly of that ship has commenced comprising at least 50 tonnes or 1% of the estimated mass of all structural material, whichever is less.

3   For the purpose of this chapter:

    .1   the expression *ships constructed* means "ships the keels of which are laid or which are at a similar stage of construction";

    .2   the expression *all ships* means ships constructed before, on or after 1 July 1998; the expressions *all passenger ships* and *all cargo ships* shall be construed accordingly;

    .3   a cargo ship, whenever built, which is converted to a passenger ship shall be treated as a passenger ship constructed on the date on which such a conversion commences.

4   For ships constructed before 1 July 1998, the Administration shall:

    .1   ensure that, subject to the provisions of paragraph 4.2, the requirements which are applicable under chapter III of the International Convention for the Safety of Life at Sea, 1974, in force prior to 1 July 1998 to new or existing ships as prescribed by that chapter are complied with; and

    .2   ensure that when life-saving appliances or arrangements on such ships are replaced or such ships undergo repairs, alterations or modifications of a major character which involve replacement of, or any addition to, their existing life-saving appliances or arrangements, such life-saving appliances or arrangements, in so far as is reasonable and practicable, comply with the requirements of this chapter. However, if a survival craft other than an inflatable liferaft is replaced without replacing its launching appliance, or vice versa, the survival craft or launching appliance may be of the same type as that replaced.

Regulation 2
Exemptions

1   The Administration may, if it considers that the sheltered nature and conditions of the voyage are such as to render the application of any specific requirements of this chapter unreasonable or unnecessary, exempt from those requirements individual ships or classes of ships which, in the course of their voyage, do not proceed more than 20 miles from the nearest land.

2   In the case of passenger ships which are employed in special trades for the carriage of large numbers of special trade passengers, such as the pilgrim trade, the Administration, if satisfied that it is impracticable to enforce compliance with the requirements of this chapter, may exempt such ships from those requirements, provided that such ships comply fully with the provisions of:

.1   the rules annexed to the Special Trade Passenger Ships Agreement, 1971; and

.2   the rules annexed to the Protocol on Space Requirements for Special Trade Passenger Ships, 1973.

Regulation 3
Definitions

For the purpose of this chapter, unless expressly provided otherwise:

1   *Anti-exposure suit* is a protective suit designed for use by rescue boat crews and marine evacuation system parties.

2   *Certificated person* is a person who holds a certificate of proficiency in survival craft issued under the authority of, or recognized as valid by, the Administration in accordance with the requirements of the International Convention on Standards of Training, Certification and Watchkeeping for Seafarers, in force; or a person who holds a certificate issued or recognized by the Administration of a State not a Party to that Convention for the same purpose as the convention certificate.

3   *Detection* is the determination of the location of survivors or survival craft.

4   *Embarkation ladder* is the ladder provided at survival craft embarkation stations to permit safe access to survival craft after launching.

5   *Float-free launching* is that method of launching a survival craft whereby the craft is automatically released from a sinking ship and is ready for use.

6   *Free-fall launching* is that method of launching a survival craft whereby the craft with its complement of persons and equipment on board is released and allowed to fall into the sea without any restraining apparatus.

7   *Immersion suit* is a protective suit which reduces the body heat loss of a person wearing it in cold water.

8   *Inflatable appliance* is an appliance which depends upon non-rigid, gas-filled chambers for buoyancy and which is normally kept uninflated until ready for use.

9   *Inflated appliance* is an appliance which depends upon non-rigid, gas-filled chambers for buoyancy and which is kept inflated and ready for use at all times.

10   *International Life-Saving Appliance (LSA) Code* (referred to as "the Code" in this chapter) means the International Life-Saving Appliance (LSA) Code adopted by the Maritime Safety Committee of the Organization by resolution MSC.48(66), as it may be amended by the Organization, provided that such amendments are adopted, brought into force and take effect in accordance with the provisions of article VIII of the present Convention concerning the amendment procedures applicable to the annex other than chapter I.

11   *Launching appliance or arrangement* is a means of transferring a survival craft or rescue boat from its stowed position safely to the water.

12   *Length* is 96% of the total length on a waterline at 85% of the least moulded depth measured from the top of the keel, or the length from the fore-side of the stem to the axis of the rudder stock on that waterline, if that be greater. In ships designed with a rake of keel the waterline on which this is measured shall be parallel to the designed waterline.

13   *Lightest seagoing condition* is the loading condition with the ship on even keel, without cargo, with 10% stores and fuel remaining and in the case of a passenger ship with the full number of passengers and crew and their luggage.

14   *Marine evacuation system* is an appliance for the rapid transfer of persons from the embarkation deck of a ship to a floating survival craft.

15   *Moulded depth*

.1   The *moulded depth* is the vertical distance measured from the top of the keel to the top of the freeboard deck beam at side. In wood and composite ships the distance is measured from the lower edge of the keel rabbet. Where the form at the lower part of the midship section is of a hollow character, or where thick garboards are fitted, the distance is measured from the point where the line of the flat of the bottom continued inwards cuts the side of the keel.

.2   In ships having rounded gunwales, the *moulded depth* shall be measured to the point of intersection of the moulded lines of the deck and side shell plating, the lines extending as though the gunwale were of angular design.

.3   Where the freeboard deck is stepped and the raised part of the deck extends over the point at which the moulded depth is to be determined, the *moulded depth* shall be measured to a line of reference extending from the lower part of the deck along a line parallel with the raised part.

16   *Novel life-saving appliance or arrangement* is a life-saving appliance or arrangement which embodies new features not fully covered by the provisions of this chapter or the Code but which provides an equal or higher standard of safety.

17   *Positive stability* is the ability of a craft to return to its original position after the removal of a heeling moment.

18   *Recovery time* for a rescue boat is the time required to raise the boat to a position where persons on board can disembark to the deck of the ship. Recovery time includes the time required to make preparations for recovery on board the rescue boat such as passing and securing a painter, connecting the rescue boat to the launching appliance, and the time to raise the rescue boat. Recovery time does not include the time needed to lower the launching appliance into position to recover the rescue boat.

19   *Rescue boat* is a boat designed to rescue persons in distress and to marshal survival craft.

20   *Retrieval* is the safe recovery of survivors.

21   *Ro–ro passenger ship* means a passenger ship with ro–ro cargo spaces or special category spaces as defined in regulation II-2/3.

22   *Short international voyage* is an international voyage in the course of which a ship is not more than 200 miles from a port or place in which the passengers and crew could be placed in safety. Neither the distance between the last port of call in the country in which the voyage begins and the final port of destination nor the return voyage shall exceed 600 miles. The final port of destination is the last port of call in the scheduled voyage at which the ship commences its return voyage to the country in which the voyage began.

23   *Survival craft* is a craft capable of sustaining the lives of persons in distress from the time of abandoning the ship.

24   *Thermal protective aid* is a bag or suit made of waterproof material with low thermal conductance.

Regulation 4
Evaluation, testing and approval of life-saving appliances and arrangements

1   Except as provided in paragraphs 5 and 6, life-saving appliances and arrangements required by this chapter shall be approved by the Administration.

2   Before giving approval to life-saving appliances and arrangements, the Administration shall ensure that such life-saving appliances and arrangements:

.**1**   are tested, to confirm that they comply with the requirements of this chapter and the Code, in accordance with the recommendations of the Organization;* or

.**2**   have successfully undergone, to the satisfaction of the Administration, tests which are substantially equivalent to those specified in those recommendations.

3   Before giving approval to novel life-saving appliances or arrangements, the Administration shall ensure that such appliances or arrangements:

.**1**   provide safety standards at least equivalent to the requirements of this chapter and the Code and have been evaluated and tested in accordance with the recommendations of the Organization;[†] or

.**2**   have successfully undergone, to the satisfaction of the Administration, evaluation and tests which are substantially equivalent to those recommendations.

4   Procedures adopted by the Administration for approval shall also include the conditions whereby approval would continue or would be withdrawn.

5   Before accepting life-saving appliances and arrangements that have not been previously approved by the Administration, the Administration shall be satisfied that life-saving appliances and arrangements comply with the requirements of this chapter and the Code.

---

* Refer to the Recommendation on testing of life-saving appliances adopted by the Organization by resolution A.689(17). For life-saving appliances installed on board on or after 1 July 1999, refer to the Revised Recommendations on testing of life-saving appliances adopted by the Maritime Safety Committee of the Organization by resolution MSC.81(70).

[†] Refer to the Code of Practice for the Evaluation, Testing and Acceptance of Prototype Novel Life-Saving Appliances and Arrangements adopted by the Organization by resolution A.520(13).

6 Life-saving appliances required by this chapter for which detailed specifications are not included in the Code shall be to the satisfaction of the Administration.

Regulation 5
Production tests

The Administration shall require life-saving appliances to be subjected to such production tests as are necessary to ensure that the life-saving appliances are manufactured to the same standard as the approved prototype.

Part B
Requirements for ships and life-saving appliances

SECTION I – PASSENGER SHIPS AND CARGO SHIPS

Regulation 6
Communications

1   Paragraph 2 applies to all passenger ships and to all cargo ships of 300 gross tonnage and upwards.

2   Radio life-saving appliances

2.1   *Two-way VHF radiotelephone apparatus*

2.1.1   At least 3 two-way VHF radiotelephone apparatus shall be provided on every passenger ship and on every cargo ship of 500 gross tonnage and upwards. At least 2 two-way VHF radiotelephone apparatus shall be provided on every cargo ship of 300 gross tonnage and upwards but less than 500 gross tonnage. Such apparatus shall conform to performance standards not inferior to those adopted by the Organization.* If a fixed two-way VHF radiotelephone apparatus is fitted in a survival craft it shall conform to performance standards not inferior to those adopted by the Organization.*

2.1.2   Two-way VHF radiotelephone apparatus provided on board ships prior to 1 February 1992 and not complying fully with the performance standards adopted by the Organization may be accepted by the Administration until 1 February 1999 provided the Administration is satisfied that they are compatible with approved two-way VHF radiotelephone apparatus.

2.2   *Radar transponders*

At least one radar transponder shall be carried on each side of every passenger ship and of every cargo ship of 500 gross tonnage and upwards. At least one radar transponder shall be carried on every cargo ship of 300 gross tonnage and upwards but less than 500 gross tonnage. Such radar transponders shall conform to performance standards not inferior to those

---

* Refer to the Performance standards for survival craft two-way VHF radiotelephone apparatus adopted by the Organization by resolution A.809(19), as it may be amended, annex 1 or annex 2 as applicable.

adopted by the Organization.* The radar transponders† shall be stowed in such locations that they can be rapidly placed in any survival craft other than the liferaft or liferafts required by regulation 31.1.4. Alternatively one radar transponder shall be stowed in each survival craft other than those required by regulation 31.1.4. On ships carrying at least two radar transponders and equipped with free-fall lifeboats one of the radar transponders shall be stowed in a free-fall lifeboat and the other located in the immediate vicinity of the navigation bridge so that it can be utilized on board and ready for transfer to any of the other survival craft.

3   Distress flares

Not less than 12 rocket parachute flares, complying with the requirements of section 3.1 of the Code, shall be carried and be stowed on or near the navigation bridge.

4   On-board communications and alarm systems

4.1   An emergency means comprised of either fixed or portable equipment or both shall be provided for two-way communications between emergency control stations, muster and embarkation stations and strategic positions on board.

4.2   A general emergency alarm system complying with the requirements of paragraph 7.2.1 of the Code shall be provided and shall be used for summoning passengers and crew to muster stations and to initiate the actions included in the muster list. The system shall be supplemented by either a public address system complying with the requirements of paragraph 7.2.2 of the Code or other suitable means of communication. Entertainment sound systems shall automatically be turned off when the general emergency alarm system is activated.

4.3   On passenger ships the general emergency alarm system shall be audible on all open decks.

4.4   On ships fitted with a marine evacuation system communication between the embarkation station and the platform or the survival craft shall be ensured.

5   Public address systems on passenger ships

5.1   In addition to the requirements of regulation II-2/40.5‡ or regulation II-2/41-2‡, as appropriate, and of paragraph 4.2, all passenger ships shall be fitted with a public address system. With respect to passenger ships

---

* Refer to the Performance standards for survival craft radar transponders for use in search and rescue operations adopted by the Organization by resolution A.802(19), as may be amended.

† One of these radar transponders may be the radar transponder required by regulation IV/7.1.3.

‡ These relate to the chapter II-2 in force before 1 July 2002. The equivalent for each in the amended chapter II-2 is 12.3.

constructed before 1 July 1997 the requirements of paragraphs 5.2 and 5.4, subject to the provisions of paragraph 5.5, shall apply not later than the date of the first periodical survey after 1 July 1997.

5.2   The public address system shall be clearly audible above the ambient noise in all spaces, prescribed by paragraph 7.2.2.1 of the Code, and shall be provided with an override function controlled from one location on the navigation bridge and such other places on board as the Administration deems necessary, so that all emergency messages will be broadcast if any loudspeaker in the spaces concerned has been switched off, its volume has been turned down or the public address system is used for other purposes.

5.3   On passenger ships constructed on or after 1 July 1997:

.1   the public address system shall have at least two loops which shall be sufficiently separated throughout their length and have two separate and independent amplifiers; and

.2   the public address system and its performance standards shall be approved by the Administration having regard to the recommendations adopted by the Organization.[*]

5.4   The public address system shall be connected to the emergency source of electrical power required by regulation II-1/42.2.2.

5.5   Ships constructed before 1 July 1997 which are already fitted with the public address system approved by the Administration which complies substantially with those required by sections 5.2 and 5.4 and paragraph 7.2.2.1 of the Code are not required to change their system.

Regulation 7
Personal life-saving appliances

1   Lifebuoys

1.1   Lifebuoys complying with the requirements of paragraph 2.1.1 of the Code shall be:

.1   so distributed as to be readily available on both sides of the ship and as far as practicable on all open decks extending to the ship's side; at least one shall be placed in the vicinity of the stern; and

.2   so stowed as to be capable of being rapidly cast loose, and not permanently secured in any way.

1.2   At least one lifebuoy on each side of the ship shall be fitted with a buoyant lifeline complying with the requirements of paragraph 2.1.4 of the

---

[*] Refer to MSC/Circ.808, Recommendation on performance standards for public address systems on passenger ships, including cabling.

Code equal in length to not less than twice the height at which it is stowed above the waterline in the lightest seagoing condition, or 30 m, whichever is the greater.

1.3   Not less than one half of the total number of lifebuoys shall be provided with lifebuoy self-igniting lights complying with the requirements of paragraph 2.1.2 of the Code; not less than two of these shall also be provided with lifebuoy self-activating smoke signals complying with the requirements of paragraph 2.1.3 of the Code and be capable of quick release from the navigation bridge; lifebuoys with lights and those with lights and smoke signals shall be equally distributed on both sides of the ship and shall not be the lifebuoys provided with lifelines in compliance with the requirements of paragraph 1.2.

1.4   Each lifebuoy shall be marked in block capitals of the Roman alphabet with the name and port of registry of the ship on which it is carried.

2   Lifejackets

2.1   A lifejacket complying with the requirements of paragraph 2.2.1 or 2.2.2 of the Code shall be provided for every person on board the ship and, in addition:

> **.1**   a number of lifejackets suitable for children equal to at least 10% of the number of passengers on board shall be provided or such greater number as may be required to provide a lifejacket for each child; and

> **.2**   a sufficient number of lifejackets shall be carried for persons on watch and for use at remotely located survival craft stations. The lifejackets carried for persons on watch should be stowed on the bridge, in the engine control room and at any other manned watch station.

2.2   Lifejackets shall be so placed as to be readily accessible and their position shall be plainly indicated. Where, due to the particular arrangements of the ship, the lifejackets provided in compliance with the requirements of paragraph 2.1 may become inaccessible, alternative provisions shall be made to the satisfaction of the Administration which may include an increase in the number of lifejackets to be carried.

2.3   The lifejackets used in totally enclosed lifeboats, except free-fall lifeboats, shall not impede entry into the lifeboat or seating, including operation of the seat belts in the lifeboat.

2.4   Lifejackets selected for free-fall lifeboats, and the manner in which they are carried or worn, shall not interfere with entry into the lifeboat, occupant safety or operation of the lifeboat.

3   Immersion suits and anti-exposure suits

An immersion suit, complying with the requirements of section 2.3 of the Code or an anti-exposure suit complying with section 2.4 of the Code, of an appropriate size, shall be provided for every person assigned to crew the rescue boat or assigned to the marine evacuation system party. If the ship is constantly engaged in warm climates* where, in the opinion of the Administration thermal protection is unnecessary, this protective clothing need not be carried.

Regulation 8
Muster list and emergency instructions

1   This regulation applies to all ships.

2   Clear instructions to be followed in the event of an emergency shall be provided for every person on board. In the case of passenger ships these instructions shall be drawn up in the language or languages required by the ship's flag State and in the English language.

3   Muster lists and emergency instructions complying with the requirements of regulation 37 shall be exhibited in conspicuous places throughout the ship including the navigation bridge, engine-room and crew accommodation spaces.

4   Illustrations and instructions in appropriate languages shall be posted in passenger cabins and be conspicuously displayed at muster stations and other passenger spaces to inform passengers of:

  .1   their muster station;

  .2   the essential actions they must take in an emergency; and

  .3   the method of donning lifejackets.

Regulation 9
Operating instructions

1   This regulation applies to all ships.

2   Posters or signs shall be provided on or in the vicinity of survival craft and their launching controls and shall:

  .1   illustrate the purpose of controls and the procedures for operating the appliance and give relevant instructions or warnings;

  .2   be easily seen under emergency lighting conditions; and

---

* Refer to MSC/Circ.1046, Guidelines for the assessment of thermal protection.

.3 use symbols in accordance with the recommendations of the Organization.*

Regulation 10
Manning of survival craft and supervision

1 This regulation applies to all ships.

2 There shall be a sufficient number of trained persons on board for mustering and assisting untrained persons.

3 There shall be a sufficient number of crew members, who may be deck officers or certificated persons, on board for operating the survival craft and launching arrangements required for abandonment by the total number of persons on board.

4 A deck officer or certificated person shall be placed in charge of each survival craft to be used. However, the Administration, having due regard to the nature of the voyage, the number of persons on board and the characteristics of the ship, may permit persons practised in the handling and operation of liferafts to be placed in charge of liferafts in lieu of persons qualified as above. A second-in-command shall also be nominated in the case of lifeboats.

5 The person in charge of the survival craft shall have a list of the survival craft crew and shall see that the crew under his command are acquainted with their duties. In lifeboats the second-in-command shall also have a list of the lifeboat crew.

6 Every motorized survival craft shall have a person assigned who is capable of operating the engine and carrying out minor adjustments.

7 The master shall ensure the equitable distribution of persons referred to in paragraphs 2, 3 and 4 among the ship's survival craft.

Regulation 11
Survival craft muster and embarkation arrangements

1 Lifeboats and liferafts for which approved launching appliances are required shall be stowed as close to accommodation and service spaces as possible.

2 Muster stations shall be provided close to the embarkation stations. Each muster station shall have sufficient clear deck space to accommodate all persons assigned to muster at that station, but at least 0.35 m^2 per person.

---

* Refer to the Symbols related to life-saving appliances and arrangements adopted by the Organization by resolution A.760(18), as amended by resolution MSC.82(70).

3   Muster and embarkation stations shall be readily accessible from accommodation and work areas.

4   Muster and embarkation stations shall be adequately illuminated by lighting supplied from the emergency source of electrical power required by regulation II-1/42 or II-1/43, as appropriate.

5   Alleyways, stairways and exits giving access to the muster and embarkation stations shall be lighted. Such lighting shall be capable of being supplied by the emergency source of electrical power required by regulation II-1/42 or II-1/43, as appropriate. In addition to and as part of the markings required under regulation II-2/28.1.10,* routes to muster stations shall be indicated with the muster station symbol, intended for that purpose, in accordance with the recommendations of the Organization.†

6   Davit-launched and free-fall launched survival craft muster and embarkation stations shall be so arranged as to enable stretcher cases to be placed in survival craft.

7   An embarkation ladder complying with the requirements of paragraph 6.1.6 of the Code extending, in a single length, from the deck to the waterline in the lightest seagoing condition under unfavourable conditions of trim of up to 10 and a list of up to 20 either way shall be provided at each embarkation station or at every two adjacent embarkation stations for survival craft launched down the side of the ship. However, the Administration may permit such ladders to be replaced by approved devices to afford access to the survival craft when waterborne, provided that there shall be at least one embarkation ladder on each side of the ship. Other means of embarkation enabling descent to the water in a controlled manner may be permitted for the liferafts required by regulation 31.1.4.

8   Where necessary, means shall be provided for bringing the davit-launched survival craft against the ship's side and holding them alongside so that persons can be safely embarked.

Regulation 12
Launching stations

Launching stations shall be in such positions as to ensure safe launching having particular regard to clearance from the propeller and steeply overhanging portions of the hull and so that, as far as possible, survival

---

* This relates to the chapter II-2 in force before 1 July 2002. The equivalent in the amended chapter II-2 is 13.3.2.5.1.

† Refer to the Symbols related to life-saving appliances and arrangements adopted by the Organization by resolution A.760(18), as amended by resolution MSC.82(70), and to the Guidelines for the evaluation, testing and application of low-location lighting on passenger ships adopted by the Organization by resolution A.752(18).

craft, except survival craft specially designed for free-fall launching, can be launched down the straight side of the ship. If positioned forward, they shall be located abaft the collision bulkhead in a sheltered position and, in this respect, the Administration shall give special consideration to the strength of the launching appliance.

Regulation 13
Stowage of survival craft

1   Each survival craft shall be stowed:

   .1   so that neither the survival craft nor its stowage arrangements will interfere with the operation of any other survival craft or rescue boat at any other launching station;

   .2   as near the water surface as is safe and practicable and, in the case of a survival craft other than a liferaft intended for throw over board launching, in such a position that the survival craft in the embarkation position is not less than 2 m above the waterline with the ship in the fully loaded condition under unfavourable conditions of trim of up to 10° and listed up to 20° either way, or to the angle at which the ship's weather deck edge becomes submerged, whichever is less;

   .3   in a state of continuous readiness so that two crew members can carry out preparations for embarkation and launching in less than 5 min;

   .4   fully equipped as required by this chapter and the Code; and

   .5   as far as practicable, in a secure and sheltered position and protected from damage by fire and explosion. In particular, survival craft on tankers, other than the liferafts required by regulation 31.1.4, shall not be stowed on or above a cargo tank, slop tank, or other tank containing explosive or hazardous cargoes.

2   Lifeboats for lowering down the ship's side shall be stowed as far forward of the propeller as practicable. On cargo ships of 80 m in length and upwards but less than 120 m in length, each lifeboat shall be so stowed that the after end of the lifeboat is not less than the length of the lifeboat forward of the propeller. On cargo ships of 120 m in length and upwards and passenger ships of 80 m in length and upwards, each lifeboat shall be so stowed that the after end of the lifeboat is not less than 1.5 times the length of the lifeboat forward of the propeller. Where appropriate, the ship shall be so arranged that lifeboats, in their stowed positions, are protected from damage by heavy seas.

3   Lifeboats shall be stowed attached to launching appliances.

4.1   Every liferaft shall be stowed with its painter permanently attached to the ship.

4.2   Each liferaft or group of liferafts shall be stowed with a float-free arrangement complying with the requirements of paragraph 4.1.6 of the Code so that each floats free and, if inflatable, inflates automatically when the ship sinks.

4.3   Liferafts shall be so stowed as to permit manual release of one raft or container at a time from their securing arrangements.

4.4   Paragraphs 4.1 and 4.2 do not apply to liferafts required by regulation 31.1.4.

5   Davit-launched liferafts shall be stowed within reach of the lifting hooks, unless some means of transfer is provided which is not rendered inoperable within the limits of trim and list prescribed in paragraph 1.2 or by ship motion or power failure.

6   Liferafts intended for throw-overboard launching shall be so stowed as to be readily transferable for launching on either side of the ship unless liferafts, of the aggregate capacity required by regulation 31.1 to be capable of being launched on either side, are stowed on each side of the ship.

Regulation 14
Stowage of rescue boats

Rescue boats shall be stowed:

.1   in a state of continuous readiness for launching in not more than 5 min;

.2   in a position suitable for launching and recovery;

.3   so that neither the rescue boat nor its stowage arrangements will interfere with the operation of any survival craft at any other launching station; and

.4   if it is also a lifeboat, in compliance with the requirements of regulation 13.

Regulation 15
Stowage of marine evacuation systems

1   The ship's side shall not have any openings between the embarkation station of the marine evacuation system and the waterline in the lightest seagoing condition and means shall be provided to protect the system from any projections.

2   Marine evacuation systems shall be in such positions as to ensure safe launching having particular regard to clearance from the propeller and steeply overhanging positions of the hull and so that, as far as practicable, the system can be launched down the straight side of the ship.

3   Each marine evacuation system shall be stowed so that neither the passage nor platform nor its stowage or operational arrangements will interfere with the operation of any other life-saving appliance at any other launching station.

4   Where appropriate, the ship shall be so arranged that the marine evacuation systems in their stowed positions are protected from damage by heavy seas.

Regulation 16
Survival craft launching and recovery arrangements

1   Unless expressly provided otherwise, launching and embarkation appliances complying with the requirements of section 6.1 of the Code shall be provided for all survival craft except those which are:

> **.1**   boarded from a position on deck less than 4.5 m above the waterline in the lightest seagoing condition and which have a mass of not more than 185 kg; or
>
> **.2**   boarded from a position on deck less than 4.5 m above the waterline in the lightest seagoing condition and which are stowed for launching directly from the stowed position under unfavourable conditions of trim of up to 10° and list of up to 20° either way; or
>
> **.3**   carried in excess of the survival craft for 200% of the total number of persons on board the ship and which have a mass of not more than 185 kg; or
>
> **.4**   carried in excess of the survival craft for 200% of the total number of persons on board the ship, are stowed for launching directly from the stowed position under unfavourable conditions of trim of up to 10° and list of up to 20° either way; or
>
> **.5**   provided for use in conjunction with a marine evacuation system, complying with the requirements of section 6.2 of the Code and stowed for launching directly from the stowed position under unfavourable conditions of trim of up to 10° and list of up to 20° either way.

2   Each lifeboat shall be provided with an appliance which is capable of launching and recovering the lifeboat. In addition there shall be provision for hanging-off the lifeboat to free the release gear for maintenance.

3   Launching and recovery arrangements shall be such that the appliance operator on the ship is able to observe the survival craft at all times during launching and for lifeboats during recovery.

4   Only one type of release mechanism shall be used for similar survival craft carried on board the ship.

5   Preparation and handling of survival craft at any one launching station shall not interfere with the prompt preparation and handling of any other survival craft or rescue boat at any other station.

6   Falls, where used, shall be long enough for the survival craft to reach the water with the ship in its lightest seagoing condition, under unfavourable conditions of trim of up to $10°$ and list of up to $20°$ either way.

7   During preparation and launching, the survival craft, its launching appliance, and the area of water into which it is to be launched shall be adequately illuminated by lighting supplied from the emergency source of electrical power required by regulation II-1/42 or II-1/43, as appropriate.

8   Means shall be available to prevent any discharge of water onto survival craft during abandonment.

9   If there is a danger of the survival craft being damaged by the ship's stabilizer wings, means shall be available, powered by an emergency source of energy, to bring the stabilizer wings inboard; indicators operated by an emergency source of energy shall be available on the navigating bridge to show the position of the stabilizer wings.

10   If partially enclosed lifeboats complying with the requirements of section 4.5 of the Code are carried, a davit span shall be provided, fitted with not less than two lifelines of sufficient length to reach the water with the ship in its lightest seagoing condition, under unfavourable conditions of trim of up to $10°$ and list of up 20° either way.

Regulation 17
Rescue boat embarkation, launching and recovery arrangements

1   The rescue boat embarkation and launching arrangements shall be such that the rescue boat can be boarded and launched in the shortest possible time.

2   If the rescue boat is one of the ship's survival craft, the embarkation arrangements and launching station shall comply with the requirements of regulations 11 and 12.

3   Launching arrangements shall comply with the requirements of regulation 16. However, all rescue boats shall be capable of being launched, where necessary utilizing painters, with the ship making headway at speeds up to 5 knots in calm water.

4   Recovery time of the rescue boat shall be not more than 5 min in moderate sea conditions when loaded with its full complement of persons and equipment. If the rescue boat is also a lifeboat, this recovery time shall be possible when loaded with its lifeboat equipment and the approved rescue boat complement of at least six persons.

5   Rescue boat embarkation and recovery arrangements shall allow for safe and efficient handling of a stretcher case. Foul weather recovery strops shall be provided for safety if heavy fall blocks constitute a danger.

Regulation 18
Line-throwing appliances

A line-throwing appliance complying with the requirements of section 7.1 of the Code shall be provided.

Regulation 19
Emergency training and drills

1   This regulation applies to all ships.

2   **Familiarity with safety installations and practice musters**

2.1   Every crew member with assigned emergency duties shall be familiar with these duties before the voyage begins.

2.2   On a ship engaged on a voyage where passengers are scheduled to be on board for more than 24 h, musters of the passengers shall take place within 24 h after their embarkation. Passengers shall be instructed in the use of the lifejackets and the action to take in an emergency.

2.3   Whenever new passengers embark, a passenger safety briefing shall be given immediately before sailing, or immediately after sailing. The briefing shall include the instructions required by regulations 8.2 and 8.4, and shall be made by means of an announcement, in one or more languages likely to be understood by the passengers. The announcement shall be made on the ship's public address system, or by other equivalent means likely to be heard at least by the passengers who have not yet heard it during the voyage. The briefing may be included in the muster required by paragraph 2.2 if the muster is held immediately upon departure. Information cards or posters or video programmes displayed on ships video displays may be used to supplement the briefing, but may not be used to replace the announcement.

3 Drills

3.1 Drills shall, as far as practicable, be conducted as if there were an actual emergency.

3.2 Every crew member shall participate in at least one abandon ship drill and one fire drill every month. The drills of the crew shall take place within 24 h of the ship leaving a port if more than 25% of the crew have not participated in abandon ship and fire drills on board that particular ship in the previous month. When a ship enters service for the first time, after modification of a major character or when a new crew is engaged, these drills shall be held before sailing. The Administration may accept other arrangements that are at least equivalent for those classes of ships for which this is impracticable.

3.3 *Abandon ship drill*

3.3.1 Each abandon ship drill shall include:

.1 summoning of passengers and crew to muster stations with the alarm required by regulation 6.4.2 followed by drill announcement on the public address or other communication system and ensuring that they are made aware of the order to abandon ship;

.2 reporting to stations and preparing for the duties described in the muster list;

.3 checking that passengers and crew are suitably dressed;

.4 checking that lifejackets are correctly donned;

.5 lowering of at least one lifeboat after any necessary preparation for launching;

.6 starting and operating the lifeboat engine;

.7 operation of davits used for launching liferafts;

.8 a mock search and rescue of passengers trapped in their staterooms; and

.9 instruction in the use of radio life-saving appliances.

3.3.2 Different lifeboats shall, as far as practicable, be lowered in compliance with the requirements of paragraph 3.3.1.5 at successive drills.

3.3.3 Except as provided in paragraphs 3.3.4 and 3.3.5, each lifeboat shall be launched with its assigned operating crew aboard and manoeuvred in the water at least once every three months during an abandon ship drill.

3.3.4 Lowering into the water, rather than launching of a lifeboat arranged for free-fall launching, is acceptable where free-fall launching is impracticable provided the lifeboat is free-fall launched with its assigned operating crew aboard and manoeuvred in the water at least once every six months. However, in cases where it is impracticable, the Administration may extend this period to 12 months provided that arrangements are made for simulated launching which will take place at intervals of not more than six months.

3.3.5 The Administration may allow ships operating on short international voyages not to launch the lifeboats on one side if their berthing arrangements in port and their trading patterns do not permit launching of lifeboats on that side. However, all such lifeboats shall be lowered at least once every three months and launched at least annually.

3.3.6 As far as is reasonable and practicable, rescue boats other than lifeboats which are also rescue boats, shall be launched each month with their assigned crew aboard and manoeuvred in the water. In all cases this requirement shall be complied with at least once every three months.

3.3.7 If lifeboat and rescue boat launching drills are carried out with the ship making headway, such drills shall, because of the dangers involved, be practised in sheltered waters only and under the supervision of an officer experienced in such drills.*

3.3.8 If a ship is fitted with marine evacuation systems, drills shall include exercising of the procedures required for the deployment of such a system up to the point immediately preceding actual deployment of the system. This aspect of drills should be augmented by regular instruction using the on-board training aids required by regulation 35.4. Additionally every system party member shall, as far as practicable, be further trained by participation in a full deployment of a similar system into water, either on board a ship or ashore, at intervals of not longer than two years, but in no case longer than three years. This training can be associated with the deployments required by regulation 20.8.2.

3.3.9 Emergency lighting for mustering and abandonment shall be tested at each abandon ship drill.

3.4 *Fire drills*

3.4.1 Fire drills should be planned in such a way that due consideration is given to regular practice in the various emergencies that may occur depending on the type of ships and the cargo.

3.4.2 Each fire drill shall include:

.1 reporting to stations and preparing for the duties described in the muster list required by regulation 8;

.2 starting of a fire pump, using at least the two required jets of water to show that the system is in proper working order;

---

* Refer to the Guidelines on training for the purpose of launching lifeboats and rescue boats from ships making headway through the water adopted by the Organization by resolution A.624(15).

.3   checking of fireman's outfit and other personal rescue equipment;

.4   checking of relevant communication equipment;

.5   checking the operation of watertight doors, fire doors, fire dampers and main inlets and outlets of ventilation systems in the drill area; and

.6   checking the necessary arrangements for subsequent abandoning of the ship.

3.4.3 The equipment used during drills shall immediately be brought back to its fully operational condition and any faults and defects discovered during the drills shall be remedied as soon as possible.

4   On-board training and instructions

4.1 On-board training in the use of the ship's life-saving appliances, including survival craft equipment, and in the use of the ship's fire-extinguishing appliances shall be given as soon as possible but not later than two weeks after a crew member joins the ship. However, if the crew member is on a regularly scheduled rotating assignment to the ship, such training shall be given not later than two weeks after the time of first joining the ship. Instructions in the use of the ship's fire-extinguishing appliances, life-saving appliances, and in survival at sea shall be given at the same interval as the drills. Individual instruction may cover different parts of the ship's life-saving and fire-extinguishing appliances, but all the ship's life-saving and fire-extinguishing appliances shall be covered within any period of two months.

4.2 Every crew member shall be given instructions which shall include but not necessarily be limited to:

.1   operation and use of the ship's inflatable liferafts;

.2   problems of hypothermia, first-aid treatment for hypothermia and other appropriate first-aid procedures;

.3   special instructions necessary for use of the ship's life-saving appliances in severe weather and severe sea conditions; and

.4   operation and use of fire-extinguishing appliances.

4.3 On-board training in the use of davit-launched liferafts shall take place at intervals of not more than four months on every ship fitted with such appliances. Whenever practicable this shall include the inflation and lowering of a liferaft. This liferaft may be a special liferaft intended for training purposes only, which is not part of the ship's life-saving equipment; such a special liferaft shall be conspicuously marked.

5   Records

The date when musters are held, details of abandon ship drills and fire drills, drills of other life-saving appliances and on board training shall be recorded in such log-book as may be prescribed by the Administration. If a full muster, drill or training session is not held at the appointed time, an entry shall be made in the log-book stating the circumstances and the extent of the muster, drill or training session held.

Regulation 20
Operational readiness, maintenance and inspections

1   This regulation applies to all ships. The requirements of paragraphs 3 and 6.2 shall be complied with, as far as is practicable, on ships constructed before 1 July 1986.

2   Operational readiness

Before the ship leaves port and at all times during the voyage, all life-saving appliances shall be in working order and ready for immediate use.

3   Maintenance

3.1   Instructions for on-board maintenance of life-saving appliances complying with the requirements of regulation 36 shall be provided and maintenance shall be carried out accordingly.

3.2   The Administration may accept, in lieu of the instructions required by paragraph 3.1, a shipboard planned maintenance programme which includes the requirements of regulation 36.

4   Maintenance of falls

4.1   Falls used in launching shall be turned end for end at intervals of not more than 30 months and be renewed when necessary due to deterioration of the falls or at intervals of not more than five years, whichever is the earlier.

4.2   The Administration may accept in lieu of the "end for ending" required in paragraph 4.1, periodic inspection of the falls and their renewal whenever necessary due to deterioration or at intervals of not more than four years, whichever one is earlier.

5   Spares and repair equipment

Spares and repair equipment shall be provided for life-saving appliances and their components which are subject to excessive wear or consumption and need to be replaced regularly.

6   Weekly inspection

The following tests and inspections shall be carried out weekly:

.1   all survival craft, rescue boats and launching appliances shall be visually inspected to ensure that they are ready for use;

.2   all engines in lifeboats and rescue boats shall be run for a total period of not less than 3 min provided the ambient temperature is above the minimum temperature required for starting and running the engine. During this period of time, it should be demonstrated that the gear box and gear box train are engaging satisfactorily. If the special characteristics of an outboard motor fitted to a rescue boat would not allow it to be run other than with its propeller submerged for a period of 3 min, it should be run for such period as prescribed in the manufacturer's handbook. In special cases the Administration may waive this requirement for ships constructed before 1 July 1986; and

.3   the general emergency alarm system shall be tested.

7   Monthly inspections

Inspection of the life-saving appliances, including lifeboat equipment, shall be carried out monthly using the checklist required by regulation 36.1 to ensure that they are complete and in good order. A report of the inspection shall be entered in the log-book.

8   Servicing of inflatable liferafts, inflatable lifejackets, marine evacuation systems, and inflated rescue boats

8.1   Every inflatable liferaft, inflatable lifejacket, and marine evacuation system shall be serviced:

.1   at intervals not exceeding 12 months, provided where in any case this is impracticable, the Administration may extend this period to 17 months; and

.2   at an approved servicing station which is competent to service them, maintains proper servicing facilities and uses only properly trained personnel.*

8.2   *Rotational deployment of marine evacuation systems*

In addition to or in conjunction with the servicing intervals of marine evacuation systems required by paragraph 8.1, each marine evacuation system should be deployed from the ship on a rotational basis at intervals to

---

* Refer to the Recommendation on conditions for the approval of servicing stations for inflatable liferafts adopted by the Organization by resolution A.761(18).

be agreed by the Administration provided that each system is to be deployed at least once every six years.

8.3   An Administration which approves new and novel inflatable liferaft arrangements pursuant to regulation 4 may allow for extended service intervals on the following conditions:

8.3.1   The new and novel liferaft arrangement has proved to maintain the same standard, as required by testing procedure, during extended service intervals.

8.3.2   The liferaft system shall be checked on board by certified personnel according to paragraph 8.1.1.

8.3.3   Service at intervals not exceeding five years shall be carried out in accordance with the recommendations of the Organization.*

8.4   All repairs and maintenance of inflated rescue boats shall be carried out in accordance with the manufacturer's instructions. Emergency repairs may be carried out on board the ship; however, permanent repairs shall be effected at an approved servicing station.

8.5   An Administration which permits extension of liferaft service intervals in accordance with paragraph 8.3 shall notify the Organization of such action in accordance with regulation I/5(b).

9   **Periodic servicing of hydrostatic release units**

Hydrostatic release units, other than disposable hydrostatic release units, shall be serviced:

.1   at intervals not exceeding 12 months, provided where in any case this is impracticable, the Administration may extend this period to 17 months;† and

.2   at a servicing station which is competent to service them, maintains proper servicing facilities and uses only properly trained personnel.

10   **Marking of stowage locations**

Containers, brackets, racks, and other similar stowage locations for life-saving equipment shall be marked with symbols in accordance with the recommendations of the Organization,‡ indicating the devices stowed in

---

* Refer to the Recommendation on conditions for the approval of servicing stations for inflatable liferafts adopted by the Organization by resolution A.761(18).

† Refer to MSC/Circ. 955, Servicing of life-saving appliances and radiocommunication equipment under the harmonized system of survey and certification (HSSC).

‡ Refer to the Symbols related to life-saving appliances and arrangements adopted by the Organization by resolution A.760(18).

that location for that purpose. If more than one device is stowed in that location, the number of devices shall also be indicated.

11 Periodic servicing of launching appliances and on-load release gear

11.1 Launching appliances:

  .1 shall be serviced at recommended intervals in accordance with instructions for on-board maintenance as required by regulation 36;

  .2 shall be subjected to a thorough examination at intervals not exceeding 5 years; and

  .3 shall upon completion of the examination in .2 be subjected to a dynamic test of the winch brake in accordance with paragraph 6.1.2.5.2 of the Code.

11.2 Lifeboat on-load release gear shall be:

  .1 serviced at recommended intervals in accordance with instructions for on board maintenance as required by regulation 36;

  .2 subjected to a thorough examination and test during the surveys required by regulation I/7 and I/8 by properly trained personnel familiar with the system; and

  .3 operationally tested under a load of 1.1 times the total mass of the lifeboat when loaded with its full complement of persons and equipment whenever the release gear is overhauled. Such overhauling and test shall be carried out at least once every five years.[*]

SECTION II – PASSENGER SHIPS
(Additional requirements)

Regulation 21
Survival craft and rescue boats

1 Survival craft

1.1 Passenger ships engaged on international voyages which are not short international voyages shall carry:

  .1 partially or totally enclosed lifeboats complying with the requirements of section 4.5 or 4.6 of the Code on each side

---

[*] Refer to the Recommendation on testing of life-saving appliances adopted by the Organization by resolution A.689(17). For life-saving appliances installed on board on or after 1 July 1999, refer to the Revised Recommendations on testing of life-saving appliances adopted by the Maritime Safety Committee of the Organization by resolution MSC.81(70).

of such aggregate capacity as will accommodate not less than 50% of the total number of persons on board. The Administration may permit the substitution of lifeboats by liferafts of equivalent total capacity provided that there shall never be less than sufficient lifeboats on each side of the ship to accommodate 37.5% of the total number of persons on board. The inflatable or rigid liferafts shall comply with the requirements of section 4.2 or 4.3 of the Code and shall be served by launching appliances equally distributed on each side of the ship; and

.2 in addition, inflatable or rigid liferafts complying with the requirements of section 4.2 or 4.3 of the Code of such aggregate capacity as will accommodate at least 25% of the total number of persons on board. These liferafts shall be served by at least one launching appliance on each side which may be those provided in compliance with the requirements of paragraph 1.1.1 or equivalent approved appliances capable of being used on both sides. However, stowage of these liferafts need not comply with the requirements of regulation 13.5.

1.2 Passenger ships engaged on short international voyages and complying with the special standards of subdivision prescribed by regulation II-1/6.5 shall carry:

.1 partially or totally enclosed lifeboats complying with the requirements of section 4.5 or 4.6 of the Code of such aggregate capacity as will accommodate at least 30% of the total number of persons on board. The lifeboats shall, as far as practicable, be equally distributed on each side of the ship. In addition inflatable or rigid liferafts complying with the requirements of section 4.2 or 4.3 of the Code shall be carried of such aggregate capacity that, together with the lifeboat capacity, the survival craft will accommodate the total number of persons on board. The liferafts shall be served by launching appliances equally distributed on each side of the ship; and

.2 in addition, inflatable or rigid liferafts complying with the requirements of section 4.2 or 4.3 of the Code of such aggregate capacity as will accommodate at least 25% of the total number of persons on board. These liferafts shall be served by at least one launching appliance on each side which may be those provided in compliance with the requirements of paragraph 1.2.1 or equivalent approved appliances capable of being used on both sides. However, stowage of these liferafts need not comply with the requirements of regulation 13.5.

1.3 Passenger ships engaged on short international voyages and not complying with the special standards of subdivision prescribed by regulation

II-1/6.5, shall carry survival craft complying with the requirements of paragraph 1.1.

1.4 All survival craft required to provide for abandonment by the total number of persons on board shall be capable of being launched with their full complement of persons and equipment within a period of 30 min from the time the abandon ship signal is given.

1.5 In lieu of meeting the requirements of paragraph 1.1, 1.2 or 1.3, passenger ships of less than 500 gross tonnage where the total number of persons on board is less than 200, may comply with the following:

.1 they shall carry on each side of the ship, inflatable or rigid liferafts complying with the requirements of section 4.2 or 4.3 of the Code and of such aggregate capacity as will accommodate the total number of persons on board;

.2 unless the liferafts required by paragraph 1.5.1 are stowed in a position providing for easy side-to-side transfer at a single open deck level, additional liferafts shall be provided so that the total capacity available on each side will accommodate 150% of the total number of persons on board;

.3 if the rescue boat required by paragraph 2.2 is also a partially or totally enclosed lifeboat complying with the requirements of section 4.5 or 4.6 of the Code, it may be included in the aggregate capacity required by paragraph 1.5.1, provided that the total capacity available on either side of the ship is at least 150% of the total number of persons on board; and

.4 in the event of any one survival craft being lost or rendered unserviceable, there shall be sufficient survival craft available for use on each side, including those which are stowed in a position providing for easy side-to-side transfer at a single open deck level, to accommodate the total number of persons on board.

1.6 A marine evacuation system or systems complying with section 6.2 of the Code may be substituted for the equivalent capacity of liferafts and launching appliances required by paragraph 1.1.1 or 1.2.1.

2   Rescue boats

2.1 Passenger ships of 500 gross tonnage and over shall carry at least one rescue boat complying with the requirements of section 5.1 of the Code on each side of the ship.

2.2 Passenger ships of less than 500 gross tonnage shall carry at least one rescue boat complying with the requirements of section 5.1 of the Code.

2.3 A lifeboat may be accepted as a rescue boat provided it also complies with the requirements for a rescue boat.

3   Marshalling of liferafts

3.1   The number of lifeboats and rescue boats that are carried on passenger ships shall be sufficient to ensure that in providing for abandonment by the total number of persons on board not more than six liferafts need be marshalled by each lifeboat or rescue boat.

3.2   The number of lifeboats and rescue boats that are carried on passenger ships engaged on short international voyages and complying with the special standards of subdivision prescribed by regulation II-1/6.5 shall be sufficient to ensure that in providing for abandonment by the total number of persons on board not more than nine liferafts need be marshalled by each lifeboat or rescue boat.

Regulation 22
Personal life-saving appliances

1   Lifebuoys

1.1   A passenger ship shall carry not less than the number of lifebuoys complying with the requirements of regulation 7.1 and section 2.1 of the Code prescribed in the following table:

Length of ship in metres	Minimum number of lifebuoys
Under 60	8
60 and under 120	12
120 and under 180	18
180 and under 240	24
240 and over	30

1.2   Notwithstanding regulation 7.1.3, passenger ships of under 60 m in length shall carry not less than six lifebuoys provided with self-igniting lights.

2   Lifejackets

2.1   In addition to the lifejackets required by regulation 7.2, every passenger ship shall carry lifejackets for not less than 5% of the total number of persons on board. These lifejackets shall be stowed in conspicuous places on deck or at muster stations.

2.2   Where lifejackets for passengers are stowed in staterooms which are located remotely from direct routes between public spaces and muster stations, the additional lifejackets for these passengers required under regulation 7.2.2, shall be stowed either in the public spaces, the muster stations, or on direct routes between them. The lifejackets shall be stowed so that their distribution and donning does not impede orderly movement to muster stations and survival craft embarkation stations.

3   Lifejacket lights

3.1   On all passenger ships each lifejacket shall be fitted with a light complying with the requirements of paragraph 2.2.3 of the Code.

3.2   Lights fitted on lifejackets on board passenger ships prior to 1 July 1998 and not complying fully with paragraph 2.2.3 of the Code may be accepted by the Administration until the lifejacket light would normally be replaced or until the first periodical survey after 1 July 2002, whichever is the earliest.

4   Immersion suits and thermal protective aids

4.1   All passenger ships shall carry for each lifeboat on the ship at least three immersion suits complying with the requirements of section 2.3 of the Code and, in addition, a thermal protective aid complying with the requirements of section 2.5 of the Code for every person to be accommodated in the lifeboat and not provided with an immersion suit. These immersion suits and thermal protective aids need not be carried:

   .1   for persons to be accommodated in totally or partially enclosed lifeboats; or

   .2   if the ship is constantly engaged on voyages in warm climates* where, in the opinion of the Administration, they are unnecessary.

4.2   The provisions of paragraph 4.1.1 also apply to partially or totally enclosed lifeboats not complying with the requirements of section 4.5 or 4.6 of the Code, provided they are carried on ships constructed before 1 July 1986.

Regulation 23
Survival craft and rescue boat embarkation arrangements

1   On passenger ships, survival craft embarkation arrangements shall be designed for:

   .1   all lifeboats to be boarded and launched either directly from the stowed position or from an embarkation deck but not both; and

   .2   davit-launched liferafts to be boarded and launched from a position immediately adjacent to the stowed position or from a position to which, in compliance with the requirements of regulation 13.5, the liferaft is transferred prior to launching.

---

* Refer to MSC/Circ.1046, Guidelines for the assessment of thermal protection.

2   Rescue boat arrangements shall be such that the rescue boat can be boarded and launched directly from the stowed position with the number of persons assigned to crew the rescue boat on board. Notwithstanding the requirements of paragraph 1.1, if the rescue boat is also a lifeboat and the other lifeboats are boarded and launched from an embarkation deck, the arrangements shall be such that the rescue boat can also be boarded and launched from the embarkation deck.

Regulation 24
Stowage of survival craft

The stowage height of a survival craft on a passenger ship shall take into account the requirements of regulation 13.1.2, the escape provisions of regulation II-2/28,* the size of the ship, and the weather conditions likely to be encountered in its intended area of operation. For a davit-launched survival craft, the height of the davit head with the survival craft in embarkation position, shall, as far as practicable, not exceed 15 m to the waterline when the ship is in its lightest seagoing condition.

Regulation 25
Muster stations

Every passenger ship shall, in addition to complying with the requirements of regulation 11, have passenger muster stations which shall:

.1   be in the vicinity of, and permit ready access for the passengers to, the embarkation stations unless in the same location; and

.2   have ample room for marshalling and instruction of the passengers, but at least 0.35 m² per passenger.

Regulation 26
Additional requirements for ro–ro passenger ships

1   This regulation applies to all ro–ro passenger ships. Ro–ro passenger ships constructed:

.1   on or after 1 July 1998 shall comply with the requirements of paragraphs 2.3, 2.4, 3.1, 3.2, 3.3, 4 and 5;

.2   on or after 1 July 1986 and before 1 July 1998 shall comply with the requirements of paragraph 5 not later than the first periodical survey after 1 July 1998 and with the requirements of paragraphs

---

* This relates to the chapter II-2 in force before 1 July 2002. The equivalent in the amended chapter II-2 is 13.

2.3, 2.4, 3 and 4 not later than the first periodical survey after 1 July 2000;

.3   before 1 July 1986 shall comply with the requirements of paragraph 5 not later than the first periodical survey after 1 July 1998 and with the requirements of paragraphs 2.1, 2.2, 2.3, 2.4, 3 and 4 not later than the first periodical survey after 1 July 2000; and

.4   before 1 July 2004 shall comply with the requirements of paragraph 2.5 not later than the first survey on or after that date.

2   Liferafts

2.1   The ro–ro passenger ship's liferafts shall be served by marine evacuation systems complying with the requirements of section 6.2 of the Code or launching appliances complying with the requirements of paragraph 6.1.5 of the Code, equally distributed on each side of the ship.

2.2   Every liferaft on ro–ro passenger ships shall be provided with float-free stowage arrangements complying with the requirements of regulation 13.4.

2.3   Every liferaft on ro–ro passenger ships shall be of a type fitted with a boarding ramp complying with the requirements of paragraph 4.2.4.1 or 4.3.4.1 of the Code, as appropriate.

2.4   Every liferaft on ro–ro passenger ships shall either be automatically self-righting or be a canopied reversible liferaft which is stable in a seaway and is capable of operating safely whichever way up it is floating. Alternatively, the ship shall carry automatically self-righting liferafts or canopied reversible liferafts, in addition to its normal complement of liferafts, of such aggregate capacity as will accommodate at least 50% of the persons not accommodated in lifeboats. This additional liferaft capacity shall be determined on the basis of the difference between the total number of persons on board and the number of persons accommodated in lifeboats. Every such liferaft shall be approved by the Administration having regard to the recommendations adopted by the Organization.[*]

2.5   Liferafts carried on ro–ro passenger ships shall be fitted with a radar transponder[†] in the ratio of one transponder for every four liferafts. The transponder shall be mounted inside the liferaft so its antenna is more than one metre above the sea level when the liferaft is deployed, except that for canopied reversible liferafts the transponder shall be so arranged as to be readily accessed and erected by survivors. Each transponder shall be arranged

---

[*] Refer to MSC/Circ.809, Recommendation for canopied reversible liferafts, automatically self-righting liferafts and fast rescue boats, including testing, on ro–ro passenger ships.

[†] Refer to the Performance standards for survival craft radar transponders for use in search and rescue operations, adopted by the Organization by resolution A.802(19).

to be manually erected when the liferaft is deployed. Containers of liferafts fitted with transponders shall be clearly marked.

3   Fast rescue boats

3.1   At least one of the rescue boats on a ro–ro passenger ship shall be a fast rescue boat approved by the Administration having regard to the recommendations adopted by the Organization.*

3.2   Each fast rescue boat shall be served by a suitable launching appliance approved by the Administration. When approving such launching appliances, the Administration shall take into account that the fast rescue boat is intended to be launched and retrieved even under severe adverse weather conditions, and also shall have regard to the recommendations adopted by the Organization.*

3.3   At least two crews of each fast rescue boat shall be trained and drilled regularly having regard to the Seafarers Training, Certification and Watchkeeping (STCW) Code and recommendations adopted by the Organization,† including all aspects of rescue, handling, manoeuvring, operating these craft in various conditions, and righting them after capsize.

3.4   In the case where the arrangement or size of a ro–ro passenger ship, constructed before 1 July 1997, is such as to prevent the installation of the fast rescue boat required by paragraph 3.1, the fast rescue boat may be installed in place of an existing lifeboat which is accepted as a rescue boat or, in the case of ships constructed prior to 1 July 1986, boats for use in an emergency, provided that all of the following conditions are met:

.1   the fast rescue boat installed is served by a launching appliance complying with the provisions of paragraph 3.2;

.2   the capacity of the survival craft lost by the above substitution is compensated by the installation of liferafts capable of carrying at least an equal number of persons served by the lifeboat replaced; and

.3   such liferafts are served by the existing launching appliances or marine evacuation systems.

4   Means of rescue‡

4.1   Each ro–ro passenger ship shall be equipped with efficient means for

---

* Refer to MSC/Circ.809, Recommendation for canopied reversible liferafts, automatically self-righting liferafts and fast rescue boats, including testing, on ro–ro passenger ships.

† Refer to the Recommendation on training requirements for crews of fast rescue boats adopted by the Organization by resolution A.771(18) and to section A-VI/2, table A-VI/2-2, "Specification of the minimum standard of competence in fast rescue boats", of the STCW Code.

‡ Refer to MSC/Circ. 810, Recommendation on means of rescue on ro–ro passenger ships.

320

rapidly recovering survivors from the water and transferring survivors from rescue units or survival craft to the ship.

4.2   The means of transfer of survivors to the ship may be part of a marine evacuation system, or may be part of a system designed for rescue purposes.

4.3   If the slide of a marine evacuation system is intended to provide the means of transfer of survivors to the deck of the ship, the slide shall be equipped with handlines or ladders to aid in climbing up the slide.

5   Lifejackets

5.1   Notwithstanding the requirements of regulations 7.2 and 22.2, a sufficient number of lifejackets shall be stowed in the vicinity of the muster stations so that passengers do not have to return to their cabins to collect their lifejackets.

5.2   In ro–ro passenger ships, each lifejacket shall be fitted with a light complying with the requirements of paragraph 2.2.3 of the Code.

Regulation 27
Information on passengers

1   All persons on board all passenger ships shall be counted prior to departure.

2   Details of persons who have declared a need for special care or assistance in emergency situations shall be recorded and communicated to the master prior to departure.

3   In addition, not later than 1 January 1999, the names and gender of all persons on board, distinguishing between adults, children and infants shall be recorded for search and rescue purposes.

4   The information required by paragraphs 1, 2 and 3 shall be kept ashore and made readily available to search and rescue services when needed.

5   Administrations may exempt passenger ships from the requirements of paragraph 3, if the scheduled voyages of such ships render it impracticable for them to prepare such records.

Regulation 28
Helicopter landing and pick-up areas

1   All ro–ro passenger ships shall be provided with a helicopter pick-up area approved by the Administration having regard to the recommendations adopted by the Organization.*

---

* Refer to the International Aeronautical and Maritime Search and Rescue Manual (IAMSAR Manual).

2   Ro–ro* passenger ships of 130 m in length and upwards, constructed on or after 1 July 1999, shall be fitted with a helicopter landing area approved by the Administration having regard to the recommendations adopted by the Organization.†

Regulation 29
Decision support system for masters of passenger ships

1   This regulation applies to all passenger ships. Passenger ships constructed before 1 July 1997 shall comply with the requirements of this regulation not later than the date of the first periodical survey after 1 July 1999.

2   In all passenger ships, a decision support system for emergency management shall be provided on the navigation bridge.

3   The system shall, as a minimum, consist of a printed emergency plan or plans.‡ All foreseeable emergency situations shall be identified in the emergency plan or plans, including, but not limited to, the following main groups of emergencies:

.1   fire;

.2   damage to ship;

.3   pollution;

.4   unlawful acts threatening the safety of the ship and the security of its passengers and crew;

.5   personnel accidents;

.6   cargo-related accidents; and

.7   emergency assistance to other ships.

4   The emergency procedures established in the emergency plan or plans shall provide decision support to masters for handling any combination of emergency situations.

5   The emergency plan or plans shall have a uniform structure and be easy to use. Where applicable, the actual loading condition as calculated for the passenger ship's voyage stability shall be used for damage control purposes.

6   In addition to the printed emergency plan or plans, the Administration may also accept the use of a computer-based decision support system on the navigation bridge which provides all the information contained in

---

* Refer to MSC/Circ. 907, Application of SOLAS regulation III/28.2 concerning helicopter landing areas on non-ro–ro passenger ships.

† Refer to MSC/Circ.895, Recommendation on helicopter landing areas on ro–ro passenger ships.

‡ Refer to the Guidelines for a structure of an integrated system of contingency planning for shipboard emergencies adopted by the Organization by resolution A.852(20).

the emergency plan or plans, procedures, checklists, etc., which is able to present a list of recommended actions to be carried out in foreseeable emergencies.

Regulation 30
Drills

1   This regulation applies to all passenger ships.

2   On passenger ships, an abandon ship drill and fire drill shall take place weekly. The entire crew need not be involved in every drill, but each crew member must participate in an abandon ship drill and a fire drill each month as required in regulation 19.3.2. Passengers shall be strongly encouraged to attend these drills.

SECTION III – CARGO SHIPS
(Additional requirements)

Regulation 31
Survival craft and rescue boats

1   **Survival craft**

1.1   Cargo ships shall carry:

.1   one or more totally enclosed lifeboats complying with the requirements of section 4.6 of the Code of such aggregate capacity on each side of the ship as will accommodate the total number of persons on board; and

.2   in addition, one or more inflatable or rigid liferafts, complying with the requirements of section 4.2 or 4.3 of the Code, stowed in a position providing for easy side-to-side transfer at a single open deck level, and of such aggregate capacity as will accommodate the total number of persons on board. If the liferaft or liferafts are not stowed in a position providing for easy side-to-side transfer at a single open deck level, the total capacity available on each side shall be sufficient to accommodate the total number of persons on board.

1.2   In lieu of meeting the requirements of paragraph 1.1, cargo ships may carry:

.1   one or more free-fall lifeboats, complying with the requirements of section 4.7 of the Code, capable of being free-fall launched over the stern of the ship of such aggregate capacity as will accommodate the total number of persons on board; and

.2 in addition, one or more inflatable or rigid liferafts complying with the requirements of section 4.2 or 4.3 of the Code, on each side of the ship, of such aggregate capacity as will accommodate the total number of persons on board. The liferafts on at least one side of the ship shall be served by launching appliances.

1.3 In lieu of meeting the requirements of paragraph 1.1 or 1.2, cargo ships of less than 85 m in length other than oil tankers, chemical tankers and gas carriers, may comply with the following:

.1 they shall carry on each side of the ship, one or more inflatable or rigid liferafts complying with the requirements of section 4.2 or 4.3 of the Code and of such aggregate capacity as will accommodate the total number of persons on board;

.2 unless the liferafts required by paragraph 1.3.1 are stowed in a position providing for easy side-to-side transfer at a single open deck level, additional liferafts shall be provided so that the total capacity available on each side will accommodate 150% of the total number of persons on board;

.3 if the rescue boat required by paragraph 2 is also a totally enclosed lifeboat complying with the requirements of section 4.6 of the Code, it may be included in the aggregate capacity required by paragraph 1.3.1, provided that the total capacity available on either side of the ship is at least 150% of the total number of persons on board; and

.4 in the event of any one survival craft being lost or rendered unserviceable, there shall be sufficient survival craft available for use on each side, including any which are stowed in a position providing for easy side-to-side transfer at a single open deck level, to accommodate the total number of persons on board.

1.4 Cargo ships where the horizontal distance from the extreme end of the stem or stern of the ship to the nearest end of the closest survival craft is more than 100 m shall carry, in addition to the liferafts required by paragraphs 1.1.2 and 1.2.2, a liferaft stowed as far forward or aft, or one as far forward and another as far aft, as is reasonable and practicable. Such liferaft or liferafts may be securely fastened so as to permit manual release and need not be of the type which can be launched from an approved launching device.

1.5 With the exception of the survival craft referred to in regulation 16.1.1, all survival craft required to provide for abandonment by the total number of persons on board shall be capable of being launched with their full complement of persons and equipment within a period of 10 min from the time the abandon ship signal is given.

1.6 Chemical tankers and gas carriers carrying cargoes emitting toxic vapours or gases* shall carry, in lieu of totally enclosed lifeboats complying with the requirements of section 4.6 of the Code, lifeboats with a self-contained air support system complying with the requirements of section 4.8 of the Code.

1.7 Oil tankers, chemical tankers and gas carriers carrying cargoes having a flashpoint not exceeding 60°C (closed-cup test) shall carry, in lieu of totally enclosed lifeboats complying with the requirements of section 4.6 of the Code, fire-protected lifeboats complying with the requirements of section 4.9 of the Code.

2 Rescue boats

Cargo ships shall carry at least one rescue boat complying with the requirements of section 5.1 of the Code. A lifeboat may be accepted as a rescue boat, provided that it also complies with the requirements for a rescue boat.

3 In addition to their lifeboats, all cargo ships constructed before 1 July 1986 shall carry:

.1 one or more liferafts capable of being launched on either side of the ship and of such aggregate capacity as will accommodate the total number of persons on board. The liferaft or liferafts shall be equipped with a lashing or an equivalent means of securing the liferaft which will automatically release it from a sinking ship; and

.2 where the horizontal distance from the extreme end of the stem or stern of the ship to the nearest end of the closest survival craft is more than 100 m, in addition to the liferafts required by paragraph 3.1, a liferaft stowed as far forward or aft, or one as far forward and another as far aft, as is reasonable and practicable. Notwithstanding the requirements of paragraph 3.1, such liferaft or liferafts may be securely fastened so as to permit manual release.

Regulation 32
Personal life-saving appliances

1 Lifebuoys

1.1 Cargo ships shall carry not less than the number of lifebuoys

---

* Refer to the products for which emergency escape respiratory protection is required in chapter 17 of the International Code for the Construction and Equipment of Ships Carrying Dangerous Chemicals in Bulk (IBC Code), adopted by the Maritime Safety Committee by resolution MSC.4(48), as amended, and in chapter 19 of the International Code for the Construction and Equipment of Ships Carrying Liquefied Gases in Bulk (IGC Code), adopted by the Maritime Safety Committee by resolution MSC.5(48), as amended.

complying with the requirements of regulation 7.1 and section 2.1 of the Code prescribed in the following table:

Length of ship in metres	Minimum number of lifebuoys
Under 100	8
100 and under 150	10
150 and under 200	12
200 and over	14

1.2   Self-igniting lights for lifebuoys on tankers required by regulation 7.1.3 shall be of an electric battery type.

2   Lifejacket lights

2.1   This paragraph applies to all cargo ships.

2.2   On cargo ships, each lifejacket shall be fitted with a lifejacket light complying with the requirements of paragraph 2.2.3 of the Code.

2.3   Lights fitted on lifejackets on board cargo ships prior to 1 July 1998 and not complying fully with paragraph 2.2.3 of the Code may be accepted by the Administration until the lifejacket light would normally be replaced or until the first periodical survey after 1 July 2001, whichever is the earliest.

3   Immersion suits and thermal protective aids

3.1   This paragraph applies to all cargo ships.

3.2   Cargo ships shall carry for each lifeboat on the ship at least three immersion suits complying with the requirements of section 2.3 of the Code or, if the Administration considers it necessary and practicable, one immersion suit complying with the requirements of section 2.3 of the Code for every person on board the ship; however, the ship shall carry in addition to the thermal protective aids required by paragraphs 4.1.5.1.24, 4.4.8.31 and 5.1.2.2.13 of the Code, thermal protective aids complying with the requirements of section 2.5 of the Code for persons on board not provided with immersion suits. These immersion suits and thermal protective aids need not be required if the ship:

.1   has totally enclosed lifeboats on each side of the ship of such aggregate capacity as will accommodate the total number of persons on board; or

.2   has totally enclosed lifeboats capable of being launched by free-fall over the stern of the ship of such aggregate capacity as will accommodate the total number of persons on board and which are boarded and launched directly from the stowed position, together with liferafts on each side of the ship of such aggregate capacity as will accommodate the total number of persons on board; or

 .3 is constantly engaged on voyages in warm climates[*] where, in the opinion of the Administration, immersion suits are unnecessary.

3.3 Cargo ships complying with the requirements of regulation 31.1.3 shall carry immersion suits complying with the requirements of section 2.3 of the Code for every person on board unless the ship:

 .1 has davit-launched liferafts; or

 .2 has liferafts served by equivalent approved appliances capable of being used on both sides of the ship and which do not require entry into the water to board the liferaft; or

 .3 is constantly engaged on voyages in warm climates where, in the opinion of the Administration, immersion suits are unnecessary.

3.4 The immersion suits required by this regulation may be used to comply with the requirements of regulation 7.3.

3.5 The totally enclosed lifeboats referred to in paragraphs 3.2.1 and 3.2.2 carried on cargo ships constructed before 1 July 1986 need not comply with the requirements of section 4.6 of the Code.

Regulation 33
Survival craft embarkation and launching arrangements

1 Cargo ship survival craft embarkation arrangements shall be so designed that lifeboats can be boarded and launched directly from the stowed position and davit-launched liferafts can be boarded and launched from a position immediately adjacent to the stowed position or from a position to which the liferaft is transferred prior to launching in compliance with the requirements of regulation 13.5.

2 On cargo ships of 20,000 gross tonnage and upwards, lifeboats shall be capable of being launched, where necessary utilizing painters, with the ship making headway at speeds up to 5 knots in calm water.

SECTION IV – LIFE-SAVING APPLIANCES AND ARRANGEMENTS REQUIREMENTS

Regulation 34

All life-saving appliances and arrangements shall comply with the applicable requirements of the Code.

---

[*] Refer to MSC/Circ.1046, Guidelines for the assessment of thermal protection.

SECTION V – MISCELLANEOUS

Regulation 35
Training manual and on-board training aids

1   This regulation applies to all ships.

2   A training manual complying with the requirements of paragraph 3 shall be provided in each crew mess room and recreation room or in each crew cabin.

3   The training manual, which may comprise several volumes, shall contain instructions and information, in easily understood terms illustrated wherever possible, on the life-saving appliances provided in the ship and on the best methods of survival. Any part of such information may be provided in the form of audio-visual aids in lieu of the manual. The following shall be explained in detail:

.1   donning of lifejackets, immersion suits and anti-exposure suits, as appropriate;

.2   muster at the assigned stations;

.3   boarding, launching, and clearing the survival craft and rescue boats, including, where applicable, use of marine evacuation systems;

.4   method of launching from within the survival craft;

.5   release from launching appliances;

.6   methods and use of devices for protection in launching areas, where appropriate;

.7   illumination in launching areas;

.8   use of all survival equipment;

.9   use of all detection equipment;

.10   with the assistance of illustrations, the use of radio life-saving appliances;

.11   use of drogues;

.12   use of engine and accessories;

.13   recovery of survival craft and rescue boats including stowage and securing;

.14   hazards of exposure and the need for warm clothing;

.15   best use of the survival craft facilities in order to survive;

.16   methods of retrieval, including the use of helicopter rescue gear (slings, baskets, stretchers), breeches-buoy and shore life-saving apparatus and ship's line-throwing apparatus;

.**17** all other functions contained in the muster list and emergency instructions; and

.**18** instructions for emergency repair of the life-saving appliances.

4 Every ship fitted with a marine evacuation system shall be provided with on-board training aids in the use of the system.

Regulation 36
Instructions for on-board maintenance

Instructions for on-board maintenance of life-saving appliances shall be easily understood, illustrated wherever possible, and, as appropriate, shall include the following for each appliance:

.**1** a checklist for use when carrying out the inspections required by regulation 20.7;

.**2** maintenance and repair instructions;

.**3** schedule of periodic maintenance;

.**4** diagram of lubrication points with the recommended lubricants;

.**5** list of replaceable parts;

.**6** list of sources of spare parts; and

.**7** log for records of inspections and maintenance.

Regulation 37
Muster list and emergency instructions

1 The muster list shall specify details of the general emergency alarm and public address system prescribed by section 7.2 of the Code and also action to be taken by crew and passengers when this alarm is sounded. The muster list shall also specify how the order to abandon ship will be given.

2 Each passenger ship shall have procedures in place for locating and rescuing passengers trapped in their staterooms.

3 The muster list shall show the duties assigned to the different members of the crew including:

.**1** closing of the watertight doors, fire doors, valves, scuppers, sidescuttles, skylights, portholes and other similar openings in the ship;

.**2** equipping of the survival craft and other life-saving appliances;

.**3** preparation and launching of survival craft;

.**4** general preparations of other life-saving appliances;

.**5** muster of passengers;

.6 use of communication equipment;

.7 manning of fire parties assigned to deal with fires; and

.8 special duties assigned in respect to the use of fire-fighting equipment and installations.

4 The muster list shall specify which officers are assigned to ensure that life-saving and fire appliances are maintained in good condition and are ready for immediate use.

5 The muster list shall specify substitutes for key persons who may become disabled, taking into account that different emergencies may call for different actions.

6 The muster list shall show the duties assigned to members of the crew in relation to passengers in case of emergency. These duties shall include:

.1 warning the passengers;

.2 seeing that they are suitably clad and have donned their lifejackets correctly;

.3 assembling passengers at muster stations;

.4 keeping order in the passageways and on the stairways and generally controlling the movements of the passengers; and

.5 ensuring that a supply of blankets is taken to the survival craft.

7 The muster list shall be prepared before the ship proceeds to sea. After the muster list has been prepared, if any change takes place in the crew which necessitates an alteration in the muster list, the master shall either revise the list or prepare a new list.

8 The format of the muster list used on passenger ships shall be approved.

CHAPTER IV
Radiocommunications

Part A
General

Regulation 1
Application

1   Unless expressly provided otherwise, this chapter applies to all ships to which the present regulations apply and to cargo ships of 300 gross tonnage and upwards.

2   This chapter does not apply to ships to which the present regulations would otherwise apply while such ships are being navigated within the Great Lakes of North America and their connecting and tributary waters as far east as the lower exit of the St Lambert Lock at Montreal in the Province of Quebec, Canada.*

3   No provision in this chapter shall prevent the use by any ship, survival craft or person in distress, of any means at their disposal to attract attention, make known their position and obtain help.

Regulation 2
Terms and definitions

1   For the purpose of this chapter, the following terms shall have the meanings defined below:

.**1**   *Bridge-to-bridge communications* means safety communications between ships from the position from which the ships are normally navigated.

.**2**   *Continuous watch* means that the radio watch concerned shall not be interrupted other than for brief intervals when the ship's receiving capability is impaired or blocked by its own communications or when the facilities are under periodical maintenance or checks.

.**3**   *Digital selective calling (DSC)* means a technique using digital codes which enables a radio station to establish contact with, and transfer information to, another station or group of stations, and

---

* Such ships are subject to special requirements relative to radio for safety purposes, as contained in the relevant agreement between Canada and the United States of America.

complying with the relevant recommendations of the International Radio Consultative Committee (CCIR).*

.4   *Direct-printing telegraphy* means automated telegraphy techniques which comply with the relevant recommendations of the International Radio Consultative Committee (CCIR).*

.5   *General radiocommunications* means operational and public correspondence traffic, other than distress, urgency and safety messages, conducted by radio.

.6   *Inmarsat*† means the Organization established by the Convention on the International Maritime Satellite Organization adopted on 3 September 1976.

.7   *International NAVTEX service* means the co-ordinated broadcast and automatic reception on 518 kHz of maritime safety information by means of narrow-band direct-printing telegraphy using the English language.‡

.8   *Locating* means the finding of ships, aircraft, units or persons in distress.

.9   *Maritime safety information* means navigational and meteorological warnings, meteorological forecasts and other urgent safety related messages broadcast to ships.

.10   *Polar orbiting satellite service* means a service which is based on polar orbiting satellites which receive and relay distress alerts from satellite EPIRBs and which provides their position.

.11   *Radio Regulations* means the Radio Regulations annexed to, or regarded as being annexed to, the most recent International Telecommunication Convention which is in force at any time.

.12   *Sea area A1* means an area within the radiotelephone coverage of at least one VHF coast station in which continuous DSC alerting is available, as may be defined by a Contracting Government.§

.13   *Sea area A2* means an area, excluding sea area A1, within the radiotelephone coverage of at least one MF coast station in which continuous DSC alerting is available, as may be defined by a Contracting Government.§

---

* The name of the Committee was changed to "ITU Radiocommunication Sector" (ITU-R) due to Article 1 of the International Telecommunication Constitution, Geneva, 1992.

† The name of the Organization was changed to "International Mobile Satellite Organization" (Inmarsat) by virtue of amendments to its Convention and Operating Agreement adopted by the 10th (extraordinary) Assembly (5–9 December 1994).

‡ Refer to the NAVTEX Manual approved by the Organization (publication IMO-951E).

§ Refer to resolution A.801(19) concerning provision of radio services for the global maritime distress and safety system (GMDSS).

.**14**   *Sea area A3* means an area, excluding sea areas A1 and A2, within the coverage of an Inmarsat geostationary satellite in which continuous alerting is available.

.**15**   *Sea area A4* means an area outside sea areas A1, A2 and A3.

.**16**   *Global maritime distress and safety system (GMDSS) identities* means maritime mobile services identity, the ship's call sign, Inmarsat identities and serial number identity which may be transmitted by the ship's equipment and used to identify the ship.

2   All other terms and abbreviations which are used in this chapter and which are defined in the Radio Regulations and in the International Convention on Maritime Search and Rescue (SAR), 1979, as may be amended, shall have the meanings as defined in those Regulations and the SAR Convention.

Regulation 3
Exemptions

1   The Contracting Governments consider it highly desirable not to deviate from the requirements of this chapter; nevertheless the Administration may grant partial or conditional exemptions to individual ships from the requirements of regulations 7 to 11 provided:

.**1**   such ships comply with the functional requirements of regulation 4; and

.**2**   the Administration has taken into account the effect such exemptions may have upon the general efficiency of the service for the safety of all ships.

2   An exemption may be granted under paragraph 1 only:

.**1**   if the conditions affecting safety are such as to render the full application of regulations 7 to 11 unreasonable or unnecessary;

.**2**   in exceptional circumstances, for a single voyage outside the sea area or sea areas for which the ship is equipped.

3   Each Administration shall submit to the Organization, as soon as possible after the first of January in each year, a report showing all exemptions granted under paragraphs 1 and 2 during the previous calendar year and giving the reasons for granting such exemptions.

Regulation 4

*Functional requirements**

1   Every ship, while at sea, shall be capable:

   .1   except as provided in regulations 8.1.1 and 10.1.4.3, of transmitting ship-to-shore distress alerts by at least two separate and independent means, each using a different radiocommunication service;

   .2   of receiving shore-to-ship distress alerts;

   .3   of transmitting and receiving ship-to-ship distress alerts;

   .4   of transmitting and receiving search and rescue co-ordinating communications;

   .5   of transmitting and receiving on-scene communications;

   .6   of transmitting and, as required by regulation V/19.2.3.2, receiving signals for locating;[†]

   .7   of transmitting and receiving[‡] maritime safety information;

   .8   of transmitting and receiving general radiocommunications to and from shore-based radio systems or networks subject to regulation 15.8; and

   .9   of transmitting and receiving bridge-to-bridge communications.

---

[*] It should be noted that ships performing GMDSS functions should use the Guidance for avoidance of false distress alerts adopted by the Organization by resolution A.814(19).

[†] Refer to resolution A.614(15) concerning carriage of radar operating in the frequency band 9,300–9,500 MHz.

[‡] It should be noted that ships may have a need for reception of certain maritime safety information while in port.

Part B
Undertakings by
*Contracting Governments**

Regulation 5
Provision of radiocommunication services

1   Each Contracting Government undertakes to make available, as it deems practical and necessary either individually or in co-operation with other Contracting Governments, appropriate shore-based facilities for space and terrestrial radiocommunication services having due regard to the recommendations of the Organization.[†] These services are:

    .1   a radiocommunication service utilizing geostationary satellites in the maritime mobile-satellite service;

    .2   a radiocommunication service utilizing polar orbiting satellites in the mobile-satellite service;

    .3   the maritime mobile service in the bands between 156 MHz and 174 MHz;

    .4   the maritime mobile service in the bands between 4,000 kHz and 27,500 kHz; and

    .5   the maritime mobile service in the bands between 415 kHz and 535 kHz[‡] and between 1,605 kHz and 4,000 kHz.

2   Each Contracting Government undertakes to provide the Organization with pertinent information concerning the shore-based facilities in the maritime mobile service, mobile-satellite service and maritime mobile-satellite service, established for sea areas which it has designated off its coasts.[§]

---

[*] 1   Each Contracting Government is not required to provide all radiocommunication services.
  2   The requirements should be specified for shore-based facilities to cover the various sea areas.

[†] Refer to resolution A.801(19) concerning provision of radio services for the global maritime distress and safety system (GMDSS).

[‡] Refer to resolution A.617(15) concerning implementation of the NAVTEX system as a component of the World-Wide Navigational Warning Service.

[§] The Master Plan of shore-based facilities for the GMDSS based on information provided by Contracting Governments is circulated to all concerned by means of GMDSS circulars.

Regulation 5-1
Global maritime distress and safety system identities

1   This regulation applies to all ships on all voyages.

2   Each Contracting Government undertakes to ensure that suitable arrangements are made for registering global maritime distress and safety system (GMDSS) identities and for making information on these identities available to rescue co-ordination centres on a 24-hour basis. Where appropriate, international organizations maintaining a registry of these identities shall be notified by the Contracting Government of these assignments.

Part C
Ship requirements

Regulation 6
Radio installations

1   Every ship shall be provided with radio installations capable of complying with the functional requirements prescribed by regulation 4 throughout its intended voyage and, unless exempted under regulation 3, complying with the requirements of regulation 7 and, as appropriate for the sea area or areas through which it will pass during its intended voyage, the requirements of either regulation 8, 9, 10 or 11.

2   Every radio installation shall:

   .1   be so located that no harmful interference of mechanical, electrical or other origin affects its proper use, and so as to ensure electromagnetic compatibility and avoidance of harmful interaction with other equipment and systems;

   .2   be so located as to ensure the greatest possible degree of safety and operational availability;

   .3   be protected against harmful effects of water, extremes of temperature and other adverse environmental conditions;

   .4   be provided with reliable, permanently arranged electrical lighting, independent of the main and emergency sources of electrical power, for the adequate illumination of the radio controls for operating the radio installation; and

   .5   be clearly marked with the call sign, the ship station identity and other codes as applicable for the use of the radio installation.

3   Control of the VHF radiotelephone channels, required for navigational safety, shall be immediately available on the navigation bridge convenient to the conning position and, where necessary, facilities should be available to permit radiocommunications from the wings of the navigation bridge. Portable VHF equipment may be used to meet the latter provision.

4   In passenger ships, a distress panel shall be installed at the conning position. This panel shall contain either one single button which, when pressed, initiates a distress alert using all radiocommunication installations required on board for that purpose or one button for each individual installation. The panel shall clearly and visually indicate whenever any button or buttons have been pressed. Means shall be provided to prevent inadvertent activation of the button or buttons. If the satellite EPIRB is used as the secondary means of distress alerting and is not remotely activated, it shall be acceptable to have an additional EPIRB installed in the wheelhouse near the conning position.

5   In passenger ships, information on the ship's position shall be continuously and automatically provided to all relevant radiocommunication equipment to be included in the initial distress alert when the button or buttons on the distress panel is pressed.

6   In passenger ships, a distress alarm panel shall be installed at the conning position. The distress alarm panel shall provide visual and aural indication of any distress alert or alerts received on board and shall also indicate through which radiocommunication service the distress alerts have been received.

Regulation 7
Radio equipment: General

1   Every ship shall be provided with:

   .1   a VHF radio installation capable of transmitting and receiving:

   .1.1   DSC on the frequency 156.525 MHz (channel 70). It shall be possible to initiate the transmission of distress alerts on channel 70 from the position from which the ship is normally navigated;* and

   .1.2   radiotelephony on the frequencies 156.300 MHz (channel 6), 156.650 MHz (channel 13) and 156.800 MHz (channel 16);

   .2   a radio installation capable of maintaining a continuous DSC watch on VHF channel 70 which may be separate from, or combined with, that required by subparagraph 1.1;*

   .3   a radar transponder capable of operating in the 9 GHz band, which:

   .3.1   shall be so stowed that it can be easily utilized; and

   .3.2   may be one of those required by regulation III/6.2.2 for a survival craft;

   .4   a receiver capable of receiving international NAVTEX service broadcasts if the ship is engaged on voyages in any area in which an international NAVTEX service is provided;

   .5   a radio facility for reception of maritime safety information by the Inmarsat enhanced group calling system† if the ship is

---

* Certain ships may be exempted from this requirement (see regulation 9.4).
† Refer to resolution A.701(17) concerning carriage of Inmarsat enhanced group call SafetyNET receivers under the GMDSS.

engaged on voyages in any area of Inmarsat coverage but in which an international NAVTEX service is not provided. However, ships engaged exclusively on voyages in areas where an HF direct-printing telegraphy maritime safety information service is provided and fitted with equipment capable of receiving such service, may be exempt from this requirement.*

.6   subject to the provisions of regulation 8.3, a satellite emergency position-indicating radio beacon (satellite EPIRB)† which shall be:

.6.1   capable of transmitting a distress alert either through the polar orbiting satellite service operating in the 406 MHz band or, if the ship is engaged only on voyages within Inmarsat coverage, through the Inmarsat geostationary satellite service operating in the 1.6 GHz band;‡

.6.2   installed in an easily accessible position;

.6.3   ready to be manually released and capable of being carried by one person into a survival craft;

.6.4   capable of floating free if the ship sinks and of being automatically activated when afloat; and

.6.5   capable of being activated manually.

2   Every passenger ship shall be provided with means for two-way on-scene radiocommunications for search and rescue purposes using the aeronautical frequencies 121.5 MHz and 123.1 MHz from the position from which the ship is normally navigated.

Regulation 8
Radio equipment: Sea area A1

1   In addition to meeting the requirements of regulation 7, every ship engaged on voyages exclusively in sea area A1 shall be provided with a radio installation capable of initiating the transmission of ship-to-shore distress alerts from the position from which the ship is normally navigated, operating either:

.1   on VHF using DSC; this requirement may be fulfilled by the EPIRB prescribed by paragraph 3, either by installing the EPIRB close to, or by remote activation from, the position from which the ship is normally navigated; or

---

* Refer to the Recommendation on promulgation of maritime safety information adopted by the Organization by resolution A.705(17).

† Refer to resolution A.616(15) concerning search and rescue homing capability.

‡ Subject to the availability of appropriate receiving and processing ground facilities for each ocean region covered by Inmarsat satellites.

.2 through the polar orbiting satellite service on 406 MHz; this requirement may be fulfilled by the satellite EPIRB, required by regulation 7.1.6, either by installing the satellite EPIRB close to, or by remote activation from, the position from which the ship is normally navigated; or

.3 if the ship is engaged on voyages within coverage of MF coast stations equipped with DSC, on MF using DSC; or

.4 on HF using DSC; or

.5 through the Inmarsat geostationary satellite service; this requirement may be fulfilled by:

.5.1 an Inmarsat ship earth station;* or

.5.2 the satellite EPIRB, required by regulation 7.1.6, either by installing the satellite EPIRB close to, or by remote activation from, the position from which the ship is normally navigated.

2   The VHF radio installation, required by regulation 7.1.1, shall also be capable of transmitting and receiving general radiocommunications using radiotelephony.

3   Ships engaged on voyages exclusively in sea area A1 may carry, in lieu of the satellite EPIRB required by regulation 7.1.6, an EPIRB which shall be:

.1 capable of transmitting a distress alert using DSC on VHF channel 70 and providing for locating by means of a radar transponder operating in the 9 GHz band;

.2 installed in an easily accessible position;

.3 ready to be manually released and capable of being carried by one person into a survival craft;

.4 capable of floating free if the ship sinks and being automatically activated when afloat; and

.5 capable of being activated manually.

Regulation 9
Radio equipment: Sea areas A1 and A2

1   In addition to meeting the requirements of regulation 7, every ship engaged on voyages beyond sea area A1, but remaining within sea area A2, shall be provided with:

.1 an MF radio installation capable of transmitting and receiving, for distress and safety purposes, on the frequencies:

---

* This requirement can be met by Inmarsat ship earth stations capable of two-way communications, such as Inmarsat-A, Inmarsat-B and Fleet-77 (resolutions A.808(19) and MSC.130(75)) or Inmarsat-C (resolution A.807(19), as amended) ship earth stations. Unless otherwise specified, this footnote applies to all requirements for an Inmarsat ship earth station prescribed by this chapter.

.1.1   2,187.5 kHz using DSC; and

.1.2   2,182 kHz using radiotelephony;

.2   a radio installation capable of maintaining a continuous DSC watch on the frequency 2,187.5 kHz which may be separate from, or combined with, that required by subparagraph .1.1; and

.3   means of initiating the transmission of ship-to-shore distress alerts by a radio service other than MF operating either:

.3.1   through the polar orbiting satellite service on 406 MHz; this requirement may be fulfilled by the satellite EPIRB, required by regulation 7.1.6, either by installing the satellite EPIRB close to, or by remote activation from, the position from which the ship is normally navigated; or

.3.2   on HF using DSC; or

.3.3   through the Inmarsat geostationary satellite service; this requirement may be fulfilled by:

.3.3.1   the equipment specified in paragraph 3.2; or

.3.3.2   the satellite EPIRB, required by regulation 7.1.6, either by installing the satellite EPIRB close to, or by remote activation from, the position from which the ship is normally navigated.

2   It shall be possible to initiate transmission of distress alerts by the radio installations specified in paragraphs 1.1 and 1.3 from the position from which the ship is normally navigated.

3   The ship shall, in addition, be capable of transmitting and receiving general radiocommunications using radiotelephony or direct-printing telegraphy by either:

.1   a radio installation operating on working frequencies in the bands between 1,605 kHz and 4,000 kHz or between 4,000 kHz and 27,500 kHz. This requirement may be fulfilled by the addition of this capability in the equipment required by paragraph 1.1; or

.2   an Inmarsat ship earth station.

4   The Administration may exempt ships constructed before 1 February 1997, which are engaged exclusively on voyages within sea area A2, from the requirements of regulations 7.1.1.1 and 7.1.2 provided such ships maintain, when practicable, a continuous listening watch on VHF channel 16. This watch shall be kept at the position from which the ship is normally navigated.

Regulation 10
Radio equipment: Sea areas A1, A2 and A3

1   In addition to meeting the requirements of regulation 7, every ship engaged on voyages beyond sea areas A1 and A2, but remaining within sea area A3, shall, if it does not comply with the requirements of paragraph 2, be provided with:

.1   an Inmarsat ship earth station capable of:

.1.1   transmitting and receiving distress and safety communications using direct-printing telegraphy;

.1.2   initiating and receiving distress priority calls;

.1.3   maintaining watch for shore-to-ship distress alerts, including those directed to specifically defined geographical areas;

.1.4   transmitting and receiving general radiocommunications, using either radiotelephony or direct-printing telegraphy; and

.2   an MF radio installation capable of transmitting and receiving, for distress and safety purposes, on the frequencies:

.2.1   2,187.5 kHz using DSC; and

.2.2   2,182 kHz using radiotelephony; and

.3   a radio installation capable of maintaining a continuous DSC watch on the frequency 2,187.5 kHz which may be separate from or combined with that required by subparagraph .2.1; and

.4   means of initiating the transmission of ship-to-shore distress alerts by a radio service operating either:

.4.1   through the polar orbiting satellite service on 406 MHz; this requirement may be fulfilled by the satellite EPIRB, required by regulation 7.1.6, either by installing the satellite EPIRB close to, or by remote activation from, the position from which the ship is normally navigated; or

.4.2   on HF using DSC; or

.4.3   through the Inmarsat geostationary satellite service, by an additional ship earth station or by the satellite EPIRB required by regulation 7.1.6, either by installing the satellite EPIRB close to, or by remote activation from, the position from which the ship is normally navigated.

2   In addition to meeting the requirements of regulation 7, every ship engaged on voyages beyond sea areas A1 and A2, but remaining within sea area A3, shall, if it does not comply with the requirements of paragraph 1, be provided with:

.1   an MF/HF radio installation capable of transmitting and receiving, for distress and safety purposes, on all distress and safety frequencies in the bands between 1,605 kHz and 4,000 kHz and between 4,000 kHz and 27,500 kHz:

.1.1   using DSC;

.1.2   using radiotelephony; and

.1.3   using direct-printing telegraphy; and

.2   equipment capable of maintaining DSC watch on 2,187.5 kHz, 8,414.5 kHz and on at least one of the distress and safety DSC frequencies 4,207.5 kHz, 6,312 kHz, 12,577 kHz or 16,804.5 kHz; at any time, it shall be possible to select any of these DSC distress and safety frequencies. This equipment may be separate from, or combined with, the equipment required by subparagraph .1; and

.3   means of initiating the transmission of ship-to-shore distress alerts by a radiocommunication service other than HF operating either:

.3.1   through the polar orbiting satellite service on 406 MHz; this requirement may be fulfilled by the satellite EPIRB, required by regulation 7.1.6, either by installing the satellite EPIRB close to, or by remote activation from, the position from which the ship is normally navigated; or

.3.2   through the Inmarsat geostationary satellite service; this requirement may be fulfilled by:

.3.2.1   an Inmarsat ship earth station; or

.3.2.2   the satellite EPIRB, required by regulation 7.1.6, either by installing the satellite EPIRB close to, or by remote activation from, the position from which the ship is normally navigated; and

.4   in addition, ships shall be capable of transmitting and receiving general radiocommunications using radiotelephony or direct-printing telegraphy by an MF/HF radio installation operating on working frequencies in the bands between 1,605 kHz and 4,000 kHz and between 4,000 kHz and 27,500 kHz. This requirement may be fulfilled by the addition of this capability in the equipment required by subparagraph .1.

3   It shall be possible to initiate transmission of distress alerts by the radio installations specified in paragraphs 1.1, 1.2, 1.4, 2.1 and 2.3 from the position from which the ship is normally navigated.

4   The Administration may exempt ships constructed before 1 February 1997, and engaged exclusively on voyages within sea areas A2 and A3, from the requirements of regulations 7.1.1.1 and 7.1.2 provided such ships maintain, when practicable, a continuous listening watch on VHF channel 16. This watch shall be kept at the position from which the ship is normally navigated.

Regulation 11
Radio equipment: Sea areas A1, A2, A3 and A4

1   In addition to meeting the requirements of regulation 7, ships engaged on voyages in all sea areas shall be provided with the radio installations and equipment required by regulation 10.2, except that the equipment required by regulation 10.2.3.2 shall not be accepted as an alternative to that required by regulation 10.2.3.1, which shall always be provided. In addition, ships engaged on voyages in all sea areas shall comply with the requirements of regulation 10.3.

2   The Administration may exempt ships constructed before 1 February 1997, and engaged exclusively on voyages within sea areas A2, A3 and A4, from the requirements of regulations 7.1.1.1 and 7.1.2 provided such ships maintain, when practicable, a continuous listening watch on VHF channel 16. This watch shall be kept at the position from which the ship is normally navigated.

Regulation 12
Watches

1   Every ship, while at sea, shall maintain a continuous watch:

.1   on VHF DSC channel 70, if the ship, in accordance with the requirements of regulation 7.1.2, is fitted with a VHF radio installation;

.2   on the distress and safety DSC frequency 2,187.5 kHz, if the ship, in accordance with the requirements of regulation 9.1.2 or 10.1.3, is fitted with an MF radio installation;

.3   on the distress and safety DSC frequencies 2,187.5 kHz and 8,414.5 kHz and also on at least one of the distress and safety DSC frequencies 4,207.5 kHz, 6,312 kHz, 12,577 kHz or 16,804.5 kHz, appropriate to the time of day and the geographical position of the ship, if the ship, in accordance with the requirements of regulation 10.2.2 or 11.1, is fitted with an MF/HF radio installation. This watch may be kept by means of a scanning receiver;

.4   for satellite shore-to-ship distress alerts, if the ship, in accordance with the requirements of regulation 10.1.1, is fitted with an Inmarsat ship earth station.

2   Every ship, while at sea, shall maintain a radio watch for broadcasts of maritime safety information on the appropriate frequency or frequencies on which such information is broadcast for the area in which the ship is navigating.

3   Until 1 February 1999 or until such other date as may be determined by the Maritime Safety Committee,* every ship while at sea shall maintain, when practicable, a continuous listening watch on VHF channel 16. This watch shall be kept at the position from which the ship is normally navigated.

Regulation 13
Sources of energy

1   There shall be available at all times, while the ship is at sea, a supply of electrical energy sufficient to operate the radio installations and to charge any batteries used as part of a reserve source or sources of energy for the radio installations.

2   A reserve source or sources of energy shall be provided on every ship, to supply radio installations, for the purpose of conducting distress and safety radiocommunications, in the event of failure of the ship's main and emergency sources of electrical power. The reserve source or sources of energy shall be capable of simultaneously operating the VHF radio installation required by regulation 7.1.1 and, as appropriate for the sea area or sea areas for which the ship is equipped, either the MF radio installation required by regulation 9.1.1, the MF/HF radio installation required by regulation 10.2.1 or 11.1, or the Inmarsat ship earth station required by regulation 10.1.1 and any of the additional loads mentioned in paragraphs 4, 5 and 8 for a period of at least:

  .1   1 h on ships provided with an emergency source of electrical power, if such source of power complies fully with all relevant provisions of regulation II-1/42 or 43, including the supply of such power to the radio installations; and

  .2   6 h on ships not provided with an emergency source of electrical power complying fully with all relevant provisions of regulation II-1/42 or 43, including the supply of such power to the radio installations.†

---

* The Maritime Safety Committee decided (resolution MSC.13(75)) that all GMDSS ships, while at sea, shall continue to maintain, when practicable, continuous listening watch on VHF channel 16.

† For guidance, the following formula is recommended for determining the electrical load to be supplied by the reserve source of energy for each radio installation required for distress conditions: 1/2 of the current consumption necessary for transmission + the current consumption necessary for reception + the current consumption of any additional loads.

The reserve source or sources of energy need not supply independent HF and MF radio installations at the same time.

3   The reserve source or sources of energy shall be independent of the propelling power of the ship and the ship's electrical system.

4   Where, in addition to the VHF radio installation, two or more of the other radio installations, referred to in paragraph 2, can be connected to the reserve source or sources of energy, they shall be capable of simultaneously supplying, for the period specified, as appropriate, in paragraph 2.1 or 2.2, the VHF radio installation and:

.1   all other radio installations which can be connected to the reserve source or sources of energy at the same time; or

.2   whichever of the other radio installations will consume the most power, if only one of the other radio installations can be connected to the reserve source or sources of energy at the same time as the VHF radio installation.

5   The reserve source or sources of energy may be used to supply the electrical lighting required by regulation 6.2.4.

6   Where a reserve source of energy consists of a rechargeable accumulator battery or batteries:

.1   a means of automatically charging such batteries shall be provided which shall be capable of recharging them to minimum capacity requirements within 10 h; and

.2   the capacity of the battery or batteries shall be checked, using an appropriate method,* at intervals not exceeding 12 months, when the ship is not at sea.

7   The siting and installation of accumulator batteries which provide a reserve source of energy shall be such as to ensure:

.1   the highest degree of service;

.2   a reasonable lifetime;

.3   reasonable safety;

.4   that battery temperatures remain within the manufacturer's specifications whether under charge or idle; and

.5   that when fully charged, the batteries will provide at least the minimum required hours of operation under all weather conditions.

---

* One method of checking the capacity of an accumulator battery is to fully discharge and recharge the battery, using normal operating current and period (e.g. 10 h). Assessment of the charge condition can be made at any time, but it should be done without significant discharge of the battery when the ship is at sea.

8   If an uninterrupted input of information from the ship's navigational or other equipment to a radio installation required by this chapter, including the navigation receiver referred to in regulation 18, is needed to ensure its proper performance, means shall be provided to ensure the continuous supply of such information in the event of failure of the ship's main or emergency source of electrical power.

Regulation 14
Performance standards

1   All equipment to which this chapter applies shall be of a type approved by the Administration. Such equipment shall conform to appropriate performance standards not inferior to those adopted by the Organization.*

---

* Refer to the following resolutions adopted by the Organization:

  .1   Resolution A.525(13): Performance standards for narrow-band direct-printing telegraph equipment for the reception of navigational and meteorological warnings and urgent information to ships.

  .2   Resolution A.694(17): General requirements for shipborne radio equipment forming part of the global maritime distress and safety system (GMDSS) and for electronic navigational aids.

  .3   Resolution A.808(19): Performance standards for ship earth stations capable of two-way communications and resolution A.570(14): Type approval of ship earth stations and MSC.130(75): Performance standards for Inmarsat ship earth stations capable of two-way communications.

  .4   Resolution A.803(19): Performance standards for shipborne VHF radio installations capable of voice communication and digital selective calling, as amended, and resolution MSC.68(68), annex 1 (valid for equipment installed on or after 1 January 2000). .5
        Resolution A.804(19): Performance standards for shipborne MF radio installations capable of voice communication and digital selective calling, as amended, and resolution MSC.68(68), annex 2 (valid for equipment installed on or after 1 January 2000).

  .6   Resolution A.806/HF(19): Performance standards for shipborne MF/HF radio installations capable of voice communication, narrow-band direct-printing and digital selective calling, as amended, and resolution MSC.68(68), annex 3 (valid for equipment installed on or after 1 January 2000).

  .7   Resolution A.810(19): Performance standards for float-free satellite emergency position-indicating radio beacons (EPIRBs) operating on 406 MHz   and MSC.120(74): Adoption of amendments to performance standards for float-free satellite emergency position-indicating radio beacons (EPIRBs) operating on 406 MHz (resolution A.810(19)) (see also Assembly resolution A.696(17): Type approval of satellite emergency position-indicating radio beacons (EPIRBs) operating in the COSPAS–SARSAT system).

  .8   Resolution A.802(19): Performance standards for survival craft radar transponders for use in search and rescue operations.

  .9   Resolution A.805(19): Performance standards for float-free VHF emergency position-indicating radio beacons.

  .10   Resolution A.807(19): Performance standards for Inmarsat-C ship earth stations capable of transmitting and receiving direct-printing communications, as amended, and resolution MSC.68(68), annex 3 (valid for equipment installed on or after 1 January 2000), and resolution A.570(14): Type approval of ship earth stations.

(continued on following page)

Regulation 15
Maintenance requirements

1   Equipment shall be so designed that the main units can be replaced readily, without elaborate recalibration or readjustment.

2   Where applicable, equipment shall be so constructed and installed that it is readily accessible for inspection and on-board maintenance purposes.

3   Adequate information shall be provided to enable the equipment to be properly operated and maintained, taking into account the recommendations of the Organization.*

4   Adequate tools and spares shall be provided to enable the equipment to be maintained.

5   The Administration shall ensure that radio equipment required by this chapter is maintained to provide the availability of the functional requirements specified in regulation 4 and to meet the recommended performance standards of such equipment.

6   On ships engaged on voyages in sea areas A1 and A2, the availability shall be ensured by using such methods as duplication of equipment, shore-based maintenance or at-sea electronic maintenance capability, or a combination of these, as may be approved by the Administration.

(footnote continued from previous page)

.11   Resolution A.664(16): Performance standards for enhanced group call equipment.

.12   Resolution A.812(19): Performance standards for float-free satellite emergency position-indicating radio beacons operating through the geostationary Inmarsat satellite system on 1.6 GHz.

.13   Resolution A.662(16): Performance standards for float-free release and activation arrangements for emergency radio equipment.

.14   Resolution A.699(17): System performance standard for the promulgation and co-ordination of maritime safety information using high-frequency narrow-band direct printing.

.15   Resolution MSC.148(77): Adoption of the revised performance standards for narrow-band direct-printing telegraph equipment for the reception of navigational and meteorological warnings and urgent information to ships (NAVTEX).

.16   Resolution A.811(19): Performance standards for a shipborne integrated radiocommunication system (IRCS) when used in the GMDSS.

.17   Resolution MSC.80(70), annex 1: Performance standards for on-scene (aeronautical) two-way portable VHF radiotelephone apparatus.

*   Refer to the Recommendation on general requirements for shipborne radio equipment forming part of the global maritime distress and safety system and for electronic navigational aids adopted by the Organization by resolution A.694(17) and to resolution A.813(19) on general requirements for electromagnetic compatibility (EMC) for all electrical and electronic ship's equipment and to MSC/Circ. 862: Clarifications of certain requirements in IMO performance standards for GMDSS equipment.

7   On ships engaged on voyages in sea areas A3 and A4, the availability shall be ensured by using a combination of at least two methods such as duplication of equipment, shore-based maintenance or at-sea electronic maintenance capability, as may be approved by the Administration, taking into account the recommendations of the Organization.*

8   While all reasonable steps shall be taken to maintain the equipment in efficient working order to ensure compliance with all the functional requirements specified in regulation 4, malfunction of the equipment for providing the general radiocommunications required by regulation 4.8 shall not be considered as making a ship unseaworthy or as a reason for delaying the ship in ports where repair facilities are not readily available, provided the ship is capable of performing all distress and safety functions.

9   Satellite EPIRBs shall be tested at intervals not exceeding 12 months for all aspects of operational efficiency with particular emphasis on frequency stability, signal strength and coding. However, in cases where it appears proper and reasonable, the Administration may extend this period to 17 months. The test may be conducted on board the ship or at an approved testing or servicing station.

Regulation 16
Radio personnel

1   Every ship shall carry personnel qualified for distress and safety radiocommunication purposes to the satisfaction of the Administration.† The personnel shall be holders of certificates specified in the Radio Regulations as appropriate, any one of whom shall be designated to have primary responsibility for radiocommunications during distress incidents.

2   In passenger ships, at least one person qualified in accordance with paragraph 1 shall be assigned to perform only radiocommunication duties during distress incidents.

Regulation 17
Radio records

A record shall be kept, to the satisfaction of the Administration and as required by the Radio Regulations, of all incidents connected with the radiocommunication service which appear to be of importance to safety of life at sea.

---

* Refer to resolution A.702(17) concerning radio maintenance guidelines for the global maritime distress and safety system related to sea areas A3 and A4.
† Refer to the STCW Code, chapter IV, section B-IV/2.

Regulation 18
Position-updating

All two-way communication equipment carried on board a ship to which this chapter applies which is capable of automatically including the ship's position in the distress alert shall be automatically provided with this information from an internal or external navigation receiver, if either is installed. If such a receiver is not installed, the ship's position and the time at which the position was determined shall be manually updated at intervals not exceeding 4 h, while the ship is under way, so that it is always ready for transmission by the equipment.

CHAPTER V
Safety of navigation

Chapter V: Safety of navigation
Contents

Regulation 1
Application

1   Unless expressly provided otherwise, this chapter shall apply to all ships on all voyages, except:

.1   warships, naval auxiliaries and other ships owned or operated by a Contracting Government and used only on Government non-commercial service; and

.2   ships solely navigating the Great Lakes of North America and their connecting and tributary waters as far east as the lower exit of the St. Lambert Lock at Montreal in the Province of Quebec, Canada.

However, warships, naval auxiliaries or other ships owned or operated by a Contracting Government and used only on Government non-commercial service are encouraged to act in a manner consistent, so far as reasonable and practicable, with this chapter.

2   The Administration may decide to what extent this chapter shall apply to ships operating solely in waters landward of the baselines which are established in accordance with international law.

3   A rigidly connected composite unit of a pushing vessel and associated pushed vessel, when designed as a dedicated and integrated tug and barge combination, shall be regarded as a single ship for the purpose of this chapter.

4   The Administration shall determine to what extent the provisions of regulations 15, 16, 17, 18, 19, 20, 21, 22, 23, 24, 25, 26, 27 and 28 do not apply to the following categories of ships:

.1   ships below 150 gross tonnage engaged on any voyage;

.2   ships below 500 gross tonnage not engaged on international voyages; and

.3   fishing vessels.

Regulation 2
Definitions

For the purpose of this chapter:

1   *Constructed* in respect of a ship means a stage of construction where:

.1   the keel is laid; or

.2   construction identifiable with a specific ship begins; or

.3 assembly of the ship has commenced comprising at least 50 tonnes or 1% of the estimated mass of all structural material, whichever is less.

2 *Nautical chart* or *nautical publication* is a special-purpose map or book, or a specially compiled database from which such a map or book is derived, that is issued officially by or on the authority of a Government, authorized Hydrographic Office or other relevant government institution and is designed to meet the requirements of marine navigation.*

3 *All ships* means any ship, vessel or craft irrespective of type and purpose.

Regulation 3
Exemptions and equivalents

1 The Administration may grant general exemptions from the requirements of regulations 15, 17, 18, 19 (except 19.2.1.7), 20, 22, 24, 25, 26, 27 and 28 to ships without mechanical means of propulsion.

2 The Administration may grant to individual ships exemptions or equivalents of a partial or conditional nature, when any such ship is engaged on a voyage where the maximum distance of the ship from the shore, the length and nature of the voyage, the absence of general navigational hazards, and other conditions affecting safety are such as to render the full application of this chapter unreasonable or unnecessary, provided that the Administration has taken into account the effect such exemptions and equivalents may have upon the safety of all other ships.

3 Each Administration shall submit to the Organization, as soon as possible after 1 January in each year, a report summarizing all new exemptions and equivalents granted under paragraph 2 of this regulation during the previous calendar year and giving the reasons for granting such exemptions and equivalents. The Organization shall circulate such particulars to other Contracting Governments for information.

Regulation 4
Navigational warnings

Each Contracting Government shall take all steps necessary to ensure that, when intelligence of any dangers is received from whatever reliable source,

---

* Refer to appropriate resolutions and recommendations of the International Hydrographic Organization concerning the authority and responsibilities of coastal States in the provision of charting in accordance with regulation 9.

it shall be promptly brought to the knowledge of those concerned and communicated to other interested Governments.[*]

Regulation 5
Meteorological services and warnings

1   Contracting Governments undertake to encourage the collection of meteorological data by ships at sea and to arrange for their examination, dissemination and exchange in the manner most suitable for the purpose of aiding navigation.[†] Administrations shall encourage the use of meteorological instruments of a high degree of accuracy and shall facilitate the checking of such instruments upon request. Arrangements may be made by appropriate national meteorological services for this checking to be undertaken, free of charge to the ship.

2   In particular, Contracting Governments undertake to carry out, in co-operation, the following meteorological arrangements:

.1   To warn ships of gales, storms and tropical cyclones by the issue of information in text and, as far as practicable, graphic form, using the appropriate shore-based facilities for terrestrial and space radiocommunications services.

.2   To issue, at least twice daily, by terrestrial and space radio-communication services,[‡] as appropriate, weather information suitable for shipping containing data, analyses, warnings and forecasts of weather, waves and ice. Such information shall be transmitted in text and, as far as practicable, graphic form, including meteorological analysis and prognosis charts transmitted by facsimile or in digital form for reconstitution on board the ship's data processing system.

.3   To prepare and issue such publications as may be necessary for the efficient conduct of meteorological work at sea and to arrange, if practicable, for the publication and making available of daily weather charts for the information of departing ships.

.4   To arrange for a selection of ships to be equipped with tested marine meteorological instruments (such as a barometer, a barograph, a psychrometer and suitable apparatus for measuring sea temperature) for use in this service, and to take, record and transmit meteorological observations at the main standard times for surface synoptic observations (i.e. at least four times daily,

---

[*] Refer to the Guidance on the IMO/IHO World-Wide Navigational Warning Service adopted by the Organization by resolution A.706(17), as amended.

[†] Refer to the Recommendation on weather routeing adopted by the Organization by resolution A.528(13).

[‡] Refer to regulations IV/7.1.4 and IV/7.1.5.

whenever circumstances permit) and to encourage other ships to take, record and transmit observations in a modified form, particularly when in areas where shipping is sparse.

.5   To encourage companies to involve as many of their ships as practicable in the making and recording of weather observations; these observations to be transmitted using the ship's terrestrial or space radiocommunications facilities for the benefit of the various national meteorological services.

.6   The transmission of these weather observations is free of charge to the ships concerned.

.7   When in the vicinity of a tropical cyclone, or of a suspected tropical cyclone, ships should be encouraged to take and transmit their observations at more frequent intervals whenever practicable, bearing in mind navigational preoccupations of ships' officers during storm conditions.

.8   To arrange for the reception and transmission of weather messages from and to ships, using the appropriate shore-based facilities for terrestrial and space radiocommunications services.

.9   To encourage masters to inform ships in the vicinity and also shore stations whenever they experience a wind speed of 50 knots or more (force 10 on the Beaufort scale).

.10   To endeavour to obtain a uniform procedure in regard to the international meteorological services already specified, and as far as practicable, to conform to the technical regulations and recommendations made by the World Meteorological Organization, to which Contracting Governments may refer, for study and advice, any meteorological question which may arise in carrying out the present Convention.

3   The information provided for in this regulation shall be furnished in a form for transmission and be transmitted in the order of priority prescribed by the Radio Regulations. During transmission "to all stations" of meteorological information, forecasts and warnings, all ship stations must conform to the provisions of the Radio Regulations.

4   Forecasts, warnings, synoptic and other meteorological data intended for ships shall be issued and disseminated by the national meteorological service in the best position to serve various coastal and high seas areas, in accordance with mutual arrangements made by Contracting Governments, in particular as defined by the World Meteorological Organization's system for the preparation and dissemination of meteorological forecasts and warnings for the high seas under the global maritime distress and safety system (GMDSS).

Regulation 6
Ice Patrol Service

1   The Ice Patrol contributes to safety of life at sea, safety and efficiency of navigation and protection of the marine environment in the North Atlantic. Ships transiting the region of icebergs guarded by the Ice Patrol during the ice season are required to make use of the services provided by the Ice Patrol.

2   The Contracting Governments undertake to continue an ice patrol and a service for study and observation of ice conditions in the North Atlantic. During the whole of the ice season, i.e., for the period from 15 February through 1 July of each year, the south-eastern, southern and south-western limits of the region of icebergs in the vicinity of the Grand Banks of Newfoundland shall be guarded for the purpose of informing passing ships of the extent of this dangerous region; for the study of ice conditions in general; and for the purpose of affording assistance to ships and crews requiring aid within the limits of operation of the patrol ships and aircraft. During the rest of the year the study and observation of ice conditions shall be maintained as advisable.

3   Ships and aircraft used for the Ice Patrol Service and the study and observation of ice conditions may be assigned other duties provided that such other duties do not interfere with the primary purpose or increase the cost of this service.

4   The Government of the United States of America agrees to continue the overall management of the Ice Patrol Service and the study and observation of ice conditions, including the dissemination of information therefrom.

5   The terms and conditions governing the management, operation and financing of the Ice Patrol are set forth in the Rules for the management, operation and financing of the North Atlantic Ice Patrol appended to this chapter, which shall form an integral part of this chapter.

6   If, at any time, the United States and/or Canadian Governments should desire to discontinue providing these services, it may do so and the Contracting Governments shall settle the question of continuing these services in accordance with their mutual interests. The United States and/or Canadian Governments shall provide 18 months' written notice to all Contracting Governments whose ships entitled to fly their flag and whose ships are registered in territories to which those Contracting Governments have extended this regulation benefit from these services before discontinuing providing these services.

Regulation 7
Search and rescue services

1   Each Contracting Government undertakes to ensure that necessary arrangements are made for distress communication and co-ordination in their area of responsibility and for the rescue of persons in distress at sea around its coasts. These arrangements shall include the establishment, operation and maintenance of such search and rescue facilities as are deemed practicable and necessary, having regard to the density of the seagoing traffic and the navigational dangers, and shall, so far as possible, provide adequate means of locating and rescuing such persons.*

2   Each Contracting Government undertakes to make available information to the Organization concerning its existing search and rescue facilities and the plans for changes therein, if any.

3   Passenger ships to which chapter I applies shall have on board a plan for co-operation with appropriate search and rescue services in the event of an emergency. The plan shall be developed in co-operation between the ship, the company, as defined in regulation IX/1, and the search and rescue services. The plan shall include provisions for periodic exercises to be undertaken to test its effectiveness. The plan shall be developed based on the guidelines developed by the Organization.

Regulation 8
Life-saving signals

Contracting Governments undertake to arrange that life-saving signals are used by search and rescue facilities engaged in search and rescue operations when communicating with ships or persons in distress.

Regulation 9
Hydrographic services

1   Contracting Governments undertake to arrange for the collection and compilation of hydrographic data and the publication, dissemination and keeping up to date of all nautical information necessary for safe navigation.

2   In particular, Contracting Governments undertake to co-operate in

---

* Refer to the International Convention on Maritime Search and Rescue (SAR), 1979, and to the following resolutions adopted by the Organization: Homing capability of search and rescue (SAR) aircraft (resolution A.225(VII)), Use of radar transponders for search and rescue purposes (resolution A.530(13)), Search and rescue homing capability (resolution A.616(15)) and International Aeronautical and Maritime Search and Rescue (IAMSAR) Manual (resolution A.894(21)).

carrying out, as far as possible, the following nautical and hydrographic services, in the manner most suitable for the purpose of aiding navigation:

.1   to ensure that hydrographic surveying is carried out, as far as possible, adequate to the requirements of safe navigation;

.2   to prepare and issue nautical charts, sailing directions, lists of lights, tide tables and other nautical publications, where applicable, satisfying the needs of safe navigation;

.3   to promulgate notices to mariners in order that nautical charts and publications are kept, as far as possible, up to date; and

.4   to provide data management arrangements to support these services.

3   Contracting Governments undertake to ensure the greatest possible uniformity in charts and nautical publications and to take into account, whenever possible, relevant international resolutions and recommendations.[*]

4   Contracting Governments undertake to co-ordinate their activities to the greatest possible degree in order to ensure that hydrographic and nautical information is made available on a world-wide scale as timely, reliably, and unambiguously as possible.

Regulation 10
Ships' routeing

1   Ships' routeing systems contribute to safety of life at sea, safety and efficiency of navigation and/or protection of the marine environment. Ships' routeing systems are recommended for use by, and may be made mandatory for, all ships, certain categories of ships or ships carrying certain cargoes, when adopted and implemented in accordance with the guidelines and criteria developed by the Organization.[†]

2   The Organization is recognized as the only international body for developing guidelines, criteria and regulations on an international level for ships' routeing systems. Contracting Governments shall refer proposals for the adoption of ships' routeing systems to the Organization. The Organization will collate and disseminate to Contracting Governments all relevant information with regard to any adopted ships' routeing systems.

3   The initiation of action for establishing a ships' routeing system is the responsibility of the Government or Governments concerned. In develop-

---

[*] Refer to the appropriate resolutions and recommendations adopted by the International Hydrographic Organization.

[†] Refer to the General provisions on ships' routeing adopted by the Organization by resolution A.572(14), as amended.

ing such systems for adoption by the Organization, the guidelines and criteria developed by the Organization* shall be taken into account.

4   Ships' routeing systems should be submitted to the Organization for adoption. However, a Government or Governments implementing ships' routeing systems not intended to be submitted to the Organization for adoption or which have not been adopted by the Organization are encouraged to take into account, wherever possible, the guidelines and criteria developed by the Organization.*

5   Where two or more Governments have a common interest in a particular area, they should formulate joint proposals for the delineation and use of a routeing system therein on the basis of an agreement between them. Upon receipt of such proposal and before proceeding with consideration of it for adoption, the Organization shall ensure that details of the proposal are disseminated to the Governments which have a common interest in the area, including countries in the vicinity of the proposed ships' routeing system.

6   Contracting Governments shall adhere to the measures adopted by the Organization concerning ships' routeing. They shall promulgate all information necessary for the safe and effective use of adopted ships' routeing systems. A Government or Governments concerned may monitor traffic in those systems. Contracting Governments shall do everything in their power to secure the appropriate use of ships' routeing systems adopted by the Organization.

7   A ship shall use a mandatory ships' routeing system adopted by the Organization as required for its category or cargo carried and in accordance with the relevant provisions in force unless there are compelling reasons not to use a particular ships' routeing system. Any such reason shall be recorded in the ships' log.

8   Mandatory ships' routeing systems shall be reviewed by the Contracting Government or Governments concerned in accordance with the guidelines and criteria developed by the Organization.*

9   All adopted ships' routeing systems and actions taken to enforce compliance with those systems shall be consistent with international law, including the relevant provisions of the 1982 United Nations Convention on the Law of the Sea.

10   Nothing in this regulation nor its associated guidelines and criteria shall prejudice the rights and duties of Governments under international law or the legal regimes of straits used for international navigation and archipelagic sea lanes.

---

* Refer to the General provisions on ships' routeing adopted by the Organization by resolution A.572(14), as amended.

Regulation 11
*Ship reporting systems**

1   Ship reporting systems contribute to safety of life at sea, safety and efficiency of navigation and/or protection of the marine environment. A ship reporting system, when adopted and implemented in accordance with the guidelines and criteria developed by the Organization[†] pursuant to this regulation, shall be used by all ships or certain categories of ships or ships carrying certain cargoes in accordance with the provisions of each system so adopted.

2   The Organization is recognized as the only international body for developing guidelines, criteria and regulations on an international level for ship reporting systems. Contracting Government shall refer proposals for the adoption of ship reporting systems to the Organization. The Organization will collate and disseminate to Contracting Governments all relevant information with regard to any adopted ship reporting system.

3   The initiation of action for establishing a ship reporting system is the responsibility of the Government or Governments concerned. In developing such systems, provision of the guidelines and criteria developed by the Organization[†] shall be taken into account.

4   Ship reporting systems not submitted to the Organization for adoption do not necessarily need to comply with this regulation. However, Governments implementing such systems are encouraged to follow, wherever possible, the guidelines and criteria developed by the Organization.[†] Contracting Governments may submit such systems to the Organization for recognition.

5   Where two or more Governments have a common interest in a particular area, they should formulate proposals for a co-ordinated ship reporting system on the basis of agreement between them. Before proceeding with a proposal for adoption of a ship reporting system, the Organization shall disseminate details of the proposal to those Governments which have a common interest in the area covered by the proposed system. Where a co-ordinated ship reporting system is adopted and established, it shall have uniform procedures and operations.

---

[*] This regulation does not address ship reporting systems established by Governments for search and rescue purposes, which are covered by chapter 5 of the 1979 SAR Convention, as amended.

[†] Refer to the Guidelines and criteria adopted by the Maritime Safety Committee of the Organization by resolution MSC.43(64), as amended by resolution MSC.111(73). Refer also to the General principles for ship reporting systems and ship reporting requirements, including guidelines for reporting incidents involving dangerous goods, harmful substances and/or marine pollutants, adopted by the Organization by resolution A.851(20).

6   After adoption of a ship reporting system in accordance with this regulation, the Government or Governments concerned shall take all measures necessary for the promulgation of any information needed for the efficient and effective use of the system. Any adopted ship reporting system shall have the capability of interaction and the ability to assist ships with information when necessary. Such systems shall be operated in accordance with the guidelines and criteria developed by the Organization* pursuant to this regulation.

7   The master of a ship shall comply with the requirements of adopted ship reporting systems and report to the appropriate authority all information required in accordance with the provisions of each such system.

8   All adopted ship reporting systems and actions taken to enforce compliance with those systems shall be consistent with international law, including the relevant provisions of the United Nations Convention on the Law of the Sea.

9   Nothing in this regulation or its associated guidelines and criteria shall prejudice the rights and duties of Governments under international law or the legal regimes of straits used for international navigation and archipelagic sea lanes.

10   The participation of ships in accordance with the provisions of adopted ship reporting systems shall be free of charge to the ships concerned.

11   The Organization shall ensure that adopted ship reporting systems are reviewed under the guidelines and criteria developed by the Organization.

Regulation 12
Vessel traffic services

1   Vessel traffic services (VTS) contribute to safety of life at sea, safety and efficiency of navigation and protection of the marine environment, adjacent shore areas, work sites and offshore installations from possible adverse effects of maritime traffic.

2   Contracting Governments undertake to arrange for the establishment of VTS where, in their opinion, the volume of traffic or the degree of risk justifies such services.

---

* Refer to the Guidelines and criteria adopted by the Maritime Safety Committee of the Organization by resolution MSC.43(64), as amended by resolution MSC.111(73). Refer also to the General principles for ship reporting systems and ship reporting requirements, including guidelines for reporting incidents involving dangerous goods, harmful substances and/or marine pollutants, adopted by the Organization by resolution A.851(20).

3   Contracting Governments planning and implementing VTS shall, wherever possible, follow the guidelines developed by the Organization.* The use of VTS may only be made mandatory in sea areas within the territorial seas of a coastal State.

4   Contracting Governments shall endeavour to secure the participation in, and compliance with, the provisions of vessel traffic services by ships entitled to fly their flag.

5   Nothing in this regulation or the guidelines adopted by the Organization shall prejudice the rights and duties of Governments under international law or the legal regimes of straits used for international navigation and archipelagic sea lanes.

Regulation 13
Establishment and operation of aids to navigation

1   Each Contracting Government undertakes to provide, as it deems practical and necessary, either individually or in co-operation with other Contracting Governments, such aids to navigation as the volume of traffic justifies and the degree of risk requires.

2   In order to obtain the greatest possible uniformity in aids to navigation, Contracting Governments undertake to take into account the international recommendations and guidelines† when establishing such aids.

3   Contracting Governments undertake to arrange for information relating to aids to navigation to be made available to all concerned. Changes in the transmissions of position-fixing systems which could adversely affect the performance of receivers fitted in ships shall be avoided as far as possible and only be effected after timely and adequate notice has been promulgated.

Regulation 14
Ships' manning

1   Contracting Governments undertake, each for its national ships, to maintain, or, if it is necessary, to adopt, measures for the purpose of ensuring that, from the point of view of safety of life at sea, all ships shall be sufficiently and efficiently manned.‡

2   Every ship to which chapter I applies shall be provided with an appropriate minimum safe manning document or equivalent issued by the

---

* Refer to the Guidelines on vessel traffic services adopted by the Organization by resolution A.857(20).

† Refer to the appropriate Recommendations and guidelines of IALA and to SN/Circ.107, Maritime buoyage system.

‡ Refer to the Principles of safe manning adopted by the Organization by resolution A.890(21), as amended by resolution A.955(23).

Administration as evidence of the minimum safe manning considered necessary to comply with the provisions of paragraph 1.

3   On all ships, to ensure effective crew performance in safety matters, a working language shall be established and recorded in the ship's log-book. The company, as defined in regulation IX/1, or the master, as appropriate, shall determine the appropriate working language. Each seafarer shall be required to understand and, where appropriate, give orders and instructions and to report back in that language. If the working language is not an official language of the State whose flag the ship is entitled to fly, all plans and lists required to be posted shall include a translation into the working language.

4   On ships to which chapter I applies, English shall be used on the bridge as the working language for bridge-to-bridge and bridge-to-shore safety communications as well as for communications on board between the pilot and bridge watchkeeping personnel,* unless those directly involved in the communication speak a common language other than English.

Regulation 15
Principles relating to bridge design, design and arrangement of navigational systems and equipment and bridge procedures

All decisions which are made for the purpose of applying the requirements of regulations 19, 22, 24, 25, 27 and 28 and which affect bridge design, the design and arrangement of navigational systems and equipment on the bridge and bridge procedures† shall be taken with the aim of:

.1   facilitating the tasks to be performed by the bridge team and the pilot in making full appraisal of the situation and in navigating the ship safely under all operational conditions;

.2   promoting effective and safe bridge resource management;

.3   enabling the bridge team and the pilot to have convenient and continuous access to essential information which is presented in a clear and unambiguous manner, using standardized symbols and coding systems for controls and displays;

.4   indicating the operational status of automated functions and integrated components, systems and/or sub-systems;

---

* The IMO Standard Marine Communication Phrases (resolution A.918(22)), as amended, may be used in this respect.

† Refer to the Guidelines on ergonomic criteria for bridge equipment and layout (MSC/Circ.982) and the Performance standards for IBS (resolution MSC.64(67), annex 1) and for INS (resolution MSC.86(70), annex 3).

.5   allowing for expeditious, continuous and effective information processing and decision-making by the bridge team and the pilot;

.6   preventing or minimizing excessive or unnecessary work and any conditions or distractions on the bridge which may cause fatigue or interfere with the vigilance of the bridge team and the pilot; and

.7   minimizing the risk of human error and detecting such error, if it occurs, through monitoring and alarm systems, in time for the bridge team and the pilot to take appropriate action.

Regulation 16
Maintenance of equipment

1   The Administration shall be satisfied that adequate arrangements are in place to ensure that the performance of the equipment required by this chapter is maintained.

2   Except as provided in regulations I/7(b)(ii), I/8 and I/9, while all reasonable steps shall be taken to maintain the equipment required by this chapter in efficient working order, malfunctions of that equipment shall not be considered as making the ship unseaworthy or as a reason for delaying the ship in ports where repair facilities are not readily available, provided suitable arrangements are made by the master to take the inoperative equipment or unavailable information into account in planning and executing a safe voyage to a port where repairs can take place.

Regulation 17
Electromagnetic compatibility

1   Administrations shall ensure that all electrical and electronic equipment on the bridge or in the vicinity of the bridge, on ships constructed on or after 1 July 2002, is tested for electromagnetic compatibility, taking into account the recommendations developed by the Organization.[*]

2   Electrical and electronic equipment shall be so installed that electromagnetic interference does not affect the proper function of navigational systems and equipment.

3   Portable electrical and electronic equipment shall not be operated on the bridge if it may affect the proper function of navigational systems and equipment.

---

[*] Refer to the *General requirements for electromagnetic compatibility for all electrical and electronic ship's equipment* adopted by the Organization by resolution A.813(19).

Regulation 18

Approval, surveys and performance standards of navigational systems and equipment and voyage data recorder

1   Systems and equipment required to meet the requirements of regulations 19 and 20 shall be of a type approved by the Administration.

2   Systems and equipment, including associated back-up arrangements, where applicable, installed on or after 1 July 2002 to perform the functional requirements of regulations 19 and 20 shall conform to appropriate performance standards not inferior to those adopted by the Organization.*

** Refer to the following recommendations adopted by the Organization by the resolutions indicated:

> Recommendations on general requirements for shipborne radio equipment forming part of the global maritime distress and safety system (GMDSS) and for electronic navigational aids (resolution A.694(17));
> Recommendation on performance standards for gyro-compasses (resolution A.424(XI));
> Recommendation on performance standards for radar equipment (resolution MSC.64(67), annex 4;
> Performance standards for automatic radar plotting aids (resolution A.823(19));
> Recommendation on performance standards for electronic chart display and information systems (ECDIS) (resolution A.817(19), as amended by resolutions MSC.64(67), annex 5, and MSC.86(70), annex 4, as appropriate);
> Recommendation on accuracy standards for navigation (resolution A.529(13));
> Recommendation on performance standards for shipborne Loran-C and Chayka receivers (resolution A.818(19));
> Recommendation on performance standards for shipborne global positioning system receiver equipment (resolution A.819(19), as amended by resolution MSC.112(73));
> Recommendation on performance standards for shipborne GLONASS receiver equipment (resolution MSC.53(66) as amended by resolution MSC.113(73));
> Recommendation on performance standards for shipborne DGPS and DGLONASS maritime radio beacon receiver equipment (resolution MSC.64(67), annex 2, as amended by resolution MSC.114(73));
> Recommendation on performance standards for combined GPS/GLONASS receiver equipment (resolution MSC.74(69), annex 1, as amended by resolution MSC.115(73));
> Recommendation on performance standards for heading control systems (resolution MSC.64(67), annex 3);
> Recommendation on performance standards for track control systems (resolution MSC.74(69), annex 2);
> Recommendation on performance standards for a universal shipborne automatic identification system (AIS) (resolution MSC.74(69), annex 3);
> Recommendation on performance standards for echo-sounding equipment (resolution A.224(VII), as amended by resolution MSC.74(69), annex 4);
> Recommendation on performance standards for devices to indicate speed and distance (resolution A.824(19), as amended by resolution MSC.96(72));
> Performance standards for rate-of-turn indicators (resolution A.526(13));
> Recommendation on unification of performance standards for navigational equipment (resolution A.575(14));
> Recommendation on methods of measuring noise levels at listening posts (resolution A.343(IX));

(continued)

3   When systems and equipment are replaced or added to on ships constructed before 1 July 2002, such systems and equipment shall, in so far as is reasonable and practicable, comply with the requirements of paragraph 2.

4   Systems and equipment installed prior to the adoption of performance standards by the Organization may subsequently be exempted from full compliance with such standards at the discretion of the Administration, having due regard to the recommended criteria adopted by the Organization. However, for an electronic chart display and information system (ECDIS) to be accepted as satisfying the chart carriage requirement of regulation 19.2.1.4, that system shall conform to the relevant performance standards not inferior to those adopted by the Organization in effect on the date of installation, or, for systems installed before 1 January 1999, not inferior to the performance standards adopted by the Organization on 23 November 1995.*

5   The Administration shall require that the manufacturers have a quality control system audited by a competent authority to ensure continuous compliance with the type approval conditions. Alternatively, the Administration may use final product verification procedures where the compliance with the type approval certificate is verified by a competent authority before the product is installed on board ships.

6   Before giving approval to systems or equipment embodying new features not covered by this chapter, the Administration shall ensure that such features support functions at least as effective as those required by this chapter.

7   When equipment, for which performance standards have been developed by the Organization, is carried on ships in addition to those items of equipment required by regulations 19 and 20, such equipment shall be subject to approval and shall, as far as practicable, comply with performance standards not inferior to those adopted by the Organization.

(footnote continued)

> Recommendation on performance standards for radar reflectors (resolution A.384(X));
> Recommendation on performance standards for magnetic compasses (resolution A.382(X));
> Recommendation on performance standards for daylight signalling lamps (resolution MSC.95(72));
> Recommendation on performance standards for sound reception systems (resolution MSC.86(70), annex 1);
> Recommendation on performance standards for marine transmitting magnetic heading devices (TMHDs) (resolution MSC.86(70), annex 2);
> Recommendation on performance standards for voyage data recorders (VDRs) (resolution A.861(20));
> Recommendations on performance standards for marine transmitting heading devices (THDs) (resolution MSC.116(73)).

* Recommendation on performance standards for electronic chart display and information systems (ECDIS) (resolution A.817(19)).

8   The voyage data recorder system, including all sensors, shall be subjected to an annual performance test. The test shall be conducted by an approved testing or servicing facility to verify the accuracy, duration and recoverability of the recorded data. In addition, tests and inspections shall be conducted to determine the serviceability of all protective enclosures and devices fitted to aid location. A copy of the certificate of compliance issued by the testing facility, stating the date of compliance and the applicable performance standards, shall be retained on board the ship.

Regulation 19
Carriage requirements for shipborne navigational systems and equipment

1   Application and requirements

Subject to the provisions of regulation 1.4:

1.1   Ships constructed on or after 1 July 2002 shall be fitted with navigational systems and equipment which will fulfil the requirements prescribed in paragraphs 2.1 to 2.9.

1.2   Ships constructed before 1 July 2002 shall:

    .1   subject to the provisions of paragraphs 1.2.2 and 1.2.3, unless they comply fully with this regulation, continue to be fitted with equipment which fulfils the requirements prescribed in regulations V/11, V/12 and V/20 of the International Convention for the Safety of Life at Sea, 1974 in force prior to 1 July 2002;

    .2   be fitted with the equipment or systems required in paragraph 2.1.6 not later than the first survey after 1 July 2002, at which time the radio direction-finding apparatus referred to in V/12(p) of the International Convention for the Safety of Life at Sea, 1974 in force prior to 1 July 2002 shall no longer be required; and

    .3   be fitted with the system required in paragraph 2.4 not later than the dates specified in paragraphs 2.4.2 and 2.4.3.

2   Shipborne navigational equipment and systems

2.1   All ships, irrespective of size, shall have:

    .1   a properly adjusted standard magnetic compass, or other means, independent of any power supply, to determine the ship's heading and display the reading at the main steering position;

.2   a pelorus or compass bearing device, or other means, independent of any power supply, to take bearings over an arc of the horizon of 360°;

.3   means of correcting heading and bearings to true at all times;

.4   nautical charts and nautical publications to plan and display the ship's route for the intended voyage and to plot and monitor positions throughout the voyage; an electronic chart display and information system (ECDIS) may be accepted as meeting the chart carriage requirements of this subparagraph;

.5   back-up arrangements to meet the functional requirements of subparagraph .4, if this function is partly or fully fulfilled by electronic means;*

.6   a receiver for a global navigation satellite system or a terrestrial radionavigation system, or other means, suitable for use at all times throughout the intended voyage to establish and update the ship's position by automatic means;

.7   if less than 150 gross tonnage and if practicable, a radar reflector, or other means, to enable detection by ships navigating by radar at both 9 and 3 GHz;

.8   when the ship's bridge is totally enclosed and unless the Administration determines otherwise, a sound reception system, or other means, to enable the officer in charge of the navigational watch to hear sound signals and determine their direction;

.9   a telephone, or other means, to communicate heading information to the emergency steering position, if provided.

2.2   All ships of 150 gross tonnage and upwards and passenger ships irrespective of size shall, in addition to the requirements of paragraph 2.1, be fitted with:

.1   a spare magnetic compass, interchangeable with the magnetic compass as referred to in paragraph 2.1.1, or other means to perform the function referred to in paragraph 2.1.1 by means of replacement or duplicate equipment;

.2   a daylight signalling lamp, or other means, to communicate by light during day and night using an energy source of electrical power not solely dependent upon the ship's power supply.

---

* An appropriate folio of paper nautical charts may be used as a back-up arrangement for ECDIS. Other back-up arrangements for ECDIS are acceptable (see appendix 6 to resolution A.817(19), as amended).

2.3   All ships of 300 gross tonnage and upwards and passenger ships irrespective of size shall, in addition to meeting the requirements of paragraph 2.2, be fitted with:

.1   an echo-sounding device, or other electronic means, to measure and display the available depth of water;

.2   a 9 GHz radar, or other means, to determine and display the range and bearing of radar transponders and of other surface craft, obstructions, buoys, shorelines and navigational marks to assist in navigation and in collision avoidance;

.3   an electronic plotting aid, or other means, to plot electronically the range and bearing of targets to determine collision risk;

.4   speed and distance measuring device, or other means, to indicate speed and distance through the water;

.5   a properly adjusted transmitting heading device, or other means, to transmit heading information for input to the equipment referred to in paragraphs 2.3.2, 2.3.3 and 2.4.

2.4   All ships of 300 gross tonnage and upwards engaged on international voyages and cargo ships of 500 gross tonnage and upwards not engaged on international voyages and passenger ships irrespective of size shall be fitted with an automatic identification system (AIS), as follows:

.1   ships constructed on or after 1 July 2002;

.2   ships engaged on international voyages constructed before 1 July 2002:

.2.1   in the case of passenger ships, not later than 1 July 2003;

.2.2   in the case of tankers, not later than the first survey for safety equipment* on or after 1 July 2003;

.2.3   in the case of ships, other than passenger ships and tankers, of 50,000 gross tonnage and upwards, not later than 1 July 2004;

.2.4   in the case of ships, other than passenger ships and tankers, of 300 gross tonnage and upwards but less than 50,000 gross tonnage, not later than the first safety equipment survey† after 1 July 2004 or by 31 December 2004, whichever occurs earlier; and

.3   ships not engaged on international voyages constructed before 1 July 2002, not later than 1 July 2008;

---

* Refer to regulation I/8.

† *The first safety equipment survey* means the first annual survey, the first periodical survey or the first renewal survey for safety equipment, whichever is due first after 1 July 2004, and, in addition, in the case of ships under construction, the initial survey.

.4   the Administration may exempt ships from the application of
the requirements of this paragraph when such ships will be taken
permanently out of service within two years after the
implementation date specified in subparagraphs .2 and .3;

.5   AIS shall:

.1   provide automatically to appropriately equipped shore
stations, other ships and aircraft information, including the
ship's identity, type, position, course, speed, navigational
status and other safety-related information;

.2   receive automatically such information from similarly
fitted ships;

.3   monitor and track ships; and

.4   exchange data with shore-based facilities;

.6   the requirements of paragraph 2.4.5 shall not be applied to cases
where international agreements, rules or standards provide for
the protection of navigational information; and

.7   AIS shall be operated taking into account the guidelines adopted
by the Organization.* Ships fitted with AIS shall maintain AIS in
operation at all times except where international agreements,
rules or standards provide for the protection of navigational
information.

2.5   All ships of 500 gross tonnage and upwards shall, in addition to
meeting the requirements of paragraph 2.3, with the exception of
paragraphs 2.3.3 and 2.3.5, and the requirements of paragraph 2.4, have:

.1   a gyro-compass, or other means, to determine and display their
heading by shipborne non-magnetic means and to transmit
heading information for input to the equipment referred in
paragraphs 2.3.2, 2.4 and 2.5.5;

.2   a gyro-compass heading repeater, or other means, to supply
heading information visually at the emergency steering position
if provided;

.3   a gyro-compass bearing repeater, or other means, to take
bearings, over an arc of the horizon of 360°, using the gyro-
compass or other means referred to in subparagraph .1.
However, ships of less than 1,600 gross tonnage shall be fitted
with such means as far as possible;

.4   rudder, propeller, thrust, pitch and operational mode indicators,
or other means, to determine and display rudder angle, propeller

---

* Refer to the Guidelines for the on-board operational use of shipborne Automatic
Identification Systems (AIS) adopted by the Organization by resolution A.917(22), as amended
by resolution A.956(23).

revolutions, the force and direction of thrust and, if applicable, the force and direction of lateral thrust and the pitch and operational mode, all to be readable from the conning position; and

.5   an automatic tracking aid, or other means, to plot automatically the range and bearing of other targets to determine collision risk.

2.6   On all ships of 500 gross tonnage and upwards, failure of one piece of equipment should not reduce the ship's ability to meet the requirements of paragraphs 2.1.1, 2.1.2 and 2.1.4.

2.7   All ships of 3,000 gross tonnage and upwards shall, in addition to meeting the requirements of paragraph 2.5, have:

.1   a 3 GHz radar or, where considered appropriate by the Administration, a second 9 GHz radar, or other means, to determine and display the range and bearing of other surface craft, obstructions, buoys, shorelines and navigational marks to assist in navigation and in collision avoidance, which are functionally independent of those referred to in paragraph 2.3.2; and

.2   a second automatic tracking aid, or other means, to plot automatically the range and bearing of other targets to determine collision risk which are functionally independent of those referred to in paragraph 2.5.5.

2.8   All ships of 10,000 gross tonnage and upwards shall, in addition to meeting the requirements of paragraph 2.7 with the exception of paragraph 2.7.2, have:

.1   an automatic radar plotting aid, or other means, to plot automatically the range and bearing of at least 20 other targets, connected to a device to indicate speed and distance through the water, to determine collision risks and simulate a trial manoeuvre; and

.2   a heading or track control system, or other means, to automatically control and keep to a heading and/or straight track.

2.9   All ships of 50,000 gross tonnage and upwards shall, in addition to meeting the requirements of paragraph 2.8, have:

.1   a rate-of-turn indicator, or other means, to determine and display the rate of turn; and

.2   a speed and distance measuring device, or other means, to indicate speed and distance over the ground in the forward and athwartships direction.

3   When "other means" are permitted under this regulation, such means must be approved by the Administration in accordance with regulation 18.

4   The navigational equipment and systems referred to in this regulation shall be so installed, tested and maintained as to minimize malfunction.

5   Navigational equipment and systems offering alternative modes of operation shall indicate the actual mode of use.

6   Integrated bridge systems* shall be so arranged that failure of one sub-system is brought to the immediate attention of the officer in charge of the navigational watch by audible and visual alarms and does not cause failure to any other sub-system. In case of failure in one part of an integrated navigational system,† it shall be possible to operate each other individual item of equipment or part of the system separately.

Regulation 20
Voyage data recorders

1   To assist in casualty investigations, ships, when engaged on international voyages, subject to the provisions of regulation 1.4, shall be fitted with a voyage data recorder (VDR) as follows:

.1   passenger ships constructed on or after 1 July 2002;

.2   ro–ro passenger ships constructed before 1 July 2002, not later than the first survey on or after 1 July 2002;

.3   passenger ships, other than ro–ro passenger ships, constructed before 1 July 2002, not later than 1 January 2004; and

.4   ships, other than passenger ships, of 3,000 gross tonnage and upwards constructed on or after 1 July 2002.

2   Administrations may exempt ships, other than ro–ro passenger ships, constructed before 1 July 2002 from being fitted with a VDR where it can be demonstrated that interfacing a VDR with the existing equipment on the ship is unreasonable and impracticable.

Regulation 21
International Code of Signals and IAMSAR Manual

1   All ships which, in accordance with the present Convention, are required to carry a radio installation shall carry the International Code of Signals as may be amended by the Organization. The Code shall also be carried by any other ship which, in the opinion of the Administration, has a need to use it.

---

* Refer to resolution MSC.64(67), annex 1, Performance standard for integrated bridge systems.

† Refer to resolution MSC.86(70), annex 3, Performance standard for integrated navigational systems.

2   All ships shall carry an up-to-date copy of Volume III of the International Aeronautical and Maritime Search and Rescue (IAMSAR) Manual.

Regulation 22
Navigation bridge visibility

1   Ships of not less than 45 m in length, as defined in regulation III/3.12, constructed on or after 1 July 1998, shall meet the following requirements:

   .1   The view of the sea surface from the conning position shall not be obscured by more than two ship lengths, or 500 m, whichever is less, forward of the bow to 10° on either side under all conditions of draught, trim and deck cargo;

   .2   No blind sector, caused by cargo, cargo gear or other obstructions outside of the wheelhouse forward of the beam which obstructs the view of the sea surface as seen from the conning position, shall exceed 10°. The total arc of blind sectors shall not exceed 20°. The clear sectors between blind sectors shall be at least 5°. However, in the view described in .1, each individual blind sector shall not exceed 5°;

   .3   The horizontal field of vision from the conning position shall extend over an arc of not less than 225°, that is from right ahead to not less than 22.5° abaft the beam on either side of the ship;

   .4   From each bridge wing, the horizontal field of vision shall extend over an arc of at least 225°, that is from at least 45° on the opposite bow through right ahead and then from right ahead to right astern through 180° on the same side of the ship;

   .5   From the main steering position, the horizontal field of vision shall extend over an arc from right ahead to at least 60° on each side of the ship;

   .6   The ship's side shall be visible from the bridge wing;

   .7   The height of the lower edge of the navigation bridge front windows above the bridge deck shall be kept as low as possible. In no case shall the lower edge present an obstruction to the forward view as described in this regulation;

   .8   The upper edge of the navigation bridge front windows shall allow a forward view of the horizon, for a person with a height of eye of 1,800 mm above the bridge deck at the conning position, when the ship is pitching in heavy seas. The Administration, if satisfied that a 1,800 mm height of eye is unreasonable and impractical, may allow reduction of the height of eye but not to less than 1,600 mm;

.9   Windows shall meet the following requirements:

.9.1   To help avoid reflections, the bridge front windows shall be inclined from the vertical plane top out, at an angle of not less than 10° and not more than 25°;

.9.2   Framing between navigation bridge windows shall be kept to a minimum and not be installed immediately forward of any work station;

.9.3   Polarized and tinted windows shall not be fitted;

.9.4   A clear view through at least two of the navigation bridge front windows and, depending on the bridge configuration, an additional number of clear-view windows shall be provided at all times, regardless of weather conditions.

2   Ships constructed before 1 July 1998 shall, where practicable, meet the requirements of paragraphs 1.1 and 1.2. However, structural alterations or additional equipment need not be required.

3   On ships of unconventional design which, in the opinion of the Administration, cannot comply with this regulation, arrangements shall be provided to achieve a level of visibility that is as near as practical to that prescribed in this regulation.

Regulation 23
Pilot transfer arrangements

1   **Application**

1.1   Ships engaged on voyages in the course of which pilots are likely to be employed shall be provided with pilot transfer arrangements.

1.2   Equipment and arrangements for pilot transfer which are installed on or after 1 January 1994 shall comply with the requirements of this regulation, and due regard shall be paid to the standards adopted by the Organization.*

1.3   Equipment and arrangements for pilot transfer which are provided on ships before 1 January 1994 shall at least comply with the requirements of regulation 17 of the International Convention for the Safety of Life at Sea, 1974 in force prior to that date, and due regard shall be paid to the standards adopted by the Organization prior to that date.

1.4   Equipment and arrangements which are replaced after 1 January 1994 shall, in so far as is reasonable and practicable, comply with the requirements of this regulation.

---

* Refer to the Recommendation on pilot transfer arrangements adopted by the Organization by resolution A.889(21) and to MSC/Circ.568/Rev.1, Required boarding arrangements for pilots.

2   General

2.1   All arrangements used for pilot transfer shall efficiently fulfil their purpose of enabling pilots to embark and disembark safely. The appliances shall be kept clean, properly maintained and stowed and shall be regularly inspected to ensure that they are safe to use. They shall be used solely for the embarkation and disembarkation of personnel.

2.2   The rigging of the pilot transfer arrangements and the embarkation of a pilot shall be supervised by a responsible officer having means of communication with the navigation bridge who shall also arrange for the escort of the pilot by a safe route to and from the navigation bridge. Personnel engaged in rigging and operating any mechanical equipment shall be instructed in the safe procedures to be adopted and the equipment shall be tested prior to use.

3   Transfer arrangements

3.1   Arrangements shall be provided to enable the pilot to embark and disembark safely on either side of the ship.

3.2   In all ships where the distance from sea level to the point of access to, or egress from, the ship exceeds 9 m, and when it is intended to embark and disembark pilots by means of the accommodation ladder, or by means of mechanical pilot hoists or other equally safe and convenient means in conjunction with a pilot ladder, the ship shall carry such equipment on each side, unless the equipment is capable of being transferred for use on either side.

3.3   Safe and convenient access to, and egress from, the ship shall be provided by either:

  .1   a pilot ladder requiring a climb of not less than 1.5 m and not more than 9 m above the surface of the water, so positioned and secured that:

  .1.1   it is clear of any possible discharges from the ship;

  .1.2   it is within the parallel body length of the ship and, as far as is practicable, within the mid-ship half length of the ship;

  .1.3   each step rests firmly against the ship's side; where constructional features, such as rubbing bands, would prevent the implementation of this provision, special arrangements shall, to the satisfaction of the Administration, be made to ensure that persons are able to embark and disembark safely;

  .1.4   the single length of pilot ladder is capable of reaching the water from the point of access to, or egress from, the ship and due allowance is made for all conditions of loading and trim of the ship, and for an adverse list of 15°; the securing strong point, shackles and securing ropes shall be at least as strong as the side ropes;

.2   an accommodation ladder in conjunction with the pilot ladder, or other equally safe and convenient means, whenever the distance from the surface of the water to the point of access to the ship is more than 9 m. The accommodation ladder shall be sited leading aft. When in use, the lower end of the accommodation ladder shall rest firmly against the ship's side within the parallel body length of the ship and, as far as is practicable, within the mid-ship half length and clear of all discharges; or

.3   a mechanical pilot hoist so located that it is within the parallel body length of the ship and, as far as is practicable, within the mid-ship half length of the ship and clear of all discharges.

4   Access to the ship's deck

Means shall be provided to ensure safe, convenient and unobstructed passage for any person embarking on, or disembarking from, the ship between the head of the pilot ladder, or of any accommodation ladder or other appliance, and the ship's deck. Where such passage is by means of:

.1   a gateway in the rails or bulwark, adequate handholds shall be provided;

.2   a bulwark ladder, two handhold stanchions rigidly secured to the ship's structure at or near their bases and at higher points shall be fitted. The bulwark ladder shall be securely attached to the ship to prevent overturning.

5   Shipside doors

Shipside doors used for pilot transfer shall not open outwards.

6   Mechanical pilot hoists

6.1   The mechanical pilot hoist and its ancillary equipment shall be of a type approved by the Administration. The pilot hoist shall be designed to operate as a moving ladder to lift and lower one person on the side of the ship, or as a platform to lift and lower one or more persons on the side of the ship. It shall be of such design and construction as to ensure that the pilot can be embarked and disembarked in a safe manner, including a safe access from the hoist to the deck and vice versa. Such access shall be gained directly by a platform securely guarded by handrails.

6.2   Efficient hand gear shall be provided to lower or recover the person or persons carried, and kept ready for use in the event of power failure.

6.3   The hoist shall be securely attached to the structure of the ship. Attachment shall not be solely by means of the ship's side rails. Proper and strong attachment points shall be provided for hoists of the portable type on each side of the ship.

6.4   If belting is fitted in the way of the hoist position, such belting shall be cut back sufficiently to allow the hoist to operate against the ship's side.

6.5   A pilot ladder shall be rigged adjacent to the hoist and be available for immediate use so that access to it is available from the hoist at any point of its travel. The pilot ladder shall be capable of reaching the sea level from its own point of access to the ship.

6.6   The position on the ship's side where the hoist will be lowered shall be indicated.

6.7   An adequate protected stowage position shall be provided for the portable hoist. In very cold weather, to avoid the danger of ice formation, the portable hoist shall not be rigged until its use is imminent.

7   **Associated equipment**

7.1   The following associated equipment shall be kept at hand ready for immediate use when persons are being transferred:

   .1   two man-ropes of not less than 28 mm in diameter, properly secured to the ship, if required by the pilot;

   .2   a lifebuoy equipped with a self-igniting light;

   .3   a heaving line.

7.2   When required by paragraph 4, stanchions and bulwark ladders shall be provided.

8   **Lighting**

Adequate lighting shall be provided to illuminate the transfer arrangements overside, the position on deck where a person embarks or disembarks and the controls of the mechanical pilot hoist.

Regulation 24
Use of heading and/or track control systems

1   In areas of high traffic density, in conditions of restricted visibility and in all other hazardous navigational situations where heading and/or track control systems are in use, it shall be possible to establish manual control of the ship's steering immediately.

2   In circumstances as above, the officer in charge of the navigational watch shall have available without delay the services of a qualified helmsperson who shall be ready at all times to take over steering control.

3 The change-over from automatic to manual steering and vice versa shall be made by, or under the supervision of, a responsible officer.

4 The manual steering shall be tested after prolonged use of heading and/or track control systems and before entering areas where navigation demands special caution.

Regulation 25
Operation of steering gear

In areas where navigation demands special caution, ships shall have more than one steering gear power unit in operation when such units are capable of simultaneous operation.

Regulation 26
Steering gear: testing and drills

1 Within 12 hours before departure, the ship's steering gear shall be checked and tested by the ship's crew. The test procedure shall include, where applicable, the operation of the following:

.1   the main steering gear;

.2   the auxiliary steering gear;

.3   the remote steering gear control systems;

.4   the steering positions located on the navigation bridge;

.5   the emergency power supply;

.6   the rudder angle indicators in relation to the actual position of the rudder;

.7   the remote steering gear control system power failure alarms;

.8   the steering gear power unit failure alarms; and

.9   automatic isolating arrangements and other automatic equipment.

2 The checks and tests shall include:

.1   the full movement of the rudder according to the required capabilities of the steering gear;

.2   a visual inspection of the steering gear and its connecting linkage; and

.3   the operation of the means of communication between the navigation bridge and steering gear compartment.

3.1   Simple operating instructions with a block diagram showing the change-over procedures for remote steering gear control systems and steering gear power units shall be permanently displayed on the navigation bridge and in the steering compartment.

3.2   All ships' officers concerned with the operation and/or maintenance of steering gear shall be familiar with the operation of the steering systems fitted on the ship and with the procedures for changing from one system to another.

4   In addition to the routine checks and tests prescribed in paragraphs 1 and 2, emergency steering drills shall take place at least once every three months in order to practise emergency steering procedures. These drills shall include direct control within the steering gear compartment, the communications procedure with the navigation bridge and, where applicable, the operation of alternative power supplies.

5   The Administration may waive the requirements to carry out the checks and tests prescribed in paragraphs 1 and 2 for ships which regularly engage on voyages of short duration. Such ships shall carry out these checks and tests at least once every week.

6   The date upon which the checks and tests prescribed in paragraphs 1 and 2 are carried out and the date and details of emergency steering drills carried out under paragraph 4 shall be recorded.

Regulation 27
Nautical charts and nautical publications

Nautical charts and nautical publications, such as sailing directions, lists of lights, notices to mariners, tide tables and all other nautical publications necessary for the intended voyage, shall be adequate and up to date.

Regulation 28
Records of navigational activities

All ships engaged on international voyages shall keep on board a record of navigational activities and incidents which are of importance to safety of navigation and which must contain sufficient detail to restore a complete record of the voyage, taking into account the recommendations adopted by the Organization.[*] When such information is not maintained in the ship's log-book, it shall be maintained in another form approved by the Administration.

---

[*] Refer to the Guidelines for recording events related to navigation adopted by the Organization by resolution A.916(22).

Regulation 29
Life-saving signals to be used by ships, aircraft or persons in distress

An illustrated table describing the life-saving signals* shall be readily available to the officer of the watch of every ship to which this chapter applies. The signals shall be used by ships or persons in distress when communicating with life-saving stations, maritime rescue units and aircraft engaged in search and rescue operations.

Regulation 30
Operational limitations

1　This regulation applies to all passenger ships to which chapter I applies.

2　A list of all limitations on the operation of a passenger ship, including exemptions from any of these regulations, restrictions in operating areas, weather restrictions, sea state restrictions, restrictions in permissible loads, trim, speed and any other limitations, whether imposed by the Administration or established during the design or the building stages, shall be compiled before the passenger ship is put in service. The list, together with any necessary explanations, shall be documented in a form acceptable to the Administration, which shall be kept on board readily available to the master. The list shall be kept updated. If the language used is not English or French, the list shall be provided in one of the two languages.

Regulation 31
Danger messages

1　The master of every ship which meets with dangerous ice, a dangerous derelict, or any other direct danger to navigation, or a tropical storm, or encounters sub-freezing air temperatures associated with gale force winds causing severe ice accretion on superstructures, or winds of force 10 or above on the Beaufort scale for which no storm warning has been received, is bound to communicate the information by all means at his disposal to ships in the vicinity, and also to the competent authorities. The form in which the information is sent is not obligatory. It may be transmitted either in plain language (preferably English) or by means of the International Code of Signals.

---

* Such life-saving signals are described in the International Aeronautical and Maritime Search and Rescue (IAMSAR) Manual, volume III, Mobile Facilities, and illustrated in the International Code of Signals, as amended pursuant to resolution A.80(IV).

2   Each Contracting Government will take all steps necessary to ensure that when intelligence of any of the dangers specified in paragraph 1 is received, it will be promptly brought to the knowledge of those concerned and communicated to other interested Governments.

3   The transmission of messages regarding the dangers specified is free of cost to the ships concerned.

4   All radio messages issued under paragraph 1 shall be preceded by the safety signal, using the procedure as prescribed by the Radio Regulations as defined in regulation IV/2.

Regulation 32
Information required in danger messages

The following information is required in danger messages:

1   Ice, derelicts and other direct dangers to navigation:

   .1   The kind of ice, derelict or danger observed.

   .2   The position of the ice, derelict or danger when last observed.

   .3   The time and date (Universal Co-ordinated Time) when the danger was last observed.

2   Tropical cyclones (storms):[*]

   .1   A statement that a tropical cyclone has been encountered. This obligation should be interpreted in a broad spirit, and information transmitted whenever the master has good reason to believe that a tropical cyclone is developing or exists in the neighbourhood.

   .2   Time, date (Universal Co-ordinated Time) and position of ship when the observation was taken.

   .3   As much of the following information as is practicable should be included in the message:
   – barometric pressure,[†] preferably corrected (stating millibars, millimetres, or inches, and whether corrected or uncorrected);
   – barometric tendency (the change in barometric pressure during the past three hours);
   – true wind direction;
   – wind force (Beaufort scale);

---

[*] The term *tropical cyclone* is the generic term used by national meteorological services of the World Meterological Organization. The terms *hurricane, typhoon, cyclone, severe tropical storm*, etc., may also be used, depending on the geographical location.

[†] The standard international unit for barometric pressure is the hectopascal (hPa), which is numerically equivalent to the millibar (mbar).

- state of the sea (smooth, moderate, rough, high);
- swell (slight, moderate, heavy) and the true direction from which it comes. Period or length of swell (short, average, long) would also be of value;
- true course and speed of ship.

Subsequent observations

3   When a master has reported a tropical cyclone or other dangerous storm, it is desirable, but not obligatory, that further observations be made and transmitted hourly, if practicable, but in any case at intervals of not more than 3 hours, so long as the ship remains under the influence of the storm.

4   Winds of force 10 or above on the Beaufort scale for which no storm warning has been received. This is intended to deal with storms other than the tropical cyclones referred to in paragraph 2; when such a storm is encountered, the message should contain similar information to that listed under the paragraph but excluding the details concerning sea and swell.

5   Sub-freezing air temperatures associated with gale force winds causing severe ice accretion on superstructures:

  .1   Time and date (Universal Co-ordinated Time).

  .2   Air temperature.

  .3   Sea temperature (if practicable).

  .4   Wind force and direction.

Examples

Ice
TTT ICE. LARGE BERG SIGHTED IN 4506 N, 4410 W, AT 0800 UTC. MAY 15.

Derelicts
TTT DERELICT. OBSERVED DERELICT ALMOST SUBMERGED IN 4006 N, 1243 W, AT 1630 UTC. APRIL 21.

Danger to navigation
TTT NAVIGATION. ALPHA LIGHTSHIP NOT ON STATION. 1800 UTC. JANUARY 3.

Tropical cyclone
TTT STORM. 0030 UTC. AUGUST 18. 2004 N, 11354 E. BAROMETER CORRECTED 994 MILLIBARS, TENDENCY DOWN 6 MILLIBARS. WIND NW, FORCE 9, HEAVY SQUALLS. HEAVY EASTERLY SWELL. COURSE 067, 5 KNOTS.

TTT STORM. APPEARANCES INDICATE APPROACH OF HURRI-CANE. 1300 UTC. SEPTEMBER 14. 2200 N, 7236 W. BAROM-

ETER CORRECTED 29.64 INCHES, TENDENCY DOWN .015 INCHES. WIND NE, FORCE 8, FREQUENT RAIN SQUALLS. COURSE 035, 9 KNOTS.

TTT STORM. CONDITIONS INDICATE INTENSE CYCLONE HAS FORMED. 0200 UTC. MAY 4. 1620 N, 9203 E. BAROMETER UNCORRECTED 753 MILLIMETRES, TENDENCY DOWN 5 MILLIMETRES. WIND S BY W, FORCE 5. COURSE 300, 8 KNOTS.

TTT STORM. TYPHOON TO SOUTHEAST. 0300 UTC. JUNE 12. 1812 N, 12605 E. BAROMETER FALLING RAPIDLY. WIND INCREASING FROM N.

TTT STORM. WIND FORCE 11, NO STORM WARNING RE-CEIVED. 0300 UTC. MAY 4. 4830 N, 30 W. BAROMETER CORRECTED 983 MILLIBARS, TENDENCY DOWN 4 MILLI-BARS. WIND SW, FORCE 11 VEERING. COURSE 260, 6 KNOTS.

Icing
TTT EXPERIENCING SEVERE ICING. 1400 UTC. MARCH 2. 69 N, 10 W. AIR TEMPERATURE 18°F (−7.8°C). SEA TEM-PERATURE 29°F (−1.7°C). WIND NE, FORCE 8.

Regulation 33
Distress messages: obligations and procedures

1   The master of a ship at sea which is in a position to be able to provide assistance, on receiving a signal from any source that persons are in distress at sea, is bound to proceed with all speed to their assistance, if possible informing them or the search and rescue service that the ship is doing so. If the ship receiving the distress alert is unable or, in the special circumstances of the case, considers it unreasonable or unnecessary to proceed to their assistance, the master must enter in the log-book the reason for failing to proceed to the assistance of the persons in distress, taking into account the recommendation of the Organization to inform the appropriate search and rescue service accordingly.

2   The master of a ship in distress or the search and rescue service concerned, after consultation, so far as may be possible, with the masters of ships which answer the distress alert, has the right to requisition one or more of those ships as the master of the ship in distress or the search and rescue service considers best able to render assistance, and it shall be the duty of the master or masters of the ship or ships requisitioned to comply with the requisition by continuing to proceed with all speed to the assistance of persons in distress.

3   Masters of ships shall be released from the obligation imposed by paragraph 1 on learning that their ships have not been requisitioned and that one or more other ships have been requisitioned and are complying with the requisition. This decision shall, if possible, be communicated to the other requisitioned ships and to the search and rescue service.

4   The master of a ship shall be released from the obligation imposed by paragraph 1 and, if his ship has been requisitioned, from the obligation imposed by paragraph 2 on being informed by the persons in distress or by the search and rescue service or by the master of another ship which has reached such persons that assistance is no longer necessary.

5   The provisions of this regulation do not prejudice the Convention for the Unification of Certain Rules of Law relating to Assistance and Salvage at Sea, signed at Brussels on 23 September 1910, particularly the obligation to render assistance imposed by article 11 of that Convention.*

Regulation 34
Safe navigation and avoidance of dangerous situations

1   Prior to proceeding to sea, the master shall ensure that the intended voyage has been planned using the appropriate nautical charts and nautical publications for the area concerned, taking into account the guidelines and recommendations developed by the Organization.†

2   The voyage plan shall identify a route which:

.1   takes into account any relevant ships' routeing systems;

.2   ensures sufficient sea room for the safe passage of the ship throughout the voyage;

.3   anticipates all known navigational hazards and adverse weather conditions; and

.4   takes into account the marine environmental protection measures that apply, and avoids, as far as possible, actions and activities which could cause damage to the environment.

3   The owner, the charterer, or the company, as defined in regulation IX/1, operating the ship or any other person shall not prevent or restrict the master of the ship from taking or executing any decision which, in the master's professional judgement, is necessary for safe navigation and protection of the marine environment.

---

* International Convention on Salvage, 1989, done at London on 28 April 1989, entered into force on 14 July 1996.

† Refer to the Guidelines for voyage planning adopted by the Organization by resolution A.893(21).

Regulation 35
Misuse of distress signals

The use of an international distress signal, except for the purpose of indicating that a person or persons are in distress, and the use of any signal which may be confused with an international distress signal are prohibited.

Appendix to chapter V
Rules for the management, operation and financing of the North Atlantic Ice Patrol

1   In these Rules:

   .1   *Ice season* means the annual period between 15 February and 1 July.

   .2   *Region of icebergs guarded by the Ice Patrol* means the south-eastern, southern and south-western limits of the region of icebergs in the vicinity of the Grand Banks of Newfoundland.

   .3   *Routes passing through regions of icebergs guarded by the Ice Patrol* means:

      .3.1   routes between Atlantic coast ports of Canada (including inland ports approached from the North Atlantic through the Gut of Canso and Cabot Straits) and ports of Europe, Asia or Africa approached from the North Atlantic through or north of the Straits of Gibraltar (except routes which pass south of the extreme limits of ice of all types);

      .3.2   routes via Cape Race, Newfoundland, between Atlantic coast ports of Canada (including inland ports approached from the North Atlantic through the Gut of Canso and Cabot Straits) west of Cape Race, Newfoundland, and Atlantic coast ports of Canada north of Cape Race, Newfoundland;

      .3.3   routes between Atlantic and Gulf Coast ports of the United States of America (including inland ports approached from the North Atlantic through the Gut of Canso and Cabot Straits) and ports of Europe, Asia or Africa approached from the North Atlantic through or north of the Straits of Gibraltar (except routes which pass south of the extreme limits of ice of all types);

      .3.4   routes via Cape Race, Newfoundland, between Atlantic and Gulf Coast ports of the United States of America (including inland ports approached from the North Atlantic through the Gut of Canso and Cabot Straits) and Atlantic Coast ports of Canada north of Cape Race, Newfoundland.

.4   *Extreme limits of ice of all types* in the North Atlantic Ocean is defined by a line connecting the following points:

A	–	42° 23'.00 N, 59° 25'.00 W	J – 39° 49'.00 N, 41° 00'.00 W
B	–	41° 23'.00 N, 57° 00'.00 W	K – 40° 39'.00 N, 39° 00'.00 W
C	–	40° 47'.00 N, 55° 00'.00 W	L – 41° 19'.00 N, 38° 00'.00 W
D	–	40° 07'.00 N, 53° 00'.00 W	M – 43° 00'.00 N, 37° 27'.00 W
E	–	39° 18'.00 N, 49° 39'.00 W	N – 44° 00'.00 N, 37° 29'.00 W
F	–	38° 00'.00 N, 47° 35'.00 W	O – 46° 00'.00 N, 37° 55'.00 W
G	–	37° 41'.00 N, 46° 40'.00 W	P – 48° 00'.00 N, 38° 28'.00 W
H	–	38° 00'.00 N, 45° 33'.00 W	Q – 50° 00'.00 N, 39° 07'.00 W
I	–	39° 05'.00 N, 43° 00'.00 W	R – 51° 25'.00 N, 39° 45'.00 W.

.5   *Managing and operating* means maintaining, administering and operating the Ice Patrol, including the dissemination of information received therefrom.

.6   *Contributing Government* means a Contracting Government undertaking to contribute to the costs of the Ice Patrol Service pursuant to these Rules.

2   Each Contracting Government specially interested in these services whose ships pass through the region of icebergs during the ice season undertakes to contribute to the Government of the United States of America its proportionate share of the costs for the management and operation of the Ice Patrol Service. The contribution to the Government of the United States of America shall be based on the ratio which the average annual gross tonnage of that contributing Government's ships passing through the region of icebergs guarded by the Ice Patrol during the previous three ice seasons bears to the combined average annual gross tonnage of all ships that passed through the region of icebergs guarded by the Ice Patrol during the previous three ice seasons.

3   All contributions shall be calculated by multiplying the ratio described in paragraph 2 by the average actual annual cost incurred by the Governments of the United States of America and Canada of managing and operating ice patrol services during the previous three years. This ratio shall be computed annually, and shall be expressed in terms of a lump sum per-annum fee.

4   Each of the contributing Governments has the right to alter or discontinue its contribution, and other interested Governments may undertake to contribute to the expense. The contributing Government which avails itself of this right will continue to be responsible for its current contribution up to 1 September following the date of giving notice of intention to alter or discontinue its contribution. To take advantage of the said right it must give notice to the managing Government at least six months before the said 1 September.

5   Each contributing Government shall notify the Secretary-General of its undertaking pursuant to paragraph 2, who shall notify all Contracting Governments.

6   The Government of the United States of America shall furnish annually to each contributing Government a statement of the total cost incurred by the Governments of the United States of America and Canada of managing and operating the Ice Patrol for that year and of the average percentage share for the past three years of each contributing Government.

7   The managing Government shall publish annual accounts including a statement of costs incurred by the Governments providing the services for the past three years and the total gross tonnage using the service for the past three years. The accounts shall be publicly available. Within three months after having received the cost statement, contributing Governments may request more detailed information regarding the costs incurred in managing and operating the Ice Patrol.

8   These Rules shall be operative beginning with the ice season of 2002.

CHAPTER VI
Carriage of cargoes

Part A
General provisions

Regulation 1
Application

1   This chapter applies to the carriage of cargoes (except liquids in bulk, gases in bulk and those aspects of carriage covered by other chapters) which, owing to their particular hazards to ships or persons on board, may require special precautions in all ships to which the present regulations apply and in cargo ships of less than 500 gross tonnage. However, for cargo ships of less than 500 gross tonnage, the Administration, if it considers that the sheltered nature and conditions of voyage are such as to render the application of any specific requirements of part A or B of this chapter unreasonable or unnecessary, may take other effective measures to ensure the required safety for these ships.

2   To supplement the provisions of parts A and B of this chapter, each Contracting Government shall ensure that appropriate information on cargo and its stowage and securing is provided, specifying, in particular, precautions necessary for the safe carriage of such cargoes.[*]

Regulation 2
Cargo information

1   The shipper shall provide the master or his representative with appropriate information on the cargo sufficiently in advance of loading to enable the precautions which may be necessary for proper stowage and safe carriage of the cargo to be put into effect. Such information[†] shall be

---

[*] Refer to:
    .1   the Code of Safe Practice for Cargo Stowage and Securing adopted by the Organization by resolution A.714(17), as amended;
    .2   the Code of Safe Practice for Ships Carrying Timber Deck Cargoes adopted by the Organization by resolution A.715(17), as amended; MSC/Circ.525, Guidance note on precautions to be taken by the masters of ships of below 100 metres in length engaged in the carriage of logs; and MSC/Circ.548, Guidance note on precautions to be taken by masters of ships engaged in the carriage of timber cargoes; and
    .3   the Code of Safe Practice for Solid Bulk Cargoes (BC Code) adopted by the Organization by resolution A.434(XI), as amended.
[†] Refer to MSC/Circ.663, Form for cargo information.

confirmed in writing* and by appropriate shipping documents prior to loading the cargo on the ship.

2   The cargo information shall include:

.1   in the case of general cargo, and of cargo carried in cargo units, a general description of the cargo, the gross mass of the cargo or of the cargo units, and any relevant special properties of the cargo. For the purpose of this regulation the cargo information required in sub-chapter 1.9 of the Code of Safe Practice for Cargo Stowage and Securing, adopted by the Organization by resolution A.714(17), as may be amended, shall be provided. Any such amendment to sub-chapter 1.9 shall be adopted, brought into force and take effect in accordance with the provisions of article VIII of the present Convention concerning the amendment procedures applicable to the annex other than chapter I;

.2   in the case of bulk cargo, information on the stowage factor of the cargo, the trimming procedures, likelihood of shifting including angle of repose, if applicable, and any other relevant special properties. In the case of a concentrate or other cargo which may liquefy, additional information in the form of a certificate on the moisture content of the cargo and its transportable moisture limit.

.3   in the case of a bulk cargo not classified in accordance with the provisions of the IMDG Code, as defined in regulation VII/1.1, but which has chemical properties that may create a potential hazard, in addition to the information required by the preceding subparagraphs, information on its chemical properties.

3   Prior to loading cargo units on board ships, the shipper shall ensure that the gross mass of such units is in accordance with the gross mass declared on the shipping documents.

Regulation 3
Oxygen analysis and gas detection equipment

1   When transporting a bulk cargo which is liable to emit a toxic or flammable gas, or cause oxygen depletion in the cargo space, an appropriate instrument for measuring the concentration of gas or oxygen in the air shall be provided together with detailed instructions for its use. Such an instrument shall be to the satisfaction of the Administration.

---

* Reference to documents in this regulation does not preclude the use of electronic data processing (EDP) and electronic data interchange (EDI) transmission techniques as an aid to paper documentation.

2   The Administration shall take steps to ensure that crews of ships are trained in the use of such instruments.

Regulation 4
*The use of pesticides in ships**

Appropriate precautions shall be taken in the use of pesticides in ships, in particular for the purposes of fumigation.

Regulation 5
Stowage and securing

1   Cargo, cargo units[†] and cargo transport units[‡] carried on or under deck shall be so loaded, stowed and secured as to prevent as far as is practicable, throughout the voyage, damage or hazard to the ship and the persons on board, and loss of cargo overboard.

2   Cargo, cargo units and cargo transport units shall be so packed and secured within the unit as to prevent, throughout the voyage, damage or hazard to the ship and the persons on board.

3   Appropriate precautions shall be taken during loading and transport of heavy cargoes or cargoes with abnormal physical dimensions to ensure that no structural damage to the ship occurs and to maintain adequate stability throughout the voyage.

4   Appropriate precautions shall be taken during loading and transport of cargo units and cargo transport units on board ro–ro ships, especially with regard to the securing arrangements on board such ships and on the cargo units and cargo transport units and with regard to the strength of the securing points and lashings.

5   Freight containers shall not be loaded to more than the maximum gross weight indicated on the Safety Approval Plate under the International Convention for Safe Containers (CSC), as amended.

6   All cargoes, other than solid and liquid bulk cargoes, cargo units and cargo transport units, shall be loaded, stowed and secured throughout the voyage in accordance with the Cargo Securing Manual approved by the Administration. In ships with ro–ro spaces, as defined in regulation II-2/3.41, all securing of such cargoes, cargo units, and cargo transport units, in accordance with the Cargo Securing Manual, shall be completed before the

---

* Refer to the IMO Recommendations on the Safe Use of Pesticides in Ships, as amended.

† Refer to the Code of Safe Practice for Cargo Stowage and Securing, adopted by the Organization by resolution A.714(17) as amended.

‡ Refer to the International Maritime Dangerous Goods (IMDG) Code, adopted by the Organization by resolution MSC.122(75).

ship leaves the berth. The Cargo Securing Manual shall be drawn up to a standard at least equivalent to relevant guidelines developed by the Organization.[*]

---

[*] Refer to the Guidelines on the preparation of the Cargo Securing Manual (MSC/Circ.745).

Part B
*Special provisions
for bulk cargoes other than grain*

Regulation 6
Acceptability for shipment

1   Prior to loading a bulk cargo, the master shall be in possession of comprehensive information on the ship's stability and on the distribution of cargo for the standard loading conditions. The method of providing such information shall be to the satisfaction of the Administration.*

2   Concentrates or other cargoes which may liquefy shall only be accepted for loading when the actual moisture content of the cargo is less than its transportable moisture limit. However, such concentrates and other cargoes may be accepted for loading even when their moisture content exceeds the above limit, provided that safety arrangements to the satisfaction of the Administration are made to ensure adequate stability in the case of cargo shifting and further provided that the ship has adequate structural integrity.

3   Prior to loading a bulk cargo which is not a cargo classified in accordance with the provisions of the IMDG Code, as defined in regulation VII/1.1 but which has chemical properties that may create a potential hazard, special precautions for its safe carriage shall be taken.

Regulation 7
Loading, unloading and stowage of bulk cargoes†

1   For the purpose of this regulation, *terminal representative* means a person appointed by the terminal or other facility, where the ship is loading or unloading, who has responsibility for operations conducted by that terminal or facility with regard to the particular ship.

---

* Refer to:
   .1   the Recommendation on intact stability for passenger and cargo ships under 100 metres in length adopted by the Organization by resolution A.167(ES.IV) and to amendments to this Recommendation adopted by the Organization by resolution A.206(VII); and
   .2   the Recommendation on a severe wind and rolling criterion (weather criterion) for the intact stability of passenger and cargo ships of 24 metres in length and over adopted by the Organization by resolution A.562(14).
† Refer to the Code of Practice for the Safe Loading and Unloading of Bulk Carriers (BLU Code) adopted by the Organization by resolution A.862(20).

2   To enable the master to prevent excessive stresses in the ship's structure, the ship shall be provided with a booklet, which shall be written in a language with which the ship's officers responsible for cargo operations are familiar. If this language is not English, the ship shall be provided with a booklet written also in the English language. The booklet shall, as a minimum, include:

.1   stability data, as required by regulation II-1/22 ;

.2   ballasting and deballasting rates and capacities;

.3   maximum allowable load per unit surface area of the tank top plating;

.4   maximum allowable load per hold;

.5   general loading and unloading instructions with regard to the strength of the ship's structure including any limitations on the most adverse operating conditions during loading, unloading, ballasting operations and the voyage;

.6   any special restrictions such as limitations on the most adverse operating conditions imposed by the Administration or organization recognized by it, if applicable; and

.7   where strength calculations are required, maximum permissible forces and moments on the ship's hull during loading, unloading and the voyage.

3   Before a solid bulk cargo is loaded or unloaded, the master and the terminal representative shall agree on a plan* which shall ensure that the permissible forces and moments on the ship are not exceeded during loading or unloading, and shall include the sequence, quantity and rate of loading or unloading, taking into consideration the speed of loading or unloading, the number of pours and the deballasting or ballasting capability of the ship. The plan and any subsequent amendments thereto shall be lodged with the appropriate authority of the port State.

4   Bulk cargoes shall be loaded and trimmed reasonably level, as necessary, to the boundaries of the cargo space so as to minimize the risk of shifting and to ensure that adequate stability will be maintained throughout the voyage.

5   When bulk cargoes are carried in 'tween-decks, the hatchways of such 'tween-decks shall be closed in those cases where the loading information indicates an unacceptable level of stress of the bottom structure if the hatchways are left open. The cargo shall be trimmed reasonably level and shall either extend from side to side or be secured by additional longitudinal divisions of sufficient strength. The safe load-carrying capacity of the

---

* Refer to the Code of Practice for the Safe Loading and Unloading of Bulk Carriers (BLU Code) adopted by the Organization by resolution A.862(20).

'tween-decks shall be observed to ensure that the deck-structure is not overloaded.

6   The master and terminal representative shall ensure that loading and unloading operations are conducted in accordance with the agreed plan.

7   If during loading or unloading any of the limits of the ship referred to in paragraph 2 are exceeded or are likely to become so if the loading or unloading continues, the master has the right to suspend operation and the obligation to notify accordingly the appropriate authority of the port State with which the plan has been lodged. The master and the terminal representative shall ensure that corrective action is taken. When unloading cargo, the master and terminal representative shall ensure that the unloading method does not damage the ship's structure.

8   The master shall ensure that ship's personnel continuously monitor cargo operations. Where possible, the ship's draught shall be checked regularly during loading or unloading to confirm the tonnage figures supplied. Each draught and tonnage observation shall be recorded in a cargo log-book. If significant deviations from the agreed plan are detected, cargo or ballast operations or both shall be adjusted to ensure that the deviations are corrected.

Part C
Carriage of grain

Regulation 8
Definitions

For the purposes of this part, unless expressly provided otherwise:

1   *International Grain Code* means the International Code for the Safe Carriage of Grain in Bulk adopted by the Maritime Safety Committee of the Organization by resolution MSC.23(59) as may be amended by the Organization, provided that such amendments are adopted, brought into force and take effect in accordance with the provisions of article VIII of the present Convention concerning the amendment procedures applicable to the annex other than chapter I.

2   The term *grain* includes wheat, maize (corn), oats, rye, barley, rice, pulses, seeds and processed forms thereof whose behaviour is similar to that of grain in its natural state.

Regulation 9
Requirements for cargo ships carrying grain

1   In addition to any other applicable requirements of the present regulations, a cargo ship carrying grain shall comply with the requirements of the International Grain Code, and hold a document of authorization as required by that Code. For the purpose of this regulation, the requirements of the Code shall be treated as mandatory.

2   A ship without such a document shall not load grain until the master satisfies the Administration, or the Contracting Government of the port of loading on behalf of the Administration, that the ship will comply with the requirements of the International Grain Code in its proposed loaded condition.

CHAPTER VII
Carriage of dangerous goods*

---

* See also resolution A.851(20), General principles for ship reporting systems and ship reporting requirements, including guidelines for reporting incidents involving dangerous goods, harmful substances and/or marine pollutants.

Part C – *Construction and equipment of ships
carrying liquefied gases in bulk*

Part D – *Special requirements for the carriage of
packaged irradiated nuclear fuel,
plutonium and high-level radioactive
wastes on board ships*

Part A
Carriage of dangerous goods in packaged form

Regulation 1
Definitions

For the purpose of this chapter, unless expressly provided otherwise:

1 *IMDG Code* means the International Maritime Dangerous Goods (IMDG) Code adopted by the Maritime Safety Committee of the Organization by resolution MSC.122(75), as may be amended by the Organization, provided that such amendments are adopted, brought into force and take effect in accordance with the provisions of article VIII of the present Convention concerning the amendment procedures applicable to the annex other than chapter I.

2 *Dangerous goods* mean the substances, materials and articles covered by the IMDG Code.

3 *Packaged form* means the form of containment specified in the IMDG Code.

Regulation 2
Application*

1 Unless expressly provided otherwise, this part applies to the carriage of dangerous goods in packaged form in all ships to which the present regulations apply and in cargo ships of less than 500 gross tonnage.

2 The provisions of this part do not apply to ships' stores and equipment.

3 The carriage of dangerous goods in packaged form is prohibited except in accordance with the provisions of this chapter.

---

* Refer to:
.1 part D, which contains special requirements for the carriage of INF cargo; and
.2 regulation II-2/19, which contains special requirements for ships carrying dangerous goods.

4   To supplement the provisions of this part, each Contracting Government shall issue, or cause to be issued, detailed instructions on emergency response and medical first aid relevant to incidents involving dangerous goods in packaged form, taking into account the guidelines developed by the Organization.[*]

Regulation 3
Requirements for the carriage of dangerous goods

The carriage of dangerous goods in packaged form shall be in compliance with the relevant provisions of the IMDG Code.

Regulation 4
Documents

1   In all documents relating to the carriage of dangerous goods in packaged form by sea, the Proper Shipping Name of the goods shall be used (trade names alone shall not be used) and the correct description given in accordance with the classification set out in the IMDG Code.

2   The transport documents prepared by the shipper shall include, or be accompanied by, a signed certificate or a declaration that the consignment, as offered for carriage, is properly packaged, marked, labelled or placarded, as appropriate, and in proper condition for carriage.

3   The person(s) responsible for the packing/loading of dangerous goods in a cargo transport unit[†] shall provide a signed container/vehicle packing certificate stating that the cargo in the unit has been properly packed and secured and that all applicable transport requirements have been met. Such a certificate may be combined with the document referred to in paragraph 2.

4   Where there is due cause to suspect that a cargo transport unit in which dangerous goods are packed is not in compliance with the requirements of paragraph 2 or 3, or where a container/vehicle packing certificate is not available, the cargo transport unit shall not be accepted for carriage.

---

[*] Refer to:
　.1 the *Emergency Response Procedures for Ships Carrying Dangerous Goods (EmS Guide)* (MSC/Circ.1025); and
　.2 the *Medical First Aid Guide for Use in Accidents Involving Dangerous Goods (MFAG)* (MSC/Circ.857)
published by the Organization.
[†] Refer to the International Maritime Dangerous Goods (IMDG) Code, adopted by the Organization by resolution MSC.122(75).

5   Each ship carrying dangerous goods in packaged form shall have a special list or manifest setting forth, in accordance with the classification set out in the IMDG Code, the dangerous goods on board and the location thereof. A detailed stowage plan, which identifies by class and sets out the location of all dangerous goods on board, may be used in place of such a special list or manifest. A copy of one of these documents shall be made available before departure to the person or organization designated by the port State authority.

Regulation 5
Cargo Securing Manual

Cargo, cargo units* and cargo transport units shall be loaded, stowed and secured throughout the voyage in accordance with the Cargo Securing Manual approved by the Administration. The Cargo Securing Manual shall be drawn up to a standard at least equivalent to the guidelines developed by the Organization.†

Regulation 6
Reporting of incidents involving dangerous goods

1   When an incident takes place involving the loss or likely loss overboard of dangerous goods in packaged form into the sea, the master, or other person having charge of the ship, shall report the particulars of such an incident without delay and to the fullest extent possible to the nearest coastal State. The report shall be drawn up based on general principles and guidelines developed by the Organization.‡

2   In the event of the ship referred to in paragraph 1 being abandoned, or in the event of a report from such a ship being incomplete or unobtainable, the company, as defined in regulation IX/1.2, shall, to the fullest extent possible, assume the obligations placed upon the master by this regulation.

---

* As defined in the Code of Safe Practice for Cargo Stowage and Securing, adopted by the Organization by resolution A.715(17), as amended.

† Refer to the Guidelines for the preparation of the Cargo Securing Manual (MSC/Circ.745).

‡ Refer to the General principles for ship reporting systems and ship reporting requirements, including Guidelines for reporting incidents involving dangerous goods, harmful substances and/or marine pollutants, adopted by the Organization by resolution A.851(20).

Part A-1
Carriage of dangerous goods in solid form in bulk

Regulation 7
Definitions

Dangerous goods in solid form in bulk means any material, other than liquid or gas, consisting of a combination of particles, granules or any larger pieces of material, generally uniform in composition, which is covered by the IMDG Code and is loaded directly into the cargo spaces of a ship without any intermediate form of containment, and includes such materials loaded in a barge on a barge-carrying ship.

Regulation 7-1
*Application**

1   Unless expressly provided otherwise, this part applies to the carriage of dangerous goods in solid form in bulk in all ships to which the present regulations apply and in cargo ships of less than 500 gross tonnage.

2   The carriage of dangerous goods in solid form in bulk is prohibited except in accordance with the provisions of this part.

3   To supplement the provisions of this part, each Contracting Government shall issue, or cause to be issued, detailed instructions on the safe carriage of dangerous goods in solid form in bulk[†] which shall include instructions on emergency response and medical first aid relevant to incidents involving dangerous goods in solid form in bulk, taking into account the guidelines developed by the Organization.[‡]

---

[*] Refer to regulation II-2/19, which contains special requirements for ship carrying dangerous goods.
[†] Refer to the Code of Safe Practice for Solid Bulk Cargoes (BC Code), adopted by the Organization by resolution A.434(XI), as amended.
[‡] Refer to the *Medical First Aid Guide for Use in Accidents involving Dangerous Goods (MFAG)* (MSC/Circ.857).

Regulation 7-2
Documents

1   In all documents relating to the carriage of dangerous goods in solid form in bulk by sea, the bulk cargo shipping name of the goods shall be used (trade names alone shall not be used).

2   Each ship carrying dangerous goods in solid form in bulk shall have a special list or manifest setting forth the dangerous goods on board and the location thereof. A detailed stowage plan, which identifies by class and sets out the location of all dangerous goods on board, may be used in place of such a special list or manifest. A copy of one of these documents shall be made available before departure to the person or organization designated by the port State authority.

Regulation 7-3
Stowage and segregation requirements

1   Dangerous goods in solid form in bulk shall be loaded and stowed safely and appropriately in accordance with the nature of the goods. Incompatible goods shall be segregated from one another.

2   Dangerous goods in solid form in bulk, which are liable to spontaneous heating or combustion, shall not be carried unless adequate precautions have been taken to minimize the likelihood of the outbreak of fire.

3   Dangerous goods in solid form in bulk, which give off dangerous vapours, shall be stowed in a well ventilated cargo space.

Regulation 7-4
Reporting of incidents involving dangerous goods

1   When an incident takes place involving the loss or likely loss overboard of dangerous goods in solid form in bulk into the sea, the master, or other person having charge of the ship, shall report the particulars of such an incident without delay and to the fullest extent possible to the nearest coastal State. The report shall be drawn up based on general principles and guidelines developed by the Organization.[*]

2   In the event of the ship referred to in paragraph 1 being abandoned, or in the event of a report from such a ship being incomplete or unobtainable, the company, as defined in regulation IX/1.2, shall, to the fullest extent possible, assume the obligations placed upon the master by this regulation.

---

[*] Refer to the General principles for ship reporting systems and ship reporting requirements, including Guidelines for reporting incidents involving dangerous goods, harmful substances and/or marine pollutants, adopted by the Organization by resolution A.851(20).

Part B
Construction and equipment of ships carrying dangerous liquid chemicals in bulk

Regulation 8
Definitions

For the purpose of this part, unless expressly provided otherwise:

1   *International Bulk Chemical Code (IBC Code)* means the International Code for the Construction and Equipment of Ships Carrying Dangerous Chemicals in Bulk adopted by the Maritime Safety Committee of the Organization by resolution MSC.4(48), as may be amended by the Organization, provided that such amendments are adopted, brought into force and take effect in accordance with the provisions of article VIII of the present Convention concerning the amendment procedures applicable to the annex other than chapter I.

2   *Chemical tanker* means a cargo ship constructed or adapted and used for the carriage in bulk of any liquid product listed in chapter 17 of the International Bulk Chemical Code.

3   For the purpose of regulation 9, *ship constructed* means a ship the keel of which is laid or which is at a similar stage of construction.

4   *At a similar stage of construction* means the stage at which:

    .1   construction identifiable with a specific ship begins; and

    .2   assembly of that ship has commenced comprising at least 50 tonnes or 1% of the estimated mass of all structural material, whichever is less.

Regulation 9
Application to chemical tankers

1   Unless expressly provided otherwise, this part applies to chemical tankers constructed on or after 1 July 1986 including those of less than 500 gross tonnage. Such tankers shall comply with the requirements of this part in addition to any other applicable requirements of the present regulations.

2   Any chemical tanker, irrespective of the date of construction, which undergoes repairs, alterations, modifications and outfitting related thereto shall continue to comply with at least the requirements previously applicable to the ship. Such a ship, if constructed before 1 July 1986, shall, as a rule, comply with the requirements for a ship constructed on or after that date to at least the same extent as before undergoing such repairs, alterations, modifications or outfitting. Repairs, alterations and modifications of a major character, and outfitting related thereto, shall meet the requirements for a ship constructed on or after 1 July 1986 in so far as the Administration deems reasonable and practicable.

3   A ship, irrespective of the date of construction, which is converted to a chemical tanker shall be treated as a chemical tanker constructed on the date on which such conversion commenced.

Regulation 10
Requirements for chemical tankers

1   A chemical tanker shall comply with the requirements of the International Bulk Chemical Code and shall, in addition to the requirements of regulation I/8, I/9, and I/10, as applicable, be surveyed and certified as provided for in that Code. For the purpose of this regulation, the requirements of the Code shall be treated as mandatory.

2   A chemical tanker holding a certificate issued pursuant to the provisions of paragraph 1 shall be subject to the control established in regulation I/19. For this purpose such certificate shall be treated as a certificate issued under regulation I/12 or I/13.

Part C
Construction and equipment of ships carrying liquefied gases in bulk

Regulation 11
Definitions

For the purpose of this part, unless expressly provided otherwise:

1 *International Gas Carrier Code (IGC Code)* means the International Code for the Construction and Equipment of Ships Carrying Liquefied Gases in Bulk as adopted by the Maritime Safety Committee of the Organization by resolution MSC.5(48), as may be amended by the Organization, provided that such amendments are adopted, brought into force and take effect in accordance with the provisions of article VIII of the present Convention concerning the amendment procedures applicable to the annex other than chapter I.

2 *Gas carrier* means a cargo ship constructed or adapted and used for the carriage in bulk of any liquefied gas or other product listed in chapter 19 of the International Gas Carrier Code.

3 For the purpose of regulation 12, *ship constructed* means a ship the keel of which is laid or which is at a similar stage of construction.

4 *At a similar stage of construction* means the stage at which:

    .1 construction identifiable with a specific ship begins; and

    .2 assembly of that ship has commenced comprising at least 50 tonnes or 1% of the estimated mass of all structural material, whichever is less.

Regulation 12
Application to gas carriers

1 Unless expressly provided otherwise, this part applies to gas carriers constructed on or after 1 July 1986 including those of less than 500 gross tonnage. Such gas carriers shall comply with the requirements of this part in addition to any other applicable requirements of the present regulations.

2 Any gas carrier, irrespective of the date of construction, which undergoes repairs, alterations, modifications and outfitting related thereto shall continue to comply with at least the requirements previously applicable to the ship. Such a ship if constructed before 1 July 1986 shall, as a rule, comply with the requirements for a ship constructed on or after that date to at least the same extent as before undergoing such repairs, alterations, modifications or outfitting. Repairs, alterations and modifications of a major character, and outfitting related thereto, shall meet the requirements for a ship constructed on or after 1 July 1986 in so far as the Administration deems reasonable and practicable.

3   A ship, irrespective of the date of construction, which is converted to a gas carrier shall be treated as a gas carrier constructed on the date on which such conversion commenced.

Regulation 13
Requirements for gas carriers

1   A gas carrier shall comply with the requirements of the International Gas Carrier Code and shall, in addition to the requirements of regulation I/8, I/9 and I/10, as applicable, be surveyed and certified as provided for in that Code. For the purpose of this regulation, the requirements of the Code shall be treated as mandatory.

2   A gas carrier holding a certificate issued pursuant to the provisions of paragraph 1 shall be subject to the control established in regulation I/19. For this purpose such certificate shall be treated as a certificate issued under regulation I/12 or I/13.

Part D
Special requirements for the carriage of packaged irradiated nuclear fuel, plutonium and high-level radioactive wastes on board ships

Regulation 14
Definitions

For the purpose of this part, unless expressly provided otherwise:

1   *INF Code* means the International Code for the Safe Carriage of Packaged Irradiated Nuclear Fuel, Plutonium and High-Level Radioactive Wastes on Board Ships, adopted by the Maritime Safety Committee of the Organization by resolution MSC.88(71), as may be amended by the Organization, provided that such amendments are adopted, brought into force and take effect in accordance with the provisions of article VIII of the present Convention concerning the amendment procedures applicable to the annex other than chapter I.

2   *INF cargo* means packaged irradiated nuclear fuel, plutonium and high-level radioactive wastes carried as cargo in accordance with class 7 of the IMDG Code.

3   *Irradiated nuclear fuel* means material containing uranium, thorium and/or plutonium isotopes which has been used to maintain a self-sustaining nuclear chain reaction.

4   *Plutonium* means the resultant mixture of isotopes of that material extracted from irradiated nuclear fuel from reprocessing.

5   *High-level radioactive wastes* means liquid wastes resulting from the operation of the first stage extraction system or the concentrated wastes from subsequent extraction stages, in a facility for reprocessing irradiated nuclear fuel, or solids into which such liquid wastes have been converted.

Regulation 15
Application to ships carrying INF cargo

1   Except as provided for in paragraph 2, this part shall apply to all ships regardless of the date of construction and size, including cargo ships of less than 500 gross tonnage, engaged in the carriage of INF cargo.

2   This part and the INF Code do not apply to warships, naval auxiliary or other vessels owned or operated by a Contracting Government and used, for the time being, only on government non-commercial service; however, each Administration shall ensure, by the adoption of appropriate measures not impairing operations or operational capabilities of such ships owned or operated by it, that such ships carrying INF cargo act in a manner consistent, so far as reasonable and practicable, with this part and the INF Code.

3   Nothing in this part or the INF Code shall prejudice the rights and duties of governments under international law and any action taken to enforce compliance shall be consistent with international law.

Regulation 16
Requirements for ships carrying INF cargo

1   A ship carrying INF cargo shall comply with the requirements of the INF Code in addition to any other applicable requirements of the present regulations and shall be surveyed and certified as provided for in that Code.

2   A ship holding a certificate issued pursuant to the provisions of paragraph 1 shall be subject to the control established in regulations I/19 and XI/4. For this purpose, such certificate shall be treated as a certificate issued under regulation I/12 or I/13.

CHAPTER VIII
Nuclear ships

Regulation 1
Application

This chapter applies to all nuclear ships except ships of war.

Regulation 2
Application of other chapters

The regulations contained in the other chapters of the present Convention apply to nuclear ships except as modified by this chapter.*

Regulation 3
Exemptions

A nuclear ship shall not, in any circumstances, be exempted from compliance with any regulations of this Convention.

Regulation 4
Approval of reactor installation

The design, construction and standards of inspection and assembly of the reactor installation shall be subject to the approval and satisfaction of the Administration and shall take account of the limitations which will be imposed on surveys by the presence of radiation.

Regulation 5
Suitability of reactor installation
for service on board ship

The reactor installation shall be designed having regard to the special conditions of service on board ship both in normal and exceptional circumstances of navigation.

Regulation 6
Radiation safety

The Administration shall take measures to ensure that there are no unreasonable radiation or other nuclear hazards, at sea or in port, to the crew, passengers or public, or to the waterways or food or water resources.

---

* Refer to the Code of Safety for Nuclear Merchant Ships (resolution A.491(XII)), which supplements the requirements of this chapter.

Regulation 7
Safety assessment

(a) A safety assessment shall be prepared to permit evaluation of the nuclear power plant and safety of the ship to ensure that there are no unreasonable radiation or other hazards, at sea or in port, to the crew, passengers or public, or to the waterways or food or water resources. The Administration, when satisfied, shall approve such safety assessment which shall always be kept up to date.

(b) The safety assessment shall be made available sufficiently in advance to the Contracting Governments of the countries which a nuclear ship intends to visit so that they may evaluate the safety of the ship.

Regulation 8
Operating manual

A fully detailed operating manual shall be prepared for the information and guidance of the operating personnel in their duties on all matters relating to the operation of the nuclear power plant and having an important bearing on safety. The Administration, when satisfied, shall approve such operating manual and a copy shall be kept on board the ship. The operating manual shall always be kept up to date.

Regulation 9
Surveys

Survey of nuclear ships shall include the applicable requirements of regulation 7 of chapter I, or of regulations 8, 9 and 10 of chapter I, except in so far as surveys are limited by the presence of radiation. In addition, the surveys shall include any special requirements of the safety assessment. They shall in all cases, notwithstanding the provisions of regulations 8 and 10 of chapter I, be carried out not less frequently than once a year.

Regulation 10
Certificates

(a) The provisions of paragraph (a) of regulation 12 of chapter I and of regulation 14 of chapter I shall not apply to nuclear ships.

(b) A certificate, called a Nuclear Passenger Ship Safety Certificate shall be issued after inspection and survey to a nuclear passenger ship which complies with the requirements of chapters II-1, II-2, III, IV and VIII, and any other relevant requirements of the present regulations.

(c) A certificate, called a Nuclear Cargo Ship Safety Certificate shall be issued after inspection and survey to a nuclear cargo ship which satisfies the requirements for cargo ships on survey set out in regulation 10 of chapter I, and complies with the requirements of chapters II-1, II-2, III, IV and VIII and any other relevant requirements of the present regulations.

(d) Nuclear Passenger Ship Safety Certificates and Nuclear Cargo Ship Safety Certificates shall state: "That the ship, being a nuclear ship, complied with all requirements of chapter VIII of the Convention and conformed to the Safety Assessment approved for the ship".

(e) Nuclear Passenger Ship Safety Certificates and Nuclear Cargo Ship Safety Certificates shall be valid for a period of not more than 12 months.

(f) Nuclear Passenger Ship Safety Certificates and Nuclear Cargo Ship Safety Certificates shall be issued either by the Administration or by any person or organization duly authorized by it. In every case, that Administration assumes full responsibility for the certificate.

Regulation 11
Special control*

In addition to the control established by regulation 19 of chapter I, nuclear ships shall be subject to special control before entering the ports and in the ports of Contracting Governments, directed towards verifying that there is on board a valid Nuclear Ship Safety Certificate and that there are no unreasonable radiation or other hazards at sea or in port, to the crew, passengers or public, or to the waterways or food or water resources.

Regulation 12
Casualties

In the event of any accident likely to lead to an environmental hazard the master of a nuclear ship shall immediately inform the Administration. The master shall also immediately inform the competent governmental authority of the country in whose waters the ship may be, or whose waters the ship approaches in a damaged condition.

---

* Refer to the IMO/IAEA Safety Recommendation on the Use of Ports by Nuclear Merchant Ships.

CHAPTER IX
Management for the
safe operation of ships

Regulation 1
Definitions

For the purpose of this chapter, unless expressly provided otherwise:

1   *International Safety Management (ISM) Code* means the International Management Code for the Safe Operation of Ships and for Pollution Prevention adopted by the Organization by resolution A.741(18), as may be amended by the Organization, provided that such amendments are adopted, brought into force and take effect in accordance with the provisions of article VIII of the present Convention concerning the amendment procedures applicable to the annex other than chapter I.

2   *Company* means the owner of the ship or any other organization or person such as the manager, or the bareboat charterer, who has assumed the responsibility for operation of the ship from the owner of the ship and who on assuming such responsibility has agreed to take over all the duties and responsibilities imposed by the International Safety Management Code.

3   *Oil tanker* means an oil tanker as defined in regulation II-1/2.12.

4   *Chemical tanker* means a chemical tanker as defined in regulation VII/8.2.

5   *Gas carrier* means a gas carrier as defined in regulation VII/11.2.

6   *Bulk carrier* means a ship which is constructed generally with single deck, top-side tanks and hopper side tanks in cargo spaces, and is intended primarily to carry dry cargo in bulk, and includes such types as ore carriers and combination carriers.[*]

7   *Mobile offshore drilling unit (MODU)* means a vessel capable of engaging in drilling operations for the exploration for or exploitation of resources beneath the sea-bed such as liquid or gaseous hydrocarbons, sulphur or salt.

8   *High-speed craft* means a craft as defined in regulation X/1.

Regulation 2
Application

1   This chapter applies to ships, regardless of the date of construction, as follows:

    .1   passenger ships including passenger high-speed craft, not later than 1 July 1998;

---

[*] Refer to resolution MSC.79(70) relating to interpretation of provisions of SOLAS chapter XII on additional safety measures for bulk carriers.

    .2   oil tankers, chemical tankers, gas carriers, bulk carriers and cargo high-speed craft of 500 gross tonnage and upwards, not later than 1 July 1998; and

    .3   other cargo ships and mobile offshore drilling units of 500 gross tonnage and upwards, not later than 1 July 2002.*

2   This chapter does not apply to government-operated ships used for non-commercial purposes.

Regulation 3
Safety management requirements

1   The company and the ship shall comply with the requirements of the International Safety Management Code. For the purpose of this regulation, the requirements of the Code shall be treated as mandatory.

2   The ship shall be operated by a company holding a Document of Compliance referred to in regulation 4.

Regulation 4
Certification

1   A Document of Compliance shall be issued to every company which complies with the requirements of the International Safety Management Code. This document shall be issued by the Administration, by an organization recognized by the Administration, or at the request of the Administration by another Contracting Government.

2   A copy of the Document of Compliance shall be kept on board the ship in order that the master can produce it on request for verification.

3   A Certificate, called a Safety Management Certificate, shall be issued to every ship by the Administration or an organization recognized by the Administration. The Administration or organization recognized by it shall, before issuing the Safety Management Certificate, verify that the company and its shipboard management operate in accordance with the approved safety-management system.

---

* The Maritime Safety Committee, at its sixty-sixth session, decided that mobile offshore drilling units not propelled by mechanical means need not comply with the requirements of the chapter.

Regulation 5
Maintenance of conditions

The safety-management system shall be maintained in accordance with the provisions of the International Safety Management Code.

Regulation 6
Verification and control

1　The Administration, another Contracting Government at the request of the Administration or an organization recognized by the Administration shall periodically verify the proper functioning of the ship's safety-management system.

2　A ship required to hold a certificate issued pursuant to the provisions of regulation 4.3 shall be subject to control in accordance with the provisions of regulation XI/4. For this purpose such certificate shall be treated as a certificate issued under regulation I/12 or I/13.

CHAPTER X
Safety measures for high-speed craft

429

Regulation 1
Definitions

For the purpose of this chapter:

1 *High-Speed Craft Code, 1994 (1994 HSC Code)* means the International Code of Safety for High-Speed Craft adopted by the Maritime Safety Committee of the Organization by resolution MSC.36(63), as may be amended by the Organization, provided that such amendments are adopted, brought into force and take effect in accordance with the provisions of article VIII of the present Convention concerning the amendment procedures applicable to the annex other than chapter I.

2 *High-Speed Craft Code, 2000 (2000 HSC Code)* means the International Code of Safety for High-Speed Craft, 2000, adopted by the Maritime Safety Committee of the Organization by resolution MSC.97(73), as may be amended by the Organization, provided that such amendments are adopted, brought into force and take effect in accordance with the provisions of article VIII of the present Convention concerning the amendment procedures applicable to the annex other than chapter I.

3 *High-speed craft* is a craft capable of a maximum speed, in metres per second (m/s), equal to or exceeding:

$$3.7\nabla^{0.1667}$$

where: ∇ = volume of displacement corresponding to the design waterline (m^3),

excluding craft the hull of which is supported completely clear above the water surface in non-displacement mode by aerodynamic forces generated by ground effect.

4 *Craft constructed* means a craft the keel of which is laid or which is at a similar stage of construction.

5 *Similar stage of construction* means a stage at which:

    .1 construction identifiable with a specific craft begins; and

    .2 assembly of that craft has commenced comprising at least 50 tonnes or 3% of the estimated mass of all structural material, whichever is the less.

Regulation 2
Application

1 This chapter applies to high-speed craft constructed on or after 1 January 1996, as follows:

.1   passenger craft which do not proceed in the course of their voyage more than 4 h at operational speed from a place of refuge when fully laden; and

.2   cargo craft of 500 gross tonnage and upwards which do not proceed in the course of their voyage more than 8 h at operational speed from a place of refuge when fully laden.

2   Any craft, irrespective of the date of construction, which undergoes repairs, alterations, modifications and outfitting related thereto shall continue to comply with at least the requirements previously applicable to the craft. Such a craft, if constructed before 1 July 2002, shall, as a rule, comply with the requirements for a craft constructed on or after that date to at least the same extent as it did before undergoing such repairs, alterations, modifications or outfitting. Repairs, alterations and modifications of a major character, and outfitting related thereto, shall meet the requirements for a craft constructed on or after 1 July 2002 in so far as the Administration deems reasonable and practicable.

Regulation 3
Requirements for high-speed craft

1   Notwithstanding the provisions of chapters I to IV and regulations V/18, 19 and 20:

.1   a high-speed craft constructed on or after 1 January 1996 but before 1 July 2002 which complies with the requirements of the High-Speed Craft Code, 1994 in its entirety and which has been surveyed and certified as provided in that Code shall be deemed to have complied with the requirements of chapters I to IV and regulations V/18, 19 and 20. For the purpose of this regulation, the requirements of that Code shall be treated as mandatory;

.2   a high-speed craft constructed on or after 1 July 2002 which complies with the requirements of the High-Speed Craft Code, 2000 in its entirety and which has been surveyed and certified as provided in that Code shall be deemed to have complied with the requirements of chapters I to IV and regulations V/18, 19 and 20.

2   The certificates and permits issued under the High-Speed Craft Code shall have the same force and the same recognition as the certificates issued under chapter I.

CHAPTER XI-1
Special measures to enhance maritime safety

Regulation 1
Authorization of recognized organizations

Organizations referred to in regulation I/6 shall comply with the guidelines adopted by the Organization by resolution A.739(18), as may be amended by the Organization, and the specifications adopted by the Organization by resolution A.789(19), as may be amended by the Organization, provided that such amendments are adopted, brought into force and take effect in accordance with the provisions of article VIII of the present Convention concerning the amendment procedures applicable to the annex other than chapter I.

Regulation 2
Enhanced surveys[*]

Bulk carriers as defined in regulation IX/1.6 and oil tankers as defined in regulation II-1/2.12 shall be subject to an enhanced programme of inspections in accordance with the guidelines adopted by the Assembly of the Organization by resolution A.744(18), as may be amended by the Organization, provided that such amendments are adopted, brought into force and take effect in accordance with the provisions of article VIII of the present Convention concerning the amendment procedures applicable to the annex other than chapter I.

Regulation 3
Ship identification number

(Paragraphs 4 and 5 apply to all ships to which this regulation applies. For ships constructed before 1 July 2004, the requirements of paragraphs 4 and 5 shall be complied with not later than the first scheduled dry-docking of the ship after 1 July 2004)

1   This regulation applies to all passenger ships of 100 gross tonnage and upwards and to all cargo ships of 300 gross tonnage and upwards.

2   Every ship shall be provided with an identification number which conforms to the IMO ship identification number scheme adopted by the Organization.[†]

---

[*] Refer to MSC/Circ.655 on guidance for planning the enhanced programme of inspections surveys of bulk carriers and oil tankers and MSC/Circ.686, Guidelines on the means of access to structures for inspection and maintenance of oil tankers and bulk carriers.
[†] Refer to the IMO ship identification number scheme adopted by the Organization by resolution A.600(15).

3   The ship's identification number shall be inserted on the certificates and certified copies thereof issued under regulation I/12 or regulation I/13.

4   The ship's identification number shall be permanently marked:

.1   in a visible place either on the stern of the ship or on either side of the hull, amidships port and starboard, above the deepest assigned load line or either side of the superstructure, port and starboard or on the front of the superstructure or, in the case of passenger ships, on a horizontal surface visible from the air; and

.2   in an easily accessible place either on one of the end transverse bulkheads of the machinery spaces, as defined in regulation II-2/3.30, or on one of the hatchways or, in the case of tankers, in the pump-room or, in the case of ships with ro–ro spaces, as defined in regulation II-2/3.41, on one of the end transverse bulkheads of the ro–ro spaces.

5.1   The permanent marking shall be plainly visible, clear of any other markings on the hull and shall be painted in a contrasting colour.

5.2   The permanent marking referred to in paragraph 4.1 shall be not less than 200 mm in height. The permanent marking referred to in paragraph 4.2 shall not be less than 100 mm in height. The width of the marks shall be proportionate to the height.

5.3   The permanent marking may be made by raised lettering or by cutting it in or by centre-punching it or by any other equivalent method of marking the ship identification number which ensures that the marking is not easily expunged.

5.4   On ships constructed of material other than steel or metal, the Administration shall approve the method of marking the ship identification number.

Regulation 4
*Port State control on operational requirements**

1   A ship when in a port of another Contracting Government is subject to control by officers duly authorized by such Government concerning operational requirements in respect of the safety of ships, when there are clear grounds for believing that the master or crew are not familiar with essential shipboard procedures relating to the safety of ships.

2   In the circumstances defined in paragraph 1 of this regulation, the Contracting Government carrying out the control shall take such steps as

---

* Refer to the Procedures for port State control adopted by the Organization by resolution A.787(19), as amended by resolution A.882(21).

will ensure that the ship shall not sail until the situation has been brought to order in accordance with the requirements of the present Convention.

3 Procedures relating to the port State control prescribed in regulation I/19 shall apply to this regulation.

4 Nothing in the present regulation shall be construed to limit the rights and obligations of a Contracting Government carrying out control over operational requirements specifically provided for in the regulations.

Regulation 5
Continuous Synopsis Record

1 Every ship to which chapter I applies shall be issued with a Continuous Synopsis Record.

2.1 The Continuous Synopsis Record is intended to provide an on-board record of the history of the ship with respect to the information recorded therein.

2.2 For ships constructed before 1 July 2004, the Continuous Synopsis Record shall, at least, provide the history of the ship as from 1 July 2004.

3 The Continuous Synopsis Record shall be issued by the Administration to each ship that is entitled to fly its flag and it shall contain, at least, the following information:

.1 the name of the State whose flag the ship is entitled to fly;

.2 the date on which the ship was registered with that State;

.3 the ship's identification number in accordance with regulation 3;

.4 the name of the ship;

.5 the port at which the ship is registered;

.6 the name of the registered owner(s) and their registered address(es);

.7 the name of the registered bareboat charterer(s) and their registered address(es), if applicable;

.8 the name of the Company, as defined in regulation IX/1, its registered address and the address(es) from where it carries out the safety-management activities;

.9 the name of all classification society(ies) with which the ship is classed;

.10 the name of the Administration or of the Contracting Government or of the recognized organization which has issued the Document of Compliance (or the Interim Document of

Compliance), specified in the ISM Code as defined in regulation IX/1, to the Company operating the ship and the name of the body which has carried out the audit on the basis of which the Document was issued, if other than that issuing the Document;

.11 the name of the Administration or of the Contracting Government or of the recognized organization that has issued the Safety Management Certificate (or the Interim Safety Management Certificate), specified in the ISM Code as defined in regulation IX/1, to the ship and the name of the body which has carried out the audit on the basis of which the Certificate was issued, if other than that issuing the Certificate;

.12 the name of the Administration or of the Contracting Government or of the recognized security organization that has issued the International Ship Security Certificate (or the Interim International Ship Security Certificate), specified in part A of the ISPS Code as defined in regulation XI-2/1, to the ship and the name of the body which has carried out the verification on the basis of which the Certificate was issued, if other than that issuing the Certificate; and

.13 the date on which the ship ceased to be registered with that State.

4.1 Any changes relating to the entries referred to in paragraphs 3.4 to 3.12 shall be recorded in the Continuous Synopsis Record so as to provide updated and current information together with the history of the changes.

4.2 In case of any changes relating to the entries referred to in paragraph 4.1, the Administration shall issue, as soon as is practically possible but not later than three months from the date of the change, to the ships entitled to fly its flag either a revised and updated version of the Continuous Synopsis Record or appropriate amendments thereto.

4.3 In case of any changes relating to the entries referred to in paragraph 4.1, the Administration, pending the issue of a revised and updated version of the Continuous Synopsis Record, shall authorize and require either the Company as defined in regulation IX/1 or the master of the ship to amend the Continuous Synopsis Record to reflect the changes. In such cases, after the Continuous Synopsis Record has been amended, the Company shall, without delay, inform the Administration accordingly.

5.1 The Continuous Synopsis Record shall be in English, French or Spanish language. Additionally, a translation of the Continuous Synopsis Record into the official language or languages of the Administration may be provided.

5.2 The Continuous Synopsis Record shall be in the format developed by the Organization and shall be maintained in accordance with guidelines developed by the Organization*. Any previous entries in the Continuous Synopsis Record shall not be modified, deleted or, in any way, erased or defaced.

6   Whenever a ship is transferred to the flag of another State or the ship is sold to another owner (or is taken over by another bareboat charterer) or another Company assumes the responsibility for the operation of the ship, the Continuous Synopsis Record shall be left on board.

7   When a ship is to be transferred to the flag of another State, the Company shall notify the Administration of the name of the State under whose flag the ship is to be transferred so as to enable the Administration to forward to that State a copy of the Continuous Synopsis Record covering the period during which the ship was under its jurisdiction.

8   When a ship is transferred to the flag of another State the Government of which is a Contracting Government, the Contracting Government of the State whose flag the ship was flying hitherto shall transmit to the Administration, as soon as possible after the transfer takes place, a copy of the relevant Continuous Synopsis Record covering the period during which the ship was under their jurisdiction together with any Continuous Synopsis Records previously issued to the ship by other States.

9   When a ship is transferred to the flag of another State, the Administration shall append the previous Continuous Synopsis Records to the Continuous Synopsis Record the Administration will issue to the ship so to provide the continuous history record intended by this regulation.

10   The Continuous Synopsis Record shall be kept on board the ship and shall be available for inspection at all times.

---

* Refer to resolution A.959(23) on format and guidelines for the maintenance of the the continuous synopsis record (CSR).

CHAPTER XI-2
Special measures to enhance
maritime security

Regulation 1
Definitions

1   For the purpose of this chapter, unless expressly provided otherwise:

   .1   *Bulk carrier* means a bulk carrier as defined in regulation IX/1.6.

   .2   *Chemical tanker* means a chemical tanker as defined in regulation VII/8.2.

   .3   *Gas carrier* means a gas carrier as defined in regulation VII/11.2.

   .4   *High-speed craft* means a craft as defined in regulation X/1.2.

   .5   *Mobile offshore drilling unit* means a mechanically propelled mobile offshore drilling unit, as defined in regulation IX/1, not on location.

   .6   *Oil tanker* means an oil tanker as defined in regulation II-1/2.12.

   .7   *Company* means a Company as defined in regulation IX/1.

   .8   *Ship/port interface* means the interactions that occur when a ship is directly and immediately affected by actions involving the movement of persons, goods or the provisions of port services to or from the ship.

   .9   *Port facility* is a location, as determined by the Contracting Government or by the Designated Authority, where the ship/port interface takes place. This includes areas such as anchorages, waiting berths and approaches from seaward, as appropriate.

   .10   *Ship-to-ship activity* means any activity not related to a port facility that involves the transfer of goods or persons from one ship to another.

   .11   *Designated Authority* means the organization(s) or the administration(s) identified, within the Contracting Government, as responsible for ensuring the implementation of the provisions of this chapter pertaining to port facility security and ship/port interface, from the point of view of the port facility.

   .12   *International Ship and Port Facility Security (ISPS) Code* means the International Code for the Security of Ships and of Port Facilities consisting of part A (the provisions of which shall be treated as mandatory) and part B (the provisions of which shall be treated as recommendatory), as adopted, on 12 December 2002, by resolution 2 of the Conference of Contracting Governments to the International Convention for the Safety of Life at Sea, 1974 as may be amended by the Organization, provided that:

      .1   amendments to part A of the Code are adopted, brought into force and take effect in accordance with article VIII of the present Convention concerning the amendment procedures applicable to the annex other than chapter I; and

.2 amendments to part B of the Code are adopted by the Maritime Safety Committee in accordance with its Rules of Procedure.

.13 *Security incident* means any suspicious act or circumstance threatening the security of a ship, including a mobile offshore drilling unit and a high-speed craft, or of a port facility or of any ship/port interface or any ship-to-ship activity.

.14 *Security level* means the qualification of the degree of risk that a security incident will be attempted or will occur.

.15 *Declaration of Security* means an agreement reached between a ship and either a port facility or another ship with which it interfaces, specifying the security measures each will implement.

.16 *Recognized security organization* means an organization with appropriate expertize in security matters and with appropriate knowledge of ship and port operations authorized to carry out an assessment, or a verification, or an approval or a certification activity, required by this chapter or by part A of the ISPS Code.

2   The term "ship", when used in regulations 3 to 13, includes mobile offshore drilling units and high-speed craft.

3   The term "all ships", when used in this chapter, means any ship to which this chapter applies.

4   The term "Contracting Government", when used in regulations 3, 4, 7 and 10 to 13, includes a reference to the Designated Authority.

Regulation 2
Application

1   This chapter applies to:

.1   the following types of ships engaged on international voyages:

.1.1   passenger ships, including high-speed passenger craft;

.1.2   cargo ships, including high-speed craft, of 500 gross tonnage and upwards; and

.1.3   mobile offshore drilling units; and

.2   port facilities serving such ships engaged on international voyages.

2   Notwithstanding the provisions of paragraph 1.2, Contracting Governments shall decide the extent of application of this chapter and of the relevant sections of part A of the ISPS Code to those port facilities within their territory which, although used primarily by ships not engaged on international voyages, are required, occasionally, to serve ships arriving or departing on an international voyage.

2.1 Contracting Governments shall base their decisions, under paragraph 2, on a port facility security assessment carried out in accordance with the provisions of part A of the ISPS Code.

2.2 Any decision which a Contracting Government makes, under paragraph 2, shall not compromise the level of security intended to be achieved by this chapter or by part A of the ISPS Code.

3 This chapter does not apply to warships, naval auxiliaries or other ships owned or operated by a Contracting Government and used only on Government non-commercial service.

4 Nothing in this chapter shall prejudice the rights or obligations of States under international law.

Regulation 3
Obligations of Contracting Governments with respect to security

1 Administrations shall set security levels and ensure the provision of security-level information to ships entitled to fly their flag. When changes in security level occur, security-level information shall be updated as the circumstance dictates.

2 Contracting Governments shall set security levels and ensure the provision of security-level information to port facilities within their territory, and to ships prior to entering a port or whilst in a port within their territory. When changes in security level occur, security-level information shall be updated as the circumstance dictates.

Regulation 4
Requirements for Companies and ships

1 Companies shall comply with the relevant requirements of this chapter and of part A of the ISPS Code, taking into account the guidance given in part B of the ISPS Code.

2 Ships shall comply with the relevant requirements of this chapter and of part A of the ISPS Code, taking into account the guidance given in part B of the ISPS Code, and such compliance shall be verified and certified as provided for in part A of the ISPS Code.

3   Prior to entering a port or whilst in a port within the territory of a Contracting Government, a ship shall comply with the requirements for the security level set by that Contracting Government, if such security level is higher than the security level set by the Administration for that ship.

4   Ships shall respond without undue delay to any change to a higher security level.

5   Where a ship is not in compliance with the requirements of this chapter or of part A of the ISPS Code, or cannot comply with the requirements of the security level set by the Administration or by another Contracting Government and applicable to that ship, then the ship shall notify the appropriate competent authority prior to conducting any ship/port interface or prior to entry into port, whichever occurs earlier.

Regulation 5
Specific responsibility of Companies

The Company shall ensure that the master has available on board, at all times, information through which officers duly authorized by a Contracting Government can establish:

> **.1**   who is responsible for appointing the members of the crew or other persons currently employed or engaged on board the ship in any capacity on the business of that ship;
>
> **.2**   who is responsible for deciding the employment of the ship; and
>
> **.3**   in cases where the ship is employed under the terms of charter party(ies), who are the parties to such charter party(ies).

Regulation 6
*Ship security alert system**

1   All ships shall be provided with a ship security alert system, as follows:

> **.1**   ships constructed on or after 1 July 2004;
>
> **.2**   passenger ships, including high-speed passenger craft, constructed before 1 July 2004, not later than the first survey of the radio installation after 1 July 2004;
>
> **.3**   oil tankers, chemical tankers, gas carriers, bulk carriers and cargo high-speed craft, of 500 gross tonnage and upwards constructed before 1 July 2004, not later than the first survey of the radio installation after 1 July 2004; and

---

* Refer to the performance standards for a ship security alert system adopted by resolution MSC.136(76) and to revised performance standards for ship security alert systems adopted by resolution MSC.147(77).

  .4 other cargo ships of 500 gross tonnage and upward and mobile offshore drilling units constructed before 1 July 2004, not later than the first survey of the radio installation after 1 July 2006.

2 The ship security alert system, when activated, shall:

  .1 initiate and transmit a ship-to-shore security alert to a competent authority designated by the Administration, which in these circumstances may include the Company, identifying the ship, its location and indicating that the security of the ship is under threat or it has been compromised;

  .2 not send the ship security alert to any other ships;

  .3 not raise any alarm on board the ship; and

  .4 continue the ship security alert until deactivated and/or reset.

3 The ship security alert system shall:

  .1 be capable of being activated from the navigation bridge and in at least one other location; and

  .2 conform to performance standards not inferior to those adopted by the Organization.

4 The ship security alert system activation points shall be designed so as to prevent the inadvertent initiation of the ship security alert.

5 The requirement for a ship security alert system may be complied with by using the radio installation fitted for compliance with the requirements of chapter IV, provided all requirements of this regulation are complied with.

6 When an Administration receives notification of a ship security alert, that Administration shall immediately notify the State(s) in the vicinity of which the ship is presently operating.

7 When a Contracting Government receives notification of a ship security alert from a ship which is not entitled to fly its flag, that Contracting Government shall immediately notify the relevant Administration and, if appropriate, the State(s) in the vicinity of which the ship is presently operating.

Regulation 7
Threats to ships

1 Contracting Governments shall set security levels and ensure the provision of security-level information to ships operating in their territorial sea or having communicated an intention to enter their territorial sea.

2 Contracting Governments shall provide a point of contact through which such ships can request advice or assistance and to which such ships can report any security concerns about other ships, movements or communications.

3   Where a risk of attack has been identified, the Contracting Government concerned shall advise the ships concerned and their Administrations of:

    .1   the current security level;

    .2   any security measures that should be put in place by the ships concerned to protect themselves from attack, in accordance with the provisions of part A of the ISPS Code; and

    .3   security measures that the coastal State has decided to put in place, as appropriate.

Regulation 8
Master's discretion for ship safety and security

1   The master shall not be constrained by the Company, the charterer or any other person from taking or executing any decision which, in the professional judgement of the master, is necessary to maintain the safety and security of the ship. This includes denial of access to persons (except those identified as duly authorized by a Contracting Government) or their effects and refusal to load cargo, including containers or other closed cargo transport units.

2   If, in the professional judgement of the master, a conflict between any safety and security requirements applicable to the ship arises during its operations, the master shall give effect to those requirements necessary to maintain the safety of the ship. In such cases, the master may implement temporary security measures and shall forthwith inform the Administration and, if appropriate, the Contracting Government in whose port the ship is operating or intends to enter. Any such temporary security measures under this regulation shall, to the highest possible degree, be commensurate with the prevailing security level. When such cases are identified, the Administration shall ensure that such conflicts are resolved and that the possibility of recurrence is minimized.

Regulation 9
Control and compliance measures

1   Control of ships in port

1.1   For the purpose of this chapter, every ship to which this chapter applies is subject to control when in a port of another Contracting Government by officers duly authorized by that Government, who may be the same as those carrying out the functions of regulation I/19. Such control shall be limited to verifying that there is on board a valid International Ship Security Certificate or a valid Interim International Ship Security Certificate issued under the provisions of part A of the ISPS Code ("Certificate"), which if valid shall be accepted, unless there are clear grounds for believing that the ship is not in compliance with the requirements of this chapter or part A of the ISPS Code.

1.2 When there are such clear grounds, or when no valid Certificate is produced when required, the officers duly authorized by the Contracting Government shall impose any one or more control measures in relation to that ship as provided in paragraph 1.3. Any such measures imposed must be proportionate, taking into account the guidance given in part B of the ISPS Code.

1.3 Such control measures are as follows: inspection of the ship, delaying the ship, detention of the ship, restriction of operations, including movement within the port, or expulsion of the ship from port. Such control measures may additionally or alternatively include other lesser administrative or corrective measures.

2 **Ships intending to enter a port of another
     Contracting Government**

2.1 For the purpose of this chapter, a Contracting Government may require that ships intending to enter its ports provide the following information to officers duly authorized by that Government to ensure compliance with this chapter prior to entry into port with the aim of avoiding the need to impose control measures or steps:

   .1 that the ship possesses a valid Certificate and the name of its issuing authority;

   .2 the security level at which the ship is currently operating;

   .3 the security level at which the ship operated in any previous port where it has conducted a ship/port interface within the timeframe specified in paragraph 2.3;

   .4 any special or additional security measures that were taken by the ship in any previous port where it has conducted a ship/port interface within the timeframe specified in paragraph 2.3;

   .5 that the appropriate ship security procedures were maintained during any ship-to-ship activity within the timeframe specified in paragraph 2.3; or

   .6 other practical security-related information (but not details of the ship security plan), taking into account the guidance given in part B of the ISPS Code.

If requested by the Contracting Government, the ship or the Company shall provide confirmation, acceptable to that Contracting Government, of the information required above.

2.2   Every ship to which this chapter applies intending to enter the port of another Contracting Government shall provide the information described in paragraph 2.1 on the request of the officers duly authorized by that Government. The master may decline to provide such information on the understanding that failure to do so may result in denial of entry into port.

2.3   The ship shall keep records of the information referred to in paragraph 2.1 for the last 10 calls at port facilities.

2.4   If, after receipt of the information described in paragraph 2.1, officers duly authorized by the Contracting Government of the port in which the ship intends to enter have clear grounds for believing that the ship is in non-compliance with the requirements of this chapter or part A of the ISPS Code, such officers shall attempt to establish communication with and between the ship and the Administration in order to rectify the non-compliance. If such communication does not result in rectification, or if such officers have clear grounds otherwise for believing that the ship is in non-compliance with the requirements of this chapter or part A of the ISPS Code, such officers may take steps in relation to that ship as provided in paragraph 2.5. Any such steps taken must be proportionate, taking into account the guidance given in part B of the ISPS Code.

2.5   Such steps are as follows:

.1   a requirement for the rectification of the non-compliance;

.2   a requirement that the ship proceed to a location specified in the territorial sea or internal waters of that Contracting Government;

.3   inspection of the ship, if the ship is in the territorial sea of the Contracting Government the port of which the ship intends to enter; or

.4   denial of entry into port.

Prior to initiating any such steps, the ship shall be informed by the Contracting Government of its intentions. Upon this information the master may withdraw the intention to enter that port. In such cases, this regulation shall not apply.

3   **Additional provisions**

3.1   In the event:

.1   of the imposition of a control measure, other than a lesser administrative or corrective measure, referred to in paragraph 1.3; or

.2   any of the steps referred to in paragraph 2.5 are taken,

an officer duly authorized by the Contracting Government shall forthwith inform in writing the Administration specifying which control measures have been imposed or steps taken and the reasons thereof. The Contracting Government imposing the control measures or steps shall also notify the recognized security organization which issued the Certificate relating to the ship concerned and the Organization when any such control measures have been imposed or steps taken.

3.2   When entry into port is denied or the ship is expelled from port, the authorities of the port State should communicate the appropriate facts to the authorities of the State of the next appropriate ports of call, when known, and any other appropriate coastal States, taking into account guidelines to be developed by the Organization. Confidentiality and security of such notification shall be ensured.

3.3   Denial of entry into port, pursuant to paragraphs 2.4 and 2.5, or expulsion from port, pursuant to paragraphs 1.1 to 1.3, shall only be imposed where the officers duly authorized by the Contracting Government have clear grounds to believe that the ship poses an immediate threat to the security or safety of persons, or of ships or other property and there are no other appropriate means for removing that threat.

3.4   The control measures referred to in paragraph 1.3 and the steps referred to in paragraph 2.5 shall only be imposed, pursuant to this regulation, until the non-compliance giving rise to the control measures or steps has been corrected to the satisfaction of the Contracting Government, taking into account actions proposed by the ship or the Administration, if any.

3.5   When Contracting Governments exercise control under paragraph 1 or take steps under paragraph 2:

.1   all possible efforts shall be made to avoid a ship being unduly detained or delayed. If a ship is thereby unduly detained, or delayed, it shall be entitled to compensation for any loss or damage suffered; and

.2   necessary access to the ship shall not be prevented for emergency or humanitarian reasons and for security purposes.

Regulation 10
Requirements for port facilities

1   Port facilities shall comply with the relevant requirements of this chapter and part A of the ISPS Code, taking into account the guidance given in part B of the ISPS Code.

2   Contracting Governments with a port facility or port facilities within their territory, to which this regulation applies, shall ensure that:

.1   port facility security assessments are carried out, reviewed and approved in accordance with the provisions of part A of the ISPS Code; and

.2   port facility security plans are developed, reviewed, approved and implemented in accordance with the provisions of part A of the ISPS Code.

3   Contracting Governments shall designate and communicate the measures required to be addressed in a port facility security plan for the various security levels, including when the submission of a Declaration of Security will be required.

Regulation 11
Alternative security agreements

1   Contracting Governments may, when implementing this chapter and part A of the ISPS Code, conclude in writing bilateral or multilateral agreements with other Contracting Governments on alternative security arrangements covering short international voyages on fixed routes between port facilities located within their territories.

2   Any such agreement shall not compromise the level of security of other ships or of port facilities not covered by the agreement.

3   No ship covered by such an agreement shall conduct any ship-to-ship activities with any ship not covered by the agreement.

4   Such agreements shall be reviewed periodically, taking into account the experience gained as well as any changes in the particular circumstances or the assessed threats to the security of the ships, the port facilities or the routes covered by the agreement.

Regulation 12
Equivalent security arrangements

1   An Administration may allow a particular ship or a group of ships entitled to fly its flag to implement other security measures equivalent to those prescribed in this chapter or in part A of the ISPS Code, provided such security measures are at least as effective as those prescribed in this chapter or part A of the ISPS Code. The Administration which allows such security measures shall communicate to the Organization particulars thereof.

2   When implementing this chapter and part A of the ISPS Code, a Contracting Government may allow a particular port facility or a group of port facilities located within its territory, other than those covered by an agreement concluded under regulation 11, to implement security measures equivalent to those prescribed in this chapter or in part A of the ISPS Code, provided such security measures are at least as effective as those prescribed in this chapter or part A of the ISPS Code. The Contracting Government which allows such security measures shall communicate to the Organization particulars thereof.

Regulation 13
Communication of information

1   Contracting Governments shall, not later than 1 July 2004, communicate to the Organization and shall make available for the information of Companies and ships:

   .1   the names and contact details of their national authority or authorities responsible for ship and port facility security;

   .2   the locations within their territory covered by approved port facility security plans;

   .3   the names and contact details of those who have been designated to be available at all times to receive and act upon the ship-to-shore security alerts referred to in regulation 6.2.1;

   .4   the names and contact details of those who have been designated to be available at all times to receive and act upon any communications from Contracting Governments exercising control and compliance measures referred to in regulation 9.3.1; and

   .5   the names and contact details of those who have been designated to be available at all times to provide advice or assistance to ships and to whom ships can report any security concerns referred to in regulation 7.2

and thereafter update such information as and when changes relating thereto occur. The Organization shall circulate such particulars to other Contracting Governments for the information of their officers.

2   Contracting Governments shall, not later than 1 July 2004, communicate to the Organization the names and contact details of any recognized security organizations authorized to act on their behalf together with details of the specific responsibility and conditions of authority delegated to such organizations. Such information shall be updated as and when changes relating thereto occur. The Organization shall circulate such particulars to other Contracting Governments for the information of their officers.

3   Contracting Governments shall, not later than 1 July 2004, communicate to the Organization a list showing the approved port facility security plans for the port facilities located within their territory together with the location or locations covered by each approved port facility security plan and the corresponding date of approval and thereafter shall further communicate when any of the following changes take place:

.1 changes in the location or locations covered by an approved port facility security plan are to be introduced or have been introduced. In such cases the information to be communicated shall indicate the changes in the location or locations covered by the plan and the date as of which such changes are to be introduced or were implemented;

.2 an approved port facility security plan, previously included in the list submitted to the Organization, is to be withdrawn or has been withdrawn. In such cases, the information to be communicated shall indicate the date on which the withdrawal will take effect or was implemented. In these cases, the communication shall be made to the Organization as soon as is practically possible; and

.3 additions are to be made to the list of approved port facility security plans. In such cases, the information to be communicated shall indicate the location or locations covered by the plan and the date of approval.

4 Contracting Governments shall, at five year intervals after 1 July 2004, communicate to the Organization a revised and updated list showing all the approved port facility security plans for the port facilities located within their territory together with the location or locations covered by each approved port facility security plan and the corresponding date of approval (and the date of approval of any amendments thereto) which will supersede and replace all information communicated to the Organization, pursuant to paragraph 3, during the preceding five years.

5 Contracting Governments shall communicate to the Organization information that an agreement under regulation 11 has been concluded. The information communicated shall include:

.1 the names of the Contracting Governments which have concluded the agreement;

.2 the port facilities and the fixed routes covered by the agreement;

.3 the periodicity of review of the agreement;

.4 the date of entry into force of the agreement; and

.5 information on any consultations which have taken place with other Contracting Governments

and thereafter shall communicate, as soon as practically possible, to the Organization information when the agreement has been amended or has ended.

6   Any Contracting Government which allows, under the provisions of regulation 12, any equivalent security arrangements with respect to a ship entitled to fly its flag or with respect to a port facility located within its territory shall communicate to the Organization particulars thereof.

7   The Organization shall make available the information communicated under paragraphs 3 to 6 to other Contracting Governments upon request.

CHAPTER XII
Additional safety measures for bulk carriers

Regulation 1
Definitions

For the purpose of this chapter:

1   *Bulk carrier* means a bulk carrier as defined in regulation IX/1.6.

2   *Bulk carrier of single side skin construction* means a bulk carrier in which a cargo hold is bounded by the side shell.

3   *Length* of a bulk carrier means the length as defined in the International Convention on Load Lines in force.

4   *Solid bulk cargo* means any material, other than liquid or gas, consisting of a combination of particles, granules or any larger pieces of material, generally uniform in composition, which is loaded directly into the cargo spaces of a ship without any intermediate form of containment.

5   *Bulk carrier bulkhead and double bottom strength standards* means the "Standards for the evaluation of scantlings of the transverse watertight vertically corrugated bulkhead between the two foremost cargo holds and for the evaluation of allowable hold loading of the foremost cargo hold" adopted by resolution 4 of the Conference of Contracting Governments to the International Convention for the Safety of Life at Sea, 1974, on 27 November 1997, as may be amended by the Organization, provided that such amendments are adopted, brought into force and take effect in accordance with the provisions of article VIII of the present Convention concerning the amendment procedures applicable to the annex other than chapter I.

6   The term *ships constructed* has the same meaning as defined in regulation II-1/1.1.3.1.

Regulation 2
Application[*]

Bulk carriers shall comply with the requirements of this chapter in addition to the applicable requirements of other chapters.

Regulation 3
Implementation schedule

(This regulation applies to bulk carriers constructed before 1 July 1999)

Bulk carriers to which regulations 4 or 6 apply shall comply with the provisions of such regulations according to the following schedule, with

---

[*] Refer to the Interpretations of the provisions of SOLAS chapter XII on additional safety measures for bulk carriers, adopted by the Maritime Safety Committee of the Organization by resolutions MSC.79(70) and MSC.89(71).

reference to the enhanced programme of inspections required by regulation XI/2:

.1 bulk carriers which are 20 years of age and over on 1 July 1999, by the date of the first intermediate survey or the first periodical survey after 1 July 1999, whichever comes first;

.2 bulk carriers which are 15 years of age and over but less than 20 years of age on 1 July 1999, by the date of the first periodical survey after 1 July 1999, but not later than 1 July 2002; and

.3 bulk carriers which are less than 15 years of age on 1 July 1999, by the date of the first periodical survey after the date on which the ship reaches 15 years of age, but not later than the date on which the ship reaches 17 years of age.

Regulation 4
Damage stability requirements applicable to bulk carriers

1   Bulk carriers of 150 m in length and upwards of single side skin construction, designed to carry solid bulk cargoes having a density of 1,000 kg/m^3 and above, constructed on or after 1 July 1999 shall, when loaded to the summer load line, be able to withstand flooding of any one cargo hold in all loading conditions and remain afloat in a satisfactory condition of equilibrium, as specified in paragraph 3.

2   Bulk carriers of 150 m in length and upwards of single side skin construction, carrying solid bulk cargoes having a density of 1,780 kg/m^3 and above, constructed before 1 July 1999 shall, when loaded to the summer load line, be able to withstand flooding of the foremost cargo hold in all loading conditions and remain afloat in a satisfactory condition of equilibrium, as specified in paragraph 3. This requirement shall be complied with in accordance with the implementation schedule specified in regulation 3.

3   Subject to the provisions of paragraph 6, the condition of equilibrium after flooding shall satisfy the condition of equilibrium laid down in the annex to resolution A.320(IX), Regulation equivalent to regulation 27 of the International Convention on Load Lines, 1966, as amended by resolution A.514(13). The assumed flooding need only take into account flooding of the cargo hold space. The permeability of a loaded hold shall be assumed as 0.9 and the permeability of an empty hold shall be assumed as 0.95, unless a permeability relevant to a particular cargo is assumed for the volume of a flooded hold occupied by cargo and a permeability of 0.95 is assumed for the remaining empty volume of the hold.

4   Bulk carriers constructed before 1 July 1999 which have been assigned a reduced freeboard in compliance with regulation 27(7) of the International Convention on Load Lines, 1966, as adopted on 5 April 1966, may be considered as complying with paragraph 2 of this regulation.

5   Bulk carriers which have been assigned a reduced freeboard in compliance with the provisions of paragraph (8) of the regulation equivalent to regulation 27 of the International Convention on Load Lines, 1966, adopted by resolution A.320(IX), as amended by resolution A.514(13), may be considered as complying with paragraphs 1 or 2, as appropriate.

6   On bulk carriers which have been assigned reduced freeboard in compliance with the provisions of regulation 27(8) set out in annex B of the Protocol of 1988 relating to the International Convention on Load Lines, 1966, the condition of equilibrium after flooding shall satisfy the relevant provisions of that Protocol.

Regulation 5
Structural strength of bulk carriers

(This regulation applies to bulk carriers constructed on or after 1 July 1999)

Bulk carriers of 150 m in length and upwards of single side skin construction, designed to carry solid bulk cargoes having a density of 1,000 kg/m^3 and above, shall have sufficient strength to withstand flooding of any one cargo hold in all loading and ballast conditions, taking also into account dynamic effects resulting from the presence of water in the hold, and taking into account the recommendations adopted by the Organization.[*]

Regulation 6
Structural and other requirements for bulk carriers

(This regulation applies to bulk carriers constructed before 1 July 1999)

1   Bulk carriers of 150 m in length and upwards of single side skin construction, carrying solid bulk cargoes having a density of 1,780 kg/m^3 and above, shall comply with the requirements of this regulation in accordance with the implementation schedule specified in regulation 3.

2   The transverse watertight bulkhead between the two foremost cargo holds and the double bottom of the foremost cargo hold shall have sufficient strength to withstand flooding of the foremost cargo hold, taking also into account dynamic effects resulting from the presence of water in the hold, in compliance with the bulk carrier bulkhead and double bottom strength standards. For the purpose of this regulation, the bulk carrier bulkhead and double bottom strength standards shall be treated as mandatory.

---

[*] Refer to resolution 3, Recommendation on compliance with SOLAS regulation XII/5, adopted by the 1997 SOLAS Conference.

3   In considering the need for, and the extent of, strengthening of the transverse watertight bulkhead or double bottom to meet the requirements of paragraph 2, the following restrictions may be taken into account:

.1   restrictions on the distribution of the total cargo weight between the cargo holds; and

.2   restrictions on the maximum deadweight.

4   For bulk carriers using either of, or both, the restrictions given in paragraphs 3.1 and 3.2 above for the purpose of fulfilling the requirements of paragraph 2, these restrictions shall be complied with whenever solid bulk cargoes having a density of 1,780 kg/m³ and above are carried.

Regulation 7
Survey of the cargo hold structure of bulk carriers

(This regulation applies to bulk carriers constructed before 1 July 1999)

A bulk carrier of 150 m in length and upwards of single side skin construction, of 10 years of age and over, shall not carry solid bulk cargoes having a density of 1,780 kg/m³ and above unless it has satisfactorily undergone either:

.1   a periodical survey in accordance with the enhanced programme of inspections required by regulation XI/2; or

.2   a survey of all cargo holds to the same extent as required for periodical surveys in the enhanced survey programme of inspections required by regulation XI/2.

Regulation 8
Information on compliance with requirements
for bulk carriers

1   The booklet required by regulation VI/7.2 shall be endorsed by the Administration or on its behalf to indicate that regulations 4, 5, 6 and 7 as appropriate, are complied with.

2   Any restrictions imposed on the carriage of solid bulk cargoes having a density of 1,780 kg/m³ and above in accordance with the requirements of regulation 6 shall be identified and recorded in the booklet referred to in paragraph 1.

3   A bulk carrier to which paragraph 2 applies shall be permanently marked on the side shell at amidships, port and starboard, with a solid equilateral triangle having sides of 500 mm and its apex 300 mm below the deck line, and painted a contrasting colour to that of the hull.

Regulation 9

*Requirements for bulk carriers not being capable
of complying with regulation 4.2 due to the
design configuration of their cargo holds*

(This regulation applies to bulk carriers constructed before 1 July 1999)

For bulk carriers being within the application limits of regulation 4.2, which
have been constructed with an insufficient number of transverse watertight
bulkheads to satisfy that regulation, the Administration may allow relaxation
from the application of regulations 4.2 and 6 on condition that they shall
comply with the following requirements:

.1 for the foremost cargo hold, the inspections prescribed for the
annual survey in the enhanced programme of inspections
required by regulation XI/2 shall be replaced by the inspections
prescribed therein for the intermediate survey of cargo holds;

.2 are provided with bilge well high water level alarms in all cargo
holds, or in cargo conveyor tunnels, as appropriate, giving an
audible and visual alarm on the navigation bridge, as approved
by the Administration or an organization recognized by it in
accordance with the provisions of regulation XI/1; and

.3 are provided with detailed information on specific cargo hold
flooding scenarios. This information shall be accompanied by
detailed instructions on evacuation preparedness under the
provisions of section 8 of the International Safety Management
(ISM) Code and be used as the basis for crew training and drills.

Regulation 10

Solid bulk cargo density declaration

1   Prior to loading bulk cargo on a bulk carrier, the shipper shall declare
the density of the cargo, in addition to providing the cargo information
required by regulation VI/2.

2   For bulk carriers to which regulation 6 applies, unless such bulk
carriers comply with all the relevant requirements of this chapter applicable
to the carriage of solid bulk cargoes having a density of 1,780 kg/m^3 and
above, any cargo declared to have a density within the range 1,250 kg/m^3 to
1,780 kg/m^3 shall have its density verified by an accredited testing
organization.*

---

* In verifying the density of solid bulk cargoes, reference may be made to MSC/Circ.908,
Uniform method of measurement of the density of bulk cargoes.

Regulation 11
Loading instrument
(This regulation applies to bulk carriers regardless of their date of construction)

1   Bulk carriers of 150 m in length and upwards shall be fitted with a loading instrument capable of providing information on hull girder shear forces and bending moments, taking into account the recommendation adopted by the Organization.*

2   Bulk carriers of 150 m in length and upwards constructed before 1 July 1999 shall comply with the requirements of paragraph 1 not later than the date of the first intermediate or periodical survey of the ship to be carried out after 1 July 1999.

Regulation 12
Hold, ballast and dry space water level detectors†
(This regulation applies to bulk carriers regardless of their date of construction)

1   Bulk carriers shall be fitted with water level detectors:

　　.1   in each cargo hold, giving audible and visual alarms, one when the water level above the inner bottom in any hold reaches a height of 0.5 m and another at a height not less than 15% of the depth of the cargo hold but not more than 2 m. On bulk carriers to which regulation 9.2 applies, detectors with only the latter alarm need be installed. The water level detectors shall be fitted in the aft end of the cargo holds. For cargo holds which are used for water ballast, an alarm overriding device may be installed. The visual alarms shall clearly discriminate between the two different water levels detected in each hold;

　　.2   in any ballast tank forward of the collision bulkhead required by regulation II-1/11, giving an audible and visual alarm when the liquid in the tank reaches a level not exceeding 10% of the tank capacity. An alarm overriding device may be installed to be activated when the tank is in use; and

　　.3   in any dry or void space other than a chain cable locker, any part of which extends forward of the foremost cargo hold, giving an audible and visual alarm at a water level of 0.1 m above the deck. Such alarms need not be provided in enclosed spaces the volume of which does not exceed 0.1% of the ship's maximum displacement volume.

---

* Refer to resolution 5, Recommendation on loading instruments, adopted by the 1997 SOLAS Conference.

† Refer to the Performance standards for water level detectors on bulk carriers, adopted by the Maritime Safety Committee of the Organization by resolution MSC.145(77).

2   The audible and visual alarms specified in paragraph 1 shall be located on the navigation bridge.

3   Bulk carriers constructed before 1 July 2004 shall comply with the requirements of this regulation not later than the date of the annual, intermediate or renewal survey of the ship to be carried out after 1 July 2004, whichever comes first.

Regulation 13
*Availability of pumping systems**

(This regulation applies to bulk carriers regardless of their date of construction)

1   On bulk carriers, the means for draining and pumping ballast tanks forward of the collision bulkhead and bilges of dry spaces any part of which extends forward of the foremost cargo hold, shall be capable of being brought into operation from a readily accessible enclosed space, the location of which is accessible from the navigation bridge or propulsion machinery control position without traversing exposed freeboard or superstructure decks. Where pipes serving such tanks or bilges pierce the collision bulkhead, valve operation by means of remotely operated actuators may be accepted, as an alternative to the valve control specified in regulation II-1/11.4, provided that the location of such valve controls complies with this regulation.

2   Bulk carriers constructed before 1 July 2004 shall comply with the requirements of this regulation not later than the date of the first intermediate or renewal survey of the ship to be carried out after 1 July 2004, but in no case later than 1 July 2007.

---

* Refer to MSC/Circ.1069, Interpretation of SOLAS regulation XII/13.

APPENDIX
Certificates*

---

* The regulations relating to life-saving appliances and arrangements referred to in the forms of certificates and related records of equipment are those of SOLAS chapter III as amended by resolution MSC.47(66).

P88 Form of Safety Certificate for Passenger Ships

PASSENGER SHIP SAFETY CERTIFICATE

This Certificate shall be supplemented by a Record of Equipment
(Form P)

(Official seal)   *(State)*

for $\dfrac{\text{an}^1}{\text{a short}}$ international voyage

Issued under the provisions of the

INTERNATIONAL CONVENTION FOR THE SAFETY OF LIFE
AT SEA, 1974, as modified by the Protocol of 1988 relating thereto

under the authority of the Government of

_____

(name of the State)

by   _____

(person or organization authorized)

---

[1] Delete as appropriate

469

Appendix
Certificates

Particulars of ship[2]

Name of ship . . . .

Distinctive number or letters . . . .

Port of registry . . . .

Gross tonnage . . . .

Sea areas in which ship is certified to operate (regulation IV/2) . . . .

IMO Number[3] . . . .

Date on which keel was laid or ship was at a similar
stage of construction or, where applicable, date on
which work for a conversion or an alteration or
modification of a major character was commenced . . . .

THIS IS TO CERTIFY:

1   That the ship has been surveyed in accordance with the requirements of regulation I/7 of the Convention.

2   That the survey showed that:

2.1   the ship complied with the requirements of the Convention as regards:

    .1   the structure, main and auxiliary machinery, boilers and other pressure vessels;

    .2   the watertight subdivision arrangements and details;

    .3   the following subdivision load lines:

Subdivision load lines assigned and marked on the ship's side amidships (regulation II-1/13)	Freeboard	To apply when the spaces in which passengers are carried include the following alternative spaces
C.1	. . . . .	. . . .
C.2	. . . . .	. . . .
C.3	. . . . .	. . . .

2.2   the ship complied with the requirements of the Convention as regards structural fire protection, fire safety systems and appliances and fire control plans;

---

[2] Alternatively, the particulars of the ship may be placed horizontally in boxes.

[3] In accordance with IMO ship identification number scheme adopted by the Organization by resolution A.600(15).

2.3   the life-saving appliances and the equipment of the lifeboats, liferafts and rescue boats were provided in accordance with the requirements of the Convention;

2.4   the ship was provided with a line-throwing appliance and radio installations used in life-saving appliances in accordance with the requirements of the Convention;

2.5   the ship complied with the requirements of the Convention as regards radio installations;

2.6   the functioning of the radio installations used in life-saving appliances complied with the requirements of the Convention;

2.7   the ship complied with the requirements of the Convention as regards shipborne navigational equipment, means of embarkation for pilots and nautical publications;

2.8   the ship was provided with lights, shapes, means of making sound signals and distress signals, in accordance with the requirements of the Convention and the International Regulations for Preventing Collisions at Sea in force;

2.9   in all other respects the ship complied with the relevant requirements of the Convention.

3   That an Exemption Certificate has/has not[1] been issued.

This certificate is valid until . . . .

Issued at . . . .
(Place of issue of certificate)

. . . .
(Date of issue)   *(Signature of authorized official issuing the certificate)*

(Seal or stamp of the issuing authority, as appropriate)

---

[1] Delete as appropriate.

Endorsement where the renewal survey has been completed and regulation I/14(d) applies

The ship complies with the relevant requirements of the Convention, and this certificate shall, in accordance with regulation I/14(d) of the Convention, be accepted as valid until. . . . .

Signed: . . . .
(Signature of authorized official)

Place: . . . .

Date: . . . .

(Seal or stamp of the authority, as appropriate)

Endorsement to extend the validity of the certificate until reaching the port of survey or for a period of grace where regulation I/14(e) or I/14(f) applies

This certificate shall, in accordance with regulation I/14(e)/I/14(f)[1] of the Convention, be accepted as valid until. . . . .

Signed: . . . .
(Signature of authorized official)

Place: . . . .

Date: . . . .

(Seal or stamp of the authority, as appropriate)

---

[1] Delete as appropriate.

RECORD OF EQUIPMENT FOR THE PASSENGER SHIP SAFETY CERTIFICATE (FORM P)

This Record shall be permanently attached to the
Passenger Ship Safety Certificate

RECORD OF EQUIPMENT FOR COMPLIANCE WITH
THE INTERNATIONAL CONVENTION FOR THE SAFETY
OF LIFE AT SEA, 1974, AS MODIFIED BY THE PROTOCOL
OF 1988 RELATING THERETO

1   *Particulars of ship*

Name of ship . . . .

Distinctive number or letters . . . .

Number of passengers for which certified . . . .

Minimum number of persons with required qualifications to operate the radio installations. . . . .

2   *Details of life-saving appliances*

1	Total number of persons for which life-saving appliances are provided	. . . .	
		Port side	Starboard side
2	Total number of lifeboats	. . . .	. . . .
2.1	Total number of persons accommodated by them	. . . .	. . . .
2.2	Number of partially enclosed lifeboats (regulation III/21 and LSA Code, section 4.5)	. . . .	. . . .
2.3	Number of totally enclosed lifeboats (regulation III/21 and LSA Code, section 4.6)	. . . .	. . . .
2.4	Other lifeboats	. . . .	. . . .
2.4.1	Number	. . . .	. . . .
2.4.2	Type	. . . .	. . . .

2   *Details of life-saving appliances (continued)*

3	Number of motor lifeboats included in the total lifeboats shown above	. . . .
3.1	Number of lifeboats fitted with searchlights	. . . .
4	Number of rescue boats	. . . .
4.1	Number of boats which are included in the total lifeboats shown above	. . . .
5	Liferafts	. . . .
5.1	Those for which approved launching appliances are required	. . . .
5.1.1	Number of liferafts	. . . .
5.1.2	Number of persons accommodated by them	. . . .
5.2	Those for which approved launching appliances are not required	. . . .
5.2.1	Number of liferafts	. . . .
5.2.2	Number of persons accommodated by them	. . . .
6	Buoyant apparatus	. . . .
6.1	Number of apparatus	. . . .
6.2	Number of persons capable of being supported	. . . .
7	Number of lifebuoys	. . . .
8	Number of lifejackets	. . . .
9	Immersion suits	. . . .
9.1	Total number	. . . .
9.2	Number of suits complying with the requirements for lifejackets	. . . .
10	Number of thermal protective aids[1]	. . . .
11	Radio installations used in life-saving appliances	. . . .
11.1	Number of radar transponders	. . . .
11.2	Number of two-way VHF radiotelephone apparatus	. . . .

---

[1] Excluding those required by the LSA Code, paragraphs 4.1.5.1.24, 4.4.8.31 and 5.1.2.2.13.

3   *Details of radio facilities*

Item		Actual provision
1	Primary systems	. . . .
1.1	VHF radio installation	. . . .
1.1.1	DSC encoder	. . . .
1.1.2	DSC watch receiver	. . . .
1.1.3	Radiotelephony	. . . .
1.2	MF radio installation	. . . .
1.2.1	DSC encoder	. . . .
1.2.2	DSC watch receiver	. . . .
1.2.3	Radiotelephony	. . . .
1.3	MF/HF radio installation	. . . .
1.3.1	DSC encoder	. . . .
1.3.2	DSC watch receiver	. . . .
1.3.3	Radiotelephony	. . . .
1.3.4	Direct-printing radiotelegraphy	. . . .
1.4	INMARSAT ship earth station	. . . .
2	Secondary means of alerting	. . . .
3	Facilities for reception of maritime safety information	. . . .
3.1	NAVTEX receiver	. . . .
3.2	EGC receiver	. . . .
3.3	HF direct-printing radiotelegraph receiver	. . . .
4	Satellite EPIRB	. . . .
4.1	COSPAS–SARSAT	. . . .
4.2	INMARSAT	. . . .
5	VHF EPIRB	. . . .
6	Ship's radar transponder	. . . .

4   *Methods used to ensure availability of radio facilities*
(regulations IV/15.6 and 15.7)

4.1   Duplication of equipment . . . .

4.2   Shore-based maintenance . . . .

4.3   At-sea maintenance capability . . . .

5   *Details of navigational systems and equipment*

Item	Actual provision
1.1 Standard magnetic compass[2]	....
1.2 Spare magnetic compass[2]	....
1.3 Gyro-compass[2]	....
1.4 Gyro-compass heading repeater[2]	....
1.5 Gyro-compass bearing repeater[2]	....
1.6 Heading or track control system[2]	....
1.7 Pelorus or compass bearing device[2]	....
1.8 Means of correcting heading and bearings	....
1.9 Transmitting heading device (THD)[2]	....
2.1 Nautical charts/Electronic chart display and information system (ECDIS)[3]	....
2.2 Back-up arrangements for ECDIS	....
2.3 Nautical publications	....
2.4 Back-up arrangements for electronic nautical publications	....
3.1 Receiver for a global navigation satellite system/terrestrial radionavigation system[2,3]	....
3.2 9 GHz radar[2]	....
3.3 Second radar (3 GHz/9 GHz[3])[2]	....
3.4 Automatic radar plotting aid (ARPA)[2]	....
3.5 Automatic tracking aid[2]	....
3.6 Second automatic tracking aid[2]	....
3.7 Electronic plotting aid[2]	....
4 Automatic identification system (AIS)	....
5 Voyage data recorder (VDR)	....
6.1 Speed and distance measuring device (through the water)*	....
6.2 Speed and distance measuring device (over the ground in the forward and athwartship direction)[2]	....
7 Echo-sounding device[2]	....
8.1 Rudder, propeller, thrust, pitch and operational mode indicator[2]	....
8.2 Rate-of-turn indicator[2]	....

---

[2] Alternative means of meeting this requirement are permitted under regulation V/19. In case of other means they shall be specified.

[3] Delete as appropriate.

5   *Details of navigational systems and equipment* (continued)

Item	Actual provision
9 Sound reception system[2]	....
10 Telephone to emergency steering position[2]	....
11 Daylight signalling lamp[2]	....
12 Radar reflector[2]	....
13 International Code of Signals	....

THIS IS TO CERTIFY that this Record is correct in all respects

Issued at . . . .
(Place of issue of the Record)

. . . .
  (Date of issue)   *(Signature of duly authorized official
                                              issuing the Record)*

(Seal or stamp of the issuing authority, as appropriate)

---

[2] Alternative means of meeting this requirement are permitted under regulation V/19. In case of other means they shall be specified.

[P88] Form of Safety Construction Certificate for Cargo Ships

CARGO SHIP SAFETY CONSTRUCTION CERTIFICATE

(Official seal)   *(State)*

Issued under the provisions of the

INTERNATIONAL CONVENTION FOR THE SAFETY OF LIFE AT SEA, 1974,
as modified by the Protocol of 1988 relating thereto

under the authority of the Government of

_____

(name of the State)

by   _____

(person or organization authorized)

Particulars of ship[1]

Name of ship . . . .

Distinctive number or letters . . . .

Port of registry . . . .

Gross tonnage . . . .

Deadweight of ship (metric tons)[2] . . . .

IMO Number[3] . . . .

---

[1] Alternatively, the particulars of the ship may be placed horizontally in boxes.

[2] For oil tankers, chemical tankers and gas carriers only.

[3] In accordance with IMO ship identification number scheme adopted by the Organization by resolution A.600(15).

Type of ship[4]

  Bulk carrier

  Oil tanker

  Chemical tanker

  Gas carrier

  Cargo ship other than any of the above

Date on which keel was laid or ship was at a similar
stage of construction or, where applicable, date on
which work for a conversion or an alteration or
modification of a major character was commenced. . . . .

THIS IS TO CERTIFY:

1   That the ship has been surveyed in accordance with the requirements of
     regulation I/10 of the Convention.

2   That the survey showed that the condition of the structure, machinery and
     equipment as defined in the above regulation was satisfactory and the ship
     complied with the relevant requirements of chapters II-1 and II-2 of the
     Convention (other than those relating to fire safety systems and appliances and
     fire control plans).

3   That the last two inspections of the outside of the ship's bottom took place

     on . . . . and . . . .
                                        (dates)

4   That an Exemption Certificate has/has not[4] been issued.

This certificate is valid until . . . .[5] subject
to the annual and intermediate surveys and inspections of the outside of the ship's
bottom in accordance with regulation I/10 of the Convention

Issued at. . . . .
                         (Place of issue of certificate)

. . . .

      (Date of issue)   *(Signature of authorized official*
                                                issuing the certificate)

           (Seal or stamp of the issuing authority, as appropriate)

---

[4] Delete as appropriate.

[5] Insert the date of expiry as specified by the Administration in accordance with regulation
I/14(a) of the Convention. The day and the month of this date correspond to the anniversary
date, as defined in regulation I/2(n) of the Convention, unless amended in accordance with
regulation I/4(h).

Endorsement for annual and intermediate surveys

THIS IS TO CERTIFY that, at a survey required by regulation I/10 of the Convention, the ship was found to comply with the relevant requirements of the Convention.

Annual survey: Signed: . . . .
                                         (Signature of authorized official)

                                Place: . . . .

                                Date: . . . .

          (Seal or stamp of the authority, as appropriate)

Annual/Intermediate[4] survey: Signed: . . . .
                                         (Signature of authorized official)

                                Place: . . . .

                                Date: . . . .

          (Seal or stamp of the authority, as appropriate)

Annual/Intermediate[4] survey: Signed: . . . .
                                         (Signature of authorized official)

                                Place: . . . .

                                Date: . . . .

          (Seal or stamp of the authority, as appropriate)

Annual survey: Signed: . . . .
                                         (Signature of authorized official)

                                Place: . . . .

                                Date: . . . .

          (Seal or stamp of the authority, as appropriate)

---

[4] Delete as appropriate.

Annual/intermediate survey in accordance with regulation I/14(h)(iii)

THIS IS TO CERTIFY that, at an annual/intermediate survey[4] in accordance with regulation I/14(h)(iii) of the Convention, this ship was found to comply with the relevant requirements of the Convention.

Signed: . . . .
(Signature of authorized official)

Place: . . . .

Date: . . . .

(Seal or stamp of the authority, as appropriate)

Endorsement for inspections of the outside of the ship's bottom[6]

THIS IS TO CERTIFY that, at an inspection required by regulation I/10 of the Convention, the ship was found to comply with the relevant requirements of the Convention.

First inspection: Signed: . . . .
                                            (Signature of authorized official)

                                    Place: . . . .

                                    Date: . . . .

(Seal or stamp of the authority, as appropriate)

Second inspection: Signed: . . . .
                                            (Signature of authorized official)

                                    Place: . . . .

                                    Date: . . . .

(Seal or stamp of the authority, as appropriate)

---

[4] Delete as appropriate.

[6] Provision may be made for additional inspections.

Endorsement to extend the certificate if valid for less than 5 years where regulation I/14(c) applies

The ship complies with the relevant requirements of the Convention, and this certificate shall, in accordance with regulation I/14(c) of the Convention, be accepted as valid until . . . .

Signed: . . . .
(Signature of authorized official)

Place: . . . .

Date: . . . .

(Seal or stamp of the authority, as appropriate)

Endorsement where the renewal survey has been completed and regulation I/14(d) applies

The ship complies with the relevant requirements of the Convention, and this certificate shall, in accordance with regulation I/14(d) of the Convention, be accepted as valid until . . . .

Signed: . . . .
(Signature of authorized official)

Place: . . . .

Date: . . . .

(Seal or stamp of the authority, as appropriate)

Endorsement to extend the validity of the certificate until reaching the port of survey or for a period of grace where regulation I/14(e) or I/14(f) applies

The certificate shall, in accordance with regulation I/14(e)/I/14(f)[4] of the Convention, be accepted as valid until . . . .

Signed: . . . .
(Signature of authorized official)

Place: . . . .

Date: . . . .

(Seal or stamp of the authority, as appropriate)

---

[4] Delete as appropriate.

Endorsement for advancement of anniversary date where regulation I/14(h) applies

In accordance with regulation I/14(h) of the Convention, the new anniversary date is
. . . .

> Signed: . . . .
> *(Signature of authorized official)*
>
> Place: . . . .
>
> Date: . . . .

(Seal or stamp of the authority, as appropriate)

In accordance with regulation I/14(h) of the Convention, the new anniversary date is
. . . .

> Signed: . . . .
> *(Signature of authorized official)*
>
> Place: . . . .
>
> Date: . . . .

(Seal or stamp of the authority, as appropriate)

P88 Form of Safety Equipment Certificate for Cargo Ships

CARGO SHIP SAFETY EQUIPMENT CERTIFICATE

This Certificate shall be supplemented by a Record of Equipment
(Form E)

(Official seal)   *(State)*

Issued under the provisions of the

INTERNATIONAL CONVENTION FOR THE SAFETY OF LIFE AT SEA, 1974,
as modified by the Protocol of 1988 relating thereto

under the authority of the Government of

_____

(name of the State)

by   _____

(person or organization authorized)

Particulars of ship[1]

Name of ship . . . .

Distinctive number or letters . . . .

Port of registry . . . .

Gross tonnage . . . .

---

[1] Alternatively, the particulars of the ship may be placed horizontally in boxes.

Deadweight of ship (metric tons)[2] . . . .

Length of ship (regulation III/3.12) . . . .

IMO Number[3] . . . .

Type of ship[4]

Bulk carrier

Oil tanker

Chemical tanker

Gas carrier

Cargo ship other than any of the above

Date on which keel was laid or ship was at a similar
stage of construction or, where applicable, date on
which work for a conversion or an alteration or
modification of a major character was commenced . . . .

THIS IS TO CERTIFY:

1   That the ship has been surveyed in accordance with the requirements of
       regulation I/8 of the Convention.

2   That the survey showed that:

2.1   the ship complied with the requirements of the Convention as regards fire
       safety systems and appliances and fire control plans;

2.2   the life-saving appliances and the equipment of the lifeboats, liferafts and
       rescue boats were provided in accordance with the requirements of the
       Convention;

2.3   the ship was provided with a line-throwing appliance and radio installations
       used in life-saving appliances in accordance with the requirements of the
       Convention;

2.4   the ship complied with the requirements of the Convention as regards
       shipborne navigational equipment, means of embarkation for pilots and
       nautical publications;

---

[2] For oil tankers, chemical tankers and gas carriers only.

[3] In accordance with IMO ship identification number scheme adopted by the Organization by
resolution A.600(15).

[4] Delete as appropriate.

2.5   the ship was provided with lights, shapes and means of making sound signals and distress signals in accordance with the requirements of the Convention and the International Regulations for Preventing Collisions at Sea in force;

2.6   in all other respects the ship complied with the relevant requirements of the Convention.

3   That an Exemption Certificate has/has not[4] been issued.

This certificate is valid until . . . . [5] subject to the annual and periodical surveys in accordance with regulation I/8 of the Convention.

Issued at. . . . .
(Place of issue of certificate)

. . . .
(Date of issue)   *(Signature of authorized official*
issuing the certificate)

(Seal or stamp of the issuing authority, as appropriate)

---

[4] Delete as appropriate.

[5] Insert the date of expiry as specified by the Administration in accordance with regulation I/14(a) of the Convention. The day and the month of this date correspond to the anniversary date as defined in regulation I/2(n) of the Convention, unless amended in accordance with regulation I/14(h).

Endorsement for annual and periodical surveys

THIS IS TO CERTIFY that, at a survey required by regulation I/8 of the Convention, the ship was found to comply with the relevant requirements of the Convention.

Annual survey: Signed: ....
                                           (Signature of authorized official)

                                   Place: ....

                                   Date: ....

(Seal or stamp of the authority, as appropriate)

Annual/Periodical[4] survey: Signed: ....
                                           (Signature of authorized official)

                                   Place: ....

                                   Date: ....

(Seal or stamp of the authority, as appropriate)

Annual/Periodical[4] survey: Signed: ....
                                           (Signature of authorized official)

                                   Place: ....

                                   Date: ....

(Seal or stamp of the authority, as appropriate)

Annual survey: Signed: ....
                                           (Signature of authorized official)

                                   Place: ....

                                   Date: ....

(Seal or stamp of the authority, as appropriate)

---

[4] Delete as appropriate.

Annual/periodical survey in accordance with regulation I/14(h)(iii)

THIS IS TO CERTIFY that, at an annual/periodical[4] survey in accordance with regulation I/14(h)(iii) of the Convention, this ship was found to comply with the relevant requirements of the Convention.

Signed: . . . .
(Signature of authorized official)

Place: . . . .

Date: . . . .

(Seal or stamp of the authority, as appropriate)

Endorsement to extend the certificate if valid for less than 5 years where regulation I/14(c) applies

The ship complies with the relevant requirements of the Convention, and this certificate shall, in accordance with regulation I/14(c) of the Convention, be accepted as valid until . . . .

Signed: . . . .
(Signature of authorized official)

Place: . . . .

Date: . . . .

(Seal or stamp of the authority, as appropriate)

Endorsement where the renewal survey has been completed and regulation I/14(d) applies

The ship complies with the relevant requirements of the Convention, and this certificate shall, in accordance with regulation I/14(d) of the Convention, be accepted as valid until . . . .

Signed: . . . .
(Signature of authorized official)

Place: . . . .

Date: . . . .

(Seal or stamp of the authority, as appropriate)

---

[4] Delete as appropriate.

Endorsement to extend the validity of the certificate until reaching the port of survey or for a period of grace where regulation I/14(e) or I/14(f) applies

The certificate shall, in accordance with regulation I/14(e)/I/14(f)[4] of the Convention, be accepted as valid until . . . .

Signed: . . . .
(Signature of authorized official)

Place: . . . .

Date: . . . .

(Seal or stamp of the authority, as appropriate)

Endorsement for advancement of anniversary date where regulation I/14(h) applies

In accordance with regulation I/14(h) of the Convention, the new anniversary date is . . . .

Signed: . . . .
(Signature of authorized official)

Place: . . . .

Date: . . . .

(Seal or stamp of the authority, as appropriate)

In accordance with regulation I/14(h) of the Convention, the new anniversary date is . . . .

Signed: . . . .
(Signature of authorized official)

Place: . . . .

Date: . . . .

(Seal or stamp of the authority, as appropriate)

---

[4] Delete as appropriate.

**RECORD OF EQUIPMENT FOR THE CARGO SHIP SAFETY
EQUIPMENT CERTIFICATE
(FORM E)**

This Record shall be permanently attached to the
Cargo Ship Safety Equipment Certificate

RECORD OF EQUIPMENT FOR COMPLIANCE WITH
THE INTERNATIONAL CONVENTION FOR THE SAFETY
OF LIFE AT SEA, 1974, AS MODIFIED BY THE PROTOCOL
OF 1988 RELATING THERETO

1   *Particulars of ship*

Name of ship . . . .

Distinctive number or letters . . . .

2   *Details of life-saving appliances*

1	Total number of persons for which life-saving appliances are provided	. . . .	
		Port side	Starboard side
2	Total number of lifeboats	. . . .	. . . .
2.1	Total number of persons accommodated by them	. . . .	. . . .
2.2	Number of totally enclosed lifeboats (regulation III/31 and LSA Code, section 4.6)	. . . .	. . . .
2.3	Number of lifeboats with a self-contained air support system (regulation III/31 and LSA Code, section 4.8)	. . . .	. . . .
2.4	Number of fire-protected lifeboats (regulation III/31 and LSA Code, section 4.9)	. . . .	. . . .
2.5	Other lifeboats	. . . .	. . . .
2.5.1	Number	. . . .	. . . .
2.5.2	Type	. . . .	. . . .

490

2   *Details of life-saving appliances (continued)*

2.6	Number of freefall lifeboats	. . . .
2.6.1	Totally enclosed (regulation III/31 and LSA Code, section 4.7)	. . . .
2.6.2	Self-contained (regulation III/31 and LSA Code, section 4.8)	. . . .
2.6.3	Fire-protected (regulation III/31 and LSA Code, section 4.9)	. . . .
3	Number of motor lifeboats (included in the total lifeboats shown above)	. . . .
3.1	Number of lifeboats fitted with searchlights	. . . .
4	Number of rescue boats	. . . .
4.1	Number of boats which are included in the total lifeboats shown above	. . . .
5	Liferafts	. . . .
5.1	Those for which approved launching appliances are required	. . . .
5.1.1	Number of liferafts	. . . .
5.1.2	Number of persons accommodated by them	. . . .
5.2	Those for which approved launching appliances are not required	. . . .
5.2.1	Number of liferafts	. . . .
5.2.2	Number of persons accommodated by them	. . . .
5.3	Number of liferafts required by regulation III/31.1.4	. . . .
6	Number of lifebuoys	. . . .
7	Number of lifejackets	. . . .
8	Immersion suits	. . . .
8.1	Total number	. . . .
8.2	Number of suits complying with the requirements for lifejackets	. . . .
9	Number of thermal protective aids[1]	. . . .
10	Radio installations used in life-saving appliances	. . . .
10.1	Number of radar transponders	. . . .
10.2	Number of two-way VHF radiotelephone apparatus	. . . .

---

[1] Excluding those required by the LSA Code, paragraphs 4.1.5.1.24, 4.4.8.31 and 5.1.2.2.13.

3   *Details of navigational systems and equipment*

Item	Actual provision
1.1 Standard magnetic compass[2]	....
1.2 Spare magnetic compass[2]	....
1.3 Gyro-compass[2]	....
1.4 Gyro-compass heading repeater[2]	....
1.5 Gyro-compass bearing repeater[2]	....
1.6 Heading or track control system[2]	....
1.7 Pelorus or compass bearing device[2]	....
1.8 Means of correcting heading and bearings	....
1.9 Transmitting heading device (THD)[2]	....
2.1 Nautical charts/Electronic chart display and information system (ECDIS)[3]	....
2.2 Back-up arrangements for ECDIS	....
2.3 Nautical publications	....
2.4 Back-up arrangements for electronic nautical publications	....
3.1 Receiver for a global navigation satellite system/terrestrial radionavigation system[2, 3]	....
3.2 9 GHz radar[2]	....
3.3 Second radar (3 GHz/9 GHz[3])[2]	....
3.4 Automatic radar plotting aid (ARPA)[2]	....
3.5 Automatic tracking aid[2]	....
3.6 Second automatic tracking aid[2]	....
3.7 Electronic plotting aid[2]	....
4 Automatic identification system (AIS)	....
5 Voyage data recorder (VDR)	....
6.1 Speed and distance measuring device (through the water)[2]	....
6.2 Speed and distance measuring device (over the ground in the forward and athwartship direction)[2]	....
7 Echo-sounding device[2]	....
8.1 Rudder, propeller, thrust, pitch and operational mode indicator[2]	....
8.2 Rate-of-turn indicator[2]	....

---

[2] Alternative means of meeting this requirement are permitted under regulation V/19. In case of other means they shall be specified.
[3] Delete as appropriate.

3   *Details of navigational systems and equipment (continued)*

Item		Actual provision
9	Sound reception system[2]	....
10	Telephone to emergency steering position[2]	....
11	Daylight signalling lamp[2]	....
12	Radar reflector[2]	....
13	International Code of Signals	....

THIS IS TO CERTIFY that this Record is correct in all respects

Issued at ....
                          (Place of issue of the Record)

....
    (Date of issue)   *(Signature of duly authorized official
                                             issuing the Record)*

        (Seal or stamp of the issuing authority, as appropriate)

---

[2] Alternative means of meeting this requirement are permitted under regulation V/19. In case
of other means they shall be specified.

[P88] Form of Safety Radio Certificate for Cargo Ships

CARGO SHIP SAFETY RADIO CERTIFICATE

This Certificate shall be supplemented by a Record of Equipment
of Radio Facilities (Form R)

(Official seal)   *(State)*

Issued under the provisions of the

INTERNATIONAL CONVENTION FOR THE SAFETY OF LIFE
AT SEA, 1974, as modified by the Protocol of 1988 relating thereto

under the authority of the Government of

_____

(name of the State)

by   _____

(person or organization authorized)

Particulars of ship[1]

Name of ship . . . .

Distinctive number or letters . . . .

Port of registry . . . .

Gross tonnage . . . .

_____
[1] Alternatively, the particulars of the ship may be placed horizontally in boxes.

494

Sea areas in which ship is certified to operate (regulation IV/2) . . . .

IMO Number[2] . . . .

Date on which keel was laid or ship was at a similar
stage of construction or, where applicable, date on
which work for a conversion or an alteration or
modification of a major character was commenced . . . .

THIS IS TO CERTIFY:

1   That the ship has been surveyed in accordance with the requirements of regulation I/9 of the Convention.

2   That the survey showed that:

2.1   the ship complied with the requirements of the Convention as regards radio installations;

2.2   the functioning of the radio installations used in life-saving appliances complied with the requirements of the Convention.

3   That an Exemption Certificate has/has not[3] been issued.

This certificate is valid until . . . . [4] subject to the periodical surveys in accordance with regulation I/9 of the Convention.

Issued at. . . . .
(Place of issue of certificate)

. . . .
(Date of issue)   *(Signature of authorized official
issuing the certificate)*

(Seal or stamp of the issuing authority, as appropriate)

---

[2] In accordance with the IMO ship identification number scheme adopted by the Organization by resolution A.600(15).

[3] Delete as appropriate.

[4] Insert the date of expiry as specified by the Administration in accordance with regulation I/14(a) of the Convention. The day and the month of this date correspond to the anniversary date as defined in regulation 1/2(n) of the Convention, unless amended in accordance with regulation I/14(h).

Endorsement for periodical surveys

THIS IS TO CERTIFY that, at a survey required by regulation I/9 of the Convention, the ship was found to comply with the relevant requirements of the Convention.

Periodical survey: Signed: . . . .
(Signature of authorized official)

Place: . . . .

Date: . . . .

(Seal or stamp of the authority, as appropriate)

Periodical survey: Signed: . . . .
(Signature of authorized official)

Place: . . . .

Date: . . . .

(Seal or stamp of the authority, as appropriate)

Periodical survey: Signed: . . . .
(Signature of authorized official)

Place: . . . .

Date: . . . .

(Seal or stamp of the authority, as appropriate)

Periodical survey: Signed: . . . .
(Signature of authorized official)

Place: . . . .

Date: . . . .

(Seal or stamp of the authority, as appropriate)

Periodical survey in accordance with regulation I/14(h)(iii)

THIS IS TO CERTIFY that, at a periodical survey in accordance with regulation I/14(h)(iii) of the Convention, the ship was found to comply with the relevant requirements of the Convention.

Signed: . . . .
(Signature of authorized official)

Place: . . . .

Date: . . . .

(Seal or stamp of the authority, as appropriate)

Endorsement to extend the certificate if valid for less than 5 years where regulation I/14(c) applies

The ship complies with the relevant requirements of the Convention, and this certificate shall, in accordance with regulation I/14(c) of the Convention, be accepted as valid until . . . .

Signed: . . . .
(Signature of authorized official)

Place: . . . .

Date: . . . .

(Seal or stamp of the authority, as appropriate)

Endorsement where the renewal survey has been completed and regulation I/14(d) applies

The ship complies with the relevant requirements of the Convention, and this certificate shall, in accordance with regulation I/14(d) of the Convention, be accepted as valid until . . . .

Signed: . . . .
(Signature of authorized official)

Place: . . . .

Date: . . . .

(Seal or stamp of the authority, as appropriate)

Endorsement to extend the validity of the certificate until reaching the port of survey or for a period of grace where regulation I/14(e) or I/14(f) applies

The certificate shall, in accordance with regulation I/14(e)/I/14(f)[3] of the Convention, be accepted as valid until . . . .

Signed: . . . .
(Signature of authorized official)

Place: . . . .

Date: . . . .

(Seal or stamp of the authority, as appropriate)

Endorsement for advancement of anniversary date where regulation I/14(h) applies

In accordance with regulation I/14(h) of the Convention, the new anniversary date is . . . .

Signed: . . . .
(Signature of authorized official)

Place: . . . .

Date: . . . .

(Seal or stamp of the authority, as appropriate)

In accordance with regulation I/14(h) of the Convention, the new anniversary date is . . . .

Signed: . . . .
(Signature of authorized official)

Place: . . . .

Date: . . . .

(Seal or stamp of the authority, as appropriate)

---

[3] Delete as appropriate.

RECORD OF EQUIPMENT FOR THE CARGO SHIP
SAFETY RADIO CERTIFICATE (FORM R)

This Record shall be permanently attached to the
Cargo Ship Safety Radio Certificate

RECORD OF EQUIPMENT OF RADIO FACILITIES FOR COMPLIANCE
WITH THE INTERNATIONAL CONVENTION FOR THE SAFETY
OF LIFE AT SEA, 1974, AS MODIFIED BY THE PROTOCOL
OF 1988 RELATING THERETO

1   *Particulars of ship*

Name of ship . . . .

Distinctive number or letters . . . .

Minimum number of persons with required
qualifications to operate the radio installations . . . .

2   *Details of radio facilities*

Item	Actual provision
1 Primary systems	
1.1 VHF radio installation	
1.1.1 DSC encoder	. . . .
1.1.2 DSC watch receiver	. . . .
1.1.3 Radiotelephony	. . . .
1.2 MF radio installation	. . . .
1.2.1 DSC encoder	. . . .
1.2.2 DSC watch receiver	. . . .
1.2.3 Radiotelephony	. . . .
1.3 MF/HF radio installation	. . . .
1.3.1 DSC encoder	. . . .
1.3.2 DSC watch receiver	. . . .
1.3.3 Radiotelephony	. . . .
1.3.4 Direct-printing telegraphy	. . . .
1.4 INMARSAT ship earth station	. . . .
2 Secondary means of alerting	. . . .
3 Facilities for reception of maritime safety information	
3.1 NAVTEX receiver	. . . .
3.2 EGC receiver	. . . .
3.3 HF direct-printing radiotelegraph receiver	. . . .
4 Satellite EPIRB	
4.1 COSPAS–SARSAT	. . . .
4.2 INMARSAT	. . . .

2   *Details of radio facilities* *(continued)*

Item	Actual provision
5 VHF EPIRB	. . . .
6 Ship's radar transponder	. . . .

3   *Methods used to ensure availability of radio facilities*
(regulations IV/15.6 and 15.7)

3.1   Duplication of equipment . . . .

3.2   Shore-based maintenance . . . .

3.3   At-sea maintenance capability . . . .

THIS IS TO CERTIFY that this Record is correct in all respects

Issued at . . . .
(Place of issue of the Record)

. . . .
(Date of issue)   *(Signature of duly authorized official*
issuing the Record)

(Seal or stamp of the issuing authority, as appropriate)

P88 Form of Safety Certificate for Cargo Ships

CARGO SHIP SAFETY CERTIFICATE

This Certificate shall be supplemented by a Record of Equipment
(Form C)

(Official seal)   *(State)*

Issued under the provisions of the

INTERNATIONAL CONVENTION FOR THE SAFETY OF LIFE
AT SEA, 1974, as modified by the Protocol of 1988 relating thereto

under the authority of the Government of

_____

(name of the State)

by   _____

(person or organization authorized)

Particulars of ship[1]

Name of ship . . . .

Distinctive number or letters . . . .

Port of registry . . . .

Gross tonnage . . . .

---

[1] Alternatively, the particulars of the ship may be placed horizontally in boxes.

501

Deadweight of ship (metric tons)[2] . . . .

Length of ship (regulation III/3.12) . . . .

Sea areas in which ship is certified to operate (regulation IV/2) . . . .

IMO Number[3] . . . .

Type of ship[4]

> Bulk carrier
>
> Oil tanker
>
> Chemical tanker
>
> Gas carrier
>
> Cargo ship other than any of the above

Date on which keel was laid or ship was at a similar
stage of construction or, where applicable, date on
which work for an alteration or modification of a
major character was commenced . . . .

THIS IS TO CERTIFY:

1   That the ship has been surveyed in accordance with the requirements of regulations I/8, I/9 and I/10 of the Convention.

2   That the survey showed that:

2.1   the condition of the structure, machinery and equipment as defined in regulation I/10 was satisfactory and the ship complied with the relevant requirements of chapter II-1 and chapter II-2 of the Convention (other than those relating to fire safety systems and appliances and fire control plans);

2.2   the last two inspections of the outside of the ship's bottom took place on

. . . . and . . . .
(dates)

2.3   the ship complied with the requirements of the Convention as regards fire safety systems and appliances and fire control plans;

2.4   the life-saving appliances and the equipment of the lifeboats, liferafts and rescue boats were provided in accordance with the requirements of the Convention;

---

[2] For oil tankers, chemical tankers and gas carriers only.

[3] In accordance with IMO ship identification number scheme adopted by the Organization by resolution A.600(15).

[4] Delete as appropriate.

2.5 the ship was provided with a line-throwing appliance and radio installations used in life-saving appliances in accordance with the requirements of the Convention;

2.6 the ship complied with the requirements of the Convention as regards radio installations;

2.7 the functioning of the radio installations used in life-saving appliances complied with the requirements of the Convention;

2.8 the ship complied with the requirements of the Convention as regards shipborne navigational equipment, means of embarkation for pilots and nautical publications;

2.9 the ship was provided with lights, shapes, means of making sound signals and distress signals in accordance with the requirements of the Convention and the International Regulations for Preventing Collisions at Sea in force;

2.10 in all other respects the ship complied with the relevant requirements of the Convention.

3 That an Exemption Certificate has/has not[4] been issued.

This certificate is valid until . . . . [5] subject to the annual, intermediate and periodical surveys and inspections of the outside of the ship's bottom in accordance with regulations I/8, I/9 and I/10 of the Convention.

Issued at . . . .
(Place of issue of certificate)

. . . .
(Date of issue)   *(Signature of authorized official
issuing the certificate)*

(Seal or stamp of the issuing authority, as appropriate)

---

[4] Delete as appropriate.

[5] Insert the date of expiry as specified by the Administration in accordance with regulation I/14(a) of the Convention. The day and the month of this date correspond to the anniversary date as defined in regulation I/2(n) of the Convention, unless amended in accordance with regulation I/14(h).

Endorsement for annual and intermediate surveys relating to structure, machinery and equipment referred to in paragraph 2.1 of this certificate

THIS IS TO CERTIFY that, at a survey required by regulation I/10 of the Convention, the ship was found to comply with the relevant requirements of the Convention.

Annual survey: Signed: . . . .
                                                    (Signature of authorized official)

                                Place: . . . .

                                Date: . . . .

(Seal or stamp of the authority, as appropriate)

Annual/Intermediate[4] survey: Signed: . . . .
                                                    (Signature of authorized official)

                                Place: . . . .

                                Date: . . . .

(Seal or stamp of the authority, as appropriate)

Annual/Intermediate[4] survey: Signed: . . . .
                                                    (Signature of authorized official)

                                Place: . . . .

                                Date: . . . .

(Seal or stamp of the authority, as appropriate)

Annual survey: Signed: . . . .
                                                     (Signature of authorized official)

                                Place: . . . .

                                Date: . . . .

(Seal or stamp of the authority, as appropriate)

---

[4] Delete as appropriate.

Annual/intermediate survey in accordance with regulation I/14(h)(iii)

THIS IS TO CERTIFY that, at an annual/intermediate[4] survey in accordance with regulations I/10 and I/14(h)(iii) of the Convention, the ship was found to comply with the relevant requirements of the Convention.

Signed: . . . .
(Signature of authorized official)

Place: . . . .

Date: . . . .

(Seal or stamp of the authority, as appropriate)

Endorsement for inspections of the outside of the ship's bottom[6]

THIS IS TO CERTIFY that, at an inspection required by regulation I/10 of the Convention, the ship was found to comply with the relevant requirements of the Convention.

First inspection:

Signed: . . . .
(Signature of authorized official)

Place: . . . .

Date: . . . .

(Seal or stamp of the authority, as appropriate)

Second inspection:

Signed: . . . .
(Signature of authorized official)

Place: . . . .

Date: . . . .

(Seal or stamp of the authority, as appropriate)

---

[4] Delete as appropriate.

[6] Provision may be made for additional inspections.

Endorsement for annual and periodical surveys relating to life-saving appliances and other equipment referred to in paragraphs 2.3, 2.4, 2.5, 2.8 and 2.9 of this certificate

THIS IS TO CERTIFY that, at a survey required by regulation I/8 of the Convention, the ship was found to comply with the relevant requirements of the Convention.

Annual survey: Signed: . . . .

                                                       (Signature of authorized official)

                              Place: . . . .

                              Date: . . . .

(Seal or stamp of the authority, as appropriate)

Annual/Periodical[4] survey: Signed: . . . .

                                                         (Signature of authorized official)

                              Place: . . . .

                              Date: . . . .

(Seal or stamp of the authority, as appropriate)

Annual/Periodical[4] survey: Signed: . . . .

                                                         (Signature of authorized official)

                              Place: . . . .

                              Date: . . . .

(Seal or stamp of the authority, as appropriate)

Annual survey: Signed: . . . .

                                                       (Signature of authorized official)

                              Place: . . . .

                              Date: . . . .

(Seal or stamp of the authority, as appropriate)

---

[4] Delete as appropriate.

Annual/periodical survey in accordance with regulation I/14(h)(iii)

THIS IS TO CERTIFY that, at an annual/periodical[4] survey in accordance with regulations I/8 and I/14(h)(iii) of the Convention, the ship was found to comply with the relevant requirements of the Convention.

Signed: . . . .
(Signature of authorized official)

Place: . . . .

Date: . . . .

(Seal or stamp of the authority, as appropriate)

---

[4] Delete as appropriate.

Endorsement for periodical surveys relating to radio installations referred to in paragraphs 2.6 and 2.7 of this certificate

THIS IS TO CERTIFY that, at a survey required by regulation I/9 of the Convention, the ship was found to comply with the relevant requirements of the Convention.

Periodical survey: Signed: . . . .
                                     (Signature of authorized official)

                          Place: . . . .

                          Date: . . . .

          (Seal or stamp of the authority, as appropriate)

Periodical survey: Signed: . . . .
                                     (Signature of authorized official)

                          Place: . . . .

                          Date: . . . .

          (Seal or stamp of the authority, as appropriate)

Periodical survey: Signed: . . . .
                                     (Signature of authorized official)

                          Place: . . . .

                          Date: . . . .

          (Seal or stamp of the authority, as appropriate)

Periodical survey: Signed: . . . .
                                     (Signature of authorized official)

                          Place: . . . .

                          Date: . . . .

          (Seal or stamp of the authority, as appropriate)

Periodical survey in accordance with regulation I/14(h)(iii)

THIS IS TO CERTIFY that, at a periodical survey in accordance with regulations I/9 and I/14(h)(iii) of the Convention, the ship was found to comply with the relevant requirements of the Convention.

Signed: . . . .
(Signature of authorized official)

Place: . . . .

Date: . . . .

(Seal or stamp of the authority, as appropriate)

Endorsement to extend the certificate if valid for less than 5 years where regulation I/14(c) applies

The ship complies with the relevant requirements of the Convention, and this certificate shall, in accordance with regulation I/14(c) of the Convention, be accepted as valid until . . . .

Signed: . . . .
(Signature of authorized official)

Place: . . . .

Date: . . . .

(Seal or stamp of the authority, as appropriate)

Endorsement where the renewal survey has been completed and regulation I/14(d) applies

The ship complies with the relevant requirements of the Convention, and this certificate shall, in accordance with regulation I/14(d) of the Convention, be accepted as valid until . . . .

Signed: . . . .
(Signature of authorized official)

Place: . . . .

Date: . . . .

(Seal or stamp of the authority, as appropriate)

Endorsement to extend the validity of the certificate until reaching the port of survey or for a period of grace where regulation I/14(e) or I/14(f) applies

The certificate shall, in accordance with regulation I/14(e)/I/14(f)[4] of the Convention, be accepted as valid until . . . .

Signed: . . . .
(Signature of authorized official)

Place: . . . .

Date: . . . .

(Seal or stamp of the authority, as appropriate)

Endorsement for advancement of anniversary date where regulation I/14(h) applies

In accordance with regulation I/14(h) of the Convention, the new anniversary date is
. . . .

Signed: . . . .
(Signature of authorized official)

Place: . . . .

Date: . . . .

(Seal or stamp of the authority, as appropriate)

In accordance with regulation I/14(h) of the Convention, the new anniversary date is
. . . .

Signed: . . . .
(Signature of authorized official)

Place: . . . .

Date: . . . .

(Seal or stamp of the authority, as appropriate)

---

[4] Delete as appropriate.

**RECORD OF EQUIPMENT FOR THE
CARGO SHIP SAFETY CERTIFICATE (FORM C)**

This Record shall be permanently attached to the
Cargo Ship Safety Certificate

RECORD OF EQUIPMENT FOR COMPLIANCE WITH
THE INTERNATIONAL CONVENTION FOR THE SAFETY
OF LIFE AT SEA, 1974, AS MODIFIED BY THE PROTOCOL
OF 1988 RELATING THERETO

1   *Particulars of ship*

Name of ship . . . .

Distinctive number or letters . . . .

Minimum number of persons with required qualifications to operate the radio
installations. . . . .

2   *Details of life-saving appliances*

1	Total number of persons for which life-saving appliances are provided	. . . .	
		Port side	Starboard side
2	Total number of lifeboats	. . . .	. . . .
2.1	Total number of persons accommodated by them	. . . .	. . . .
2.2	Number of totally enclosed lifeboats (regulation III/31 and LSA Code, section 4.6)	. . . .	. . . .
2.3	Number of lifeboats with a self-contained air support system (regulation III/31 and LSA Code, section 4.8)	. . . .	. . . .
2.4	Number of fire-protected lifeboats (regulation III/31 and LSA Code, section 4.9)	. . . .	. . . .
2.5	Other lifeboats	. . . .	. . . .
2.5.1	Number	. . . .	. . . .
2.5.2	Type	. . . .	. . . .

2   *Details of life-saving appliances* *(continued)*

2.6	Number of freefall lifeboats	. . . .
2.6.1	Totally enclosed (regulation III/31 and LSA Code, section 4.7)	. . . .
2.6.2	Self-contained (regulation III/31 and LSA Code, section 4.8)	. . . .
2.6.3	Fire-protected (regulation III/31 and LSA Code, section 4.9)	. . . .
3	Number of motor lifeboats included in the total lifeboats shown above	. . . .
3.1	Number of lifeboats fitted with searchlights	. . . .
4	Number of rescue boats	. . . .
4.1	Number of boats which are included in the total lifeboats shown above	. . . .
5	Liferafts	. . . .
5.1	Those for which approved launching appliances are required	. . . .
5.1.1	Number of liferafts	. . . .
5.1.2	Number of persons accommodated by them	. . . .
5.2	Those for which approved launching appliances are not required	. . . .
5.2.1	Number of liferafts	. . . .
5.2.2	Number of persons accommodated by them	. . . .
5.3	Number of liferafts required by regulation III/31.1.4	. . . .
6	Number of lifebuoys	. . . .
7	Number of lifejackets	. . . .
8	Immersion suits	. . . .
8.1	Total number	. . . .
8.2	Number of suits complying with the requirements for lifejackets	. . . .
9	Number of thermal protective aids[1]	. . . .
10	Radio installations used in life-saving appliances	. . . .
10.1	Number of radar transponders	. . . .
10.2	Number of two-way VHF radiotelephone apparatus	. . . .

---

[1] Excluding those required by the LSA Code, paragraphs 4.1.5.1.24, 4.4.8.31 and 5.1.2.2.13.

3   *Details of radio facilities*

	Item	Actual provision
1	Primary systems	
1.1	VHF radio installation	
1.1.1	DSC encoder	. . . .
1.1.2	DSC watch receiver	. . . .
1.1.3	Radiotelephony	. . . .
1.2	MF radio installation	. . . .
1.2.1	DSC encoder	. . . .
1.2.2	DSC watch receiver	. . . .
1.2.3	Radiotelephony	. . . .
1.3	MF/HF radio installation	. . . .
1.3.1	DSC encoder	. . . .
1.3.2	DSC watch receiver	. . . .
1.3.3	Radiotelephony	. . . .
1.3.4	Direct-printing telegraphy	. . . .
1.4	INMARSAT ship earth station	. . . .
2	Secondary means of alerting	. . . .
3	Facilities for reception of maritime safety information	
3.1	NAVTEX receiver	. . . .
3.2	EGC receiver	. . . .
3.3	HF direct-printing radiotelegraph receiver	. . . .
4	Satellite EPIRB	
4.1	COSPAS–SARSAT	. . . .
4.2	INMARSAT	. . . .
5	VHF EPIRB	. . . .
6	Ship's radar transponder	. . . .

4   *Methods used to ensure availability of radio facilities*
(regulations IV/15.6 and 15.7)

4.1   Duplication of equipment . . . .

4.2   Shore-based maintenance . . . .

4.3   At-sea maintenance capability . . . .

5   *Details of navigational systems and equipment*

Item	Actual provision
1.1 Standard magnetic compass[2]	....
1.2 Spare magnetic compass[2]	....
1.3 Gyro-compass[2]	....
1.4 Gyro-compass heading repeater[2]	....
1.5 Gyro-compass bearing repeater[2]	....
1.6 Heading or track control system[2]	....
1.7 Pelorus or compass bearing device[2]	....
1.8 Means of correcting heading and bearings	....
1.9 Transmitting heading device (THD)[2]	....
2.1 Nautical charts/Electronic chart display and information system (ECDIS)[3]	....
2.2 Back-up arrangements for ECDIS	....
2.3 Nautical publications	....
2.4 Back-up arrangements for electronic nautical publications	....
3.1 Receiver for a global navigation satellite system/terrestrial radionavigation system[2, 3]	....
3.2 9 GHz radar[2]	....
3.3 Second radar (3 GHz/9 GHz[3])[2]	....
3.4 Automatic radar plotting aid (ARPA)[2]	....
3.5 Automatic tracking aid[2]	....
3.6 Second automatic tracking aid[2]	....
3.7 Electronic plotting aid[2]	....
4 Automatic identification system (AIS)	....
5 Voyage data recorder (VDR)	....
6.1 Speed and distance measuring device (through the water)[2]	....
6.2 Speed and distance measuring device (over the ground in the forward and athwartship direction)[2]	....
7 Echo-sounding device[2]	....
8.1 Rudder, propeller, thrust, pitch and operational mode indicator[2]	....
8.2 Rate-of-turn indicator[2]	....

---

[2] Alternative means of meeting this requirement are permitted under regulation V/19. In case of other means they shall be specified.
[3] Delete as appropriate

5   *Details of navigational systems and equipment* (continued)

Item	Actual provision
9 Sound reception system[2]	....
10 Telephone to emergency steering position[2]	....
11 Daylight signalling lamp[2]	....
12 Radar reflector[2]	....
13 International Code of Signals	....

THIS IS TO CERTIFY that this Record is correct in all respects

Issued at . . . .
                                    (Place of issue of the Record)

. . . .
    (Date of issue)   *(Signature of duly authorized official
                                                       issuing the Record)*

(Seal or stamp of the issuing authority, as appropriate)

---

[2] Alternative means of meeting this requirement are permitted under regulation V/19. In case of other means they shall be specified.

▣P88 Form of Exemption Certificate

EXEMPTION CERTIFICATE

(Official seal)   *(State)*

Issued under the provisions of the
INTERNATIONAL CONVENTION FOR THE SAFETY OF LIFE
AT SEA, 1974, as modified by the Protocol of 1988 relating thereto,

under the authority of the Government of

_____
(name of the State)

by   _____
(person or organization authorized)

Particulars of ship[1]

Name of ship . . . .

Distinctive number or letters . . . .

_____

[1] Alternatively, the particulars of the ship may be placed horizontally in boxes.

Port of registry . . . .

Gross tonnage . . . .

IMO Number[2] . . . .

THIS IS TO CERTIFY:

That the ship is, under the authority conferred by regulation . . . .
of the Convention, exempted from the requirements of . . . .
. . . . of the Convention.

Conditions, if any, on which the Exemption Certificate is granted:
. . . .
. . . .

Voyages, if any, for which the Exemption Certificate is granted:
. . . .
. . . .

This certificate is valid until . . . . subject
to the . . . . .Certificate,
to which this certificate is attached, remaining valid.

Issued at . . . .
(Place of issue of certificate)

. . . .
(Date of issue)   *(Signature of authorized official*
issuing the certificate)

(Seal or stamp of the issuing authority, as appropriate)

---

[2] In accordance with IMO ship identification number scheme adopted by the Organization by resolution A.600(15)

Endorsement to extend the certificate if valid for less than 5 years where regulation I/14(c) applies

This certificate shall, in accordance with regulation I/14(c) of the Convention, be accepted as valid until . . . . subject to the . . . . Certificate, to which this certificate is attached, remaining valid.

Signed: . . . .
(Signature of authorized official)

Place: . . . .

Date: . . . .

(Seal or stamp of the authority, as appropriate)

Endorsement where the renewal survey has been completed and regulation I/14(d) applies

This certificate shall, in accordance with regulation I/14(d) of the Convention, be accepted as valid until . . . . subject to the . . . . Certificate, to which this certificate is attached, remaining valid.

Signed: . . . .
(Signature of authorized official)

Place: . . . .

Date: . . . .

(Seal or stamp of the authority, as appropriate)

Endorsement to extend the validity of the certificate until reaching the port of survey or for a period of grace where regulation I/14(e) or I/14(f) applies

The certificate shall, in accordance with regulation I/14(e)/I/14(f)[3] of the Convention, be accepted as valid until . . . . subject to the . . . . Certificate, to which this certificate is attached, remaining valid.

Signed: . . . .
(Signature of authorized official)

Place: . . . .

Date: . . . .

(Seal or stamp of the authority, as appropriate)

---

[3] Delete as appropriate.

Form of Nuclear Passenger Ship Safety Certificate

NUCLEAR PASSENGER SHIP SAFETY CERTIFICATE

(Official seal)   *(State)*

Issued under the provisions of the

INTERNATIONAL CONVENTION FOR THE SAFETY OF LIFE AT SEA, 1974

Name of ship	Distinctive number or letters	Port of registry	Gross tonnage	Particulars of voyages, if any, sanctioned under regulation 27(c)(vii) of chapter III*	Date on which keel was laid (see NOTE below)

The _____ *(Name)* Government certifies
I, the undersigned *(Name)* certify

I.   that the above-mentioned ship has been duly surveyed in accordance with the provisions of the Convention referred to above.

II.   that the ship, being a nuclear ship, complied with all the requirements of chapter VIII of the Convention and conformed to the safety assessment approved for the ship.

III.   that the survey showed that the ship complied with the requirements of the regulations annexed to the said Convention as regards:

---
* Now regulation III/21.1.2.

519

(1)   the structure, main and auxiliary boilers and other pressure vessels and machinery;

(2)   the watertight subdivision arrangements and details;

(3)   the following subdivision load lines:

Subdivision load lines assigned and marked on the ship's side at amidships (regulation 11 of chapter II-1)*	Freeboard	To apply when the spaces in which passengers are carried include the following alternative spaces
C.1	. . . . .	. . . .
C.2	. . . . .	. . . .
C.3	. . . . .	. . . .

IV.   that the life-saving appliances provide for a total number of . . . . persons and no more, viz.:

    . . . . . lifeboats (including . . . . . . motor lifeboats) capable of accommodating . . . . . persons, and . . . . . motor lifeboats fitted with radiotelegraph installation and searchlight (included in the total lifeboats shown above) and . . . . . motor lifeboats fitted with searchlight only (also included in the total lifeboats shown above), requiring . . . . . certificated lifeboatmen;

    . . . . . liferafts, for which approved launching devices are required, capable of accommodating . . . . . persons; and

    . . . . . liferafts, for which approved launching devices are not required, capable of accommodating . . . . . persons;

    . . . . . buoyant apparatus capable of supporting . . . . . persons;

    . . . . . lifebuoys;

    . . . . . lifejackets.

V.   that the lifeboats and liferafts were equipped in accordance with the provisions of the regulations.

VI.   that the ship was provided with a line-throwing appliance and portable radio apparatus for survival craft, in accordance with the provisions of the regulations.

VII.   that the ship complied with the requirements of the regulations as regards radiotelegraph installations, viz.:

---

* Now regulation II-1/13.

	Requirements of regulations	Actual provision
Hours of listening by operator	. . . .	. . . .
Number of operators	. . . .	. . . .
Whether auto alarm fitted	. . . .	. . . .
Whether main installation fitted	. . . .	. . . .
Whether reserve installation fitted	. . . .	. . . .
Whether main and reserve transmitters electrically separated or combined	. . . .	. . . .
Whether direction-finder fitted	. . . .	. . . .
Whether radio equipment for homing on the radio-telephone distress frequency fitted	. . . .	. . . .
Whether radar fitted	. . . .	. . . .
Number of passengers for which certificated	. . . .	. . . .

VIII.   that the functioning of the radiotelegraph installations for motor lifeboats and/or the portable radio apparatus for survival craft, if provided, complied with the provisions of the regulations.

IX.   that the ship complied with the requirements of the regulations as regards fire-detecting and fire-extinguishing appliances, radar, echo-sounding device and gyro-compass and was provided with navigation lights and shapes, pilot ladder, and means of making sound signals, and distress signals in accordance with the provisions of the regulations and also the International Regulations for Preventing Collisions at Sea in force.

X.   that in all other respects the ship complied with the requirements of the regulations, so far as these requirements apply thereto.

This certificate is issued under the authority of the . . . . Government. It will remain in force until. . . . .

Issued at . . . . the . . . . day of . . . . 19. . . . .

Here follows the seal or signature of the authority entitled to issue the certificate.

(Seal)

If signed, the following paragraph is to be added:

The undersigned declares that he is duly authorized by the said Government to issue this certificate.

(Signature)

NOTE: In the case of a ship which is converted as provided in regulation 1(b)(i) of chapter II-1* or regulation 1(a)(i) of chapter II-2[†], the date on which the work of conversion was begun should be given.

---

* Now regulation II-1/1.1.3.3.
[†] Now regulation II-2/1.1.2.3.

Form of Nuclear Cargo Ship Safety Certificate

NUCLEAR CARGO SHIP SAFETY CERTIFICATE

(Official seal)   *(State)*

Issued under the provisions of the
INTERNATIONAL CONVENTION FOR THE SAFETY OF LIFE AT
SEA, 1974

Name of ship	Distinctive number or letters	Port of registry	Gross tonnage	Date on which keel was laid

The
I, the undersigned

(Name) Government certifies
(Name) certify

I.   that the above-mentioned ship has been duly surveyed in accordance with the provisions of the Convention referred to above.

II.   that the ship, being a nuclear ship, complied with all the requirements of chapter VIII of the Convention and conformed to the safety assessment approved for the ship.

III.   that the survey showed that the ship satisfied the requirements set out in regulation 10 of chapter I of the Convention as to hull, machinery and equipment, and complied with the relevant requirements of chapter II-1 and chapter II-2.

IV.   that the life-saving appliances provide for a total number of . . . . persons and no more, viz.:

. . . . . lifeboats on port side capable of accommodating . . . . . persons;

. . . . . lifeboats on starboard side capable of accommodating . . . . . persons;

. . . . . motor lifeboats (included in the total lifeboats shown above) including . . . . . motor lifeboats fitted with radiotelegraph installation and searchlight, and . . . . . motor lifeboats fitted with searchlight only;

. . . . . liferafts, for which approved launching devices are required, capable of accommodating . . . . . persons; and

. . . . . liferafts, for which approved launching devices are not required, capable of accommodating . . . . . persons;

. . . . . lifebuoys;

. . . . . lifejackets.

V. that the lifeboats and liferafts were equipped in accordance with the provisions of the regulations annexed to the Convention.

VI. that the ship was provided with a line-throwing apparatus and portable radio apparatus for survival craft in accordance with the provisions of the regulations.

VII. that the ship complied with the requirements of the regulations as regards radiotelegraph installations, viz.:

	Requirements of regulations	Actual provision
Hours of listening by operator	. . . .	. . . .
Number of operators	. . . .	. . . .
Whether auto alarm fitted	. . . .	. . . .
Whether main installation fitted	. . . .	. . . .
Whether reserve installation fitted	. . . .	. . . .
Whether main and reserve transmitters electrically separated or combined	. . . .	. . . .
Whether direction-finder fitted	. . . .	. . . .
Whether radio equipment for homing on the radio-telephone distress frequency fitted	. . . .	. . . .
Whether radar fitted	. . . .	. . . .

VIII. that the functioning of the radiotelegraph installations for motor lifeboats and/ or the portable radio apparatus for survival craft, if provided, complied with the provisions of the regulations.

IX. that the inspection showed that the ship complied with the requirements of the said Convention as regards fire-extinguishing appliances, radar, echo-sounding device and gyro-compass and was provided with navigation lights and shapes, pilot ladder, and means of making sound signals and distress signals in accordance with the provisions of the regulations and the International Regulations for Preventing Collisions at Sea in force.

X.   that in all other respects the ship complied with the requirements of the regulations, so far as these requirements apply thereto.

This certificate is issued under the authority of the . . . . Government. It will remain in force until . . . .

Issued at . . . . the . . . . day of . . . . 19. . . .

Here follows the seal or signature of the authority entitled to issue the certificate.

(Seal)

If signed, the following paragraph is to be added:

The undersigned declares that he is duly authorized by the said Government to issue this certificate.

(Signature)

NOTE: In the case of a ship which is converted as provided in regulation 1(b)(i) of chapter II-1[*] or regulation 1(a)(i) of chapter II-2[†], the date on which the work of conversion was begun should be given.

---

[*] Now regulation II-1/1.1.3.3.
[†] Now regulation II-2/1.1.2.3.

Part 2

CONTENTS

Annex 1

Resolution A.883(21)
Global and uniform implementation of the harmonized system of survey and certification (HSSC)

THE ASSEMBLY,

RECALLING Article 15(j) of the Convention on the International Maritime Organization concerning the functions of the Assembly in relation to regulations and guidelines concerning maritime safety and the prevention and control of marine pollution from ships,

RECALLING ALSO that the International Conference on the Harmonized System of Survey and Certification, 1988 (1988 HSSC Conference), adopted the Protocol of 1988 relating to the International Convention for the Safety of Life at Sea, 1974 (1988 SOLAS Protocol), and the Protocol of 1988 relating to the International Convention on Load Lines, 1966 (1988 Load Line Protocol), which introduce, *inter alia*, the harmonized system of survey and certification under the International Convention for the Safety of Life at Sea, 1974 (1974 SOLAS Convention) and the International Convention on Load Lines, 1966 (1966 Load Line Convention),

NOTING that the 1988 SOLAS and Load Line Protocols are due to enter into force on 3 February 2000, resulting in the harmonized system of survey and certification taking effect as from that date with respect to ships entitled to fly the flag of States Parties to the 1988 SOLAS and Load Line Protocols,

NOTING ALSO that, by the resolutions given below, amendments have been adopted to introduce the harmonized system of survey and certification in the following instruments:

(a)   Annexes I and II of the International Convention for the Prevention of Pollution from Ships, 1973, as modified by the Protocol of 1978 relating thereto (MARPOL 73/78), by resolution MEPC.39(29);

(b)   the International Code for the Construction and Equipment of Ships Carrying Dangerous Chemicals in Bulk (IBC Code), by resolutions MEPC.40(29) and MSC.16(58);

(c)   the International Code for the Construction and Equipment of Ships Carrying Liquefied Gases in Bulk (IGC Code), by resolution MSC.17(58); and

(d)   the Code for the Construction and Equipment of Ships Carrying Dangerous Chemicals in Bulk (BCH Code), by resolutions MEPC.41(29) and MSC.18(58),

NOTING FURTHER that the aforementioned amendments to the above instruments will also enter into force on 3 February 2000, and that:

(a)   amendments to MARPOL 73/78, the IBC Code and BCH Code will take effect with respect to ships entitled to fly the flags of States Parties to MARPOL 73/78; and

(b)   amendments to the IBC Code and the IGC Code will take effect with respect to ships entitled to fly the flags of States the Governments of which are Contracting Governments of the 1974 SOLAS Convention,

irrespective of whether or not they are also Parties to the 1988 SOLAS and Load Line Protocols,

BEING DESIROUS that all States apply a single and uniform system of survey and certification to all types of ships entitled to fly their flags,

RECOGNIZING the need for the change-over from the existing system of survey and certification to the harmonized system in a uniform manner,

RECALLING resolution A.718(17) on early implementation of the harmonized system of survey and certification, which encourages States to introduce the harmonized system of survey and certification prior to the entry into force of the 1988 SOLAS and Load Line Protocols,

BEING CONVINCED that the harmonized system of survey and certification is at least equivalent to the system prescribed in the existing SOLAS and Load Line Conventions,

BELIEVING that the implementation of a single and uniform system of survey and certification could best be achieved through the introduction of the harmonized system of survey and certification also by States which are not Parties to the 1988 SOLAS and Load Line Protocols, as equivalent to the existing system,

BELIEVING ALSO that the global and uniform implementation of the harmonized system of survey and certification by all States could avoid possible problems or confusion by contributing to the determination of the duration and validity of certificates issued,

HAVING CONSIDERED the recommendations made by the Maritime Safety Committee at its seventy-first session and by the Marine Environment Protection Committee at its forty-third session,

1.   INVITES States to introduce the harmonized system of survey and certification in the manner provided for in annex 1 to the present resolution;

2.   AGREES that States which are Contracting Governments to the 1974 SOLAS Convention and the 1966 Load Line Convention, but not Parties to the 1988 SOLAS and Load Line Protocols, may:

(a)   implement the harmonized system of survey and certification as from 3 February 2000; and

(b)   issue certificates in the form prescribed by the 1988 SOLAS and Load Line Protocols as modified in accordance with annex 2 to the present resolution;

3.   INVITES port States, whether or not they are Parties to the 1988 SOLAS and Load Line Protocols, to accept the certificates issued in accordance with paragraph 1 above as equivalent to the certificates issued under the SOLAS and Load Line Convention or Protocols in force for those States;

4.   REQUESTS Governments that implement the harmonized system of survey and certification in accordance with the provisions of this resolution to inform the Secretary-General of their action and of the date when it will take effect;

5.   REQUESTS ALSO that the Secretary-General keep Governments informed of those Governments that are introducing the harmonized system of survey and certification in accordance with the provisions of this resolution;

6.   URGES States which have not yet become Party to the 1988 SOLAS and Load Line Protocols to do so as soon as possible.

Annex 1

Introduction of the harmonized system of survey and certification

1   The current certificates that are on board a particular ship on 3 February 2000 will remain valid until they expire.

2   The date for the introduction of the harmonized system of survey and certification (HSSC) after 3 February 2000 should normally be the latest expiry date of certificates issued under the SOLAS, Load Line and MARPOL Conventions, unless another convenient date, e.g. the expiry date of the Cargo Ship Safety Construction Certificate, the date of dry-docking or date of repair or renovation, is agreed upon between the shipowner or company and the Administration.

3   In the case where an existing certificate has expired before the date of introduction of the harmonized system, a new certificate using the form prescribed under the harmonized system may be issued after the renewal

survey has been carried out. The validity of the new certificate may be limited to the date of introduction of the harmonized system as provided for in paragraph 2 above.

4　Notwithstanding that some certificates may still be valid when the harmonized system of survey and certification is introduced on a particular ship, renewal surveys should be carried out whether or not they are due, and a new set of the relevant certificates under the harmonized system should be issued and the anniversary date common to all certificates should be specified. In general, renewal surveys completed within three months of the date of introduction of the harmonized system may be valid, and the extent of renewal surveys to be carried out may take account of the date and extent of the previous renewal surveys if carried out only recently.

5　When implementing the harmonized system of survey and certification, it should be applied to all types of ships and in respect of all relevant instruments.

Annex 2
Modifications to the forms of certificates prescribed by the 1988 SOLAS and Load Line Protocols

Passenger Ship Safety Certificate
Cargo Ship Safety Construction Certificate
Cargo Ship Safety Equipment Certificate
Cargo Ship Safety Radio Certificate
Cargo Ship Safety Certificate

After the words "Issued under the provisions of the INTERNATIONAL CONVENTION FOR THE SAFETY OF LIFE AT SEA, 1974" *delete* "as modified by the Protocol of 1988 relating thereto" *and insert* "in accordance with Assembly resolution A.883(21) relating to the global implementation of the harmonized system of survey and certification".

Record of Equipment for the Passenger Ship Safety Certificate (Form P)
Record of Equipment for the Cargo Ship Safety Equipment Certificate (Form E)
Record of Equipment for the Cargo Ship Safety Radio Certificate (Form R)
Record of Equipment for the Cargo Ship Safety Certificate (Form C)

After the words "RECORD OF EQUIPMENT FOR COMPLIANCE WITH THE INTERNATIONAL CONVENTION FOR THE SAFETY OF LIFE AT SEA, 1974" *delete* ''as modified by the Protocol of 1988 relating thereto'' *and insert* ''in accordance with Assembly resolution A.883(21) relating to the global implementation of the harmonized system of survey and certification''.

International Load Line Certificate
International Load Line Exemption Certificate

After the words ''Issued under the provisions of the INTERNATIONAL CONVENTION ON LOAD LINES, 1966'' *delete* ''as modified by the Protocol of 1988 relating thereto'' *and insert* ''in accordance with Assembly resolution A.883(21) relating to the global implementation of the harmonized system of survey and certification''.

Annex 2
Certificates and documents required to be carried on board ships

(Note: All certificates to be carried on board must be originals)

Reference

1 All ships

International Tonnage Certificate (1969)

An International Tonnage Certificate (1969) shall be issued to every ship, the gross and net tonnage of which have been determined in accordance with the Convention.	Tonnage Convention, art. 7

International Load Line Certificate

An International Load Line Certificate shall be issued under the provisions of the International Convention on Load Lines, 1966, to every ship which has been surveyed and marked in accordance with the Convention or the Convention as modified by the 1988 LL Protocol, as appropriate.	LL Convention, art. 16; 1988 LL Protocol, art. 18

International Load Line Exemption Certificate

An International Load Line Exemption Certificate shall be issued to any ship to which an exemption has been granted under and in accordance with article 6 of the Load Line Convention or the Convention as modified by the 1988 LL Protocol, as appropriate.	LL Convention, art. 6; 1988 LL Protocol, art. 18

Intact Stability Booklet

Every passenger ship regardless of size and every cargo ship of 24 m and over shall be inclined on completion and the elements of their stability determined. The master shall be supplied with a Stability Booklet containing such information as is necessary to enable him, by rapid and simple procedures, to obtain accurate guidance as to the ship under varying conditions of loading. For bulk carriers, the information required in a bulk carrier booklet may be contained in the stability booklet.	SOLAS 1974, regs. II-1/22 and II-1/25-8; 1988 LL Protocol, reg. 10

Damage control booklets
On passenger and cargo ships, there shall be permanently exhibited plans showing clearly for each deck and hold the boundaries of the watertight compartments, the openings therein with the means of closure and position of any controls thereof, and the arrangements for the correction of any list due to flooding. Booklets containing the aforementioned information shall be made available to the officers of the ship.

SOLAS 1974, regs. II-1/23, 23-1, 25-8

Minimum safe manning document
Every ship to which chapter I of the Convention applies shall be provided with an appropriate safe manning document or equivalent issued by the Administration as evidence of the minimum safe manning.

SOLAS 1974 (1989 amdts.), reg. V/13(b)

Certificates for masters, officers or ratings
Certificates for masters, officers or ratings shall be issued to those candidates who, to the satisfaction of the Administration, meet the requirements for service, age, medical fitness, training, qualifications and examinations in accordance with the provisions of the STCW Code annexed to the Convention on Standards of Training, Certification and Watchkeeping for Seafarers, 1978. Formats of certificates are given in section A-I/2 of the STCW Code. Certificates must be kept available in their original form on board the ships on which the holder is serving.

STCW 1978 (1995 amdts.), art. VI, reg. I/2; STCW Code, section A-I/2

International Oil Pollution Prevention Certificate
An International Oil Pollution Prevention Certificate shall be issued after survey in accordance with regulation 4 of Annex I of MARPOL 73/78, to any oil tanker of 150 gross tonnage and above and any other ship of 400 gross tonnage and above which are engaged in voyages to ports or offshore terminals under the jurisdiction of other Parties to MARPOL 73/78. The certificate is supplemented by a Record of Construction and Equipment for Ships Other Than Oil Tankers (Form A) or a Record of Construction and Equipment for Oil Tankers (Form B), as appropriate.

MARPOL 73/78, Annex I, reg. 5

Oil Record Book
Every oil tanker of 150 gross tonnage and above and
every ship of 400 gross tonnage and above other than
an oil tanker shall be provided with an Oil Record
Book, Part I (Machinery space operations). Every oil
tanker of 150 gross tonnage and above shall also be
provided with an Oil Record Book, Part II (Cargo/
ballast operations).

MARPOL 73/78,
Annex I, reg. 20

Shipboard Oil Pollution Emergency Plan
Every oil tanker of 150 gross tonnage and above and
every ship other than an oil tanker of 400 gross
tonnage and above shall carry on board a Shipboard
Oil Pollution Emergency Plan approved by the
Administration.

MARPOL 73/78,
Annex I, reg. 26

Garbage Management Plan
Every ship of 400 gross tonnage and above and every
ship which is certified to carry 15 persons or more
shall carry a garbage management plan which the
crew shall follow.

MARPOL 73/78,
Annex V, reg. 9

Garbage Record Book
Every ship of 400 gross tonnage and above and every
ship which is certified to carry 15 persons or more
engaged in voyages to ports or offshore terminals
under the jurisdiction of other Parties to the
Convention and every fixed and floating platform
engaged in exploration and exploitation of the sea-
bed shall be provided with a Garbage Record Book.

MARPOL 73/78,
Annex V, reg. 9

Cargo Securing Manual
Cargo units, including containers, shall be loaded,
stowed and secured throughout the voyage in
accordance with the Cargo Securing Manual approved by the Administration. The Cargo Securing
Manual is required on all types of ships engaged in
the carriage of all cargoes other than solid and liquid
bulk cargoes, which shall be drawn up to a standard
at least equivalent to the guidelines developed by the
Organization.

SOLAS 1974,
regs. VI/5, VII/6;
MSC/Circ.745

Document of Compliance
A document of compliance shall be issued to every
company which complies with the requirements of
the ISM Code. A copy of the document shall be kept
on board.

SOLAS 1974,
reg. IX/4;
ISM Code,
paragraph 13

Reference

Safety Management Certificate

A Safety Management Certificate shall be issued to every ship by the Administration or an organization recognized by the Administration. The Administration or an organization recognized by it shall, before issuing the Safety Management Certificate, verify that the company and its shipboard management operate in accordance with the approved safety management system.

SOLAS 1974, reg. IX/4; ISM Code, paragraph 13

2   In addition to the certificates listed in section 1 above, passenger ships shall carry:

Passenger Ship Safety Certificate*

A certificate called a Passenger Ship Safety Certificate shall be issued after inspection and survey to a passenger ship which complies with the requirements of chapters II-1, II-2, III and IV and any other relevant requirements of SOLAS 1974. A Record of Equipment for the Passenger Ship Safety Certificate (Form P) shall be permanently attached.

SOLAS 1974, reg. I/12, as amended by the GMDSS amdts.; 1988 SOLAS Protocol, reg. I/12

Exemption Certificate†

When an exemption is granted to a ship under and in accordance with the provisions of SOLAS 1974, a certificate called an Exemption Certificate shall be issued in addition to the certificates listed above.

SOLAS 1974, reg. I/12; 1988 SOLAS Protocol, reg. I/12

Special trade passenger ships

A form of safety certificate for special trade passenger ships, issued under the provisions of the Special Trade Passenger Ships Agreement, 1971.

STP Agreement, reg. 6

Special Trade Passenger Ships Space Certificate issued under the provisions of the Protocol on Space Requirements for Special Trade Passenger Ships, 1973.

SSTP 73, rule 5

Search and rescue co-operation plan

Passenger ships to which chapter I of the Convention applies, trading on fixed routes, shall have on board a plan for co-operation with appropriate search and rescue services in event of an emergency.

SOLAS 1974 (1995 Conference amdts), reg. V/15(c)

---

* The form of the certificate and its Record of Equipment may be found in the GMDSS amendments to SOLAS 1974.
† SLS.14/Circ.115 and Add. 1 refers to the issue of exemption certificates.

Reference

List of operational limitations

Passenger ships to which chapter I of the Convention applies shall keep on board a list of all limitations on the operation of the ship, including exemptions from any of the SOLAS regulations, restrictions in operating areas, weather restrictions, sea state restrictions, restrictions in permissible loads, trim, speed and any other limitations, whether imposed by the Administration or established during the design or the building stages.

SOLAS 1974 (1995 Conference amdts), reg. V/23

Decision support system for masters

In all passenger ships, a decision support system for emergency management shall be provided on the navigation bridge.

SOLAS 1974, reg. III/29

3   **In addition to the certificates listed in section 1 above, cargo ships shall carry:**

*Cargo Ship Safety Construction Certificate**

A certificate called a Cargo Ship Safety Construction Certificate shall be issued after survey to a cargo ship of 500 gross tonnage and over which satisfies the requirements for cargo ships on survey, set out in regulation I/10 of SOLAS 1974, and complies with the applicable requirements of chapters II-1 and II-2, other than those relating to fire-extinguishing appliances and fire control plans.

SOLAS 1974, reg. I/12, as amended by the GMDSS amdts.; 1988 SOLAS Protocol, reg. I/12

Cargo Ship Safety Equipment Certificate†*

A certificate called a Cargo Ship Safety Equipment Certificate shall be issued after survey to a cargo ship of 500 gross tonnage and over which complies with the relevant requirements of chapters II-1, II-2 and III and any other relevant requirements of SOLAS 1974. A Record of Equipment for the Cargo Ship Safety Equipment Certificate (Form E) shall be permanently attached.

SOLAS 1974, reg. I/12, as amended by the GMDSS amdts.; 1988 SOLAS Protocol, reg. I/12

---

* The form of the certificate may be found in the GMDSS amendments to SOLAS 1974.

† The form of the certificate and its Record of Equipment may be found in the GMDSS amendments to SOLAS 1974.

Reference

Cargo Ship Safety Radio Certificate*
A certificate called a Cargo Ship Safety Radio
Certificate shall be issued after survey to a cargo
ship of 300 gross tonnage and over, fitted with a
radio installation, including those used in life-saving
appliances which complies with the requirements of
chapters III and IV and any other relevant requirements of SOLAS 1974. A Record of Equipment for
the Cargo Ship Safety Radio Certificate (Form R)
shall be permanently attached.

SOLAS 1974,
reg. I/12,
as amended by the
GMDSS amdts.;
1988 SOLAS
Protocol, reg. I/12

Cargo Ship Safety Certificate
A certificate called a Cargo Ship Safety Certificate
may be issued after survey to a cargo ship which
complies with the relevant requirements of chapters
II-1, II-2, III, IV and V and other relevant
requirements of SOLAS 1974 as modified by the
1988 SOLAS Protocol, as an alternative to the above
cargo ship safety certificates.

1988 SOLAS
Protocol, reg. I/12

Exemption Certificate†
When an exemption is granted to a ship under and in
accordance with the provisions of SOLAS 1974, a
certificate called an Exemption Certificate shall be
issued in addition to the certificates listed above.

SOLAS 1974,
reg. I/12;
1988 SOLAS
Protocol, reg. I/12

Document of compliance with the special requirements
for ships carrying dangerous goods
An appropriate document as evidence of compliance
with the construction and equipment requirements
of that regulation.

SOLAS 1974,
reg. II-2/54.3

Dangerous goods manifest or stowage plan
Each ship carrying dangerous goods shall have a
special list or manifest setting forth, in accordance
with the classification set out in regulation VII/2, the
dangerous goods on board and the location thereof.
A detailed stowage plan which identifies by class and
sets out the location of all dangerous goods on board,
may be used in place of such a special list or manifest.
A copy of one of these documents shall be made
available before departure to the person or organization designated by the port State authority.

SOLAS 1974,
reg. VII/5(5);
MARPOL 73/78,
Annex III, reg. 4

---

* The form of the Certificate and its Record of Equipment may be found in the GMDSS
amendments to SOLAS 1974.
† SLS.14/Circ.115 and Add. 1 refers to the issue of exemption certificates.

Reference

Document of authorization for the carriage of grain
A document of authorization shall be issued for every
ship loaded in accordance with the regulations of the
International Code for the Safe Carriage of Grain in
Bulk either by the Administration or an organization
recognized by it or by a Contracting Government on
behalf of the Administration. The document shall
accompany or be incorporated into the grain loading
manual provided to enable the master to meet the
stability requirements of the Code.

SOLAS 1974,
reg. VI/9;
International
Code for the Safe
Carriage of Grain
in Bulk, section 3

*Certificate of insurance or other financial security in
respect of civil liability for oil pollution damage*
A certificate attesting that insurance or other financial
security is in force shall be issued to each ship
carrying more than 2,000 tons of oil in bulk as cargo.
It shall be issued or certified by the appropriate
authority of the State of the ship's registry after
determining that the requirements of article VII,
paragraph 1, of the CLC Convention have been
complied with.

CLC 69,
art. VII

Enhanced survey report file
Bulk carriers and oil tankers shall have a survey
report file and supporting documents complying
with paragraphs 6.2 and 6.3 of annex A and annex B
of resolution A.744(18), Guidelines on the enhanced
programme of inspections during surveys of bulk
carriers and oil tankers.

MARPOL 73/78,
Annex I,
reg. 13G;
SOLAS 1974,
reg. XI/2

*Record of oil discharge monitoring and control system for
the last ballast voyage*
Subject to provisions of paragraphs (4), (5), (6) and
(7) of regulation 15 of Annex I of MARPOL 73/78,
every oil tanker of 150 gross tonnage and above shall
be fitted with an oil discharge monitoring and
control system approved by the Administration.
The system shall be fitted with a recording device
to provide a continuous record of the discharge in
litres per nautical mile and total quantity discharged,
or the oil content and rate of discharge. This record
shall be identifiable as to time and date and shall be
kept for at least three years.

MARPOL 73/78,
Annex I,
reg. 15(3)(a)

Bulk Carrier Booklet
To enable the master to prevent excessive stress in the ship's structure, the ship loading and unloading of solid bulk cargoes shall be provided with a booklet referred to in SOLAS regulation VI/7.2. As an alternative to a separate booklet, the required information may be contained in the intact stability booklet.

SOLAS 1974 (1996 amdts), reg. VI/7; the Code of Practice for the Safe Loading and Unloading of Bulk Carriers (BLU Code)

4   In addition to the certificates listed in sections 1
and 3 above, where appropriate, any ship carrying noxious liquid chemical substances in bulk shall carry:

International Pollution Prevention Certificate for the Carriage of Noxious Liquid Substances in Bulk (NLS Certificate)
An international pollution prevention certificate for the carriage of noxious liquid substances in bulk (NLS Certificate) shall be issued, after survey in accordance with the provisions of regulation 10 of Annex II of MARPOL 73/78, to any ship carrying noxious liquid substances in bulk and which is engaged in voyages to ports or terminals under the jurisdiction of other Parties to MARPOL 73/78. In respect of chemical tankers, the Certificate of Fitness for the Carriage of Dangerous Chemicals in Bulk and the International Certificate of Fitness for the Carriage of Dangerous Chemicals in Bulk, issued under the provisions of the Bulk Chemical Code and the International Bulk Chemical Code, respectively, shall have the same force and receive the same recognition as the NLS Certificate.

MARPOL 73/78 Annex II, regs. 12 and 12A

Cargo Record Book
Every ship to which Annex II of MARPOL 73/78 applies shall be provided with a Cargo Record Book, whether as part of the ship's official log-book or otherwise, in the form specified in appendix IV to the Annex.

MARPOL 73/78, Annex II, reg. 9

Procedures and Arrangements Manual (P & A Manual)
Every ship certified to carry noxious liquid substances in bulk shall have on board a Procedures and Arrangements Manual approved by the Administration.

Resolution
MEPC.18(22),
chapter 2;
MARPOL 73/78,
Annex II, regs. 5,
5A and 8

Shipboard Marine Pollution Emergency Plan for Noxious Liquid Substances
Every ship of 150 gross tonnage and above certified to carry noxious liquid substances in bulk shall carry on board a shipboard marine pollution emergency plan for noxious liquid substances approved by the Administration. This requirement shall apply to all such ships not later than 1 January 2003.

MARPOL 73/78,
Annex II, reg. 16

5   In addition to the certificates listed in
    sections 1
    and 3 above, where applicable, any chemical
    tanker shall carry:

Certificate of Fitness for the Carriage of Dangerous Chemicals in Bulk
A certificate called a Certificate of Fitness for the Carriage of Dangerous Chemicals in Bulk, the model form of which is set out in the appendix to the Bulk Chemical Code, should be issued after an initial or periodical survey to a chemical tanker engaged in international voyages which complies with the relevant requirements of the Code.

BCH Code,
section 1.6;
BCH Code as
modified by
resolution
MSC.18(58)
section 1.6

Note: The Code is mandatory under Annex II of MARPOL 73/78 for chemical tankers constructed before 1 July 1986.

or

International Certificate of Fitness for the Carriage of Dangerous Chemicals in Bulk
A certificate called an International Certificate of Fitness for the Carriage of Dangerous Chemicals in Bulk, the model form of which is set out in the appendix to the International Bulk Chemical Code, should be issued after an initial or periodical survey to a chemical tanker engaged in international voyages which complies with the relevant requirements of the Code.

IBC Code,
section 1.5; IBC
Code as modified
by resolutions
MSC.16(58) and
MEPC.40(29),
section 1.5

Note: The Code is mandatory under both chapter VII of SOLAS 1974 and Annex II of MARPOL 73/78 for chemical tankers constructed on or after 1 July 1986.

6 **In addition to the certificates listed in sections 1 and 3 above, where applicable, any gas carrier shall carry:**

Certificate of Fitness for the Carriage of Liquefied Gases in Bulk
A certificate called a Certificate of Fitness for the Carriage of Liquefied Gases in Bulk, the model form of which is set out in the appendix to the Gas Carrier Code, should be issued after an initial or periodical survey to a gas carrier which complies with the relevant requirements of the Code.

GC Code,
section 1.6

or

International Certificate of Fitness for the Carriage of Liquefied Gases in Bulk
A certificate called an International Certificate of Fitness for the Carriage of Liquefied Gases in Bulk, the model form of which is set out in the appendix to the International Gas Carrier Code, should be issued after an initial or periodical survey to a gas carrier which complies with the relevant requirements of the Code.

IGC Code,
section 1.5;
IGC Code as
modified by
resolution
MSC.17(58),
section 1.5

Note: The Code is mandatory under chapter VII of SOLAS 1974 for gas carriers constructed on or after 1 July 1986.

7 **In addition to the certificates listed in sections 1 and 3 above, where applicable, high-speed craft shall carry:**

High-Speed Craft Safety Certificate
A certificate called a High-Speed Craft Safety Certificate should be issued after completion of an initial or renewal survey to a craft which complies with the requirements of the High-Speed Craft (HSC) Code in its entirety.

SOLAS 1974,
reg. X/3;
HSC Code,
paragraph 1.8

Reference

Permit to Operate High-Speed Craft
A certificate called a Permit to Operate High-Speed Craft should be issued to a craft which complies with the requirements set out in paragraphs 1.2.2 to 1.2.7 and 1.8 of the HSC Code.

HSC Code, paragraph 1.9

8   In addition to the certificates listed in sections 1
and 3 above, where applicable, any ship carrying INF cargo shall carry:

International Certificate of Fitness for the Carriage of INF Cargo
A ship carrying INF cargo shall comply with the requirements of the International Code for the Safe Carriage of Packaged Irradiated Nuclear Fuel, Plutonium and High-Level Radioactive Wastes on Board Ships (INF Code) in addition to any other applicable requirements of the SOLAS regulations and shall be surveyed and be provided with the International Certificate of Fitness for the Carriage of INF Cargo.

SOLAS 1974 (1999 amdts), reg. 16; INF Code (resolution MSC.88(71)), paragraph 1.3

Other miscellaneous certificates

Special purpose ships

Special Purpose Ship Safety Certificate
In addition to SOLAS certificates as specified in paragraph 7 of the Preamble of the Code of Safety for Special Purpose Ships, a Special Purpose Ship Safety Certificate shall be issued after survey in accordance with the provisions of paragraph 1.6 of the Code of Safety for Special Purpose Ships. The duration and validity of the certificate should be governed by the respective provisions for cargo ships in SOLAS 1974. If a certificate is issued for a special purpose ship of less than 500 gross tonnage, this certificate should indicate to what extent relaxations in accordance with 1.2 were accepted.

Resolution A.534(13) as amended by MSC/Circ.739; SOLAS 1974, reg. I/12; 1988 SOLAS Protocol, reg. I/12

Offshore support vessels

Certificate of Fitness for Offshore Support Vessels
When carrying such cargoes, offshore support vessels should carry a Certificate of Fitness issued under the "Guidelines for the transport and handling of limited amounts of hazardous and noxious liquid substances in bulk on offshore support vessels".

Resolution A.673(16); MARPOL 73/78, Annex II, reg. 13(4)

If an offshore support vessel carries only noxious liquid substances, a suitably endorsed International Pollution Prevention Certificate for the Carriage of Noxious Liquid Substances in Bulk may be issued instead of the above Certificate of Fitness.

Diving systems

Diving System Safety Certificate
A certificate should be issued either by the Administration or any person or organization duly authorized by it after survey or inspection to a diving system which complies with the requirements of the Code of Safety for Diving Systems. In every case, the Administration should assume full responsibility for the certificate.

Resolution A.536(13), section 1.6

Dynamically supported craft

Dynamically Supported Craft Construction and Equipment Certificate
To be issued after survey carried out in accordance with paragraph 1.5.1(a) of the Code of Safety for Dynamically Supported Craft.

Resolution A.373(X), section 1.6

Mobile offshore drilling units

Mobile Offshore Drilling Unit Safety Certificate
To be issued after survey carried out in accordance with the provisions of the Code for the Construction and Equipment of Mobile Offshore Drilling Units, 1979, or, for units constructed on or after 1 May 1991, the Code for the Construction and Equipment of Mobile Offshore Drilling Units, 1989.

Resolution A.414(XI), section 1.6; resolution A.649(16), section 1.6; resolution A.649(16) as modified by resolution MSC.38(63), section 1.6

Reference

Noise levels

Noise Survey Report
A noise survey report should be made for each ship in accordance with the Code on Noise Levels on Board Ships.

Resolution A.468(XII), section 4.3

Annex 3
List of resolutions adopted
by the SOLAS Conferences

International Conference on Safety of Life at Sea, 1974 *(October 1974)*

Resolution 1 – Comprehensive revision of the International Convention for the Safety of Life at Sea, 1974

Resolution 2 – Rapid amendment procedure and entry into force of the International Convention for the Safety of Life at Sea, 1974

Resolution 3 – Voting rights in the Maritime Safety Committee for the adoption of amendments

Resolution 4 – Recommendations of the 1960 Safety Conference and resolutions of the Assembly of the Organization related to regulations of the International Convention for the Safety of Life at Sea, 1974

Resolution 5 – Recommendations on the use of a system of units in the International Convention for the Safety of Life at Sea, 1974

Conference of Contracting Governments to the International Convention for the Safety of Life at Sea, 1974 *(May 1994)*

Resolution 1 – Adoption of amendments to the annex to the International Convention for the Safety of Life at Sea, 1974

Resolution 2 – Implementation of chapter IX of the 1974 SOLAS Convention on management for the safe operation of ships

Resolution 3 – Implementation of the International Safety Management (ISM) Code for cargo ships of less than 500 gross tonnage

Resolution 4 – Accelerated tacit acceptance procedure under the 1974 SOLAS Convention in exceptional circumstances

Resolution 5 – Future amendments to chapter XI of the 1974 SOLAS Convention on special measures to enhance maritime safety

Conference of Contracting Governments to the International Convention for the Safety of Life at Sea, 1974 *(November 1995)*

Resolution 1 – Adoption of amendments to the annex to the International Convention for the Safety of Life at Sea, 1974

Resolution 2 – Fire-extinguishing arrangements in machinery spaces of passenger ships

Resolution 3 – Escape arrangements in ships constructed before 1 July 1997

Resolution 4 – Maximum evacuation time for new ro–ro passenger ships

Resolution 5 – Amendments to chapter III of the 1974 SOLAS Convention

Resolution 6 – Low-powered radio homing devices for liferafts on ro–ro passenger ships

Resolution 7 – Development of requirements, guidelines and performance standards

Resolution 8 – Distress messages: obligations and procedures

Resolution 9 – Automatic ship identification transponder/transceiver systems

Resolution 10 – Establishment of working languages on ships

Resolution 11 – Operational limitations on passenger ships

Resolution 12 – Voyage data recorders

Resolution 13 – Cargo securing equipment

Resolution 14 – Regional agreements on specific stability requirements for ro–ro passenger ships

Conference of Contracting Governments to the International Convention for the Safety of Life at Sea, 1974 *(November 1997)*

Resolution 1 – Adoption of amendments to the annex to the International Convention for the Safety of Life at Sea, 1974

Resolution 2 – Adoption of amendments to the Guidelines on the enhanced programme of inspections during surveys of bulk carriers and oil tankers (resolution A.744(18))

Resolution 3 – Recommendation on compliance with SOLAS regulation XII/5

Resolution 4 – Standards for the evaluation of scantlings of the transverse watertight vertically corrugated bulkhead between the two foremost cargo holds and for the evaluation of allowable hold loading of the foremost cargo hold

Resolution 5 – Recommendation on loading instruments

Resolution 6 – Interpretation of the definition of "bulk carrier", as given in chapter IX of SOLAS 1974, as amended in 1994

Resolution 7 – Enhanced surveys carried out prior to entry into force of the amendments

Resolution 8 – Further work on the safety of bulk carriers

Resolution 9 – Implementation of the International Safety Management (ISM) Code

Conference of Contracting Governments to the International Convention for the Safety of Life at Sea, 1974 *(December 2002)*

Resolution 1 – Adoption of amendments to the Annex to the International Convention for the Safety of Life at Sea, 1974

Resolution 2 – Adoption of the International Code for the Security of Ships and of Port Facilities

Resolution 3 – Further work by the International Maritime Organization pertaining to the enhancement of maritime security

Resolution 4 – Future amendments to chapters XI-1 and XI-2 of the 1974 SOLAS Convention on special measures to enhance maritime safety and security

Resolution 5 – Promotion of technical co-operation and assistance

Resolution 6 – Early implementation of the special measures to enhance maritime security

Resolution 7 – Establishment of appropriate measures to enhance the security of ships, port facilities, mobile offshore drilling units on location and fixed and floating platforms not covered by chapter XI-2 of the 1974 SOLAS Convention

Resolution 8 – Enhancement of security in co-operation with the International Labour Organization

Resolution 9 – Enhancement of security in co-operation with the World Customs Organization

Resolution 10 – Early implementation of long-range ship's identification and tracking

Resolution 11 – Human-element-related aspects and shore leave for seafarers

Annex 4
Regulation 12-2 of chapter II-1
*(adopted 11 December 1992 by MSC.27(61))**

Regulation 12-2
Access to spaces in the cargo area of oil tankers

1   This regulation applies to oil tankers constructed on or after 1 October 1994.

2   Access to cofferdams, ballast tanks, cargo tanks and other spaces in the cargo area shall be direct from the open deck and such as to ensure their complete inspection. Access to double bottom spaces may be through a cargo pump-room, pump-room, deep cofferdam, pipe tunnel or similar compartments, subject to consideration of ventilation aspects.

3   For access through horizontal openings, hatches or manholes, the dimensions shall be sufficient to allow a person wearing a self-contained air-breathing apparatus and protective equipment to ascend or descend any ladder without obstruction and also to provide a clear opening to facilitate the hoisting of an injured person from the bottom of the space. The minimum clear opening should be not less than 600 mm × 600 mm.

4   For access through vertical openings, or manholes providing passage through the length and breadth of the space, the minimum clear opening should be not less than 600 mm × 800 mm at a height of not more than 600 mm from the bottom shell plating unless gratings or other footholds are provided.

5   For oil tankers of less than 5,000 tonnes deadweight smaller dimensions may be approved by the Administration in special circumstances, if the ability to traverse such openings or to remove an injured person can be proved to the satisfaction of the Administration.

---

* This regulation was adopted in December 1992, entered into force on 1 October 1994, and was removed by resolution MSC.134(76). Although the date of entry into force of resolution MSC.134(76) is 1 July 2004, oil tankers of 500 gross tonnage and over constructed on or after 1 October 1994 but before 1 January 2005 must comply with the provisions of this regulation.

Index